Capitalism and Schizophrenia in the Later Novels of Louis-Ferdinand Céline

Currents in Comparative Romance Languages and Literatures

Tamara Alvarez-Detrell and Michael G. Paulson
General Editors

Vol. 100

PETER LANG
New York • Washington, D.C./Baltimore • Bern
Frankfurt am Main • Berlin • Brussels • Vienna • Oxford

Greg Hainge

Capitalism and Schizophrenia in the Later Novels of Louis-Ferdinand Céline

D'un...l'autre

PETER LANG
New York • Washington, D.C./Baltimore • Bern
Frankfurt am Main • Berlin • Brussels • Vienna • Oxford

Library of Congress Cataloging-in-Publication Data

Hainge, Greg.
Capitalism and schizophrenia in the later novels
of Louis-Ferdinand Céline: d'un…l'autre / Greg Hainge.
p. cm. — (Currents in comparative Romance languages and literatures; vol. 100)
Includes bibliographical references.
1. Céline, Louis-Ferdinand, 1894–1961—Criticism and interpretation.
2. Capitalism in literature. 3. Schizophrenia in literature. I. Title. II. Series.
PQ2607.E834 Z684 843'.912—dc21 00-062964
ISBN 0-8204-5195-9
ISSN 0893-5963

Die Deutsche Bibliothek-CIP-Einheitsaufnahme

Hainge, Greg:
Capitalism and schizophrenia in the later novels
of Louis-Ferdinand Céline: d'un…l'autre / Greg Hainge.
–New York; Washington, D.C./Baltimore; Bern;
Frankfurt am Main; Berlin; Brussels; Vienna; Oxford: Lang.
(Currents in comparative Romance languages and literatures; Vol. 100)
ISBN 0-8204-5195-9

The paper in this book meets the guidelines for permanence and durability
of the Committee on Production Guidelines for Book Longevity
of the Council of Library Resources.

Printed in the United States of America

Table of Contents

Foreword

Nicholas Hewitt

This excellent book is an important contribution to our understanding of Céline's writing from a psychoanalytic perspective. Céline's concern with madness in his writing is one of the major features of his work, and one which has been consistently recognised by his critics. In fact, Céline's "madness" takes two forms, one clinical and covering a wide range of psychological symptoms, and the other aesthetic and stylistic, operating in the domain of hallucination and dream and often expressed through the means of "délire".

His professional interest in psychology is well-documented. The correspondence with Cillie Pam in the 1930s, following his visit to Vienna in 1933, when he met a number of Viennese (and Jewish) psychoanalysts, demonstrates an above average knowledge of Freud's work and refers specifically to the essay 'Mourning and Melancholia', of 1916. At the same time, by 1936 and the publication of *Bagatelles pour un massacre*, Céline, through his narrator Ferdinand, is at pains to distance himself from Freud and invokes instead a non-Freudian interpretation of dreams, embodied in Léon Daudet's *Le Rêve éveillé*, of 1926.

Similarly, in Céline's fiction the interest in psychological abnormality is present right from the beginning. In the long essay *La Quinine en thérapeutique*, of 1926, Dr Destouches recounts the strange case of the obsessive and Molièresque Dr Bazire, who is so convinced of the healing properties of quinine that, when it fails to effect an immediate cure on his own ailment, proceeds to increase the dose until he dies. Similarly, Céline's doctoral thesis on Semmelweis fictionalises the career of the Hungarian scientist, signified by the inversion of the name Ignace-Fulop to Philippe-Ignace, by turning him, literally, into a madman. This concern with abnormal psychology continues into the fiction signed under the name of Céline: *Voyage au bout de la nuit* can not merely be interpreted as a dream and hallucination, it deploys a first-person narrator who spends much of his time, literally, delirious: from the light-headedness on the café terrace which opens the novel, through the literal nervous collapse in Paris during the War, to the fever in the African jungle and the hallucinatory crossing of the Atlantic on a slave-galley. Much more obviously Freudian in inspiration, *Mort à crédit* is a chronicle of madness: the neurotic Auguste, the fanciful Courtial des Pereires, the despairing Nora, the retarded child Jonkind, and, finally, the narrator Ferdinand himself, whose response to the misery of his family-life and economic situation is autism. This classic psychoanalytical tale ends significantly enough with a classic nervous collapse and a retreat into non-being, or back to the womb, under Oncle Edouard's pile of 'pardessus'. That this is no resolution is conveyed by the madness and delirium still tracking the mature narrator. Finally, from *Bagatelles pour un massacre* onwards explores the use of a deranged first-person narrator whose madness is both exculpatory and blindingly insightful.

Unsurprisingly, Céline's critics have paid considerable attention to this body of psychological material at the heart of his writing. As early as 1971, Albert Chesneau, in *Psychocritique de Céline*, saw Céline's work as highly susceptible to analysis on the lines of Charles Mauron. Similarly, Nicole Debrie, Willy Szafran, Henri Godard and Marie-Christine Bellosta have explored in considerable detail Céline's debt to Freud in particular and psychology in general.

A psychological or, indeed, psychoanalytical, approach to Céline's work presents problems, however. In the first place, most psychological studies of Céline have tended at some time to be backed into a biographical or autobiographical interpretation, as if the neuroses portrayed and worked out in the novels could only stem from a reality grounded in biography. Here, the letters from Céline to Joseph Garcin are highly revealing: not only do they confirm his extensive knowledge of Freud, but they also an exclusively writerly relish for pastiching the 1930s vogue for psychoanalytical fiction. Not that this should be taken totally seriously—no more so that his claims that *Voyage* was a merely a response to fashionable First World War fiction—but it does indicate that the gallery of psychological victims in Mort à crédit, along with the neurotic, and often mad, narrator, in full "délire", from *Bagatelles* onwards is the result of conscious artifice and not emotional momentum.

Similarly, psychological studies of Céline have rarely succeeded in integrating the psychological features of the work to is socio-economic concerns. *Mort à crédit*, with its acute awareness of the importance of gold and its extensive reflection of the life of petit-bourgeois turn-of-the-century Paris, is one of France's major historical novels. And that historical dimension is intimately connected to the neurosis of its characters and the autism of its child-narrator and the delirium of his mature counterpart. In this respect, Ferdinand must be seen as literally and metaphorically schizophrenic.

Here, and it is the great merit of this book, the work of Deleuze and Guattari provides a compelling framework for the analysis of Céline's writing, in that it enables the psychological, the socio-economic and, above all, the stylistic, to be fully integrated into one reading. Dr Hainge, with meticulous care and highly intelligent insight, takes us closer than we have ever been before to the psychological centre of Céline's work.

Acknowledgments

In preparing and publishing this study, I have benefited from the advice and help of a number of individuals and institutions to whom I wish to express my sincere gratitude: the British Academy, the Australian Academy of the Humanities and Adelaide University for their generous funding; Éditions Gallimard for their permission to quote extensively from Céline's novels; the British Library; the Bibliothèque Nationale; the Hallward Library at the University of Nottingham; l'Institut Mémoires de l'Édition Contemporaine, the holders of an invaluable and unparalleled Célinian research library; the Société d'Études Céliniennes and all of its members with whom I have come into contact at its biennial conferences.

Finally, my deepest gratitude and respect go out to my mentor Professor Bernard McGuirk, a seemingly inexhaustible well of inspiration, and to Professor Nick Hewitt whose infectious passion for the Célinian corpus inspired this work.

List of Abbreviations

The following works by Louis-FerdinandCéline are referred to in the text under these indications:

CA *D'un château l'autre*, in *Romans* II, ed. by Henri Godard, coll. La Pléiade (Paris: Gallimard, 1974)

EY *Entretiens avec le professeur Y*, in *Romans* IV, ed. by Henri Godard, coll. La Pléiade (Paris: Gallimard, 1993)

*F*I *Féerie pour une autre fois* I, in *Romans* IV, ed. by Henri Godard, coll. La Pléiade (Paris: Gallimard, 1993)

*F*II *Féerie pour une autre fois* II [*Normance*], in *Romans* IV, ed. by Henri Godard, coll. La Pléiade (Paris: Gallimard, 1993)

*GB*I *Guignol's band* I, in *Romans* III, ed. by Henri Godard, coll. La Pléiade (Paris: Gallimard, 1988)

*GB*II *Guignol's band* II [*Le Pont de Londres*], in *Romans* III, ed. by Henri Godard, coll. La Pléiade (Paris: Gallimard, 1988)

MC *Mort à crédit*, in *Romans* I, ed. by Henri Godard, coll. La Pléiade (Paris: Gallimard, 1981)

N *Nord*, in *Romans* II, ed. by Henri Godard, coll. La Pléiade (Paris: Gallimard, 1974)

R *Rigodon*, in *Romans* II, ed. by Henri Godard, coll. La Pléiade (Paris: Gallimard, 1974)

V *Voyage au bout de la nuit*, in *Romans* I, ed. by Henri Godard, coll. La Pléiade (Paris: Gallimard, 1981)

Introduction

Capitalism and Schizophrenia

> Nous voici parvenus au bout de vingt siècles de haute civilisation et, cependant, aucun régime ne résisterait à deux mois de vérité. Je veux dire la société marxiste aussi bien que nos sociétés bourgeoises et fascistes.
>
> L'homme ne peut persister, en effet, dans aucune de ces formes sociales, entièrement brutales, toutes masochistes, sans la violence d'un mensonge permanent et de plus en plus massif, répété, frénétique, «totalitaire» comme on l'intitule.
>
> —Louis-Ferdinand Céline,
> *Céline et l'actualité littéraire, 1932–1957*

> Nous avons vu que la production désirante était la limite de la production sociale, toujours contrariée dans la formation capitaliste: le corps sans organes à la limite du socius déterritorialisé, le désert aux portes de la ville... Mais justement il est urgent, il est essentiel que la limite soit déplacée, qu'elle soit rendue inoffensive et passe, ait l'air de passer à l'intérieur de la formation sociale elle-même. La schizophrénie ou la production désirante, c'est la limite entre l'organisation molaire et la multiplicité moléculaire du désir; il faut que cette limite de déterritorialisation passe maintenant à l'intérieur de l'organisation molaire, qu'elle s'applique à une territorialité factice et soumise. On pressent alors ce que signifie Œdipe: il déplace la limite, il l'intériorise. Plutôt un peuple de névrosés qu'un seul schizophrène réussi, non autistisé.
>
> —Gilles Deleuze and Félix Guattari,
> *L'Anti-Œdipe: capitalisme et schizophrénie*

Louis-Ferdinand Céline is without doubt one of France's most infamous literary figures, an author both praised for his revolutionary use of the French language and reviled for his Fascistic outpourings. To interface the novels of this author with the revolutionary and resolutely anti-Fascist thought of Gilles Deleuze and Félix Guattari—co-authors of *Capitalisme et schizophrénie*, one of the key works in the ever controversial field of French post-structuralist theory—may appear to many, therefore, merely to epitomise a certain postmodern trend wherein "anything goes". As should already be clear from the epigraphs above, however, in spite of their apparent polarity, there is much common ground to be found between these seemingly disparate works on both a thematic and stylistic level. For not only is the struggle of the individual to survive within the superstructures of Capitalist society with his/her desire intact recounted in both of these *œuvres*, but both Céline and Deleuze and Guattari can be seen to conceive of the notion of style as a schizophrenic entity. It is to these aspects of these works that the present study dedicates itself, for no other reason than to further the reader's understanding of these individual *œuvres* through their juxtaspotion.

The novels of Louis-Ferdinand Céline are infused with both an acute economic awareness regarding the mechanisms of twentieth-century Capitalist society, and a quasi-professional knowledge of the psychology of man, its dysfunctions in particular. It would be, then, entirely possible to carry out a thematic study of the motifs of Capitalism and schizophrenia (when this latter is taken to signify a pathological psychological state akin to a commonly accepted notion of madness) in the works of Céline. Indeed, one might ask how else to analyse a work such as *Mort à crédit* which could be said to form the nexus of these elements in Céline's *œuvre*, Capitalism, in this novel, effectively inducing a state akin to madness/pathological schizophrenia characterised by delirium and autistic withdrawal in both the narrator and his father, Auguste. Perhaps somewhat unsurprisingly, therefore, numerous critical works on Céline and his corpus deal with precisely these subjects—examples of which will be cited throughout the present study. However, even when they clearly establish the causal link between the economic/social/historical elements of the novels and their psychological/psychoanalytic traits, as does Nicholas Hewitt's *The Golden Age of Louis-Ferdinand Céline*,[1] such studies neglect, for the most part, the novels' stylistics, an essential element of all fictional works, but one which, in the Célinian corpus, is arguably accorded an even greater importance than the thematics. This is not to say, of course, that commentators on Céline have neglected to examine the novels' stylistics, indeed, quite the opposite is the case. But just as thematic studies of Céline's *œuvre* neglect its stylistics, so stylistic studies too often neglect the thematics, as though these aspects of the novels were disembodied, autonomous, having no direct causal link between them.[2] Even when a link is established between these two levels, as is the case in the studies of, amongst others, Julia Kristeva, Paul Fortier and, in a slightly perverse manner, Bettina Knapp, it is generally considered that the stylistics serve the thematics, functioning as a secondary reinforcement of the ideological premises perceived in the works.[3] (The one notable exception to this comes with studies dealing with *Entretiens avec le professeur Y*, a work in which there is a transparent reversal of this scenario, the thematics serving to explicate the Célinian style.) In attempting to unite the thematic and stylistic levels, however, this study will argue that it is rather the case, not only in *Entretiens avec le professeur Y*, but in all of Céline's novels from *Guignol's band* onwards, that the thematic level is put to the service of the stylistics, the thematic treatment of psychology/madness being employed not only to denounce the dehumanising mechanisms of Capitalist society in all of its manifestations—for the thematic level always retains this ideological function—, but also, and above all, to privilege the works' style.

In proposing a reading of these novels in which style is accorded ultimate primacy, however, it should not be thought that this study will ultimately be little more than a structuralist, stylistic analysis. On the contrary, due to the very particular nature of Céline's conception of style, in which, it will be argued, style has to do not so much with the formal construction of the literary text as with a mode of existence, style will be seen to function as a thematic, providing the only possible non-pathological means of authentic survival amongst the omnipresent and multifarious apparatus of capture of Capitalist society. This mode of existence premised on the concept of style will be termed, after Deleuze and Guattari, schizophrenic, for just as in their conception of this term the dissolution of the boundary between interior and exterior allows thoughts to behave like bodies,[4] so the dissolution of the boundary between the thematics and the stylistics of these texts will allow the novels' very style to resolve the ideological problematic posed in the thematic level, *délire*—the most manifest trait of the dysfunctional psyche in Céline's work—being positively valorised as the stylistic and thematic foundation of his fictional universe.

Style

> Le style, chez un grand écrivain, c'est toujours aussi un style de vie, non pas du tout quelque chose de personnel, mais l'invention d'une possibilité de vie, d'un mode d'existence.
>
> —Gilles Deleuze, *Pourparlers: 1972–1990*

> Ah, turpitude! menterie éhontée!... plein de style que je suis! que oui! et pire!... bien plus! que je les rendrai tous illisibles!... tous les autres! flétrides impuissants! pourris des prix et manifesses! que je peux comploter bien tranquille, l'époque est à moi! je suis le béni des Lettres! qui m'imite pas existe pas!... simple!...
>
> —Louis-Ferdinand Céline, *Rigodon*

In his introduction to a special edition of the *South Atlantic Quarterly*, entitled *A Deleuzian Century?*—a blatant misnomer according to the sentiment expressed by Céline in the second of the above quotations—, Ian Buchanan, commenting on the first of the above quotations, speculates that, 'it is through style, as the enfolding of life and work, that the philosopher becomes imperceptible, a persona (or mediator) rather than a person', and that Deleuze's interviews might best be understood, 'as an attempt to fashion himself as (what he called) a conceptual persona'.[5] Much the same thing can be said with regard to Louis-Ferdinand Céline, for, as J.H. Matthews has noted, Céline,

> always found amusement in deliberately making inaccurate statements that, having the ring of truth, would find glad and unquestioned acceptance among the public. Such was his pleasure in disinformation that the more earnestly he asserted something, the more skeptical one needed to be about what he said;[6]

and later,

> Louis-Ferdinand Céline [a *nom de plume*] had no intention of telling his readers exactly how Louis Destouches had lived or was living. After all, he was in the habit of advising any critic or journalist who asked him for details about his past to invent them, asserting that history has no importance.[7]

Likewise, Philip Stephen Day has written that,

> La vie chaotique de Céline est en même temps son roman le plus captivant, alors que son œuvre n'est pas, comme on le croit souvent, la transposition de faits autobiographiques, mais une aventure de l'imagination au milieu d'une

> réalité semée d'embûches [....] Céline a toujours abusé ses biographes, laissant coexister dans ses écrits et dans ses propos la vérité et le mirage.[8]

But if Buchanan, who himself claims to be 'looking for a set of Deleuzian principles for reading Deleuze', conjectures that, 'if it is true that Deleuze's interviews fold his life and work into one, then perhaps what he does reveal about himself can be taken as part and parcel of how he wants philosophy to think of him and with him',[9] few seem willing to indulge such a reading of Céline, preferring to read his *œuvre* in the very Historical context he consistently implored his commentators to ignore, to privilege the story (*histoire*) over style despite the author's protestations to the contrary: 'C'est tout ce que j'ai, le style, rien d'autre. Il n'y a pas de messages dans mes livres, c'est l'affaire de l'Église'.[10] In reconciling and conflating the novels' thematic concerns with their stylistic concerns, the aim of this study will be, then, to provide a framework for a reading of the later novels of Céline that derives from precepts perceived in the works themselves, to find a set of Célinian principles for reading Céline, and to apply those principles to his post-war novels.[11]

A reading which aims to interpret a body of work solely according to precepts perceived in that very body of work itself, might be termed a metatextual reading, for it is a reading which will only be produced through a constantly renewed contact with the text that feeds back into the text itself, a feedback loop. Such a reading must, of course, remain devoid of all presuppositions and allow itself no epistemological priority. To carry out such a reading of the *œuvre* of Céline will be, for many, an unforgivable tactic, an act of provocation. The present study is not intended as such an act, nor does it aim to disregard the view shared by many that Céline was directly implicated in the worst atrocities of the Twentieth Century. This study, in the firm conviction that an understanding of Céline's work can only be arrived at when style is granted ultimate primacy, presumes solely to read Céline's *œuvre* as artifice, as metatext, and in so doing will unashamedly remain on a purely intellectual and abstract level.[12]

To claim that such an intellectualised metatextual reading of the *œuvre* of Céline is to read his work according to Célinian principles may seem to many, however, a somewhat aporetic statement, for there is much unbridled hostility to such intellectuality to be found in his writing. Take, for instance, the following passages, the first coming from

Entretiens avec le professeur Y, the second from a letter to Milton Hindus:

> —Qu'est-ce que vous diriez alors d'un petit débat philosophique?... vous sentez-vous apte?... un débat, mettons, par exemple, sur les mutations du progrès par les transformations du "soi"?...
>
> —Ah, monsieur le professeur Y, je veux bien vous respecter et tout... mais je vous le déclare: je suis hostile!... j'ai pas d'idées moi! aucune! et je trouve rien de plus vulgaire, de plus commun, de plus dégoûtant que les idées! les bibliothèques en sont pleines! et les terrasses des cafés!... tous les impuissants regorgent d'idées!... (*EY*, pp.496–497, *et passim*)

> En vérité mon apport aux lettres françaises a été je crois ceci, on le reconnaîtra plus tard; rendre le langage français écrit plus *sensible*, plus *émotif*, le désacadémiser—et ceci par le *truc* qui consiste (moins facile qu'il y paraît) en un monologue d'intimité parlé mais TRANSPOSÉ—Cette transposition immédiate spontanée voilà le hic—En réalité, c'est le retour à la poésie spontanée du sauvage. Le sauvage ne s'exprime pas sans poésie, *il ne peut pas*. Le civilisé académisé, s'exprime en ingénieur, en architecte, *en mécanisé*, plus en homme sensible.[13]

And yet, as many commentators have pointed out, behind Céline's desire to express through his writing the spontaneity and immediate sensory affect of spoken language ('*l'émotion du langage parlé à travers l'écrit!*' (*EY*, 498)), there lies a very self-conscious, meticulously constructed aesthetic.[14] Indeed, one does not need to advance much beyond the above passage from his allegorical stylistic manifesto, *Entretiens avec le professeur Y*, to come across talk of, 'rails biseautés "spécial"!' (*EY*, p.541) and other such tropes describing the degree of aesthetic reflection involved in the creation of Céline's literature, the extent to which a reflection on the very processes of production is inseparable from and essential to the very artistic product itself. This conception of the work of art is not only to be found in *Entretiens avec le professeur Y*, however; indeed, as Allen Thiher has noted,

> une perspective moderniste sur Céline fait voir que cette forme de symbolisation est une tentative de s'emparer de l'expérience de telle sorte que, comme dans le cas de l'essence proustienne, il n'y a aucune distinction entre les moyens de représentation et ce qui est représenté. La métaphore de la danse n'est là finalement que pour communiquer ce que cette image peut connoter. Ou, en d'autres termes, l'expérience et la représentation de l'expérience coïncident dans cette parole qui restitue la présence immédiate. C'est peut-être dans ce sens qu'il faut comprendre les commentaires de Céline où il prétend

> n'avoir jamais été intéressé par autre chose que des effets de style. Mais par "effets de style" il faut entendre l'expérience du langage lui-même en tant que force subjective capable de révéler le délire jubilant de l'univers.[15]

Founded on an intellectual construct, it will be possible, then, to carry out a metatextual reading of Céline's literary output based on precepts derived solely from the texts themselves, a reading which will highlight the texts' artifice to reveal their metanarratival or metafictional levels, the primacy accorded artifice over artefact.

Considered in this way, Céline's texts (like the reading of them proposed herein) might be considered as instances of schizophrenic desiring-production, as desiring-machines, concepts expounded in the respective and joint *œuvres* of Gilles Deleuze and Félix Guattari. In their account of existence, especially that found in their co-authored two-volume *Capitalisme et schizophrénie*, Deleuze and Guattari term schizophrenic a certain type of production, one that shares certain characteristics with clinical schizophrenia—clinical or pathological schizophrenia, schizophrenia as a malady and not a process, being produced, in their account, by the premature and abrupt termination of desire by the repressive mechanisms or modes of reterritorialisation erected by Capitalist societies to suppress desire for the assured continuance of the Urstaat.[16] They write:

> Ce que le schizophrène vit spécifiquement, génériquement, ce n'est pas du tout un pôle spécifique de la nature, mais la nature comme processus de production. Que veut dire ici processus? Il est probable que, à un certain niveau, la nature se distingue de l'industrie: pour une part l'industrie s'oppose à la nature, pour une autre part elle y puise des matériaux, pour une autre part elle lui restitue ses déchets, etc. Ce rapport distinctif homme-nature, industrie-nature, société-nature, conditionne même dans la société la distinction de sphères relativement autonomes qu'on appellera 'production', 'distribution', 'consommation'. Mais ce niveau de distinctions en général, considéré dans sa structure formelle développée, présuppose (comme l'a montré Marx) non seulement le capital et la division du travail, mais la fausse conscience que l'être capitaliste prend nécessairement de soi et des éléments figés d'un procès d'ensemble. Car en vérité—l'éclatante et noire vérité qui gît dans le délire—il n'y a pas de sphères ou de circuits relativement indépendants: la production est immédiatement consommation et enregistrement, l'enregistrement et la consommation déterminent directement la production, mais la déterminent au sein de la production même. Si bien que tout est production: *productions de productions*, d'actions et de passions; *productions d'enregistrements*, de distributions et de repérages; *productions de consommations*, de voluptés, d'angoisses et de douleurs. Tout est si bien production que les enregistrements sont immédia-

> tement consommés, consumés, et les consommations directement reproduites. Tel est le premier sens de processus: porter l'enregistrement et la consommation dans la production même, en faire les productions d'un même procès.[17]

Expressing 'l'éclatante et noire vérité qui gît dans le délire'—a phrase that would not look out of place in the blurb of any of Céline's novels—, pitting quasi-pathological individuals against the monstrous ideological and economic superstructures of the Twentieth Century, contemplatable only as a reflection on its own processes of production, as an expression of style, and not as an autonomous entity with its own ontological status and capacity for representation, Céline's *œuvre* invites comparison to that of Deleuze and Guattari.[18] In spite of the similarity to be found between the Célinian and Deleuzoguattarian projects, however, it is not the intention of this study merely to seek out ideological common ground between Céline and Deleuze/Guattari, but rather to draw a line of flight between them, to couple the Céline-machine with the Deleuze/Guattari-machine, so as to produce a new product:[19]

> Les machines désirantes sont des machines binaires, à règle binaire ou régime associatif; toujours une machine couplée avec une autre. La synthèse productive, la production de production, a une forme connective: "et", "et puis"... C'est qu'il y a toujours une machine productrice d'un flux, et une autre qui lui est connectée, opérant une coupure, un prélèvement de flux (le sein—la bouche). Et comme la première est à son tour connectée à une autre par rapport à laquelle elle se comporte comme coupure ou prélèvement, la série binaire est linéaire dans toutes les directions. Le désir fait couler, coule et coupe. 'J'aime tout ce qui coule, même le flux menstruel qui emporte les œufs non fécondés...', dit Miller dans son chant du désir. Poche des eaux et calculs du rein; flux de cheveu, flux de bave, flux de sperme, de merde ou d'urine qui sont produits par des objets partiels, constamment coupés par d'autres objets partiels, lesquels produisent d'autres flux, recoupés par d'autres objets partiels. Tout "objet" suppose la continuité d'un flux, tout flux, la fragmentation de l'objet. Sans doute chaque machine-organe interprète le monde entier d'après son propre flux, d'après l'énergie qui flue d'elle: l'œil interprète tout en termes de voir—le parler, l'entendre, le chier, le baiser... Mais toujours une connexion s'établit avec une autre machine, dans une transversale où la première coupe le flux de l'autre ou "voit" son flux coupé par l'autre.
>
> Le couplage de la synthèse connective, objet partiel-flux, a donc aussi bien une autre forme, produit-produire. Toujours du produire est greffé sur le produit, c'est pourquoi la production désirante est production de production, comme toute machine, machine de machine.[20]

As can be seen from this quotation, the coupling of two machines will unavoidably modify both terms of the binary set—the present work might thus be said to be as much a study of Deleuze and Guattari as it is of Céline—, and consequently render impossible all pre-ordained structure, all ready-made model for interpretation, all manner of mythification by which a text is analysed from a pre-existing semiologic chain.[21] It is to avoid such an analysis that, in the chapters to follow, lengthy and extensive quotations from primary sources will be used, allowing the reader the opportunity of performing him/herself the work of synthesis necessary to couple the two machines juxtaposed by this study.[22] Before arriving at this stage, however, it will firstly be necessary to examine briefly each of these machines.

The Deleuze/Guattari-machine

To attempt a succinct synthesis of Deleuze and Guattari's *Capitalisme et schizophrénie* is, inevitably, an exercise in self-defeat. Deleuze and Guattari may themselves appear to indulge in reductive globalisation, claiming, in *L'Anti-Œdipe*, to provide an 'histoire universelle',[23] but that phrase in its context is not so much ripe, as rotten with irony. For *L'Anti-Œdipe* and *Mille plateaux* (the two volumes which together form *Capitalisme et Schizophrénie*) are a condemnation of the normalising mechanisms of society that resist those very same mechanisms in their very expression—a term that they would no doubt reject in favour of "collective assemblage of enunciation". As Nick Heffernan notes, their 'refusal to "make sense" [...] is crucial to the book's political ambitions, for Deleuze and Guattari subscribe absolutely to the avant-garde modernist investment in the politics of style—particularly in its subversive, defamiliarizing possibilities'.[24] Like the schizophrenic whose traits inspire (or provide a convenient parallel for) much of their thought, the ideas and concepts expounded in *Capitalisme et schizophrénie* refuse to be reduced to a primal essence, they are mobile, nomadic, their boundaries incessantly shifting in a constant, irreducible state of flux (a becoming), their self-definition coming only from the incessant enfolding of an aleatory outside, capable of being grasped only in their interaction with that hyperdifferentiated outside, and then only for an evanescent instant. As they state,

> On ne peut pas, on ne devrait pas songer à décrire l'objet schizophrénique sans le rattacher au processus de production. Les *Cahiers de l'art brut* en sont la démonstration vivante (et nient du même coup qu'il y ait une entité du schizophrène).[25]

Nonetheless, as the vocabulary to be used throughout this study (which is primarily a study of Céline's novels) will be specifically Deleuzo-guattarian, an attempt briefly to explicate some of the terms to be used and the concepts to which they apply is both necessary and desirable, for all its futility.

The essence of *L'Anti-Œdipe* and *Mille plateaux* can almost be surmised by the binary set of the title that links these two works. For if, as has been suggested above, the term schizophrenia is taken to be a process and not a pathological illness, a non-transcendental, nomadic, machinic, heterogenetic mode of composition which constitutes the true and natural means of existence of the human condition, *Homo natura*,[26] then Capitalism, the apparent last stage in the logical progression of all Political systems,[27] might be said to be that mechanism which employs a whole range of repressive, reductive, transcendental, representational apparatus of capture (psychoanalysis, the police, the military), in order to re-axiomatise nature's rhizomatic structure, its a-structurality (or, rather, chaotic structurality, its structure coming from internal self-organisation) within a containable, understandable (and controllable, therefore) frame.[28]

The vision of existence that Deleuze and Guattari propose, then, is one in which there exists a fundamental antinomy, an apparently irreconcilable division of life into a schizophrenic, desiring, molecular level, in which all is fragmentary, instantaneous and intensive, and a paranoid, fascistic, extensive, molar level, ruled by

> those large, abstract, mediate and perhaps even empty and imaginary forms by which we seek to recontain the molecular: the mirage of the continuity of personal identity, the organizing unity of the psyche or the personality, the concept of society itself.[29]

Human existence can be said to oscillate between these two levels, the paranoiac and schizoid poles, for, as Deleuze and Guattari state,

> L'investissement paranoïaque et l'investissement schizoïde sont comme deux pôles opposés de l'investissement libidinal inconscient, dont l'un subordonne la production désirante à la formation de souveraineté et à l'ensemble grégaire

> qui en découle, et l'autre effectue la subordination inverse, renverse la puissance et soumet l'ensemble grégaire aux multiplicités moléculaires des productions de désir. Et, s'il est vrai que le délire est coextensif au champ social, on voit dans tout délire les deux pôles coexister, et des fragments d'investissement schizoïde révolutionnaire coïncider avec des blocs d'investissement paranoïaque réactionnaire. L'oscillation entre les deux pôles est même constitutive du délire. Toutefois, il apparaît que l'oscillation n'est pas égale, et que le pôle schizoïde est plutôt potentiel par rapport au pôle paranoïaque actuel.[30]

Implicit in their analysis, then, is a damning critique of this molar level, for in attempting to maintain this imbalance, to recontain the molecular level, to impose upon it a coherent transcendental view which, by definition, must be at odds with it, to petrify it in a structure not its own, or, to use Deleuze and Guattari's favoured term, to territorialise it, the molar level—'the level at which the profusion of libidinal energies assumes ideological forms'—[31] has the effect of denying the eminently productive nature of existence, the *real*, since, as Heffernan points out, the real 'is inseparable from *desire*, which invests and produces the real at every turn'.[32] Against this normalised, unnatural state of being, Deleuze and Guattari posit an intensive state of existence which must always start from a zero intensity, a body without organs, founded on a plane of immanence or consistency. This state, which can be thought of as a reformulation of the Thanatic drive, a model of death in the unconscious, is a moment of antiproduction in the process of production, and without which desiring-production would be impossible—the molecular level proceeding only by breaks, by a constant move forwards away from all that is fixed, stagnant, pre-ordained:

> Le corps sans organes n'est pas le témoin d'un néant originel, pas plus que le reste d'une totalité perdue. Il n'est surtout pas une projection; rien à voir avec le corps propre, ou avec une image du corps. C'est le corps sans image. Lui, l'improductif, il existe là où il est produit, au troisième temps de la série binaire-linéraire [sic]. Il est perpétuellement réinjecté dans la production. Le corps catatonique est produit dans l'eau du bain. Le corps plein sans organes est de l'anti-production; mais c'est encore un caractère de la synthèse connective ou productive, de coupler la production à l'anti-production, à un élément d'anti-production.[33]

A revolutionary text, *Capitalisme et schizophrénie* (as has been suggested) itself aspires to such an irreducible state, and exhorts its readers to do the same, to live life not as a being, but as a becoming, a body without organs, to shrug off all of those normalised patterns by which it is almost universally accepted that life is led, instead to live as a supermolecular individual governed solely by desire, by one's own individual style.[34] To live thus within a capitalist system, however, it is necessary, of course, to break free from the all-pervading axiomatics that overcode man's every action, to deterritorialise the strata in which molarity compartmentalises experience. This must be done not in a frenzied, uncontrolled manner, however, for by attempting to attain the revolutionary schizophrenic level in such a manner, one risks slipping into a state of impotence which might be likened to autism, a pathological manifestation of the schizophrenic characterised by withdrawal and an inability to interact with the dominant reality. As Deleuze and Guattari state,

> L'organisme, il faut en garder assez pour qu'il se reforme à chaque aube; et des petites provisions de signifiance et d'interprétation, il faut en garder, même pour les opposer à leur propre système, quand les circonstances l'exigent, quand les choses, les personnes, même les situations vous y forcent; et de petites rations de subjectivité, il faut en garder suffisamment pour pouvoir répondre à la réalité dominante. Mimez les strates. On n'atteint pas au CsO [corps sans organes], et à son plan de consistance, en dé[s]tratifiant à la sauvage.[35]

The end towards which the Deleuze/Guattari machine is directed, then, is the activation of desire through deterritorialisation, or, as they term it, a schizoanalysis, 'the radical practice by which schizoid investments, so far doomed either to "congeal" pathologically or remain forever "potential", can be reconnected and "actualized"'.[36] This politics of desire, concerned not with the governance of a State (Politics/*polis*) but with the immanent relations between all things (politics/*polos*), aims, in the final analysis,

> to break down the dichotomy between desire and interest, so that people can begin to desire, think, and act in their own interests, and become interested in their own desires. [...] It aims to construct a collective social space where desire is liberated, and can spread by contagion through the creation of immanent relations between heterogeneous multiplicities.[37]

Like Céline's *œuvre*, Deleuze and Guattari's *Capitalisme et schizophrénie* can thus be said to privilege style above all else, for it desires nothing other than to empower individuals to live life according to their own desire, to awaken the music in people's hearts.

The Céline-machine

On n'a plus beaucoup de musique en soi pour faire danser la vie, voilà.
—Louis-Ferdinand Céline, *Voyage au bout de la nuit*

The novels of Louis-Ferdinand Céline are infused with an intense sadness arising from the state of the world they describe, a putrid morass of misery, oppression, corruption, exploitation, violence, perversion, disease and hate. His landscapes, as Denise Aebersold has put it, are,

> des paysages urbains décomposés où les immeubles partent en détritus, où les rues fondent en boues liquides, villes des tropiques croupissant dans les fièvres moites, tous ces lieux surchargés de pourriture [qui] représentent un nouvel aspect d'un panorama unique, qui dépeint la corruption des êtres, la dissolution irrémédiable de l'existant.[38]

Yet even though death and darkness provide the canvas on which his works are painted, Céline's brush strokes are vibrant slashes of colour brimming with delirious energy and laughter. Or maybe it is because death is his canvas that his palette is so bright, for it is only when death is accepted as the ineluctable end towards which all is travelling on this *voyage au bout de la nuit* we call life, when the enlightening beams of Genetic light are eclipsed, that one is able to live in freedom and lucidity, to take desire/delirium as the guiding principle of existence, and not the dissimulating lies proffered by molarity:

> M.H. —Donc, à votre avis, une pensée lucide est une pensée eschatologique, essentiellement.
>
> L.-F.C. —Essentiellement. Il n'a qu'à se résoudre à son sort, penser à son père, sa mère, ses frères, ses cousins...[39]

Death, then, might be considered the plane of immanence of Céline's novels, their body without organs, for it is that zero intensity necessary for desiring-production, for the machinic heterogenesis of these works which will reject all pre-givens, all inscribed Histories, to traverse the ever new world of the imagination, the smooth space of fiction:[40]

Voyager, c'est bien utile, ça fait travailler l'imagination. Tout le reste n'est que déceptions et fatigues. Notre voyage à nous est entièrement imaginaire. Voilà sa force.

Il va de la vie à la mort. Hommes, bêtes, villes et choses, tout est imaginé. C'est un roman, rien qu'une histoire fictive. Littré le dit, qui ne se trompe jamais.

Et puis d'abord tout le monde peut en faire autant. Il suffit de fermer les yeux.

C'est de l'autre côté de la vie. (*V*, p.5)

If death can be said to constitute the plane of immanence of the Célinian universe, the primary mode of production on this plane is surely delirium, as many critics have noted. In Allen Thiher's study, *Céline: The Novel as Delirium*, for instance, it is suggested that Céline's novels, 'are, in essence, discourses in the delirium that springs from his intolerable awareness of human misery',[41] whilst in his article 'La Quête du délire', Michel Beaujour sees 'sous-jacente à toute écriture, la tentation permanente de la folie'.[42] Notwithstanding their individual merit, both of these studies, however, ultimately perceive Céline's *délire* to be simulated, a conscious act of mimicry employed by the author to a specific end, an interpretation which reaches its apogee in Yannic Mancel's article 'Sémiotiques de la folie et de l'écriture dans *Féerie pour une autre fois*', where it is suggested that Céline deliberately integrates into his discourse pathological traits of schizophrenia so as to attain absolution for the anti-Semitic pamphlets he wrote from 1937–1941.[43] An even greater number of Célinian commentators, meanwhile, have interpreted the delirious essence of this *œuvre* as being indicative of a pathological condition on the part of the author. Such studies include George Steiner's 'Cry Havoc', Patrick McCarthy's *Céline*, Alain Ferrant's 'D'une compulsion l'autre: écriture et rhétorique de la confusion chez L.-F. Céline', and, most strikingly, Bettina L. Knapp's *Céline: Man of Hate*.[44] Ferrant, for instance, writes,

Certains névrosés traumatiques ne rêvent pas mais écrivent. Le travail d'écriture prend chez eux la place et les fonctions assignées au rêve et se charge alors d'un rôle complémentaire. Au-delà de la "prime de séduction", le lecteur est convoqué comme acteur dans un espace qui est et n'est pas en même temps le sien. Il est confronté à une part de lui-même nécessairement refoulée dans le processus de symbolisation qui caractérise l'avènement du sujet en tant que tel.

> L.-F. Céline appartient à cette catégorie d'écrivains. Son écriture est essentiellement inductive en ce sens qu'elle est tout entière mobilisée pour agir sur le lecteur: elle est asservie à la compulsion de répétition.[45]

Knapp, meanwhile, carries out a reading of Céline's *œuvre* intended to bring to light hate complexes and other psychological deficiencies within the author, stating, for instance, that *Féerie pour une autre fois* is, 'the work of a man fighting for his sanity, a man trying to extricate the pain, anger, resentment, and unassimilated feelings that have built up within him and curdled in his subliminal world', and that, 'the unending and confused series of images—some of them archetypal—that emerge in *Fairy-Play for Another Time I* are comparable to those observed by Doctor Marie-Louise von Franz in schizophrenics'. Knapp goes on to conclude from this that, '*Fairy-Play for Another Time I* is [...the] product [...] of a mutilated psyche. It is a manifestation of the physical and psychological distortions experienced by the author in his twisted and tormented world'.[46]

In the belief that no literary analysis can nor should attempt to attribute such traits to the author of the text under consideration, and that any such analysis is of little use for a further understanding of that text, the present study will reject all such conceptions of delirium/madness in the novels of Louis-Ferdinand Céline, preferring, in the light of Deleuze and Guattari's conception of schizophrenia, to analyse this delirium not as a deliberate ploy to attain concrete ends, nor as the symptom of a pathological condition—although, like a Deleuzoguattarian schizophrenia, this delirium will constantly verge on and risk slipping into pathology—, but rather, as has been suggested, as a style, an organising principle, a mode of composition, the only possible means of survival and continuance for those refusing to conform to the simulacra of life presented by molarity:[47]

> Et où aller dehors, je vous le demande, dès qu'on a plus en soi la somme suffisante de délire? La vérité, c'est une agonie qui n'en finit pas. La vérité de ce monde c'est la mort. Il faut choisir, mourir ou mentir. Je n'ai jamais pu me tuer moi. (*V*, p.200)

In taking this approach, this study finds itself in agreement with Pierre Verdaguer who, in spite of his assertion that, in *Voyage au bout de la nuit* and *Mort à crédit*, pathology is occasionally employed by Céline to give a realistic justification to the delirious accesses of his narrators and the marvellous events they recount,[48] states, 'la fièvre et le délire offriront l'ouverture nécessaire sur un ailleurs onirique à valeur compensatoire. Chez Céline, les univers de l'au-delà onirique, produits de l'imagination déformante, se suivent et s'enchevêtrent', and that, 'le délire s'impose comme le mode privilégié de ce glissement dans le surnaturel'.[49] Such a mode of organisation might be termed, to borrow another term from Deleuze and Guattari, a war machine, the organising principle intrinsic to the nomad which can be appropriated yet never fully assimilated by the State (hence the normalised conception of war as a function of the State apparatus),[50] a suggestion lent credence by Robert Llambias' study, 'Guerre, histoire et langage dans le récit célinien', where is it suggested that war acts as the organising principle of the Célinian novel. Llambias writes,

> La guerre est surabondance de fête, voyage donc délire dans lequel le monde éprouve un monstrueux orgasme permettant la destruction de l'individu et sa fusion dans une alchimie de sexe et de violence. La fête/guerre est donc la disparition de l'homme et de l'ordre anciens;[51]

and later,

> Guerre et écriture possèdent les mêmes effets, les mêmes vertus. Elles opèrent un dédoublement de l'homme qui le transforme en mort-vivant. La guerre est une métaphore de l'écriture célinienne. Toutes deux élèvent la mort *hic et nunc* au statut de créateur: création d'une altérité irréductible à soi et au monde.[52]

Founded on a non-pathological delirium, Céline's novels will act as agents of deterritorialisation, emanating from the sedentary spaces of molarity, yet seeking to destratify those very spaces, to redefine the givens and preconceptions of everyday life at every turn, to re-imagine reality as a fiction. It is in such terms, as Henri Godard rightly notes, that Céline conceives of the role of the novelist:

> Ne jamais raconter que des histoires que l'on ait soi-même vécues, les seules à propos desquelles on puisse "lyriser", mais ne jamais les raconter telles qu'on les a vécues, c'est entre ces limites que Céline définit l'aire du roman. D'un côté, bannir l'imagination en tant que "pure invention", c'est-à-dire gratuité; de l'autre, ne rien admettre que l'imagination, mise en branle par l'émotion, n'ait "transposé". Les deux exigences peuvent paraître contradictoires; il faut semble-t-il, qu'un récit choisisse entre la vérité et la fiction. Mais il existe un point d'où elles apparaissent au contraire comme complémentaires, et c'est là que se place Céline.[53]

It is, then, by that most primordial of techniques for Céline, transposition—'Transposez ou c'est la mort' (*GB*I, p.86)—, that the apparent lacuna at the heart of the Célinian aesthetic is breached. As Robert Llambias notes,

> Cette transposition, comme la théâtralisation, dédouble le récit en une chronique où défilent, en parallèle, comme sur des rails, le déluge du quotidien et celui, plus authentique, de l'"outre-là". Cet "outre-là" n'est pas un ailleurs de notre monde; il en est la face cachée et la source intensive où s'élaborent les pulsions homicides de notre temps.[54]

Transposition will thus be that which will allow the Célinian aesthetic to come to its fruition, for it is that which injects anti-production into the process of production, which deterritorialises the strata of molarity so as to enable a movement away from the societally-constructed spaces of a reality governed by hermeneutic transcendentalisms, to an intensive, collective social space filled with immanent relations and desire, a choreographic life.[55]

The rejection of the dominant mode of reality, of molar agglomerates as the organisational principle of twentieth-century life, and the quest for alternative modes of existence ruled by desire, aesthetic principles and social relations, can be seen in the fictional spaces of Céline's first two novels, *Voyage au bout de la nuit* and *Mort à crédit*. In the former, the molar institutions of War, Nation, State, Patriotism, Colonialism, Capitalism and Religion confronted by Bardamu on his quest for a mode of existence in which individual desire is able to coexist with the dominant mode of governance, are all deterritorialised through transposition into a space where they are stripped of their naturalness, where the universally accepted tenets that normally sustain them are no longer able to provide justification for their insidious ways—or their very existence, even—, and where they thus become subject to interrogation and ridicule.[56] In spite of his terrifying lucidity which leads him to refuse the strata of molarity with their infinite number of transcendental means to dissimulate the true organic nature of human existence, however, Bardamu's inability to cast off his own refusal of death binds him to the strata, ensuring that his deterritorialisation never goes far enough, remaining an empty cry and not an expression of desire capable of accelerating the territorialisations of molarity to the point that they break apart.[57] As a result, his desire/delirium always ends up pathologised, bringing about a flight to a new strata, not a line of flight traversing and deterritorialising the strata, the dissolution of the scene and not the dissolution of self that would be required for the accession to a supermolecular state of becoming:[58]

> Décidément nous n'adorons rien de plus divin que notre odeur. Tout notre malheur vient de ce qu'il nous faut demeurer Jean, Pierre ou Gaston coûte que coûte pendant toutes sortes d'années. Ce corps à nous, travesti de *molécules agitées* et banales, tout le temps se révolte contre cette farce atroce de durer. Elles veulent aller se perdre nos *molécules*, au plus vite, parmi l'univers ces mignonnes! Elles souffrent d'être seulement «nous», cocus d'infini. On éclaterait si on avait du courage, on faille seulement d'un jour à l'autre. Notre torture chérie est enfermée là, *atomique*, dans notre peau même, avec notre orgueil. (*V*, p.337; my italics)

This same kind of deterritorialisation can be seen to take place in *Mort à crédit*—the title of which, in the context of the present study, can be said to describe Capitalist society's dissimulation of death, its attempt to postpone *ad infinitum* the final reckoning—with regard to the molar institutions of the Family (especially its Œdipal aspects), the Class system, Capitalism, Psychoanalysis, Science and Education. Rather than simply move from one strata to another, as did Bardamu in *Voyage au bout de la nuit*, however, the Ferdinand of *Mort à crédit* does seem to access a desiring mode of existence, to find an alternative lifestyle within the strata of society that nonetheless refuses to conform to them.[59] In every case, however, these alternative lives prove to be either but fleeting instances of desire, or illusory, the supposedly alternative existence they proffer being ultimately exposed as nothing more than a disguised strata, an alternative molarity that does not even offer the anaesthetic advantages that make the orthodox molar institutions such an attractive prospect. No wonder, then, that at the end of *Mort à crédit*, Ferdinand is left in a state of near catatonia—his desire pathologised by the succession of impasses it has come up against—, able to conceive of a future life only within the ultra-regimented confines of that most repressive of molar institutions, the Army (*MC*, pp.1098–1104).

It seems somehow fitting that Bardamu and Ferdinand should never find the means to achieve an existence infused with desire, to exist according to their own style, for in *Voyage au bout de la nuit* and *Mort à crédit*, the same can be said with regard to Céline and his literary style. No matter how revolutionary their style, the delirium on which Céline's aesthetic is to be constructed is never fully integrated into the writing of his first two novels, remaining primarily on the level of content and not that of style. This is perhaps more obvious in Céline's literary début, *Voyage au bout de la nuit* indubitably being the most orthodox and traditionally literary of all his works; but in *Mort à crédit* also, despite the ever-increasing proliferation of the infamous aposiopetic "trois points" and the establishment in the prologue of a delirious narrative space, the stylistic composition seems reserved in comparison to the vertiginous linguistic acrobatics and apocalyptic stylistic deconstruction of the later novels. As Henri Godard notes,

> Plus on avance dans l'œuvre romanesque de Céline, plus la forme du roman se modifie. Dans *Voyage au bout de la nuit* et dans *Mort à crédit*, le récit garde un ordre assez traditionnel: sauf dans le prologue de *Mort à crédit*, il suit fidèlement l'ordre chronologique et l'enchaînement des aventures du héros. Mais à partir de *Guignol's band*, il se complique. Entre ces aventures et le lecteur vient s'interposer un narrateur, dont le présent et la mémoire ne peuvent qu'interférer avec l'ordre des événements, le bouleverser, lui imposer leur ordre propre, c'est-à-dire leur désordre. On atteint ainsi peu à peu les derniers romans, ceux de la trilogie allemande, dans lesquels le lecteur ne trouve plus l'histoire qu'il attend qu'à travers la présence d'un narrateur constamment au premier plan (pour commencer en début de roman) et seulement au gré des caprices de sa mémoire.[60]

It is to these later novels, post-*Mort à crédit*, that the present study will limit itself, firstly because there exists such a wealth of commentary on Céline's first two novels that much of what could be said about them here would be little more than a re-statement in different terms of points made elsewhere.[61] The notions of deterritorialisation and alternative modes of existence discussed above, for instance, are, to a certain extent, but reformulations of those anarchic elements discussed by critics such as Erika Ostrovsky, who writes,

> Céline advocates a semblance of anarchy in literature mainly in order to reflect the state of the world in which we live, and rejects any doctrinaire approach. He is clearly too much of a skeptic to believe in the methodical application of anarchy or any other theory. Actually, he is "merely an anarchist out to destroy all anarchies. Surely if anarchy reigned somewhere, he would be opposed to it, just as he is opposed to everything else..." We might once again connect this attitude with the opposition or even abhorrence the author feels toward any strictly delimited action, category, or school of thought, that is, anything that resembles a state of fixity.[62]

More importantly, however, this study will concentrate solely on Céline's completed novels from *Guignol's band* on, because in them, through the reversal of the normal hierarchy between thematics and stylistics, can be traced the delirious trajectories not only of their protagonists in a fictional universe, but also the stylistic trajectories of Céline in the Historical universe.

Trajectories

If Céline's principal characters and narrators are engaged in the quest for a life lived by style, a life of intensive states limited only by desire and with an infinite number of possible points of local connection, then the same can be said of Céline himself.[63] For true to Deleuze's statement that opened this introduction, style, for Céline, author, does not merely describe the particularity of his writing, but his entire way of life, his constantly renewed struggle for a form capable of transmitting to his reader not a message—for despite the intellectual foundation of his art, Céline cared little for messages, ideas, concepts or any other construct depending on the axiomatics of intellectuality for its transfer—, but desire, emotion.[64] In this respect, the role of art for Céline can be said to coincide with that of Proust (as analysed by Deleuze), for it is the only means by which man, in a world of chaos, can access a certain unity or totality without recourse to the transcendental falsehoods of molarity:[65]

> Quel est donc ce mode très spécial d'unité irréductible à toute "unification", cette unité très spéciale qui surgit par après, qui assure l'échange des points de vue comme la communication des essences, et qui surgit suivant la loi de l'essence, elle-même comme une partie à côté des autres, coup de pinceau final ou morceau localisé? La réponse est la suivante: dans un monde réduit à une multiplicité de chaos, c'est seulement la structure formelle de l'œuvre d'art, en tant qu'elle ne renvoie pas à autre chose, qui peut servir d'unité—par après [...]. Or nous avons vu précédemment, dans les directions les plus diverses, l'importance d'une *dimension transversale* dans l'œuvre de Proust: la transversalité. C'est elle qui permet dans le train, non pas d'unifier les points de vue d'un paysage, mais de les faire communiquer suivant sa dimension propre, dans sa dimension propre, alors qu'ils restent incommunicants d'après les leurs. [...] C'est elle qui fonde les profanations et se trouve hantée par le bourdon, l'insecte transversal qui fait communiquer les sexes par eux-même cloisonnés. C'est elle qui assure la transmission d'un rayon, d'un univers à un autre aussi différents pourtant que les mondes astronomiques. La nouvelle convention linguistique, la structure formelle de l'œuvre, est donc la transversalité, qui

traverse toute la phrase, qui va d'une phrase à une autre dans tout le livre, et qui même unit le livre de Proust à ceux qu'il aimait, Nerval, Chateaubriand, Balzac... Car si une œuvre d'art communique avec un public, bien plus le suscite, si elle communique avec les autres œuvres du même artiste, et en suscite à venir, c'est toujours dans cette dimension de transversalité, où l'unité et la totalité s'établissent pour elles-mêmes, sans unifier ni totaliser objets ou sujets.[66]

This study will examine the ways in which Céline's work attempts to attain such a style premised on a transversal relation, an auto-objective style which, through a non-representational mode (itself achieved through the unity coming from the concordance of the novels' thematic and stylistic levels), will construct an aesthetic capable of carrying out the emotive transmission of Céline's 'style au plus sensible des nerfs!' (*EY*, p.537), his 'métro émotif'—the metaphorical embodiment of his ideal aesthetic found in *Entretiens avec le professeur Y*.[67] Although written after *Guignol's band* and *Féerie pour une autre fois*, it is in this fictional work that Céline's aesthetic intent can best be seen, *Entretiens avec le professeur Y* being an exercise in style at the same time as it is an explication of that very style.[68] He writes,

la Surface est plus fréquentable!... la vérité!... voilà!... alors?... j'hésite pas moi!... c'est mon génie! le coup de mon génie! pas trente-six façons... j'embarque tout mon monde dans le métro, pardon!... et je fonce avec: j'emmène tout le monde!... de gré ou de force!... avec moi!... le métro émotif, le mien! sans tous les inconvénients, les encombrements! dans un rêve!... jamais le moindre arrêt nulle part! non! au but! au but! direct! dans l'émotion!... par l'émotion! rien que le but: en pleine émotion... bout en bout! (*EY*, p.536)

This is to be made possible, as he goes on to point out, thanks to his 'rails profilés! mon style profilé!' (*EY*, p.536):

—*Exprès profilés!*... spécial! je les lui fausse ses rails au métro, moi! j'avoue!... ses rails rigides!... je leur en fous un coup!... il en faut plus!... ses phrases bien filées... il en faut plus!... son style, nous dirons!... je les lui fausse d'une certaine façon, que les voyageurs sont dans le rêve... qu'ils s'aperçoivent pas... le charme, la magie, colonel! la violence aussi!... j'avoue!... tous les voyageurs enfournés, bouclés, double-tour!... tous dans ma rame émotive!... pas de chichis!... je tolère pas de chichis! pas question qu'ils échappent!... non! non! (*EY*, p.536)

The 'métro-tout-nerfs-rails-magiques-à-traverses-trois-points' (*EY*, p.543) thus describes the manner in which Céline's aesthetic is to operate according to a transversal relation, one which passes straight into the emotive core of the reader and which, through a carefully constructed artifice, deliberately sets out to become a collective assemblage of enunciation, an auto-objective expression: 'Des rails tout à fait spéciaux, des rails qu'ont l'air tout à fait droits et qui le sont pas!... que vous avez, vous, biseautés!... vous-même! d'une façon tout à fait magique!... vicieuse!...' (*EY*, pp.539–540).[69] The transmission of such an auto-objective expression, of course, necessitates the dissolution of the fixed molar boundary of subjectivity, or, to put it another way, the recipient/exponent of such an expression must *s'oublier*—[70] a process which has hilarious consequences for the interviewer of *Entretiens avec le professeur Y*:

> —Donc gafe colonel!... horrible péril!... allez pas lancer votre rame sur des rails droits ordinaires! non! non!... non!... je vous adjure! que sur les rails biseautés "spécial"! profilés "spécial"! par vous même! vous fiez à personne pour l'ouvrage! ouvragés au poil de micron! *vzzz! vzzz!*...»
>
> Mon *vzzz! vzzz!* lui faisait de l'effet... son pantalon dégoulinait... il pataugeait bien dans sa flaque... la flaque de plus en plus grande... (*EY*, p.541)

Chapter one of this study will propose that *Guignol's band* I and II can be read, on a thematic level, as the metafictional account of Céline's quest for precisely such an auto-objective style, an affective aesthetic mode of composition intended to bypass the molar frontiers of subjectivity (*faire s'oublier*) and pass directly to the emotive core of the reader in the Historical world—who will hopefully not experience the secondary affects arising from a more figurative interpretation of this process. Through a consideration of the novels' spatial representation, especially the tropes of the bridge and the *métro*, and of the characters who inhabit the fictional spaces of the two volumes, it will be suggested that the narrative of *Guignol's band* can be seen to constitute a metanarrative which serves primarily to trace the trajectory of the very artifice and aesthetic act by which that narrative comes into being. In this respect, *Guignol's band* will be considered as a precursor to the later, more explicitly theoretical *exposé*, *Entretiens avec le professeur Y*, and, as is the case with this later work, it will be suggested that, ironically, it is precisely because the narrative serves primarily to describe its own artifice that that artifice ultimately fails to fulfil its aim, the narrative space it creates for itself being quasi-autistic, autonomous to the point of remove. Rather than provide the accomplishment of the Célinian aesthetic, then, *Guignol's band* will be said merely to lay the groundwork for that aesthetic, to provide indications as to how that aesthetic is to come to its fruition.

Chapter two will examine *Féerie pour une autre fois*, a two-volume work commenced whilst Céline was in prison in Copenhagen awaiting extradition back to France. A reading of these volumes will be proposed that sees the effect that this imprisonment has on the affective aesthetic Céline was attempting to attain as the primary concern of the novels. Confined within the centripetal boundaries of History (of which the prison of the first volume is the concrete embodiment), Céline will be seen to be unable to transmit his aesthetic to his reader as he desired (that is to say, as desire), his every word being overcoded and interpreted as but the ravings of the Fascist he had become for the French reading public. As a means to escape this overcoding and enable his aesthetic to transmit itself via the transversal relation of emotion, it will be suggested that, in the first volume of *Féerie*, Céline intensifies the centripetal forces to which his narrator is subjected in an attempt to turn them to his advantage, whilst in the second volume, he performs a scission of his first-person narrator, projecting his desire (or, it might be said, his style, the mode of composition according to which the spaces of the novel are created) into an abject double—Jules—who is not subject to the centripetal forces of History, and who can thus emit a centrifugal, desiring force of sufficient intensity to overcome the inverse force of molarity. Both volumes will ultimately be seen to fail in their attempts to deterritorialise Céline's poetic expression from the strata of History and attain a plane of consistency, however, the first creating a pathological space, and the second, much like *Guignol's band*, an autistic space removed from the dominant reality.

Céline's continued attempt to liberate his aesthetic from the centripetal forces of History so as to arrive at an aesthetic mode of composition capable of direct sensory affect, will be seen, in chapter three of the present study, on a thematic level in all of the narratives of the author's final trilogy. In the novels that make up this trilogy, Céline will be seen to subject his pseudo-autobiographical first-person narrator to a process of self-abjectification, a reformulation of the Kristevan concept of abjection by which the narrator falsely appropriates (and thus deterritorialises) the Fascist traits attributed him, whilst simultaneously accelerating the centripetal forces of History inwards to a point of infinite density (a becoming-imperceptible) from which an auto-objective expression will be possible. This auto-objective expression—and thus the Célinian aesthetic—will be seen to reach its apogee in the final volume of the trilogy, *Rigodon*, as the narrator employs various becomings to access a supermolecular mode on a plane of consistency from which a transversal relation, a connective synthesis, will finally be possible, the textual space becoming one, 'where desire is liberated, and can spread by contagion through the creation of immanent relations between heterogeneous multiplicities'.[71]

Chapter One
Guignol's band

Introduction

That the action of *Guignol's band* begins on a bridge is by no means merely incidental. Nor is it a coincidence that the second volume of *Guignol's band* ends on a bridge, for this framing device provides this work (which is generally considered to be incomplete in every sense of the term)[1] with an organic unity—a unity that denies closure, nonetheless. Indeed, it will be argued that the image of the bridge is so important in *Guignol's band*, that the decision to publish the second volume of this work under the title *Le Pont de Londres* may not be nearly as unfortunate as some critics believe.[2]

The image of the bridge in the works of Céline has been expertly analysed by Philippe Bonnefis in his article 'Passage Céline', where he remarks that bridges are paramount for Céline because they 'enjambent les cassures',[3] that, 'le pont et le chaos vont ensemble. Ils tiennent ensemble; ils s'épaulent en quelque sorte. Ordre et désordre se fortifient ici l'un l'autre, établis l'un sur l'autre...',[4] and that, 'le pont célinien cède toujours plus ou moins aux séductions du gouffre. Pas de pont, chez Céline, qui ne flirte avec l'abîme',[5] all of which leads him to the consideration that, 'les ponts de Céline sont moins destinés à nous faciliter le franchissement des gouffres, qu'ils n'ont pour fonction d'amener les gouffres, pour ainsi dire, à notre niveau'.[6] Bridges, then, are the most precarious of man-made structures, separating man from the smooth space they span, a space which threatens both the stability of the structure itself and of those who cross it; it is for this very reason that they exercise such a strong attraction on those inhabitants of Céline's universe suffering amongst the molar superstructures of Capitalist society, on none more so than the various guises of the narrator, Bardamu, Ferdinand, Céline.[7]

Bridges, allowing man access to smooth space without plunging him into it, are an intermediary between the molar and the molecular, allowing communion with the amorphousness of the fluid without breaking all contact with the fixity necessary for molar-conditioned man to be able to function in the society around him, which is, according to Céline's first two novels, invariably predominated by molar axiomatics. To give man access to this kind of space was also the aim of Céline's 'métro émotif' which, as stated in the theoretical *exposé*, *Entretiens avec le professeur Y*, was intended to carry its passengers along with it as one body, a feat which is only possible once man, with his fixed notions of identity, race, class, creed and subject, has been introduced into a smooth space—such as the underground—where stratification can never be complete:

> j'embarque tout mon monde dans le métro, pardon!... et je fonce avec: j'emmène tout le monde!... de gré ou de force!... avec moi!... le métro émotif, le mien! sans tous les inconvénients, les encombrements! dans un rêve!... jamais le moindre arrêt nulle part! (*EY*, p.536).

This 'métro émotif' takes not only people with it, however, but, 'toute la Surface! [...] tous les ingrédients de la Surface! toutes les distractions de la Surface!' (*EY*, p.536), that is to say, all those molar formations existing in striated space that serve to distract man from the biological truth of his condition. So total is this destratification by the 'métro émotif', that it even takes 'les ponts avec!' (*EY*, p.537); but this is not to say that bridges are stratifying formations, for, as Philippe Bonnefis points out, in taking the bridges in its wake, 'le métro, à vrai dire, ne fait que reprendre son bien'.[8]

It can thus be argued that there is an equivalence between bridges and the *métro* in Céline's work, an assertion which is confirmed by a reading of one of the opening scenes of *Guignol's band* depicting the bombardment of a fictitious bridge, *le pont d'Orléans*. For by situating this scene on a bridge, the text can be seen to provide a fictional expression of the stylistic aim expounded in *Entretiens avec le professeur Y* on both a stylistic and thematic level. Thematically, this scene creates a smooth space/molecular mode for itself in a number of ways. Firstly, being set in the midst of a war destroying all around, the reader is plunged into a narrative recounted by a narrator and peopled by protagonists who cannot easily indulge in the death-dissimulating illusions rife in Capitalist society and the preceding two novels. Secondly, the people observed in this scene are a people in transit, without a fixed geographical territory to call their own, and, although it would be wrong to grant them the status of nomads, there is undoubtedly something nomadic in their present temporary condition. Finally, if a bridge is already a somewhat precarious structure that suspends man above an abyss—a smooth space devoid of stratification—then the 'gouffre' that Bonnefis states is brought to man on such a structure, is brought even closer when the very foundations of that bridge are in danger of destruction, and the water it spans begins to inundate it, as can be seen in the following quotations:

> *Braoum! Vraoum!...* C'est le grand décombre!... Toute la rue qui s'effondre au bord de l'eau!... [...] Le fier pont, douze arches, titube, culbute au limon d'un seul coup! La boue du fleuve tout éclabousse!... brasse, gadouille la cohue qui hurle étouffe déborde au parapet!... (*GB*I, p.87)

> Un obus! *Vrang!...* qui rentre dans le pont! la maîtresse arche saute, éclate!... Creuse un gouffre dans la chaussée, une béance énorme... un cratère où tout s'engouffre!... (*GB*I, p.90)

There are two main effects of this introduction into a smooth space. Firstly, connective syntheses are established between the people travelling across the bridge, with the result that any breach of the spontaneous self-organising structure formed brings about a violent reaction—as Ferdinand and his companions find out when their vehicle stalls (*GB*I, p.87)—, a reaction which, furthermore, acts upon the transgressive element to integrate it into the structure: 'La cohue nous rattrape... Nous tasse... Nous emballons à sauve qui peut!... On nous soupèse, on nous étreint farouchement!...' (*GB*I, p.89). Secondly, within this smooth space in which molecularity is heightened by the unavoidable presence of death, the kind of patriotic fervour that would, in the earlier *Voyage au bout de la nuit*, have served as a means by which to attempt to dissimulate the finiteness of the human condition, is now silenced, subsumed by death: 'L'on aperçoit un colonel, des Zouaves je crois, qui se débat dans la cataracte... Il succombe sous le poids des morts!... bascule tout au fond... «Vive la France!» qu'il crie finalement... vaincu sous le tas des cadavres!...' (*GB*I, p.90). Both of these effects are fused together in the image of a mutilated soldier communing with the people around him:

> Un petit soldat prélasse au fond! sa jambe hors pendante en lambeaux... juteux... Il est arsouille ce petit pioupiou! il nous fait des signes tout canailles... On s'amuse bien avec lui! *On est ensemble dans l'atmosphère*!... tout bouillonnants en plein remous!... (*GB*I, p.89; my italics)[9]

What is interesting to note, is that this introduction into a smooth space which brings about the formation of connective syntheses, suppression of molar fictions, and increase in desiring-production, all comes about due to the direct action of the Imperial War Formation on the populus. For, as is the case in the Tuileries scene in *Mort à crédit* (*MC*, pp.814–816), the spontaneous system created through connective syntheses is conducted to the strains of music; here, though, the music emanates from the Imperial War Formation—not from the spontaneous system formed on a plane of consistency itself, as can be said to be the case in *Mort à crédit*—, or, more specifically, from the symphony of explosions raining down from the enemy warplane above them, as can be seen in the following passages:

> Le méchant du ciel nous en veut... Il revient... Il nous repique en tornade!... Il nous rarrive en toboggan, fulminant, giclant de toutes ses foudres... Le sauvage il nous décapite!... le malotru!... Il nous emporte dedans son ventre! dedans son fracas massacreur!... (*GB*I, p.89)[10]

> Et puis tic-tac!... *Rraou!... Rraou!...* C'est la musique du grand carnage!... le ciel râle de rage contre nous!... L'eau par-dessous... Et c'est l'abîme!... Tout explosionne!... (*GB*I, p.90)

> Mais le branle-monde est en musique... rien ne saurait stopper la danse!... C'est le Musette Tonnerre de Dieu!... Et l'égrènement des cent mille morts, des mille oiseaux piaillants, piaulant au vol autour, tramant les airs...
>
> Et puis c'est une autre guirlande à doux accents et sourds tromblons... ça vient tout du fond... des collines... ça roule aux échos d'artillerie... Vous ne sauriez battre entrechats tellement tout le corps vous accable bâté de vil plomb morfondu!... mais la cadence vous rattrape... le fond du pont plein de grenades trémousse pour vous... (*GB*I, p.93)

Ironically, then, in attempting to destroy individual people, this enemy bombardment of the bridge actually has the effect of creating *a* people who act as one body in a process of spontaneous self-organisation, a bond far stronger than the illusory one proffered by patriotism within its own stratified spaces demarcated by fictional boundaries and abstract concepts of Nation. Through the introduction of Capitalism's reterritorialising tendencies into doubly smooth/molecular space (the plane of immanence created by the bridge and all-pervading sense of mortality), a space in which axiomatisation becomes redundant, therefore, the fluxes decoded in the creation of the Capitalist system escape the control of the fascist paranoiac pole that constantly attempts to reterritorialise/overcode them, allowing for connective not conjunctive syntheses that bring about an expression of schizophrenic desire, of pure, spontaneous emotion.[11]

This desire is expressed libidinally by one of the characters in the text, and is interpreted by the molar agent present (who is a representative of all of the major molar axiomatics: the Family, the Judiciary, and the Economy) as madness which breaches reason. Unsurprisingly, his protestations are futile, provoking both the (female) transgressor into a statement which annihilates not only the symbolic capital of his molar positions of power, but also his belief in his own fixed subjectivity, and the crowd into a violent reaction which leads to his reintegration into the mass:

> Ah! Dans *ces remous d'hébétude* survient le cas de rébellion... D'un *élan*, voici que Brigitte, *la femme* du *Procureur* Sacagne, délaissant *d'un trait* sa voiture, s'arrache aux exhortes angoissées, relève une bonne grande fois sa jupe et saute sur le parapet, de là dominant la cohue, braille à travers toute la tourmente des mots de colère et d'insultes!...
>
> «Brigitte!... Brigitte!... je vous supplie! de grâce *revenez à moi!... votre bon mari! Revenez à la raison!...* Je vous intime! Je vous somme!...
>
> —Merde! Merde! *Vous existez pas!...*
>
> —Messieurs, mesdames! *ma femme est folle*!... Elle est enceinte! *C'est l'émotion! Je suis le Procureur* Sacagne de Montargis dans la Côte-d'*Or*!...
>
> —Merde! Eh, Chinois! Tu nous les casses! Au vent ta morue! Wagon!...»
>
> Voilà comment la foule l'appelle... Voilà qui aigrissait les choses!... *Il retombe épuisé sur le monde!* (*GB*I, pp.93–94; my italics)[12]

If the smooth space created on this bridge under attack is expressed through libidinal liberation in Brigitte, in the narrator, Ferdinand, it is experienced, as the attack reaches its climax, as a dissolution of his fixed subjectivity which, in turn, leads to a 'vision féerique' in which he fuses with the entire universe:

> Au moment juste tout redevient feu, tonnerre, éclairs!... déchirement du ciel dedans et autour... Une foudre écrase, broye la chaussée... Ah! Il était temps!... éparpille toute la panique, les personnes, les arches, les voitures, le fleuve tout bouillant vaporise.... L'enfer est là!... Les flammes nous enveloppent, nous sommes pirouettés dans l'espace!... [...] Je voyais plus haut maintenant que les nuages... là alors c'était du spécial... là en plein ciel!... en plein azur!... la vision féerique... une main coupée je voyais... une main bien pâle sur des flocons... des coussins de nuages à reflet d'or... et qui saignait au goutte à goutte... une main pâle blanche et tout autour des nuées d'oiseaux... tout rouges... voletant jaillis de ces plaies même... les doigts tout scintillant d'étoiles... semés aux

> marges de l'espace... en longs voiles tendres... clairs et de grâce... berçant les Mondes... et vous effleure... et vos beaux yeux... câlinement... tout vous emporte... tout vogue aux rêves... tout abandonne... aux fêtes du Palais des Nuits... (*GB*I, p.94)

This vision has often been neglected by critics, somewhat surprisingly.[13] For this passage can be said to constitute a pivotal moment in the novel—indeed, in Céline's literary career—for it marks the point at which the thematics (which, up until this point, have been concerned with the protagonists' search for a smooth, deterritorialised space within the striated) are put to the service of the stylistics, the narrative serving to tell of the text's attempts to introduce the *reader* into a smooth space where s/he is able to experience the same kind of direct emotive communion experienced by the protagonists. To put it another way, this passage, both retroactively and proactively, indicates that there is a certain slippage between the thematic and stylistic levels of the narrative, that the entire bombardment scene and all that is to come, describe not only a surface thematics, but also the very spaces of the text itself, that, in other words, this is a metanarrative describing a metafictional space. The first indication that this passage can be read in this manner comes from the description of this vision as 'féerique', the adjective derived from the word that seems to encapsulate best the essence of Céline's aesthetic—as he himself was to recognise in the title of his next work after *Guignol's band*. Taking this hypothesis further, it can be conjectured that, if this hand is the hand of the author, the blood flowing from it could symbolise the emotionally invested ink flowing from the author's pen, and the flocks of birds and stars that emanate from these very same wounds—from the same emotional core—his 'style émotif' '[qui] vous effleure', especially 'vos beaux yeux' (of the reader?), and 'vous emporte' as does the 'métro émotif', taking you to a place where everything is dream, a 'Palais des Nuits', that place which is 'de l'autre côté de la vie' and to enter into which, 'Il suffit de fermer les yeux' (*V*, p.5).[14]

The Smooth Space of Metafiction

This interpretation is reinforced by the strategic positioning of this scene. For the pages preceding it are little more than an explicit metanarratival address to the reader from the author, extolling the virtues, for mortal man, of emotionally-invested telegraphic writing ('vous écrirez «télégraphique» ou vous écrirez plus du tout! L'Émoi c'est tout dans la Vie! / Faut savoir en profiter! / L'Émoi c'est tout dans la Vie! / Quand on est mort c'est fini!' (*GB*I, p.85)), whilst the three short passages following on from this scene are, as Henri Godard has pointed out, intended to 'prendre en compte les positions exposées dans ses écrits les plus récents [(les pamphlets)] et assurer la transition'.[15] However, the clue to read the bombardment scene as a metanarrative is not only provided by the surrounding of it by such self-consciously self-referential sections which deliberately point up the artifice of the text. Indeed, the line preceding the bombardment scene tells the reader that this text 'sera tout ce que vous y mettrez! l'orage ou la flûte! comme aux Enfers, comme chez les Anges!' (*GB*I, p.86), that, in other words, this text can either be read as an 'orage', a Historical, Political tract (as Céline's audience did with regards to his pamphlets), or as a 'flûte', an expression of musicality, of emotion.[16]

By giving the reader this clue as to his/her own reading of the text, however, the narrator is not implying that the text can only be read in one of these two ways. For any text which is consciously written so as to elicit more than one reading cannot, by definition, be read according to the precepts of only one of the possible interpretative keys suggested. On the contrary, what this statement tells the reader is that the very essence of the text is to be found in between the two terms of the dichotomy, that the text is neither solely 'orage', nor solely 'flûte', nor is it half of one and half of the other; it is neither and both, for it is the dialogue between the two that truly matters, the process of transposition that shifts past into present, History into story, molar into molecular. Henri Godard may thus be perfectly right in his assertion that, in these initial sections, Céline's intention was to retain the polemical nature of the pamphlets which had caused him so much trouble, but in a slightly diluted form.[17] For by thus highlighting the multiplicitous nature of the text and suggesting two possible modes of reading, the text can no longer be read solely as Political/Historical comment, since the 'orage' is simultaneously 'flûte', a pure aesthetic, and thus removed from that sphere in which Politics takes effect. This downgrading of the Historical content of the text through transposition into an aesthetic, imaginary realm, would ideally ensure, of course, that *Guignol's band* did not fall prey to the unfortunate narrowly anti-Semitic reading his pamphlets had elicited, and that sensibilities would not be harmed. That this would indeed seem to be the text's intention is suggested later, as the narrator says:

> Maintenant ça risque plus grand-chose... je peux vous raconter tout en somme... toute la comédie... Y a les payes et les distances!... Ah! là là! plutôt!... C'est fini tout ça!... C'est du rêve... c'est plus que des images... imagination!... et puis y a eu la guerre 39... et puis tout ce que vous savez... C'est comme un autre monde à présent... (*GB*I, p.207)

This process of transposition into the smooth space of the text does not stop here, however, for a further thematic metafictional link—which operates both infratextually between these two sections and intertextually between this text and *Voyage au bout de la nuit*—can be seen in the first of the three short sections coming after the bombardment scene (which ends with the 'vision féerique' examined above) with the inclusion of a phrase that can only recall the prologue to Céline's first novel ('Rien ne s'affirme, rien ne luit!...' (*GB*I, p.94)).[18] This resonance between these two passages which, at first sight, seem to be linked to each other only spatially, then continues a few lines later with what would seem to be a direct address to the audience coming fresh from the linguistic acrobatics of the bombardment scene: 'Vous voici tout frémissants, / Hennissants, avides aux pirouettes, / *Sous les déluges d'artifice*' (*GB*I, p.95; my italics). Any reader who has seen in this bombardment scene an ideologically-biased portrayal of History, therefore, has been led astray. For what the reader has been witness to is not journalistic reportage, but *transposition*, not a scene of enemy bombardment, but (*feu d'*) artifice, a fireworks display, the re-enactment of a real Historical event in which all the destructive horror is converted into pure enjoyment for the spectator.[19]

The opening sections of *Guignol's band*, therefore, are primarily concerned with the creation of a smooth space—[20] an exemplary symbol of which is provided by the image of a bridge under attack—in which the paranoiac reterritorialising axiomatics of Capitalism crumble to leave room for the expression of a properly schizophrenic desire that can set up connective syntheses—either thematically between protagonists, or stylistically between text and reader. This is a space into which History, freed of fixed ideological perspectives, can be transposed and become a story with the power to move, thus conforming to the stylistic intention of the 'métro émotif', of going, 'direct dans l'émotion!... par l'émotion!' (*EY*, p.536):

Émouvez bon Dieu! Ratata! Sautez! Vibrochez! Éclatez dans vos carapaces! fouillez-vous crabes! Éventrez! Trouvez la palpite nom de foutre! La fête est là! Enfin! Quelque chose! Réveil! Allez salut! Robots la crotte! Merde! Transposez ou c'est la mort! (*GB*I, pp.85–86).

It is not only in the opening sections that this creation of a smooth narrative space is attempted, however. Indeed, the entire main body of the text deliberately constructs a smooth narrative space by employing a technique already utilised in *Mort à crédit*, namely, the retention of the present tense in an external analepsis which is interspersed with frequent metanarratival intrusions from an extra-homodiegetic narrator situated in a narrative present posterior to the events of the story (*histoire* as opposed to *récit* or *narration*).[21] Allen Thiher talks of this stratagem in terms of a 'dichotomy between his young hero's vision, set in a world of comic lyricism and *délire*, and that of his older narrator, whose concern, as always, is with death'.[22] In view of the mechanisms of transposition analysed here, however, it would seem that the operation taking place in this mode of narration has to do not so much with a dichotomy, as with the desire to establish a connective synthesis between present and past. For if the mature narrator is situated in a molecular space in which he must inevitably confront death (which is not the same as saying that he is always concerned with death), and if the story he tells takes elements from the ideologically constructed strata of History, then the narrative thread produced will be a line of flight between the plane and the strata, neither one nor the other, but an intensity produced in the connective synthesis between the two.

Nor is it merely through a stylistic manipulation of temporality that the main body of *Guignol's band* creates a smooth space. On the contrary, it will be argued that the entire plot of *Guignol's band* can be read not only as a transposed History of French society, but also (perhaps primarily) as a fictional recounting of the precepts of the 'style émotif' that prefigures many of the elements that were to come in the later, more explicit but no less fictional declaration of stylistic intent, *Entretiens avec le professeur Y*.[23] Although this reading will highlight the text's awareness of its own artifice and style, however, it will be suggested that, ultimately, the textual space created is too smooth, privileging solely the 'flûte' side of the dichotomy established in the preface, intensifying the text's schizophrenic traits to the point of remove, of autism, with the result that the stylistic intent expounded in the thematics is not translated into the style of the work, style being that which allows individual essence to become a collective assemblage of enunciation, an instance of authorial desire which can be reinvested by the reader.

A Space Too Smooth

In *Guignol's band*, as is the case in *Voyage au bout de la nuit* and *Mort à crédit*, topography is distorted so as to render the geography of the physical space in which the action takes place if not unrecognisable, then troubling. As Nicholas Hewitt puts it,

> the maps [Ferdinand] draws for his reader are more like the mythological and magical maps of [Sosthène] than a Naturalistic account of London, and they are established through the presentation of an accumulation of topographical detail which, on closer inspection, is either invented or compressed and dislocated in order to recreate, not a real city, but an autonomous world.[24]

To call the geographical space created in *Guignol's band* autonomous is, in many ways, to call it a smooth space, for it is a space in which the co-ordinates that stratify man's geographical surroundings no longer apply, a space intended to frustrate any geodetic study, being a space that is not pre-existent but created only by the trajectories passing through it in that very instant. For the descriptions of promenades or flight in *Guignol's band* do not rely on any pre-existing knowledge of the itineraries traced. On the contrary, there is a deliberate stratagem on the part of the narrator to ensure that a sense of the itineraries traced in the novel can only be gained by the active pursuit of that itinerary which, furthermore, will never be the same twice, a change in light transforming one street into another, a phenomenon which escapes all logical explanation:

> Mettons que vous venez de Piccadilly... Vous descendez à Wapping... Il faut que je vous guide... Vous trouveriez pas... En sortant du «Tub» c'est à gauche... entre les Frigos... C'est étroit comme rue... du mur de briques, des pavillons des deux côtés, la queue leu leu... comme des jours de semaine... ça finit plus... ça recommence... une ribambelle... une éternité de maisons... pas une fantaisie... un étage toutes... une petite porte au trottoir... le marteau en cuivre... ainsi des rues et puis des rues... à la traverse et la suite... Plymouth Street... Blossom Avenue... Orchard Alley... Neptune Commons... des kyrielles de la même famille... Tout ça bien aligné convenable... Certaines gens vous disent que c'est triste... Ça dépend des jours, des saisons... Avec un petit coup de soleil ça devient joujou, ça se met en frais... Y a de la misère... C'est une

> chose... Y a des géraniums plein les fenêtres... plein les croisées... ça vous égaye... C'est les briques qui font monotone... grasses... poisseuses de fumée partout... des suints de la brume, des coaltars... L'odeur par là vers les docks est insidieuse, au soufre mouillé, au tabac moite, vous rentre au poil, vous habille... au miel aussi... C'est tout des choses qui vous viennent, qui s'expliquent pas d'en parler... (*GB*I, pp.104–105)[25]

In *Guignol's band*, a further, far more comprehensive distortion of physical space is in operation, however, for the London of *Guignol's band* bears much resemblance to the Paris of *Mort à crédit*—indeed, Ferdinand himself occasionally remarks on this similarity, saying, at one point, whilst contemplating an antiques gallery, for instance, 'ça me rappelait le nôtre à Paris comme genre de passage mais alors bien plus amusant' (*GB*II, p.448). Henri Godard points out many other such similarities in the footnotes to the Pléiade edition of the novels,[26] and has also remarked that, in certain letters to Marie Canavaggia at the time of writing *Guignol's band*, Céline often referred to the second volume as 'Pantin II', a name which recalls not only the word 'Guignol', but which is also a slang designation for Paris.[27] Furthermore, not only does the London of *Guignol's band* resemble the Paris of *Mort à crédit* in many ways, it is also principally peopled—in the experience of the narrator—by Frenchmen, who, as Colin Nettelbeck points out, constitute a series of transposed images of the degenerate French society (as portrayed in *Bagatelles pour un massacre*) which Ferdinand has supposedly left behind.[28] But, just as there is a double deterritorialisation of the physical striated space described in the novel, the co-ordinates of London being destratified so as to resemble a destratified version of Paris, so the allegorical status of the criminals and whores who should represent certain French Political figures, is anything but forthcoming, their introduction into this doubly smooth space rendering them virtually unrecognisable. To take but one general example, the gas mask trials that led Ferdinand and Sosthène to the Colonel's house can surely be read as an allegorical representation of the enterprise of twentieth-century warfare which is concerned merely with the economic benefits to be reaped from the invention of new methods of murder, but which, nonetheless, trusses its soldiers up in shiny uniforms (or feathers!) to give them the illusory sense of serving abstract, fictional notions such as "defence of the realm" and "Patriotism" in order to dupe them into believing that they are not totally expendable, mere fodder for the Imperialist machine. However, the space in which these events take place is so far removed from the strata of History, that all possible historical referents are obliterated in favour of the pure fleeting *jouissance* of comedy.

As regards the main body of these novels' narratives, then, the reader is once again witness to (*feu d'*) artifice, but one which will perhaps implode rather than explode. For even though referents from specific cultural, geographical and Historical centres are displaced into a space which is not their own, rather than providing a kind of diluted pamphlet through the defusing of these referents' symbolic capital, as Henri Godard has been seen to suggest above, it may rather be the case that, just as the physical space of the text (Great Britain—GB) is abstracted to the point of misrecognition/remove, so the textual space of the narrative (*Guignol's band—GB*) is so smooth, so metafictional, as to be an essentially autistic space, its desire enclosed within itself, just as the reader's desire is enveloped in the instant gratification of laughter. (To pervert an image from *Entretiens avec le professeur Y*, it might be said that it is by plunging it into water—smooth space—that Céline breaks the stick.) Hence, as much as the narrator may claim, in the opening sections of *Guignol's band*, that this text, 'sera tout ce que vous y mettrez! l'orage ou la flûte! comme aux Enfers, comme chez les Anges!' (*GB*I, p.86), his text may only allow the latter option.

As if aware of this possibility, both volumes of *Guignol's band* contain passages which might be described as cautionary allegories, passages which seem to warn against the reduction of the text to any one meaning. In these passages, ships—awe-inspiring vessels which travel in smooth space—are brought into port and anchored, tied down, removed from the limitless space in which they belong to be grounded in the artificial fixity of Man, their seemingly infinite beauty and potential being stifled in the process:

> À va molo! gros tremblement! À quai se proche!... gémit du flanc!... doucette amène... Là tout petit énorme se borde... accoste!... Il est paré!... Ouf! C'est fini!... Un gros sanglot plein sa bedaine... Ouf! Ouf! fini! fini! gros navigot!... À triste la fin des musiques... Le chagrin qui lui saisit tout!... Retour au port!... Tout pris de partout mille filins... Chagrin monte lui recouvre tout!... anéantit!... Stop! (*GB*I, p.114)

> Le plus tragique c'est les filins qui retiennent le navire par les bouts, gros comme il est, énorme en panse, il est léger, il s'envolerait, c'est un oiseau, malgré les myrions de camelotes dans son ventre en bois, comble à en crever, le vent qui lui chante dans les hunes l'emporterait par la ramure, même ainsi tout sec, sans toile, il partirait, si les hommes s'acharnaient pas, le retenaient pas par

> cent mille cordes, souquées à rougir, il sortirait tout nu des docks, par les hauteurs, il irait se promener dans les nuages, il s'élèverait au plus haut du ciel, vive harpe aux océans d'azur, ça serait comme ça le coup d'essor, ça serait l'esprit du voyage, tout indécent, *y aurait plus qu'à fermer les yeux*, on serait emporté pour longtemps, on serait parti dans les espaces de la magie du sans-souci, passager des rêves du monde! (*GB*II, p.672; my italics)[29]

It is not the wish of this study of *Guignol's band* to tie Céline's text down to one meaning in such a manner, destroying its beauty in the process. It will be argued, however, that, in the main body of the narratives of both volumes of *Guignol's band*, the metafictional level of narrative is privileged to the detriment of the allegorical level, the scene played out being concerned not so much with a transposed image of French society, as it is with the text's own stylistic aim of finding a truly auto-objective mode of expression, of becoming a collective assemblage of enunciation capable of being shaped by the reader's desire at the same time as it shapes his/her desire. In other words, the main body of narrative will play out the stylistic intent expounded in the prefacing sections, of creating a text able to be, 'tout ce que [le lecteur] y mettr[a]! l'orage ou la flûte! comme aux Enfers, comme chez les Anges!' (*GB*I, p.86).

This struggle for an inter-polar mode of expression, a molecular, schizophrenic expression of desire capable of affect in the paranoiac strata of molarity, will be acted out by the main protagonist and narrator, Ferdinand, in his own quest for an inter-polar mode of existence in which individual desire is able to survive and act within the dominant mode of reality.[30] On this quest, Ferdinand comes across many different characters, all of whom adhere, to a greater or lesser extent, to the paranoiac or schizoid poles of existence, or a mixture of the two. Each of these protagonists acts as a possible example for Ferdinand, and he runs from them or comes under their sway just as any individual is alternately repulsed and attracted by the paranoiac and schizoid poles of existence, just as this text oscillates between 'orage' and 'flûte'.[31] These characters fall into various categories: those who strictly adhere to the paranoiac pole of existence, investing their very being in a molar structure and becoming dehumanised in the process; those who attempt to experience life in its plenitude of duality, who live life as a constant struggle between the molar/paranoiac and molecular/schizoid poles, but who, failing to find an adequate means of reconciling the two poles of existence, are unable to provide Ferdinand with a model of harmonious inter-polar existence; those who are so far removed from the molar paranoiac pole as to be completely unable to interact with it, operating instead in what might be termed an autistic space; and, finally, those characters who find a way to express their desire in spite of the reterritorialising tendencies of the molar pole, whose flute, like the Pied Piper's, is capable of causing a storm.

The Paranoiac Pole

Matthew

The first and most obvious agent of the paranoiac pole that Capitalist society employs to reterritorialise any liberated flow of desire is a policeman.[32] A policeman, furthermore, who comes from Scotland Yard, a molar institution invested—thanks to the fiction of many Edwardian writers—with great symbolic capital. Not surprisingly, then, the first time Matthew appears in the novel, he demonstrates all the intolerant, paranoiac tendencies that might be expected of such a "respectable" agent of the Law from an organisation which, as Ferdinand comments, cannot abide, 'les variations d'habitude' (*GB*I, p.160). Accordingly, enraged by Borokrom's idiosyncratic dress sense, Matthew threatens to lock him up, thereby stopping Borokrom's piano playing—that all the clients of the pub were singing along to—and provoking a riot during which Matthew ends up buried underneath a pile of drunken revellers toasting his health (*GB*I, pp.102–103). To put this another way, it might be said that Matthew, a molar agent, in attempting to curtail a liberated expression of desire, a refrain leading to a body without organs—a self-organising system in which each individual (in this case) is but a partial object of a greater whole (here, a chorus)—replaces that refrain with a paranoiac, repressive attractor that incites a violent reaction in the crowd which leads to the integration of the territorialising agent into the body without organs. This, it should be remembered, is precisely what happened to the Procureur Sacagne during the bombardment scene in the opening sections of the novel.[33]

This mobbing of Matthew gives Ferdinand a chance to escape—this time—but for the majority of the time, Matthew's presence is not so easily avoided. For even when Matthew is not present in person to check up on Ferdinand and his friends—to check that their "papers" (that most molar of inventions that facilitates the instantaneous identification and classification of individuals, especially individuals of a more nomadic nature, that is to say, immigrants) are in order (*GB*I, p.168), to try and reintegrate them into molar society (be it by way of the Imperial War Formation in his role as self-appointed recruitment officer (*GB*I, p.124), that of self-righteous moralist appealing to their better senses (*GB*I, p.126), or his official one of upholder of the Law), or to take bribes from them (*GB*I, pp.128, 168) —, the reterritorialising paranoia his position is intended to inspire ensures that his symbolic power is ever-present (hence Ferdinand's constant preoccupation with Matthew in the second volume of *Guignol's band* after the incident at Greenwich) and capable of inducing such paranoia in Ferdinand that he recreates Matthew as an illusory, fantastical presence:

> Je le voyais partout dans les portes... Pas besoin de brahmanes pour cela... de troufignoler dans les transes... gavottes et tonnerres!... Je voyais Matthew dans tous les coins... il s'amenait tout seul... il m'engueulait et plus encore... il me traitait atroce... tous les noms de la dégoûtation... il me promettait les pires supplices... J'en dégoulinais de sueur froide... hypnotisé c'est le cas de le dire par ce bourre affreux... Il s'amenait tout en rouge dans le noir, et puis jaune et vert... c'était ses couleurs... et puis il fondait dans le grand flou... (*GB*II, p.582)[34]

Cascade

Cascade, although a criminal and supposed avowed enemy of Matthew, nonetheless obeys the molar codes embodied by Matthew. Cascade's apparent rebellion, bravado and self-assured individuality, are pure rhetoric, for he is, in fact, totally subservient to Matthew no matter what he may claim to the contrary. Behind Matthew's back, he may say, 'Moi j'ai pas besoin de feuille de route! Je marche bien tout seul!... Matthew je l'emmerde! et puis les autres!...' (*GB*I, p.131), but in Matthew's presence, he makes sure that his own papers are in order and adheres strictly to their mutual understanding that he can continue conducting his affairs without official intervention for as long as he keeps paying for the privilege. At one point, he even acts as a kind of intermediary for Matthew, informing Ferdinand, Borokrom and Clodovitz that they have been called up for national service, but doing so in such a manner that his words seem more like a threat than a warning (*GB*I, p.167–168).

In other respects too, Cascade is seen to be a real stickler for 'la loi! les bonnes façons, la politesse!' (*GB*I, p.141), and even has his own symbolically-invested insignia which have to be respected as he decrees:

> Ça venait souvent propos de ses bagues les impertinences, sur ses «six carats du Brésil» et son «saphir chevalière», deux pierres magnifiques. Elles lui faisaient bien des jaloux. Les lopes le trouvaient trop paré, ils lui demandaient si c'était lourd? Si ça lui retournait pas les poignes? Il tolérait pas la malice, quand ils y revenaient deux trois fois, y avait de la baffe plein l'atmosphère... (*GB*I, p.141)

When Cascade does not impose respect for himself on others physically, he does so using another molar code, that of gold. The text states:

> il était estimé, même par ses ennemis, même par les pires bourriques du Yard qu'étaient pourtant des bas râleux, disgracieux, cupides et jaloux. [...] l'homme s'imposait bien entendu, mais y avait aussi les cadeaux, c'était le caractère généreux, il répandait l'or d'abondance... (*GB*I, p.141)

Little does it matter, therefore, that Cascade is a criminal. In all respects he can be considered to be a representative of the molar paranoiac pole that imposes itself on others through various axiomatising tactics: terrorism, purchase, morality. It is surely these similarities that have led Colin Nettelbeck to see in Cascade and his band, 'an unmistakable allegory of the degenerate French society already portrayed in *Bagatelles*', and to see 'Ferdinand's rebellion against this milieu [as] a widening of Céline's own revolt against ready-made superstructures', a rebellion which, however, 'is not a total rejection, but an effort to establish a more equitable balance between the individual and the collective [which] is possible only if the potential of the individual has been determined and realized'.[35] According to Nettelbeck, this quest for an equitable balance that restores the individual at the heart of the collective is explored in the second part of the novel, which, as Nettelbeck comments, 'explores the two major areas of experience needed to complete Ferdinand's initiation: the spiritual and the esthetic'.[36] This division seems somewhat arbitrary, however, for there is no such absolute delineation of the text, Cascade being a constant absent presence fundamental to the development of Ferdinand's paranoid persecution complex throughout the novel. Although the Political allegory that Nettelbeck highlights is undoubtedly present, then, the continuity and unity of the text would seem to suggest, rather, that Ferdinand's relations with Cascade also enlighten primarily the spiritual and aesthetic quest undertaken by the author Céline through the medium of the text.[37]

des Entrayes

Another character whose presence is experienced fantastically in the text is le colonel des Entrayes, Ferdinand's army commander from *Voyage au bout de la nuit*—who, in that text, was le général des Entrayes—[38] a character who is conjured up in Ferdinand's mind only at those times when the paranoiac pole of molarity risks engulfing Ferdinand completely.

The first time des Entrayes is invoked as a fantastical figure of Ferdinand's imagination, comes after the murder of Mille-Pattes, an episode which forms the culmination of a whole series of breaches of molar codes in which Ferdinand, when not directly and solely responsible, has been implicated.[39] At this point in the text, Ferdinand has found no mode of existence that allows him to live inside yet apart from molar society, he has not attained the desired balance between the individual and the collective, for he is still captivated by the paranoiac pole employed by the "civilised" Capitalist machine to keep its subjects in check, and thus cannot transgress its moral and judicial codes without feeling guilty and persecuted. The enormity of this latest crime of his brings this paranoiac pole into full effect, causing the onset of a paranoid delirium—marked by an increase in Ferdinand's cranial noise—[40] in which all the molar forces that have inscribed him with their morals and codes of conduct come to haunt and reproach him: Matthew, his Mother and Father, and des Entrayes (*GB*I, pp.255–256). What he specifically remembers about des Entrayes is his patriotic battle cries, '«Haut les cœurs!... [...] Cavaliers! sabres à la main! [...] Haut les cœurs!... et au galôôôp!... Châârrrge!»' (*GB*I, p.257), and, believing that such blind adherence to a molar cause that gives purpose and direction to the frightening contingency of life through complete subsumption of the individual will be enough—as did both Bardamu at the beginning of *Voyage au bout de la nuit*, and Ferdinand at the end of *Mort à crédit*—, Ferdinand 'répond[..] à son appel' and heads off to the French embassy to try and join up, all the while trying to convince himself that his decision is the right one by insisting that he knows where he's going—an obvious irony since the topography of this passage is totally distorted and the proper nouns misspelt—,[41] and shouting out patriotic slogans: 'Je sais où je vais!... Haut les cœurs!... Tout pour la Patrie!... Je le connais moi l'itinéraire!... Je me perds pas dans le cœur de Londres!' (*GB*I, p.257).

Des Entrayes' second appearance comes at a time when Ferdinand finally seems to have found a purpose in life that is not dependent on a molar structure, his love for Virginie enabling him, for the first time ever, to plan for the future (*GB*II, p.588). The elation he experiences at this new sensation is short-lived, however, for the paranoiac codes of morality and honour that Auguste, Ferdinand's father in *Mort à crédit*, suffered from so, now come to threaten Ferdinand's future with this fourteen-year-old girl:

> Ah! y a pas à dire j'avais traversé une crise, maintenant je voyais clair... Je commence donc à rebicher, à me sentir d'attaque... tout recroule! Je suis repris par la frousse... tout est à recommencer!... tremblements! je saccade je clinque de tous les membres... Dans mon baquet je ragite je remousse!... je suis un martyr des scrupules... je suis en plein supplice... c'est tout à fait comme mon père... je souffre tout pareil... Il me parlait toujours en colère les yeux hors de tête... Lui aussi c'était la conscience qui le rendait marteau... qu'il s'en bouleversait pour des riens... pour une remarque, un mot de travers, pour un coup d'œil des voisins et nous en avions des voisins! cent quarante tout le long de notre Passage... c'est dire s'il était ravagé... moi j'étais juste comme lui au poil... et puis en plus quelles aventures!... j'avais de quoi me révolutionner!... et maintenant encore quel pétrin!... ah! j'en sortirais jamais! merde! (*GB*II, p.588)

As was the case for the young Ferdinand of *Mort à crédit*, this excess of the paranoiac pole results in a spontaneous defence mechanism: defecation. For the adult Ferdinand, however, the soiled garment (which he removes) only increases the strength of the paranoiac pole—as he now feels ashamed of his stench and nudity (*GB*II, p.591)—which, in turn, exacerbates his persecution complex to the extent that he imagines Virginie to be implicated in a plot with Sosthène and the Colonel to gas him to death (*GB*II, pp.592–593). Obviously realising that molarity can only be fought with molarity, Ferdinand enlists the help of des Entrayes to combat the molar forces that he sees lined up against him, imagining himself—in a full-blown paranoid delirium—to be a horse ridden by his former Army commander (*GB*II, pp.593–598).

The paranoiac pole of the Capitalist/Imperialist machine, then, is both that which transmits paranoia to Ferdinand, and that to which he resorts in attempting to overcome that very same paranoia—just as it might be said that the paranoiac pole of the Capitalist machine was that against which *Mort à crédit* was written, yet precisely that to which Céline took recourse when the resulting expression of his liberated, deterritorialising desire, was deemed to have broached the limits of societal acceptability. Unsurprisingly, however, such recourse can only lead to a pathological reaction—Ferdinand's paranoid delirium—trapped in an autistic space, and not a schizophrenic expression able to introduce the smooth into the striated through deterritorialisation within the strata. To attempt to do precisely this, however, to destabilise the illusory fixity of the striated, is the intention of some of the other characters Ferdinand encounters in the course of the novels.

Attempts at Inter-Polarity

The majority of the minor characters that Ferdinand encounters in the novel can be said to attempt to lead an inter-polar existence, trying to create a transgressive smooth space within molar society, but ultimately returning fully to molarity—one need only think of the exodus of pimps returning to France to join up to see that this is the case.[42] But a number of the major characters in the novel attempt to conduct their whole lives as molecular beings, living within the Capitalist/Judicial/Œdipal systems in such a way that their individuality is not subsumed, constantly deviating from the status quo.[43] All such attempts, however, are ultimately doomed to fail in this life oscillating between, 'Plaisanteries, courtois devis, frais rigodons, actes aimables... et puis [...] tout ce qui n'est plus après tant d'épreuves et d'horreurs que lourd et fantasque apparat de catafalques....' (*GB*I, p.177).[44]

Sosthène

Sosthène first appears as Ferdinand is ejected from the French Embassy where he had gone to join up. Refused by the Imperial War machine, this strange-looking Frenchman in a Chinaman's clothing seems to offer an attractive alternative to the disoriented narrator. For Sosthène firstly shatters Ferdinand's illusions of transcendence through patriotic fervour ('«Vous êtes un héros, paraît-il... Vous le prétendez!... Hum! Héros de la guerre!... Proie facile!... Jouet héroïque!... Un enfant!... [...] À votre âge tout est permis!... Vaillance! Vaillance!... Pour ma part, dites-le vous bien, j'ai d'autres chats à fouetter que d'aller me ruer sous les chars!... J'ai subi toutes les épreuves!... Toutes!... La guerre n'est qu'une pétarade! La vie est brève!...» (*GB*I, p.271)), suggesting that life should, in fact, only be about 'Divertissement!...' (*GB*I, p.271), and then offers Ferdinand the chance to escape the molar forces that assail him. For the adventures in which Sosthène wishes to embroil Ferdinand—the quest for 'La Tara-Tohé, Fleur des Songes!...' which is to be found in the '"Nid de Vérité sous le Toit du Monde"' (*GB*I, p.289) – will, according to Sosthène, result in his liberation from the molar forces which persecute him so:

> « [...] Tara-Tohé! Charme de l'Être!... Le poids s'échappe de votre corps!... Vous avez saisi la Fleur!... Les Ondes vous saisissent, vous entraînent à votre tour! elles vous emportent!... elles vous transposent!... où vous voulez!»
>
> Tiens! tiens!...
>
> «Vous évoluez!... vous voyagez dans l'atmosphère à votre guise des mois... des mois... La pesanteur n'est plus pour vous! Vous êtes entré...»
>
> [...]
>
> «dans la quatrième dimension!...
>
> Ah! Ça c'était chouette!
>
> «Personne ne peut plus toucher!... Vous atteindre!... Vous mettre en prison!... Vous êtes libre!... le "Libre des Ondes!"... le choyé des accords du monde! Vous êtes tout musique en un mot!... Harmonie!...» (*GB*I, pp.289–290)

Like Céline's 'style émotif', then, Sosthène's 'ondes' carry their subject outside of himself into a smooth space where the paranoiac pole of molarity can no longer reterritorialise and terrorise, leaving the subject free to express himself as a molecular being in tune with the universe, converting him into a pure expression of his own personal music, an individual governed solely by a refrain coming from within which is nonetheless in harmony with the universe. By joining up with Sosthène, one would think, therefore, that Ferdinand would finally be able to attain the inter-polar mode of existence that has frustrated him on so many occasions. Unfortunately, however, this is not to be the case.

The ideal that Sosthène offers is indeed appealing, and might well have been able to bring its objectives to fruition were not it for the fact that Sosthène is a phoney through and through, totally untrustworthy, and denounced as a despicable liar even by his own wife (*GB*I, p.293). Despite his insistent question when he first meets Ferdinand as to whether or not he is 'initiable' (*GB*I, p.271), Sosthène himself has never been initiated into the ways he purports to practise, he merely mimics them, dressing up in Chinese robes, acting out step by step and in time to a rhythm hammered out by Ferdinand with cutlery or toothbrushes the sacred dances described in the *Végas* text he has acquired as though it were a recipe book (*GB*II, pp.414–427), pretending to drink in pubs but never touching a drop (*GB*I, p.283), claiming to cast curses through the telephone but really just yelling childish obscenities (*GB*II, pp.552–557), and transforming, as Peter Dunwoodie has noted, 'la Fleur magique [en] fleurs artificielles, le culte des morts [en] l'exploitation commericale d'une momie, le mysticisme de l'Orient [...] en une troupe de "Brahmanes" de music-hall', all of which converts the supposedly marvellous into high farce.[45] This farce is heightened even more by the disastrous effects of Sosthène's efforts; for not only does he look completely ridiculous contorting himself into all manner of positions as he attempts to invoke various demons and spirits through dance, once he has become the bodily incarnation of one of these ferocious demons, the anti-molar power with which he is supposed to be infused is pathetic in the extreme, going no way towards fulfilling its goal of liberation from the paranoiac pole.[46] To take but one example, Sosthène's *pièce de résistance* does not reverse the flow of traffic as intended, putting a spanner in the works of the neatly striated traffic systems of London, and even though he does cause minor inconvenience for a few motorists, the major effect that his antics have is to bring about a serious beating of his own person by the police.

Bettina Knapp has commented on Sosthène's phoney Orientalism, rightly noting that, 'as narrated by Céline, the religious ritual has become a broad farce whose implication is that the practice of Yoga and of Oriental religious beliefs may be salvation for the Easterner, but not for the Westerner'.[47] She goes on to state, however, that the Occidental cannot gain access to the kind of 'suprapersonal, transcendental state' actively sought in Buddhist or Hindu religious practices, since the ego is inherent to and a basic requirement of the Occidental who must be able 'to experience "the phenomenal world in his own way"', with the result that any attempt to seek Atman will end in, 'emotional or psychic disaster' which will maim him and, 'compel him [...] to limp through life rather than to walk through it at a brisk pace'.[48] But Sosthène is not turned into the kind of miserable incapacitated wretch that Knapp's reading implies, merely an object of ridicule who negates his own particular method of trying to attain a supra-personal, auto-objective mode through the dissolution of his ego, but not the attempt itself. For it is precisely such a dissolution of the ego that is actively sought by Ferdinand in his allegorical, metafictional enactment of the author Céline's aesthetic quest, and the portrayal of Sosthène as a comic figure ensures that the reader does not totally dismiss him, but instead sympathises with his earnest, if ultimately useless, attempts to overcome the forces of molarity.

Van Claben

Like Sosthène, Van Claben's mere physical appearance would seem to relinquish the grip of the paranoiac pole to some extent; for someone who runs a business 'en grand costume de pacha [...] tout paré de soie jaune et mauve avec un turban colossal et puis une canne toute en pierreries et une grosse loupe de bijoutier [...,] en grand travesti oriental' (*GB*I, p.181), cannot be said to conform to a stereotypical conception of a businessman. Similarly, the very nature of his business—Van Claben is a pawnbroker—, although a legitimate profession, is the very opposite of the more usual type of business conducted in the retail industry, especially when Van Claben is involved: whereas in the latter goods are sold to the client and the client is always right, in Van Claben's business, goods are bought off the client and the client is not only wrong, he is openly mocked, humiliated, devalued and even involved in physical altercations (*GB*I, pp.185–186, 196–197). It is appropriate, therefore, that Van Claben's business should be situated in a place whose geographical location constitutes the very antithesis of that of an archetypal business district, the City with its hustle and bustle. Van Claben's house and place of business is described in the following manner:

> Comment elle se présente la maison?... «Titus Van Claben»... [...] C'est tout tranquille... tout rassurant... Trois, quatre quidams sur le perron qui bavardent comme ça... des clients sans doute... ils attendent leur tour... Dans le parc des mômes qui galopent, qui foncent partout, se coursent à travers les allées... (*GB*I, p.180)

> Ça se trouvait situé admirable, un peu en dehors de Greenwich, en plein sur le parc et puis au loin sur la Tamise, tout le panorama du fleuve... une féerie de spectacle... De ses fenêtres au premier étage on apercevait les gréements, tout l'Indian Dock, les premières voiles, les agrès, les clippers d'Avril, les long-courriers d'Australie... Plus loin encore, passé Poplar, les cheminées ocre, les wharfs des Peninsulars, les paquebots des Straits, blanc éclatant à superponts...

> Ah! c'était l'endroit idéal, on peut pas dire le contraire, comme point de vue, coup d'œil et tout pour celui qui gamberge voyages, navigation, escampettes...
>
> Une maison située admirable, tout un théâtre devant ses fenêtres, prodigieux décor de verdure sur le plus grand port du monde... Tout de suite à la belle saison ça devenait une vraie magie... fallait voir un peu les massifs, ce déferlement de fleurs!... toutes les espèces, jaunes, rouges, mauves, éclatantes, toutes essences, de quoi bien vour monter la tête, vous redonner la pleine confiance, la sottise pépère... (*GB*I, p.189)

From this description, it might easily be thought that Ferdinand had finally found, in this place, a space in which to live a fruitful inter-polar existence, Van Claben's house being a centre of molarity surrounded by molecularity. But therein lies the problem; for just as Van Claben's business and dress sense appear to turn the hierarchical molar institutions and ways of the business world upside down, whilst his actual behaviour is even more fascistic than a modern-day multinational corporation, even more vicious than the colonial rubber plantation bosses in *Voyage au bout de la nuit*, so the introduction of smooth space into the strata of molarity that has been said to describe the aesthetic quest of *Guignol's band* is turned on its head by Van Claben and his space. For a bridge—that structure which has been said to constitute these novels' idealised metaphor of smooth space in the strata—, brings destratification (smooth space) into the midst of stratified space; Van Claben's house, however, is an unorthodox but nonetheless striated space constructed in the midst of smooth space, which, for Van Claben, is something to be held at bay, something that he wishes to banish from his life, hence his self-imposed imprisonment in his own house, his life led in a perpetual claustrophobic gloom with all windows and shutters closed to the outside world (*GB*I, p.190).

From this description of Van Claben, his appearance in this section dealing with attempted inter-polar modes of existence may seem slightly difficult to understand, for even though he appears to transgress many molar codes, his transgression is, in fact, merely an inversion of them that does not detract from their molarity in any way. There is, however, one important aspect of Van Claben that must not be neglected: his love of music. Van Claben will do almost anything, pay any price, for Borokrom to play the piano for him, such is the rapture that he feels when listening to music. Once again, there is a problem, however, for whereas the narrative style describing these piano playing sessions—

Céline's 'métro émotif' at full speed—would seem to imply that Borokrom's playing is a genuine musical (or desiring/schizophrenic) expression, Van Claben has to pay in order to procure these services, thereby reterritorialising his own desire within Capitalist axiomatics. It is precisely this commercialisation of music—or, for Céline, commercialisation of literature, the 'chromos «jours d'atelier»... faux 1900...' (*R*, p.856), talked of in the trilogy—that Ferdinand is against, its conversion into a commodity which can be mass-reproduced without any personal emotional investment:

> La revoilà!... jamais n'expire!... C'est une affaire!... riguedondonne!... Le monde halète!... pâme... se rend!... farceur d'ivoires!... façon friponne!... rêche et câline!... brute et toucheuse! à *dig! dong!*... débraille notes!... sorcière des mains! conquiert et sonne!... digue dondonne!... emporte tout!... le monde vogue!... tout ensorcelle, dissolve, papille! parpille aux ondes! *dig! dig! dong!* ne flanchez pas!... Tenez au *si!* dièse! dièse! dièse!... *dum!*...
>
> Le truc a fait fureur depuis, mille fois repris, ratatouillé, dégobillé par toutes les mécaniques du monde, par tous les jazz des continents!... par les bougnoules d'un peu partout!... à la rémoulade cafouillette... (*GB*I, p.193)[49]

In all respects, therefore, Van Claben, although surrounded by smooth space and music—even the instruments he hoards, although he refuses to sell them, are valued only as possessions, as collectibles (*GB*I, p.191)—, keeps their molecularity at bay by reterritorialising them within molar axiomatics. Such an attitude is symptomatic of the Occidental in Bettina Knapp's analysis examined above, that being in whom a fixed sense of self and ego is vital for any kind of healthy interaction in the world. Van Claben's excessive confinement within his self and his own molar space, however, is seen as far from healthy, being given metaphoric expression in his asthma (*GB*I, pp.202–203). Having tried every remedy under the sun, none of which have cured him of this terrible affliction, Claben is willing to try anything, and is therefore keen to light up the mysterious cigarettes given to his maid, Delphine, by a strange skeletal black man who assured her that they would cure him (*GB*I, pp.210–213). These drugged cigarettes, supplied with a little bone, have a liberating, deterritorialising effect not only on Van Claben, but also on Delphine, Borokrom and Ferdinand:

> Du coup on tire tous une bouffée... puis deux... puis trois... Le vieux il respire à fond toute la fumée... il l'avale... celle des autres aussi... il aspire tout... ça semble bien lui réussir... il respire mieux... ça le dégage!

> «*Feeling grand boys! Feeling grand!...*»
> Il jubile... il nous annonce... Je suis heureux du coup avec lui.
> «Ça me monte à la tête!... ça me trouble!... C'est charmant chez moi!...»
> Voilà les mots que j'ai prononcés, après peut-être dix minutes... je me souviens exact!... Et puis j'ai eu envie de vomir... pas beaucoup, une petite idée... je me suis retenu... La nausée en somme... Ça vous montait bien à la tête... Ça vous ressortait par les yeux... comme ça pleurnichant... Boro aussi il voyait trouble, il me l'a dit:
> «T'es deux! qu'il me fait... T'es deux l'enflure!...» (*GB*I, pp.213–214)

The communal joy provided by these cigarettes soon turns to vicious libidinal desire, however, as Van Claben molests Delphine, they all take Claben's trousers off, and Delphine straddles Claben (*GB*I, pp.214–215). This desire, in turn, is subsequently transmuted into suicidal and homicidal tendencies, Borokrom repeatedly throwing himself off the landing into a pile of plates (*GB*I, p.214), Ferdinand deciding he wants to kill Boro and then fighting with him (*GB*I, p.216), Ferdinand grabbing a gun to kill whomsoever he chooses (*GB*I, p.221), and, finally, Ferdinand and Boro force-feeding Van Claben the coins he had ready to pay for some music, only to attempt to recuperate these same coins by dropping Claben repeatedly on his head from a height, killing him in the process (*GB*I, pp.218–223).

That the cigarettes' effect can be described as molecular—that is to say, undermining the fixity of molar categories and perception—is undeniable, as is shown by the distortion of perception experienced by Ferdinand as he grabs the gun:

> Je retombe sur la carabine!... la grosse Winchester!... sa «Chasse»!... je l'empoigne... je la lâche plus!... elle me fond dans les mains!... positif!... je le dis juste!... elle me fond!... la crosse s'allonge en mastic, elle me dégouline dans les doigts... la guimauve!.... tout ce que je touche ça fond!... et puis tout tourne autour du globe! comme au manège... la lampe à eau... Je vois des choses dedans! Je vois des guirlandes... je vois des fleurs!... Je vois des jonquilles!... Je vois des oiseaux!... un rossignol!... Je l'entends chanter!... (*GB*I, p.221)

This evocation is reminiscent of other moments in Ferdinand's life—or those of Céline's other first-person narrators—when he has accessed a plane of consistency, but, as he himself realises, this time there is something wrong: 'Je me rends compte que c'est pas exact... Je le dis à Boro!... Il me rote!...' (*GB*I, p.221). What is wrong, of course, is that this plane of consistency has been accessed through artificial means, with the result that the connective syntheses taking place on it are converted into destructive impulses.[50] These cigarettes—and their accompanying little bone—, supplied by a skeleton, have not only cast off the death-dissimulating strategies of molarity and injected anti-production into the process of production, providing a model of death in the unconscious, they have brought death into the fray, as the desubjectification they were intended to bring about was too speedy.[51] As Nick Heffernan, paraphrasing Deleuze and Guattari, notes:

> any becoming consists in a movement towards the 'Body without Organs' (BwO), an ideal of thoroughly desubjectified desire that is the antithesis of both the monadic bourgeois subject and the relatively decentred Althusserian-Lacanian subject, locked as the latter is into ideology and language. In this sense the liberation of desire and of the body are one and the same, and the primary form inhibiting such liberation is the *organism*, understood as the particularly static 'organization' of organs and parts which Deleuze and Guattari contrast to the BwO's 'molecular multiplicities' and 'bands of intensity'. [...] Yet [...] Deleuze and Guattari are at pains to point out how the BwO can be 'botched' by a too hasty desubjectification which can result in the 'empty', 'sucked-dry' bodies of the schizo, the masochist, the hypochondriac and the drug addict. These are becomings which have been hijacked by the 'death-drive' and converted into 'self-destructions'; and it seems that subjectivity must be *worked through* rather than exploded, for, 'You have to keep enough of the organism for it to reform each dawn... and you have to keep small rations of subjectivity to enable you to respond to the dominant reality'.[52]

In light of these comments, Van Claben's demise is particularly significant. On precisely this subject, Nicholas Hewitt has suggested that, 'the enforced ingurgitation of Van Claben's gold coins constitutes a refusal both of the gold principle and of the tyranny of the father: the oral excrement of the gold is returned to the body from whence it came', and he goes on to remark that this scene constitutes, 'an exact and direct inversion of Ferdinand's assault on Auguste in *Mort à crédit*'.[53] If the Freudian trinity of gold, monarch and father was parodically deconstructed through an intensification of its own terms in *Mort à crédit*, with the result that Ferdinand takes to his father's head with a typewriter, in *Guignol's band*, it is, then, like the process of desubjectification under the influence of narcotics, completely blown apart, Ferdinand obliterating the head of the pseudo-paternal figure, Van Claben. For having not merely transgressed molar codes, but exploded them by attempting a too hasty deterritorialisation, Ferdinand, like the pathological schizophrenic (and, indeed, like the text, whose pure comedic pleasure that denies the transversal relation is rarely greater than at this point), fails to access an inter-polar, desiring mode, and succeeds only in increasing the reterritorialising tendencies of the molar pole.

The Schizoid Pole

True to the uneven process of oscillation between the poles of human existence conceived as an instance of delirium (for delirium, according to Deleuze and Guattari, is coextensive with the social field),[54] there are characters in *Guignol's band* who are attracted almost exclusively towards the schizoid/molecular pole, which is to say that they are architects and inhabitants of smooth space, of a space entirely at odds with the molar stratification all around them. The result of this excessive supermolecularity, is that these characters—when they have already been initiated into molar society—are unable to function properly in the world around them, unable to respond to the dominant reality in a way befitting that reality, and so instead display behavioural traits which appear pathological.

Borokrom

Yves Pagès sees in Borokrom, a 'guignol subversif célinien', whose 'discours alambiqué du "terroriste" [...] reprend à son compte la critique de "la servitude volontaire" tout en freudisant ses postulats sociophilosophiques'.[55] But whereas Pagès' comments are directed towards the Borokrom of *Guignol's band*, the textual quotations used to illustrate his point are heavily reliant on *Bagatelles pour un massacre*. It is self-evident that the Borokrom of *Guignol's band* and that of *Bagatelles pour un massacre* are, in many respects, one and the same; there are differences, however, differences that are explained more by the nature of the texts themselves than by the character. As was suggested at the beginning of this chapter, *Guignol's band* consciously attempts to distance itself from the pamphlets written before it, and is concerned with creating a fictional smooth space into which History can be transposed and thus, paradoxically, sterilised through an intensification of its own processes. (It could, of course, be argued that exactly the same process is in operation in the pamphlets themselves, that, regardless of the vehement reactions they elicited, their intended effect—a sterilisation of Fascist discourse through extreme intensification—was not as polemical as their actual effect.) Nonetheless, whilst they are undeniably an important part of Céline's *œuvre*, vital to a full appreciation of his work, the pamphlets remain, even for the most dedicated of Célinophiles, somehow apart from the novels and chronicles, the political content being transposed—for there is, undeniably, a process of transposition at work in the pamphlets—in a far cruder manner. So whilst Pagès' analysis of Borokrom is both extremely lucid and enlightening, it is not appropriate to talk of the two Borokroms as though they were interchangeable, for the *Guignol's band* version is never shown to command as coherent and erudite a discourse as his *Bagatelles* counterpart. Indeed, all that is really learnt about Borokrom from the two volumes of *Guignol's band*, is that he, 'avait eu tous ses diplômes à Sofia puis à Pétersbourg, mais il avait pas le sens de l'heure, ça lui a joué un mauvais tour, il pouvait pas être employé, ensuite il buvait vraiment trop, même pour l'Angleterre' (*GB*I, p.100), that he has a rather extravagant sense of dress, plays the piano in pubs along the Thames or in Cascade or Van Claben's house, that he is a compulsive liar (*GB*I, pp.239, 248), indulges his libido infrequently but excessively when he does (*GB*II, pp.719–720), and that he has a penchant for fabricating and throwing bombs (*GB*I, pp.173, 234–235).

This is not to say that Pagès' insights are totally useless for an examination of the Borokrom of *Guignol's band*, however; far from it. For if it is difficult to sustain and expand upon Pagès' discussion of the political ramifications raised by a character such as Borokrom, his analysis of Boro's character traits are still of much use. Pagès discerns an essential ambiguity in the character of Borokrom, claiming that he is both sado-masochistic and anarchic-despotic.[56] Furthermore, Pagès likens the tyrannical libertine that he sees in Boro, to a Sadian character who would, 'prendre son plaisir à exercer le pouvoir aux dépens du Pouvoir lui-même'.[57] Quoting Deleuze, Pagès goes on to note that,

> De l'autre côté du miroir des cruautés, ce qui est désiré idéalement, au terme de cette Utopie du Mal, c'est 'le délire originel, le chaos primordial fait uniquement de molécules furieuses, l'anarchie naturelle' [...]. Il y aurait, selon [Deleuze], chez Sade, deux niveaux de 'Nature': une 'Nature première' sans loi ni règle qu'un permanent flux de la matière, et une 'Nature seconde', soumise aux lois et à leur subversions, à des déconstructions qui ne sont que les

> répliques inversées de l'ordre établi. Les héros du 'boudoir' philosophique chercheraient donc à sortir des transgressions partielles pour retrouver un état de Nature originel, un terrain d'aventure où l'immoralisme ne serait plus simplement réactif ou transgressif, mais l'expression d'un état antérieur des mœurs, n'ayant jamais connu de limitations morales. La profonde intuition deleuzienne nous semble s'appliquer à la lettre au fantasme programmatique de Boro.[58]

An examination of the *Guignol's band* Borokrom reveals this same ambiguity; but rather than fusing together the two terms of a Political dichotomy, the ambiguity of *Guignol's band*'s Borokrom seems far more metaphysical in nature, containing both creation and destruction, genesis and apocalypse. As in Pagès' analysis, what drives both terms of this ambiguity is the desire to attain, 'le délire originel, le chaos primordial', 'l'expression d'un état antérieur des mœurs, n'ayant jamais connu de limitations morales', that, in other words, he wishes to destratify molar space in order to access a plane of delirium coextensive with the social field on which he will be able fully to express his desire. Attracted entirely to the molecular/schizoid pole, however, Boro's method of destratification does not operate through an intensification of the fluxes inherent in the present system in place: Borokrom, ultra-molecular, being unable to react to the dominant reality in an appropriate manner, can only act pathologically, can only deterritorialise, create a smooth space for himself, by completely wiping out the territory, exploding it in the most literal sense of this term.

And then there is the other side of Borokrom, the piano player, 'ce brio d'artiste!' (*GB*I, p.192):

> Lui plutôt loursingue de nature et franchement brutal et pénible avec sa manie d'explosifs, il devenait là tout voltigeur, tout cascadeur, tout lutin!... Il avait l'esprit dans les doigts... Des mains de fées!... des papillons sur les ivoires... Il virevolait aux harmonies!... piquait l'une et l'autre à l'envol!... songes et toquades!... guirlandes... détours... fredaines prestes... Possédé!... pas autre chose à dire!... par vingt petits diables dans les doigts!... (*GB*I, p.192)

Boro's music 'vous tinte plein les soucis... vous triche le temps, vous tille la peine, lutine, mutine, tinte aux soucis et *ptemm! ptemm!* vous la tourbillonne!... vous l'emporte... constante à galope! notes en notes!...' (*GB*I, p.192), just as the 'métro émotif' is intended to carry its passengers along 'dans le rêve... qu'ils s'aperçoivent pas... le charme, la magie' (*EY*, p.536), and whilst Boro's music 'forcerait un crocodile à la rêvasserie...' (*GB*I, p.192), Céline claims that he 'saurai[t] s'il le fallait faire danser les alligators sur la flûte de Pan'.[59] Boro, both bomber and pianist, then, marks a return to the opening sections' dichotomy of *flûte/orage*. For Borokrom has at his disposal two deterritorialising mechanisms: a pure aesthetic, *flûte*, and a pure line of destruction, *orage*. In Borokrom's case, the former always precedes the latter, as though he feels a need to transmute the smooth space of his aesthetic into the real world through direct Political action. This action, however, is pure anarchy, intended to destratify completely through violent means, to make a clean and irredeemable break from a society it intends to annihilate. This action, therefore, is molecular/schizophrenic to the point of remove, of autism, and, as such, is deemed to remain pathologic.

If Ferdinand's reactions to this character are examined, a further possible metafictional analysis becomes apparent. For if the Historical author Céline did indeed write *Guignol's band* to distance himself from the pamphlets, as Henri Godard has suggested,[60] and if Ferdinand's travails are indeed an allegorical description of Céline's own aesthetic quest, then the fact that Ferdinand sings Borokrom's praises whenever talking of his piano playing, but condemns his terrorist activities without quarter, can only be highly significant.[61] The ramifications of this parallel for a discussion of the pamphlets are, of course, highly contentious; for in this analysis, the three texts which, directly or indirectly, cost Céline his health, reputation, and material possessions, become expressions of a near pathological schizophrenia, totally removed from the real world and incapable of interacting with it in any normal manner. As has been seen in the introduction to the present study, and as will be seen later on in this study, such is precisely what many critics seem to imply when dealing with the pamphlets—or, indeed, Céline's entire *œuvre*. If the pamphlets are indeed, however, the result of a quasi-pathological condition, any study which posits such a possibility as a means to condemn the texts in question, must surely first ask whether or not pathology is punishable. To return to the primary concern of the present study, however, what remains indisputable in *Guignol's band*, is that the relationship between Ferdinand and Borokrom can be read on an allegorical, metafictional level, and ultimately reveals more about Céline's attitude towards his own creation than it does about his past or future Political affiliations.

Virginie

Virginie is molecular in that, being very young, she has not fully undergone the process of Œdipalisation and been integrated into the paranoid ways of society. She is innocence incarnate, seen by Ferdinand from the moment he sets eyes on her as perfection, pure beauty and grace (*GB*II, p.314), a creature made of pure music that vibrates in harmony with the natural universe: 'C'est là qu'on voit l'animal, au diapason d'entre les jambes... la façon qu'il vibre à la terre à chaque foulée... la musique du corps... l'irrésistible...' (*GB*II, p.397). For Ferdinand, Virginie is indeed irresistible, for this 'fée véritable' (*GB*II, p.336) inspires such ecstasy in Ferdinand, that, when he is with her, his molar sense of perception—in which fixity is paramount—is liable to dissolve:

> Ah! c'est un autre monde tout à coup!... Elle veut maintenant qu'on se promène.... on se promène autour de la table... c'est le jardin des délices... avec le vieil épagneul... tous les trois comme ça bien d'accord... je marche dans un songe... elle me guide par la main... elle nous précède dans les merveilles... d'un petit mot à l'autre... à propos du morceau de sucre... de la pâtée sur son assiette... de l'hirondelle qui doit venir... Ah! la magique comédie... Ah! que j'aime ça!... Ah! comme je l'aime!... nous nous promenons chez les fées!... Ça y est nous y sommes!... Tout le salon tout autour est un monde fées!... je ne savais pas... elle m'apprend... Ah! comme je l'adore!... tout va s'animer... parler... rire... le gros patapouf coussin aussi comme le clebs... le fauteuil aussi!... la théière avec son long cou!... tout le ménage se met en frais!... la mime à tout le monde... chacun danse à sa façon... la comédie du miracle... le gros guéridon à trois pieds... il traverse la pièce bedonnant... (*GB*II, p.336)

In this ecstatic universe, Ferdinand is able to shed all of his *amour-propre*—that molar condition that troubled Bardamu so in *Voyage au bout de la nuit*—and pretends to be her dog (*GB*II, pp.338, 394–395). In *pretending* to be her dog, however, Ferdinand does not access the kind of state Deleuze and Guattari talk of as a becoming-animal, a zone of intensity on the scale of molecular becomings in the process of desubjectification necessary to access a plane of consistency on which desire can be expressed. As they state,

> D'une certaine manière, il faut commencer par la fin: tous les devenirs sont déjà moléculaires. C'est que devenir, ce n'est pas imiter quelque chose ou quelqu'un, ce n'est pas s'identifier à lui. Ce n'est pas non plus proportionner des rapports formels. Aucune de ces deux figures d'analogie ne convient au devenir, ni l'imitation d'un sujet, ni la proportionalité d'une forme. Devenir,

> c'est, à partir des formes qu'on a, du sujet qu'on est, des organes qu'on possède ou des fonctions qu'on remplit, extraire des particules, entre lesquelles on instaure des rapports de mouvement et de repos, de vitesse et de lenteur, les plus *proches* de ce qu'on est en train de devenir, et par lesquels on devient. C'est en ce sens que le devenir est le processus du désir. Ce principe de proximité ou d'approximation est tout à fait particulier, et ne réintroduit aucune analogie. Il indique le plus rigoureusement possible une *zone de voisinage ou de co-présence* d'une particule, le mouvement que prend toute particule quand elle entre dans cette zone.
> [...]
> Par exemple: non pas imiter le chien, mais composer son organisme avec *autre chose*, de telle manière qu'on fasse sortir, de l'ensemble ainsi composé, des particules qui seront canines en fonction du rapport de mouvement et de repos, ou du voisinage moléculaire dans lequel elles entrent.[62]

Responding to Virginie's supermolecularity—a state to which he does not have immediate access having undergone the process of Œdipalisation—, therefore, Ferdinand once again rushes the process of desubjectification in the quest for spontaneous desire, enclosing himself in an autistic, non-human space, by attempting to *be* a dog, rather than embarking upon a becoming-animal. Unable to survive in the dominant reality in this space, Ferdinand comes to depend entirely upon Virginie, and claims to be unable to live without her, threatening to commit suicide if he cannot be with her (*GB*II, p.343). Unable to be always by her side, however, his transports of joy are always followed by a particularly violent fall back into the paranoiac structures of molarity, marked by a return of the head pains—which, being the result of a war wound, can be seen as a physical manifestation of the hold the molar paranoiac pole exercises over him—that Virginie is able temporarily to assuage (*GB*II, p.367).[63]

It is because of her pure supermolecularity that Virginie is always described as being futile, somehow unsuited to the world, incapable of reacting to it in a normal way, playing with a bunny rabbit as her house is being blown apart by her uncle's experiments, for instance (*GB*II, p.406), 'juste une petite fille toute joueuse... [...] absolument insoucieuse de tout ce qui s'était passé!...' (*GB*II, p.445).[64] Allen Thiher is thus right in suggesting that the 'hyperbolic élan' is 'meaningless when judged from the viewpoint of death', and that, 'the perfect coordination of body, music, and poetry is perhaps man's only hope of assuaging, momentarily at least, his constant degradation in a world given over to disease and decay'.[65] The implicit fatalism of Thiher's comments is perhaps excessive, however, for even though the pure aesthetic sensation that Virginie embodies may provide temporary relief, Ferdinand—and, indeed, Céline—does not relent his quest for a more permanent inter-polar mode of existence with Virginie. He will never attain this, however, until she has been initiated into the molar ways of society, for as long as she retains her innocence and remains pre-Œdipal, his life with her can only ever be a violent oscillation of excess from the molecular schizoid pole, that provides some temporary but impractical relief, to the molar paranoiac pole, that makes life a living hell.

Successful Inter-Polarity

Mille-Pattes

Colin Nettelbeck considers Mille-Pattes to be merely one of Cascade's band, 'a symbol of Cascade's power', and Ferdinand's murder of him as a sign of his 'rebellion against this milieu [... which] is not a total rejection, but an effort to establish a more equitable balance between the individual and the collective'.[66] But there is no evidence in the text that Mille-Pattes is merely one of Cascade's minions; he simply advises Ferdinand to go and see Cascade to sort out the situation he has got himself into (*GB*I, p.248), and explicitly states that he is not in Cascade's employ: '«Cascade il envoye personne!... Apprends ça grand con!... Il règle lui-même!... [...]»' (*GB*I, p.249). If Mille-Pattes ever appears guilty of conspiring against Ferdinand in the text, this is purely due to Ferdinand's own persecution complex that sees danger everywhere, for when Ferdinand calms down slightly, they chat and quarrel like old friends (*GB*I, pp.250–253).[67] Furthermore, for Mille-Pattes to stand as a symbol of Cascade's power, he would have to embody the same molar characteristics as his supposed leader in his very physical appearance, and this is patently not the case. For whereas Cascade places great importance on his physical appearance, especially his 'mèche' (*GB*I, p.141), Mille-Pattes is a 'nabot' (*GB*I, p.245), a trait which denies him access to the kind of symbolic power Cascade reaps from his physical traits. If Nettelbeck sees in Mille-Pattes an echo of Cascade, then, this is because Mille-Pattes is perfectly able to function within the *milieu* that Cascade has created. It is a mistake, however, to see Mille-Pattes as a kind of sub-Cascade, for he is, in many respects, the very antithesis of

Cascade, able to interact with the molar pole but really belonging to the molecular.

Nettelbeck sees in Mille-Pattes' name, 'a symbol of the widespread power of disintegration represented by the Cascade civilization myth',[68] but this name also carries in it notions of multiplicity—multiplicity being, of course, one of the effects of the abandonment of a fixed molar subjectivity, of accession to a schizophrenic molecular mode in which the boundary of self between interior and exterior is no longer absolute. Mille-Pattes can also be seen to display some schizophrenic traits, appearing to have some problems with the molar tendency to attribute value (he refuses to admit that the Louvre is better than Buckingham Palace, insisting that it depends on individual taste (*GB*I, pp.251–252)), as well as with the molar system of nomenclature (calling Ferdinand Arthur (*GB*I, p.251), and being unable to remember the name of the last French king (*GB*I, p.252)). He also harbours a deep resentment against the Educational Institutions of molarity, which, in his opinion, suppress spontaneity and natural intelligence:

> «C'est pas tout, retiens, l'instruction! Ce qui compte tu vois dans la vie c'est l'intelligence naturelle!... Moi j'en ai! ça je peux me flatter! Voilà le principal! Moi j'ai connu tiens des femmes qui savaient cinq et six langues! j'en aurais pas voulu boniches!... de la prétention! voilà tout!... Ils s'éclatent la tronche!... Regarde un peu les michés... C'est souvent hein qu'ils sont instruits!... T'as rien vu de plus con!... la preuve!... T'as qu'à voir un peu dans les clubs à quoi ils s'amusent!... Je peux te causer!... Ça joue! ça perd! et moi je gagne!... Petit je les emmerde moi je te le dis!... [...]» (*GB*I, p.252)

If Mille-Pattes is molecular in life, however, he is even more so in death.

Returning from the grave, Mille-Pattes makes his entrance from the smooth space of darkness in which the light of Reason is eclipsed, emanating from the night as though a part of it:

> Y a rien sur les pelouses... que de la flotte encore... des flaques... des longues brumes qui rôdent... Je regarde moi aussi, je m'efforce... j'aperçois rien... rien du tout... ah! puis là si, y a un bonhomme... une forme qu'avance au bout de l'allée... il vient vers nous... comme un promeneur... il longe la pelouse... il traverse l'herbe... ah! c'est bien vrai, c'est quelqu'un... comme ça tout seul qu'il avance... les buées dansent autour... il se rapproche... figé... puis il remarche... des pas lents comme ça... somnambule... tout posément... encore un pas et puis un autre... je le vois plus... c'est une rafale de pluie qui voile... la flotte reprend qu'on voit plus rien... (*GB*II, p.461)

But this is far from the only schizoid molecular trait displayed by this zombie-like figure. For whereas Ferdinand seems to find some solace in the sound of Big Ben striking the hour—an idea which would be abhorrent to the young Ferdinand of *Mort à crédit* who so despised the molar demarcation of time—, Mille-Pattes is distinctly troubled by it: 'Ah! le Mille-Pattes ça le frappe en plein chaque coup de *broum!* il vogue chancelle... l'écho on dirait lui fait mal, l'embarde le secoue tout entier, toute sa carcasse d'épouvantail... comme s'il allait tomber chaque *braoum...*' (*GB*II, pp.464–465). It is also significant that, after an initial fright, right from the start, Mille-Pattes makes Virginie (a fellow super-molecular being) laugh (*GB*II, p.462), which is not at all the case for Ferdinand: 'je palpite je peux le dire... moi qu'ai déjà le cœur patraque, maintenant c'est du galop, la charge... maintenant je palpite de partout... *tac! tac! tac! tac!* le cul qui me bat, l'oigne, j'en crierais... ah! ça me paralyse la gorge...' (*GB*II, p.464). Indeed, whilst Mille-Pattes seems to bring out a flirtatious side of Virginie not seen before that makes her giggle and dance, Ferdinand considers him to be utterly repulsive in every way (*GB*II, p.466). For described by Ferdinand, Mille-Pattes is a skeletal figure whose bones rattle as he moves, who reeks of putrefaction—in Ferdinand's nose, at least—, emits a strange yellowish light, is, 'tout vert [...] dans son cou, et puis arraché des bouts de chair... et puis une sorte d'humeur qui coule... et puis des bouts de peau rose et jaune...'(*GB*II, p.472), and someone who seems to find the whole concept of money more amusing than anything else, and yet who seems to have inordinate amounts of it in his rotten innards (*GB*II, p.485–486). He is also capable of having a desubjectifying effect on those he touches ('Il me répond pas, il me regarde, il me pose seulement la main sur le bras, sa main, son genre, des petits bouts d'os... ça y est *flof!* j'existe plus. Je suis comme vidé net... je bégaye' (*GB*II, p.468)), claims only to be able to exist in the darkness (*GB*II, p.490), and describes himself in the following manner: '«Je je suis le plus grand détenteur des passions extra!»' (*GB*II, p.490).

The repetition of the first person pronoun in this last quotation is deliberate. For Mille-Pattes is Ferdinand, or rather, he is the embodiment of Ferdinand's schizophrenic, emotive side that is still ensnared by the paranoiac molar pole. He is, in other words, that side of Ferdinand that Ferdinand knows can do him harm within molar society, that side of him of which, in a moment of excessive paranoia, he tried to rid himself by pushing Mille-Pattes under a train. This is why, when asked by Virginie how long he has known Ferdinand, Mille-Pattes replies, '«Depuis toujours chère petite! *Nobody knows him better!* Personne le connaît mieux que moi!»' (*GB*II, p.477), for they are, essentially, one and the same person at differing degrees of intensity. Mille-Pattes claims to have known Ferdinand '«Dans un autre monde!»' (*GB*II, p.477), but when Virginie asks whether he means America, he replies '«Non, non mademoiselle... à Paris...»' (*GB*II, p.477), the birthplace of Ferdinand. Mille-Pattes, then, is that side of Ferdinand that creates 'un autre monde' from within stratified space: being little more than a puddle on the *métro* rails in death, in his life after death he becomes the 'métro émotif'. For Mille-Pattes is multiplicity, he rattles with every movement like a train on its tracks, he is inevitably inscribed with his own death being dead, and elicits two very different reactions in those he meets. For those belonging to the molecular pole who have accepted their true organic state, he is a source of great amusement who provokes that most spontaneous of reactions that goes directly 'au plus sensible des nerfs!' (*EY*, p.537), laughter. To those ensnared by the molar paranoiac pole, like Ferdinand at the present time, however, he is abhorrent, for he blatantly exposes that which the paranoiac pole so desperately tries to dissimulate with its various *socii*: man's fundamental organic *pourriture*, *pourriture* which, for Mille-Pattes, is no longer *en suspens*.[69] The rotting, stinking Mille-Pattes, then, externalises and intensifies that which it is the function of molarity to dissimulate, namely, those organic (and natural, therefore) traits intimately linked to all forms of dissolution. This, as Alain Cresciucci points out, is Céline's,

> *aveu biologique* [...] que l'univers entier est soumis au visqueux. Il n'y a pas d'objet intègre, de formes fixes. Le solide renferme en lui les signes de sa déchéance qui ne demandent qu'à se manifester. Et c'est le thème largement exploité du moisi. La moisissure est la forme cutanée du pourrissement. L'extérieur corrompu témoigne de l'altération de l'intérieur... Moisir est la façon de se dissoudre de l'immobile. [...] À son tour le moisi fait le lien avec l'olfactif car il participe autant du vu ou du touché que du senti. Si le monde est toujours sur la voie de la transmutation liquide, c'est aussi un monde de la sublimation.[70]

Ferdinand's reaction when Mille-Pattes invites him to take the *métro*—that form of transport so beloved of the interviewee in *Entretiens avec le professeur Y* (*EY*, pp.535–536)—, then, signals a full-blown return of Ferdinand's paranoia when faced with yet unable to assume his molecular side, for to take the *métro*, to enter into smooth space, is to cast off the molar trappings that imbue life with a false sense of transcendence and immortality:

> «T'as l'air fatigué dis donc! Tu veux pas prendre le métro?»
>
> Métro? Métro? ah! je fais qu'un bond... ah! lui ça encore! métro?... ce fiel qu'il a!
>
> «Tante! assassin! je l'appelle, assassin!» et que je le braille! que je le crie! je veux que les gens se jettent dessus, l'emmènent! (*GB*II, p.470)

Like the 'métro émotif' that he comes to embody, then, Mille-Pattes is but a mode of transport to take the individual into a space in which desire can be liberated:

> «Je vous ai rencontrés mes chéris, je vous lâcherai plus! Vous allez voir ce beau cadeau! Promis! Juré! une veine mes anges! vous me refuserez pas?»
>
> Et là-dessus il envoie des lueurs... de tout qu'il se met à phosphorer... des guenilles de la tête des mains... et puis il retrémousse gigote... un transport de joie! et l'odeur avec ça âcre grasse...
>
> «Le plus beau voyage de la terre! Voilà mes chouchous mon cadeau! Oui, de la terrre, je m'y connais! de la terre en large et en long! ça sera de la gâterie! Plus jamais de métro Ferdinand! plus jamais de métro de l'existence! Je te retirerai tous les métros!»
>
> Ah! là là que c'est fin! Cinq minutes de craquements là-dessus, de castagnettes de tous ses membres.
>
> «Ça sera plus que du bateau mon loup! des cabines en soie! des cabines! La nuit pas de chichis alors! Petite vous irez à l'amour!» (*GB*II, p.489)

The 'métro émotif' embodied by Mille-Pattes only finds its full expression, however, in the *Touit-Touit Club*—the name of which could be said to have a nocturnal character, being the double phonetic transcription of the first half of that most nocturnal of birds' call, the owl—, the final destination of Mille-Pattes, Virginie and Ferdinand's flight through an ever-encroaching night (*GB*II, p.495), which is accessed via a flight of descending stairs ('je titube dans les marches... je descends... descends...' (*GB*II, p.496)), and the main room of which, like a train platform, is described as 'une longue cuve' (*GB*II, p.497).[71] In this dark, tunnel-like place, the 'métro émotif' picks up speed, as Dunwoodie notes, 'en effaçant tous les signes reconnaissables du normal, du réel, par la distorsion et le bouleversement',[72] wiping out stratification, therefore, and creating a plane of consistency on which a spontaneous system may erupt and a collective assemblage of enunciation be formed. Accordingly, in the Touit-Touit club, the revellers all cry '«Touit-Touit!» en refrain en cadence...', 'et tout ça chante braille en refrain', and dance as though one body, 'les gens au fond qui tournent les uns dans les autres' (*GB*II, p.497). One of these dancers fascinates Ferdinand more than the others, however, '[un] nègre... [...] tout noir sous la lumière... [...qui] beugle [...] se déhanche du coup, [...] convulse positivement' (*GB*II, p.497), contortions which make Ferdinand remark,

> Ah! si Sosthène était témoin, ça lui en ferait un partenaire... c'est autre chose que les transes hindoues! celui-là il sait faire du tic-tac! on les voit même plus ses baguettes tellement il joue vertigineux! et puis désossé de tous les membres, qu'il les projette au plafond, et qu'ils lui reviennent *pflaf!* élastique!... ça c'est quelque chose... (*GB*II, p.497)[73]

This dancer, then, succeeds in the project of desubjectification through dance that eluded Sosthène. Not to be outdone, Mille-Pattes joins in this dance of desubjectification that captivates the audience so, seeming to be either evanescent, omnipresent, or fractured, as can be seen in the following examples:

> On voit plus ses lueurs par exemple... ça se perd dans l'éblouissement... on voit que sa tête et ses loques, il est flottant effiloché... (*GB*II, p.497).
>
> ils jubilent trop avec Mille-Pattes, ils sont en transe de le regarder... c'est vrai qu'il est extraordinaire, il voltige de partout à la fois... il a plus de poids, plus de pesanteur... il flotte, c'est un paquet de guenilles au-dessus de l'assistance... c'est le vrai phénomène (*GB*II, p.498)
>
> on dirait qu'il s'éparpille, qu'il se répand en miettes... c'est des ovations à n'en plus finir... fanatiquement qu'ils l'adulent... une vraie rage qui les secoue tous, ils se jettent les uns dans les autres... ils veulent attraper Mille-Pattes, il les fascine trop... ils lèvent leurs trois cents bras en l'air... ils attrapent rien du tout!... ils attrapent de la fumée... (*GB*II, p.501)

The mood is infectious, and soon the whole club has joined in the dance:

> ça bouille là-dedans la danse à trois, à dix, à vingt! et allez donc! à mille nom de Dieu! glapissements, et la grosse caisse qui vous les retourne, et le trombone qu'est enragé! et rauque et qui râle et «Touit-Touit». Ils chantent tous en chœur hurlent tous! (*GB*II, p.498)

Like le professeur Y, exposure to this emotive aesthetic precipitates the liberation of biological fluxes as the individuals *s'oublient*, but, unlike le professeur Y, this audience does not repress this liberation, with the result that there are soon 'des grandes mares de pipi partout...' (*GB*II, p.499).[74] Ferdinand is equally captivated by this prodigious show—even though he realises that, like the 'métro émotif' with its 'rails [...] biseautés! [...] truqués!' (*EY*, pp.539–540), 'c'est une illusion [...] C'est un jeu de glaces' (*GB*II, p.500)—, and yet, still shackled by the paranoiac pole (Mille-Pattes introduces him as '*Ferdinand* [the] *jealous*' (*GB*II, p.501), jealousy being a molar mechanism), he represses his own fluxes of desire, extricating himself forcefully from the orgy that the dance floor has become (*GB*II, p.505). Ferdinand looks helplessly on, unable to participate in these orgiastic scenes being under the sway of the paranoiac pole with its repressive mechanisms of shame and guilt, until Mille-Pattes makes a fatal mistake. For taking advantage of the delirium that he has created, Mille-Pattes changes the direction of the *métro*, turning it away from its trajectory of desire to one of parasitic, Capitalistic gain. Having disappeared for a time, he returns with, 'un gros paquet de cartes, des géantes, bien plus hautes que lui...' (*GB*II, p.509), and, acting as croupier, cheats the crowd out of their possessions and very souls:

> C'est Mille-Pattes qui lance les boules... Je le gafe en plein la saloperie!... Il est tassé sous le piano... recroquevillé dans ses odeurs... il phosphore tout plein à chaque coup!... à chaque envoi de boule... Le 9!... le 9!... Il ricane... il fraudule... tout le monde... il leur ramasse tous leurs bijoux... Il couaque... couaque... couaque... Il fait le canard... C'est son genre de joie!... Son râteau passe... il écrème tout, c'est vraiment un horrible tableau... Il ramasse maintenant les âmes... Les âmes aussi jouent tout ce qu'elles ont... les Touit-Touit! Y en a plein le parquet des âmes... ça roule... c'est un peu comme des cœurs... mais tout pâles tout translucides... On voit que c'est fragile comme tout!... Ah! je le gafe dans toute son horreur le Mille-Pattes maudit!... *Il a pas volé son métro!...* Ah! Dieu foutre non!... (*GB*II, p.510; my italics)

This misappropriation of the *métro* enrages Ferdinand so much that it liberates him from the paranoiac pole that has held him in check up until now: 'Ah! plus un poil de remords!... Ils s'envolent mes remords! Tous! Ah! je suis guéri!...' (*GB*II, p.510), and he threatens to throw Mille-Pattes under a *métro* train once again. As it transpires, he does not need to carry out his threat, for Mille-Pattes' activities elicit castigation from a higher power, a 'tambourineur' with '*Cimetry*' written on his cap, who reduces Mille-Pattes to a gibbering wreck and then leads him away like an obedient dog (*GB*II, pp.510–511).

With Mille-Pattes out of the way, Ferdinand can reclaim what is rightfully his, both Virginie and the *métro*. For having loosened the bonds of the paranoiac pole which has thus far prevented him from any physical contact with Virginie, he can now give free reign to his desire (*GB*II, pp.514–516), and in doing so, he reclaims his creativity, impregnating Virginie.[75]

Ferdinand

If Ferdinand could not find an authentic inter-polar mode of existence with Virginie for as long as she retained her innocence, it is through the loss of her innocence, the destruction of her 'insouciance' (*GB*II, p.564), that he is able to attain the inter-polarity that has eluded him for so long, or, to be more precise, it is through the loss of her innocence that Ferdinand *might possibly* be able to attain a state of inter-polarity, for his quest is far from over. Ferdinand may have reclaimed the 'métro émotif' and given free reign to his desire—symbolised by Virginie's pregnancy, desire being eminently productive—that will afford him the capacity to survive with his individuality intact within the Capitalist strata, but, as he is to find out, it is sometimes far harder to assume responsibility for one's actions than it is to act.

So it is that Ferdinand returns to his old ways, living in the vain hope that either Sosthène's counterfeit mysticism or the Colonel's suicidal gas mask project will provide him with an option to spare him the shame of having to admit to himself and the world that he has impregnated a young girl, an act which once again intensifies the pull of the paranoiac pole:

> Ah! ça me cognait plein la tête tellement ça me montait en terreur les conséquences!... j'en palpitais.... dandinant là comme ça avec elle debout!... ça me sonnait les tempes!... Ah! j'aurais pas dû!... pas dû!... avec ses jupes courtes... si courtes... j'aurais dû savoir... ses mollets... ses cuisses... Ah! je savais pas!... Ah! je pensais qu'à ça! sûrement qu'elle était bien trop jeune!... Prison mon lascar!... prison!... échafaud!... prison!... corde au cou!... *couic!...* voilà!... comment ça se passe comme ça si jeune!... (*GB*II, p.576)

The predicament Ferdinand is in is not helped any by the fact that he is living in the same house as Virginie, and he spends most of his time and energy trying to avoid any contact with her, whilst simultaneously feeling guilty for what he has done. By so doing, however, Ferdinand only strengthens the stranglehold the paranoiac pole has on him, for in avoiding Virginie, he compounds his feelings of guilt, being ashamed not only of what he has done, but of not having the courage to shoulder his actions. The effects of this are as might be expected: paranoia, loss of sleep, hallucinations, 'des sifflets d'oreilles... des cauchemars aussi... des bruits... des catastrophes... des genres de trappes...' (*GB*II, pp.564–565), symptoms that are aggravated even more once Virginie tells him that she is pregnant. Take the following examples:

> tout barbouillait dans ma tête en plus des sifflets des vapeurs! (*GB*II, p.576)

> C'est trop! C'est trop! dans ma tête! *Broum!... Broum!...* et *Broum!* C'est la bombarderie perpétuelle... Tout qui me cataracte par la gueule! (*GB*II, p.577)

> mais j'ai pas dormi beaucoup!... Il m'en passait trop par la tête... je m'entendais même plus bourdonner... (*GB*II, p.580)

> Terreurs me récrasent... (*GB*II, p.581)

> Je voyais Matthew dans tous les coins... il s'amenait tout seul... il m'engueulait et plus encore... il me traitait atroce... tous les noms de la dégoûtation... il me promettait les pires supplices... J'en dégoulinais de sueur froide... hypnotisé c'est le cas de le dire par ce bourre affreux... (*GB*II, p.582)

> c'est la fièvre du sang... c'est les fantômes qui m'agressent... ils me tirent par les pieds tout d'en haut... (*GB*II, p.587)

Ferdinand's head pains, then, occur as a direct result of the persecution he feels as a result of the guilt which is one of the paranoiac molar pole's main mechanisms of reterritorialisation. As such, they could be considered a pathologically schizophrenic trait, for, like the corporeal thoughts experienced as external voices that plague a schizophrenic, Ferdinand's head pains are always trying to force him to act against his will, to comply with a fictional *socius* and not obey his own inner self, his core, his music. And yet, paradoxically, it is this very pain that roots Ferdinand in the world, that prevents him from passing into a state of pure supermolecularity/autism, of pathological schizophrenia. Ferdinand's pain, being an internalisation of the molar mechanisms that he inevitably has to deal with, therefore, has its uses, which is not to say that the paranoia it induces is not occasionally lived as unbearable, as a pain so intense, a feeling of persecution so great, that it brings about a total breakdown.

The climax of Ferdinand's paranoia comes with the scene analysed above in which he is transformed into a horse ridden by des Entrayes.[76] This massive mental delirium seems to exorcise Ferdinand's paranoia to a certain extent, for after this *crise*, he looks at Virginie with love in his eyes again—not terror as before—, and realises that it does not matter what other people think:

> Ah! je vais beaucoup mieux... je renais... Ils s'aperçoivent tout de suite les autres comment qu'elle me charme, que c'est une résurrection... Ils voyent l'effet qu'elle me produit...
>
> [...]
>
> «*Darling... Darling*» que je l'appelle comme ça tout doucement... Je me gêne plus moi devant les deux frappes... le sournois oncle et l'autre coquin... Ils en penseront ce qu'ils voudront! Faut qu'ils se rendent compte de l'amour! (*GB*II, p.599)

From this point on, Ferdinand's relationship with Virginie is no longer excessively molecular to the point of autistic remove from reality, nor governed by paranoia, but balanced between the two in a state of molecular becoming. This is shown by Ferdinand's description of his own ecstasy at this moment, for whereas before he *became* a dog in his ecstasy, removing himself from human society ('Le chien que je suis moi aussi!... un chien! c'est tout!' (*GB*II, p.338), 'Ah! je suis chien maintenant tout à fait!...' (*GB*II, p.394)), he is now only *like* a dog ('Je jouis comme un chien...' (*GB*II, p.599)). Having dealt with the mental manifestations of the paranoiac pole, Ferdinand is left to deal with its physical ones; cue the return of Cascade's band.

Nelson, Bigoudi and Mille-Pattes—who, as 'il sentait plus si fort' (*GB*II, p.618), would now seem to have been reterritorialised by the molar pole—track Ferdinand down to the Colonel's house and try to persuade him to go back with them, saying that Ferdinand owes his entire existence to Cascade (*GB*II, pp.617–635)—Cascade being attributed the status of a *socius*, a transcendental fiction that sets itself up as a quasi-cause, therefore. Refusing to comply, Ferdinand resolves to get himself, Virginie and Sosthène—who are also being pursued by the molar paranoiac pole in the form of a telephone conversation from 'le bon Dieu' and two police officers with summonses (*GB*II, p.650)—out of trouble in the only way he can think of ('Fuyez! Fuyez la gueule du loup!' (*GB*II, p.651)), and so it is that they make their way to a place from which they may be able to follow a line of flight away from molarity, to that smoothest, most *féerique* of the novels' spaces, the fog-covered river (*GB*II, pp.653–654). After much persuasion, Prosper gives Ferdinand the name of a boat that might take them away, the Kong Hamsün, which seems to be straining at its moorings, trying to take off into the sky.[77] The skipper of this ship, Jovil—who, as his name implies, is a character of pure spontaneous emotion, joviality or anger—, however, will only accept Ferdinand on board, and it is only the return of the molar paranoiac pole that prevents Ferdinand from sailing alone.

It is the party to celebrate Ferdinand's Saint's day that reunites all of Cascade's band and forces Ferdinand to miss the boat, for, like a ship straining at its moorings, Ferdinand cannot flee into smooth space for as long as he has not severed all of his ties to molarity. He cannot escape the war (symbolised by the bombs exploding throughout his party) since he has been indelibly tainted by it, nor can he flee his crimes (symbolised by the corpse of Van Claben brought to the festivities) since he never paid the consequences of his actions. Condemned to stay within molarity, Ferdinand can but attempt to convert the horrors of war into something less painful, and to cover over his crimes as best he can. Both attempts utilise the smooth space of fiction to turn horror into spectacle, since the war is described, once again, as a fireworks display (*GB*II, p.696), whilst the reappearance of Van Claben's rotting corpse and Delphine's treatment of the corpse is described in such a hyper-repulsive manner as to remove the scene completely from the realm of realism—a device which is heightened by Delphine's Shakespearean quotations—and elicit the antithesis of the expected reaction: humour (*GB*II, pp.722–727). With this scenario, it is, of course, easy to draw intertextual metafictional links to the pamphlets once again, for the disposal of the corpse of the Jew Van Claben (whose name provides a transparent link to the pamphlets' Van Bagaden) is carried out on Ferdinand's behalf. Furthermore, Van Claben's bodily remains are consigned to the smooth space of the river, just as, in Godard and Dunwoodie's view, the smooth fictional space of *Guignol's band* is created to attenuate the effects of the pamphlets without abandoning all traces of anti-Semitism. Similarly, Nettelbeck has written that, 'as an image of materialism and parasitism, Van Claben closely resembles the Jew of the pamphlets, and his murder must be seen as an act similar in kind to Céline's writing of the pamphlets'.[78] Nonetheless, if this Political affect is intended by the text, the fact remains that the excessive humour of this scene, along with the other ways in which the real is negated, privilege the metafictional levels of the text, denying the collective affectivity of the Political by enclosing the text in the private space of its own, instantly consummated *jouissance*.

With Van Claben's body out of the way, Ferdinand flees again, knowing full well by now that in stratified space, molar systems regenerate themselves at an alarming rate, reterritorialising with great ease, since those living under molarity are not aware of the true nature of existence: 'On voyait rien nous dans le local, dans cette castafouine!' (*GB*II, p.746). And so it is that Ferdinand, Virginie and Sosthène leave the party to make their way to a point situated in between the smooth and the striated from which to ponder the constant flux of life in which, when looked at from such a vantage point, the molecular always wins over the molar:

> Je regarde un peu le va-et-vient... l'eau... ça continue... ça glisse dans le noir... y a des falots dans tous les sens... le trafic... ça se croise... s'efface... rouge... jaune... vert... un écho de sirène... puis des lourds coups de poumon tout près... là comme ça *pfoo... pfoo!*... de la machine... un cargo qui pousse... frôle... nous borde... on voit son gros flanc... ombre sur ombre... passe... Ça brûle là-bas dans la Cité... C'est tombé tout de même... et pas qu'un petit peu... trois... quatre foyers... et des énormes... les flammes lèchent les nuages... la fumée rabat en panaches... des volutes si longues si immenses que ça couvre tout Londres, l'étendue, tous le rebord nord... jusqu'à Big Ben que ça voltige, entoure l'Heure, le Beffroi, les Communes, le Palais, tout... (*GB*II, p.746)

Le Pont de Londres

Le Pont de Londres finishes on the Pont de Londres, bringing the novel—and indeed, this analysis—full circle, back to that molar structure which spans the molecular and constantly threatens to plunge the individual on it into an abyss of desubjectification: 'Au milieu du pont c'est une force les jours où ça souffle, des rafales qui vous retournent emportent... Faut forcer contre...' (*GB*II, p.758). The bridge, being such a unique bi-polar structure that introduces smooth space into the striated, is also, as has been suggested, the metafictional symbol *par excellence* in Céline's *œuvre*. For aside from the metafictional self-referentiality afforded by this fortuitous choice of title, the bridge, being synonymous with the *métro* (as Philippe Bonnefis was seen to suggest at the beginning of this chapter),[79] brings smooth space into the striated structures of the novel, confounding the representational distance between protagonist and author, character and creator. As Peter Stoicheff notes,

> If language is recognized not as a neutral occasion for the direct transferral of meaning, but as a chaotic generator of significance whose interpretations are multiple, then the determinacy of the text it occasions becomes somewhat troubled. In effect, the text ceases to transmit the exterior world, and interrogates its own medium of transmission instead. This self-reflexive moment is a characteristic indicator of a metafictional text: it is a moment at which the subject under investigation is neither the ontological nor the phenomenal worlds external to it, but the complex margin of language strategy that separates the text from them.[80]

Accordingly, just before stepping on to the bridge at the end of the novel, Ferdinand-narrator/Céline-author reminds the reader of his artifice: 'Je faisais pas encore des romans. Je savais pas tirer sept cents pages comme ça en dentelles quiproquos...' (*GB*II, p.755); on the bridge, Sosthène sings a song whose lyrics asks an imaginary lady if it was indeed her in the *métro* with him: '*Est-ce vous la petite dame? / Qu'étiez l'autre tantôt? /* [...] *Tout près de moi dans le métro...*' (*GB*II, p.759); and, finally, as they/the reader approach the end of *Le Pont de Londres*, both the book, the fictional representation of that structure and the metafictional space described by the trope of the bridge, Ferdinand remarks, 'Ça y est! C'est le bout! On arrive! Le pont franchi! Ouf!... Ah! l'amusement!...' (*GB*II, p.759).

The bridge, then, is the primordial symbol in *Guignol's band*, the gravitational centre from which all begins and to which all returns, that which spans every aspect of the work; for the bridge in *Guignol's band* is used not only as a narratival frame, but also to create a link between the thematic and stylistic levels of the text. For the bridge, like Céline's 'métro émotif', is that which brings smooth space into striated space, that which annuls death not by attempting to ignore and dissimulate it, but by confronting it and converting it into a source of amusement, *divertissement*, comedy. As Céline writes to Robert Poulet:

> Voilà ce qu'il ne faut pas oublier: que ma danse macabre m'amuse, comme une immense farce. Chaque fois que l'image du fatal trépas s'impose dans mes livres, on y entend des gens qui s'esclaffent. Ma camarde, c'est un effet comique. Et aussi la réalité d'où elle sort, qu'elle éclaire!... Une réalité cocassement agencée, avec mille détails encore plus burlesques que sinistres, et à la

> surface de laquelle s'agitent quelques milliards de nœuds d'atomes, qui à peine serrés commencent à se dénouer, après avoir crié vaniteusement leur nom d'hommes: y-a-t-il rien de plus bouffon?[81]

What better space could there be for such a joyous *danse macabre*, this quasi-suicidal ballet that delights in the threat of dissipation, than the smooth space of a bridge?

> Ça les amusait au possible, tout farceurs maintenant, des démons, ils faisaient semblant de s'envoler, d'être soulevés au vide, que je coure après, que je les raccroche...
>
> Deux petits fous...
>
> «Allez! que je me fâche... ça suffit!»
>
> Ils faisaient semblant de lâcher la rampe. C'est le vieux qu'était le plus turbulent. (*GB*II, p.758)

And yet, *Guignol's band* cannot be said to constitute the accomplishment of the Célinian aesthetic which, as stated in this study's introduction, seeks an auto-objective style capable of creating a space characterised by a non-transcendental unity from which a transversal relation can emanate, a connective synthesis which will pass straight to the emotive core of the reader. The opening sections of *Guignol's band* have been said to provide a metafictional allegory of precisely such a style, for the all-pervading sense of mortality during the bombardment scene on 'Le Pont d'Orléans' establishes, as has been shown, a plane of consistency on which desire is able to form connective syntheses between individuals so as to form a spontaneous, self-organising system. Such a system is not formed in the closing scene of *Guignol's band*, however, since, for the characters on London Bridge at the end of *Le Pont de Londres*, death is nothing more than farce, a childish game. *Guignol's band* might be said, then, to move from a space of horror to one in which that horror is turned on its head and converted into a farcical game. (Incidentally, this can be said to be true with reference not only to the novels' Historical referents, but their intertextual ones too, for by bringing the novel to a close on a structurally-sound London Bridge, a significant reversal is made, it being 'Le Pont d'Avignon'—to which an explicit reference is made in the 'Le Pont d'Orléans' section of the text (*GB*I, p.90)—which is falling down, the very obverse of these bridges' nursery rhyme counterparts.)[82] Such would appear to support the thesis of Godard examined above, according to which Céline intended to retain, in *Guignol's band*, the polemical concerns of the pamphlets in a diluted form. Godard's comments referred only to the opening sections of *Guignol's band*, however, and rightly so. For if such was the intention of those (anti-novelistic) opening sections, *Guignol's band*'s main body of narrative, recounting (on a thematic level) Ferdinand's tireless journey to 'Le Pont de Londres', is concerned solely with its stylistics, with the creation of a fictional space in which to convert the horror of History into harmless farce, and not with the actual conversion of History into farce. As Nettelbeck writes,

> En ce qui concerne le renouvellement de son style, dans *Guignol's band* Céline n'y arrive qu'imparfaitement. Le livre souffre du décalage évident entre le prologue et le récit romanesque. Ce dernier, en dépit d'une évolution stylistique appréciable par rapport à *Mort à crédit*, y reste apparenté dans sa conception: c'est toujours l'histoire de Ferdinand, c'est toujours le roman de l'individu. Le prologue, lui, annonce l'esthétique des derniers romans. On le retrouve, en fait, beaucoup agrandi, mais ayant la même structure, les mêmes jeux d'espace et de temps, la même fonction romanesque, dans *Féerie pour une autre fois*.[83]

Failing to extend the mechanisms of the prologue into the main body of text, the fictional space that *Guignol's band* creates for itself becomes autistic, for in seeking to confound the boundary between interior and exterior, fiction and reality, the interior (fiction/style) miraculates the exterior (reality/thematics), becoming a full body without organs acting as a *socius*, pathologising its molecularity through an internalisation of the paranoiac traits of molarity:[84]

> les formes de production sociale impliquent elles aussi une station improductive inengendrée, un élément d'anti-production couplé avec le procès, un corps plein déterminé comme *socius*. Ce peut être le corps de la terre, ou le corps despotique, ou bien le capital. C'est de lui que Marx dit: il n'est pas le produit du travail, mais il apparaît comme son présupposé naturel ou divin. Il ne se contente pas en effet de s'opposer aux forces productives en elles-mêmes. Il se rabat sur toute la production, constitue une surface où se distribuent les forces et les agents de production, si bien qu'il s'approprie le surproduit et s'attribue l'ensemble et les parties du procès qui semblent maintenant émaner de lui comme d'une quasi-cause. Forces et agents deviennent sa puissance sous une forme miraculeuse, ils semblent *miraculés* par lui. Bref, le socius comme corps plein forme une surface où toute la production s'enregistre et semble émaner de la surface d'enregistrement.[85]

Providing a surface on which its own forces and agents of production are recorded, being above all metafictional, the unity of *Guignol's band* is one from which a transversal relation cannot emanate, for it acts as its own quasi-cause and appropriates both its own processes of production, and the surplus-desire of the reader which is instantaneously consumed in the pure pleasure of the text, in mere surface sensation, this being the very opposite to the affect intended by the Célinian aesthetic:

> la Surface est plus fréquentable!... la vérité!... voilà!... alors?... j'hésite pas moi!... c'est mon génie! le coup de mon génie! pas trente-six façons... j'embarque tout mon monde dans le métro, pardon!... et je fonce avec: j'emmène tout le monde!... de gré ou de force!... avec moi!... le métro émotif, le mien! sans tous les inconvénients, les encombrements! dans un rêve!... jamais le moindre arrêt nulle part! non! au but! au but! direct! dans l'émotion!... par l'émotion! rien que le but: en pleine émotion... bout en bout! (*EY*, p.536)[86]

Nonetheless, the end of the novel does not see Ferdinand joining in the games of the 'deux petits fous...' he is with, for having reclaimed the *métro*, having found the means to convert his desire into a productive force (symbolised by Virginie's pregnancy), he is able to master both the forces of the bridge (the smooth/the molecular), and those of the town to which the bridge leads (the striated/the molar), both weightless farce and Historical gravity:

> Je tire sur la jupe, elle était retroussée au menton dans les coups de bourrasque. Ils seraient rentrés tels quels en ville... Ils faisaient plus attention à rien... Ils veulent maintenant jouer à cache-cache... ils sont impossibles!... Y a que moi là-dedans qui glousse pas... Ils sont plus du tout fatigués... J'ai le don du comique. Ils veulent que je ronchonne pour voir. Ils veulent plus bouger du tout avant que je fasse ma figure, que je fronce les sourcils...
>
> «Ferdinand *dear! make your face!*... Ferdinand! fais-nous ta figure!
>
> —Allez hop! en route!»
>
> Je veux plus.
>
> C'est moi le pitre maintenant. C'est un monde!
>
> Moi qu'ai le souci, la discrétion! (*GB*II, p.759)

Like *Entretiens avec le professeur Y*, to which *Guignol's band* might be considered a precursor, *Guignol's band* does not balance the individual with the collective, does not emit a transversal relation which allows the reader to access a certain non-transcendental unity, for its unity is too complete, all trajectories enfolding incessantly inwards towards the very aesthetic act by which its own artifice comes into being.[87] However, if *Guignol's band* itself cannot be said to form a textual space akin to the space described by the structural trope of the bridge, it does, nonetheless, draw up the blueprint for the creation of such an architectural/architextual space—architecture being, of course, that art form in which function is inseparable from form—a space in which the collective work (*tektôn*) will be directed by the (imperceptible) author (*arkhi*).[88] This space is that of the bridge, which, therefore, can be said to define Céline's *œuvre* from this point on,[89] for, as Philippe Bonnefis notes, 'le pont est une ponctuation'.[90] In light of the present analysis, the bridge is surely not, as Bonnefis goes on to specify, 'un point', however, but three, for it is Céline's self-proclaimed sole invention, his famous '...', 'les trois points [qui] produisent [une] rupture qui mime l'ouverture immédiate à l'expérience [...], une sorte d'intensité qui serait celle de l'expérience immédiate, ou ce que nous pouvons appeler le rythme de la plénitude même',[91] that bring smooth space into the realm of the striated, that trouble the Saussurian linguistic system being non-signifying, yet speaking volumes, and that bring death into language, being silence.[92] This is what was meant when, at the beginning of this chapter, it was stated that the bridge provides this work with an organic unity that denies closure. For even though the text is closed in itself, even though no transversal relation emanates from its transcendental unity, even though the text ends with an exclamation mark, a sign of its own self-consuming autonomy, in its final scene, the Trinity of main protagonists prepare to step off the bridge, yet remain on it—the bridge as eternal passage. Likewise, Céline's *œuvre* will never leave a bridge from this point on, existing only as a passage somewhere between the smooth and the striated, as an instance of deterritorialising desiring-production in the strata, an expression proceeding by breaks and flows built on a plane of disarticulatory aposiopetic *points de suspension*.

Chapter Two
Féerie pour une autre fois

Introduction

According to the above analysis of *Guignol's band*, Ferdinand's travails through this novel and his search for an inter-polar existence in which his individual essence would be in harmony with the collective, have been read as an allegory of Céline's quest to create a textual space in which his voice would become an auto-objective expression, a collective assemblage of enunciation, a textual space characterised by a non-transcendental unity from which a transversal relation would emanate and pass directly into the reader's emotive core. The trope of the bridge has been said to provide a blueprint for the creation of such a textual space, the bridge being that which allows man, miraculated by the molar pole, access to the molecular, without plunging him into its amorphous, aqueous flux. It has been suggested, however, that the textual space of *Guignol's band* is not organised according to the blueprint that it provides, being, in the final analysis, an essentially private space, its smooth space ultimately too smooth, its trajectories, being primarily metafictional, turning back on themselves rather than emanating from the text as a transversal relation. The textual space of *Guignol's band* can be said to be, then, autistic, for whilst the trajectories taking place within a non-pathological smooth/nomadic space must, by definition, always be governed according to a centrifugal force—nomadic space being created only by the trajectories passing through it which define it in that very instant, a space of machinic heterogenesis in which there are no givens, no reduction, no hermeneutics, just a constant process of becoming, of 'fuites en avant'—,[1] the space of metafiction is, conversely, governed by a centripetal force, each trajectory constantly turning back in on itself, every surface being specular as opposed to prismatic. This is not to say that all texts that can be qualified as metafictional are condemned to remain within the constantly infolding artificial boundary that they create in their very expression, however.

There is no reason why the centripetal force of a work's metafictional aspect cannot be surpassed by the centrifugal force of another facet of the same work. (Indeed, as Nicholas Hewitt points out, 'the bridge over the Thames is also the bridge to *Féerie pour une autre fois*'.)[2] But this is not the case in *Guignol's band*, since all aspects of the work—style, content, thematics, expression, etc.—operate in tandem, with the result that no intensity that would convert the work into an appeal to the reader is created by and in the force differential. As a result, the work remains closed, and it is for this reason that it can at times feel somewhat frivolous and futile, for, although the infinite creative potential of smooth space is opened up to the characters left on/in *Le Pont de Londres*, such potential is denied the reader who cannot use the cultural artefact as a means to reinvest his/her own material reality, such being, as Debrie rightly points out, the ultimate aim of Céline's balletic writing:

> Dans la terminologie célinienne, "danser" signifie vivre en investissant ce que l'on vit; symbolisant l'enthousiasme que l'homme est capable d'éprouver, la musique est ce miel qui permet à l'homme de se ménager un espace essentiel, une distance entre lui et la sidération du vécu, un espace intérieur, seul moyen de ne pas être accablé, écrasé par la 'formidable puissance des choses absurdes'.
>
> 'Délirer juste?'. C'est être capable d'élaborer cette écriture qui va permettre aux hommes d'investir de nouveaux aspects du réel.[3]

Although this conflict will not be entirely resolved in Céline's next novel, the struggle between molarity and molecularity, centripetal and centrifugal forces that has been seen at the core of the Célinian aesthetic project in *Guignol's band*, will be conveyed, in *Féerie pour une autre fois*, precisely in a dichotomy of style governed, in the first instance, by a centripetal, then a centrifugal force. For if these forces operate, in *Voyage au bout de la nuit* and *Mort à crédit*, on a mostly thematic level within a fictional universe, the result being that the books tend too much towards the concrete, risking petrification—hence the biographical fallacy that has flawed so many studies—, and if *Guignol's band* sets these same forces against each other in the very creation of the work on both a thematic and stylistic level, effectively annulling the affective intent of the Célinian aesthetic, then these same forces will be employed, in *Féerie pour une autre fois*, in the work's style in order to combat the centripetality of the text's external thematics, the Historical narrative of Céline, author of *Bagatelles pour un massacre*, *L'École des cadavres* and *Les Beaux draps*. This is not to say, however, that the fundamental project driving *Féerie* is any different to that of *Guignol's band*, for the aim of Céline's fictional *œuvre* remains the same, namely, to find that very same inter-polarity sought by Ferdinand, to attain a means of stylistic expression (and mode of existence, therefore) that lies somewhere between molarity and molecularity, paranoia and schizophrenia, to create a pure aesthetic, a work of the imagination, a centrifugal intensity that does not spin off into a pathological condition—be it a pathological delirium or a quasi-autistic state similar to those experienced by the narrators of the previous novels—, nor allows itself to be reterritorialised by the very molar forces it denounces by its very existence, yet within which it is forced to operate. But even though *Féerie pour une autre fois* will be seen to wrestle with this problem on both a thematic and stylistic level, the solution to Céline's aesthetic quest will not be found in this work, *Féerie pour une autre fois* being a heuristic rather than algorithmic exercise.[4]

Without wishing to slip into the kind of biographical conjecturing to which the life of Céline has been subjected by some critics, it can be suggested that Céline would have found the solution to his aesthetic quest sooner had it not been for force of Historical circumstance. But, as though to prove the point that survival within molarity is a constant struggle for the molecular being who rejects all *socii*, all those fictional structures erected to dissimulate the organic nature of life, the conditions in which Céline found himself writing *Féerie pour une autre fois* led to the creation of a novel which—and this can be said with certainty—would otherwise have been a very different work. As it was, however, Céline's quest for a form in which to 'délirer juste' had another factor thrown into the equation that was to complicate matters enormously.[5] That factor was History, the molar ordering of time into a strict chronological sequence in order that the events and/or instances of desiring-production taking place within time may be subjected to a cause and effect relationship, and it is History that constitutes the subject matter of *Féerie*, a work whose title is essentially an antonym of that very word, as the inscription to this work tells us:

> L'horreur des réalités!
> Tous les lieux, noms, personnages, situations, présentés dans ce roman, sont imaginaires! Absolument imaginaires! Aucun rapport avec aucune réalité! Ce n'est là qu'une «Féerie»... et encore!... pour une autre fois! (*FI*, p.3)

It would thus seem something of a contradiction to claim that the subject matter of *Féerie pour une autre fois* is nothing other than History, even if the above inscription could, in many ways, be said to function as a disclaimer, thereby, in effect, proving the exact opposite of what it claims. This is not how this passage should be read, however, for in actuality, it provides a key to the intended reading of *Féerie*. It is obvious that many, if not all, of the events, places and characters in both volumes of *Féerie are* based on real events, places and characters, the actual names being transformed by the imagination of the author for comic (and thus deterritorialising) and stylistic effect. It is this transformation or, to use a favourite term of Céline's, transposition of History that constitutes the core of *Féerie pour une autre fois*, for it is precisely this kind of transformation that allows the reader to deterritorialise History, to re-invest History with desire.

The question is not quite so simple, however, for, as has been mentioned, Céline the author had himself become something of a Historical being, at this time, his name carrying with it, like a ball and chain, considerable symbolic capital. As Frédéric Grover notes,

> Le nom de Céline, qu'on le veuille ou non, qu'on essaye de l'en disculper ou qu'on l'en accable, est associé à un crime incontestable, enregistré par l'Histoire, le grand Massacre des Innocents de notre siècle: la liquidation de millions de Juifs. Ce *massacre*, ces millions de *cadavres* ont donné rétroactivement aux titres des deux pamphlets antisémites de Louis-Ferdinand Céline, *Bagatelles pour un massacre* et *L'École des cadavres*, un sens terriblement accusateur. On ne badine pas avec l'Histoire. Céline a joué avec un engin particulièrement explosif et, comme il arrive à Robinson dans *Voyage au bout de la nuit*, son pétard lui a explosé dans la figure.[6]

In order to deterritorialise History, therefore, Céline must first de-Historicise himself, or, as Charles Krance puts it, 'restore the balance which had been seriously threatened by the writing of the pamphlets, between the transpositional Eye and the representational I',[7] for until such time as this is done, the reader will, as certain critics have, read the attempted subversion of History purely as a means to exonerate himself, to clear his name. The most striking example of this kind of criticism can be seen in Yannic Mancel's article, 'Sémiotique de la folie et de l'écriture dans *Féerie pour une autre fois*', where it is suggested that the schizophrenic (molecular and de-Historicising) discourse found in *Féerie* I is actually a deliberate ploy to obtain leniency. He writes:

> L'ultime recours de Céline, pour se faire *pardonner* (j'insiste tout particulièrement sur le contenu *chrétien* du terme) l'*exclusion* fictive (*par l'écriture*) de ceux qui furent des victimes et/ou des libérateurs du fascisme hitlérien, mais aussi pour que *sa propre exclusion*, après la Libération, revête la forme la moins sévère possible (en un mot: pour qu'on lui accorde les "circonstances atténuantes"), cet ultime recours, donc, est de *s'exclure soi-même* non seulement par des procédés sémiotiques désormais parfaitement maîtrisés et par la simulation (avouée!) de la schizophrénie (comme nous venons de le voir), mais aussi par une écriture à caractère psychotique tant au niveau sémantique du texte qu'à ses niveaux syntaxique et narratif.[8]

To a lesser degree, Christine Sautermeister sees a similar operation at work in the humour of *Féerie* when she writes:

> Le dédoublement est une nouvelle pitrerie; il permet en effet d'établir comme seule réalité concrète celle de l'homme privé, le médecin Destouches, lequel est innocent; l'écrivain n'est qu'un fantôme qui 's'en fout', c'est-à-dire qu'il est supérieur aux événements, que le châtiment ne l'atteint pas; à la limite, il est irresponsable. C'est là le sens ultime de la pitrerie, une schizophrénie. Le pitre se déclare invulnérable puisqu'il n'est pas concerné (c'est l'autre, le fantôme, qui est touché) et cela lui permet de rire de ses malheurs, de les braver; mais le rire est de courte durée dans la mesure où la réalité reste présente pour rappeler que le dédoublement n'est pas possible; l'individu Destouches est donc atteint par les persécutions destinées à l'homme célèbre Céline. *Féerie* destinée à racheter Céline (rachat ironiquement transposé sous forme de réussite financière) vient détruire dans son contenu comme dans sa forme la thèse de l'écrivain insensible et irresponsable. [...] Le jeu de la fiction sert à masquer la réalité historique et politique au bénéfice de l'auteur.[9]

To interpret the schizophrenic expression of the narrator in this way, however, is to defeat its aim, to reterritorialise within History an expression intended to deterritorialise, to introduce smooth space into the artificially striated spaces of molarity:

> Je vous l'écris de partout par le fait! de Montmartre chez moi! du fond de ma prison baltave! et en même temps du bord de la mer, de notre cahute! Confusion des lieux, des temps! Merde! C'est la féerie vous comprenez... Féerie c'est ça... l'avenir! Passé! Faux! Vrai! Fatigue! Tout de même je réfléchis à une chose, c'est que le dernier clebs en rupture là qui vadrouille au ruisseau, fouine, mettons qu'il s'appelle Piram, a moins à redouter que mézigue!... hanté comme pas chien! Pas hanté par son nom Piram! c'est un nom supportable Piram!... Piram c'est pas une catastrophe! (*FI*, p.15)

For as long as Céline's name carries this kind of symbolic capital, his work will not be able to serve as a tool for the re-investment of people's desire in material reality, for instead, their desire will be directed into the scapegoat figure that he has become, the scapegoat being an invention of molar society that reterritorialises by channelling desire into a fictional, foreign, abject other that can be destroyed, thus providing illusory satiation and the temporary abatement of desire. Being directed solely into the figure of the author, the desire directed towards the work by the reader thus becomes a pure line of destruction that, instead of desubjectifying the reader, dismembers the author to create not a full, but an empty body without organs, an undifferentiated, amorphous plane incapable of desiring-production:

> L'indignation! Dégradation! Tout!... Le toboggan c'est une force qu'une fois aspiré par l'abîme vous prenez chaque volte des horions, de ces ruées de coups plein la gueule, et plus en plus bas, *que vous êtes plus que bouillie et larmes.*
> Réfléchissez! *la centrifugation des haines!* (*FI*, pp.15–16; my italics)

It will be the task of the two volumes of *Féerie pour une autre fois* to examine this predicament of the molecular being subjectified by and attempting to get out of History, but each volume will approach this predicament in a different way. It is for this reason that it is often difficult to see the two volumes of *Féerie pour une autre fois* as two halves of one whole, for the unity of *Féerie pour une autre fois* is anything but forthcoming—[10] indeed, if it were not for the introduction of Jules in the second half of the first volume, one could be forgiven for believing there to be no link at all between the two tomes. This difficulty in reconciling the two is undoubtedly due, in part, to the conditions in which *Féerie pour une autre fois* was written and the many successive versions and revisions the manuscript underwent.[11] But even when (as will be the case in this study) these successive versions are not taken into account, when the two volumes published in the Pléiade edition are considered to be the definitive versions and are studied as an autonomous, complete work, its unity still seems elusive, precisely because *Féerie pour une autre fois* (in its final version) is a truly atomistic work, comprehensible as a single entity only through an examination of the difference between its constituent parts. Whence the merit of taking History to be the essential subject matter of *Féerie pour une autre fois*, for it is only by examining the treatment of History in the two volumes—namely, the reversal of the subject-object relationship between History and protagonist, and of the dynamic force in the two volumes of *Féerie* I and II—that the complementarity (and thus unity) of the two volumes will become apparent.

Féerie pour une autre fois I: The Centripetal Force of History

As has been stated, any work of the imagination, any instance of desiring-production (and especially one which, like Céline's, claims to valorise emotion above all else), necessarily possesses a centrifugal force, a force which is constantly moving away from a fixed centre, away from the normalising structures orchestrated by the centripetal forces of molarity that act as a quasi-cause in order to combat the terrifying contingency of existence and to dissimulate that existence's only certainty, death.[12] Such a centrifugal force poses a particular problem for the civilised Capitalist machine—which functions by reterritorialising on deterritorialisation itself, therefore needing to employ ever more repressive structures to contain the fluxes liberated in the very processes of Capitalism—,[13] since the surplus value it creates cannot easily be reaxiomatised or miraculated so as to appear as an emanation from the full body of the *socius*/recording surface.[14] Thus, although it would be inappropriate to make historically specific comments regarding the circumstances surrounding Céline's incarceration here, it could be said that it was his increasing resistance against the forces of molarity and his accelerated deterritorialisation of those very forces that necessitated—for the smooth functioning of the paranoid Capitalist machine—the employment of a mechanism of repression whose centripetal force was inversely proportionate to the *perceived* centrifugal threat posed by Céline at that time. Being written and narrated from within that repressive structure, *Féerie pour une autre fois* I can be seen as a chronicle of the effects of an excessive centripetal force on a centrifugal (schizophrenic/desiring) subject.

The results of this containment are as might be expected. For just as the child subjected to the processes of subjectification and Œdipalisation becomes paranoid, rather than being "cured", so Céline (the narrator of *Féerie pour une autre fois*),[15] a molecular being, becomes excessively paranoid in prison. Furthermore, the paranoia and other symptoms that he exhibits being proportionate to the level of his own molecularity and the harshness of his enforced containment, his entire organism and expression become quasi-pathological. As befits a molecular being in confinement whose fluxes are forcefully contained, then, he becomes extremely constipated, reliant on the scalding hot enemas given him by the prison authorities—these authorities acting, thereby, as a *socius*, taking responsibility for the very functioning of his biological organism, taking away his autonomy, his humanity:

> Oh mais je peux tout recouvrir pardon! la ressource! le thorax! au moment où vraiment je peux plus, où je souffre trop, où j'ai pas été à la selle par exemple depuis dix, douze jours… treize jours, un coup! qu'ils veulent pas me donner mon lavement, j'aboye!
>
> Ils me l'administrent plus que chaud, presque à cinquante degrés! exprès! exprès! m'en fous! C'est du lavement!… À l'aboyement je suis sûr qu'ils viennent!… je couvre tous les hurleurs! je suis molosse de force d'aboyement!… (*FI*, p.38)

It is passages such as this that have led many critics to interpret *Féerie* as the delirious outpourings of a clinically insane subject, thereby following what Rosemarie Scullion calls, a 'semantic movement from the realm of literature to that of pathology'.[16] In doing so, however, these critics miss the deliberate and conscious nature of the writing. For just as the narrator Céline consciously feigns madness in order to procure the enemas that allow the release of his pent-up physiological flows, so the only way in which the author Céline can liberate his imagination (a desiring-flow) within such molar strictures, is by imitating the discourse of a pathological schizophrenic so as to reveal and denounce the paranoid fascistic processes of the molar regime that have accused him of Fascism and paranoia.[17]

In his study *Les Territoires céliniens*, Alain Cresciucci points out that in *Féerie*, the prison from within which the novel is written and recounted is never described as a concrete structure.[18] He attributes this, firstly, to the lack of distance between author and narrator, since,

> Pour décrire il faut être, d'une manière ou d'une autre, extérieur. Jusqu'à présent, la distance entre le narrateur et l'auteur a été une des formes de l'extériorité: l'univers de Bardamu conserve une certaine distance avec le moment de l'énonciation. Mais elle tend à se réduire dans *Féerie*; c'est même l'essentiel du procédé que de laisser croire à une énonciation qui, sans vraiment coïncider avec les faits, ne pourrait plus prendre ses distances, n'aurait ni le temps ni les capacités d'élaborer un monde romanesque… [19]

In Cresciucci's analysis, the immateriality of the prison in *Féerie* would seem to be indicative of what has here been termed the centripetal force of History—that force which prevents the conversion of Céline's work into an appeal to the desire of the reader—, for that very immateriality would prohibit the narrator from gaining autonomy from the author, and thus the subjective expression of Céline from becoming auto-objective, a collective assemblage of enunciation. Cresciucci's subsequent comments, however, allow for—and possibly intuit—a totally different understanding of the function of the prison's immateriality. He writes,

> Parler de la prison de l'intérieur, c'est vouloir en désigner l'essence. C'est pourquoi Céline élimine ce qui n'en évoque que l'enveloppe: l'architectural, le topographique, objet littéraire s'il en est. La prison, ce sont les hommes (prisonniers et gardiens), car son essence est la souffrance.[20]

This statement, according to the thesis of the present study, provides a far more convincing explanation of the immateriality of the prison in *Féerie*. And yet Cresciucci does not go far enough, this immateriality being far more complex than he suggests, serving a triple purpose. Firstly, by eliminating the material existence of the prison, Céline ensures that the brutality suffered by the inmates is attributed to the people responsible, and not to the concrete embodiment of an abstract, inanimate institution, an apparatus of capture.[21] Secondly, the lack of boundary walls in the prison described facilitates the narrator's passage out of this space (a space which remains, in spite of its immateriality, a strictly striated space), into the smooth space of the narrative—the narrative itself being that which attempts to overcome the centripetal forces of molarity—in which there is, 'Confusion des lieux, des temps!' since, 'Féerie c'est ça... l'avenir! Passé! Faux! Vrai! Fatigue!' (*F*I, p.15).[22] As Ian Noble remarks,

> The prison walls constitute a shifting boundary between the fixed, known, delimited inside and the outside. As a concrete symbol of the limits of the space immediately visible to and directly representable by the narrator, they also become the borderline (this time conceived as a starting-point) for the creation of other spaces and, in particular, for an attempt to escape [...] into a world of fantasy-gratification.[23]

But finally, and most importantly, the absent walls of the prison act as a figural device in much the same way as do the circles, boxes and parallelepipeds in the paintings of Francis Bacon, as understood by

Deleuze.[24] For these shapes, in Bacon's paintings, exert a centripetal force within the painting, isolating the figure found in the middle of them in order to, 'rompre avec la représentation, casser la narration, empêcher l'illustration, libérer la Figure',[25] without, nonetheless, condemning that figure to immobility:

> L'important est qu'ils [ces procédés] ne contraignent pas la Figure à l'immobilité; au contraire ils doivent rendre sensible une sorte de cheminement, d'exploration de la Figure dans le lieu, ou sur elle-même. C'est un champ opératoire. Le rapport de la Figure avec son lieu isolant définit un fait: le fait est..., ce qui a lieu... Et la Figure ainsi isolée devient une Image, une Icône.[26]

According to Deleuze, this centripetal movement in Bacon's paintings coexists with another converse movement coming from within the isolated figure itself:

> Mais l'autre mouvement, qui coexiste évidemment avec le premier, c'est au contraire celui de la Figure vers la structure matérielle, vers l'aplat. Depuis le début, la Figure est le corps, et le corps a lieu dans l'enceinte du rond. Mais le corps n'attend pas seulement quelque chose de la structure, il attend quelque chose en soi-même, il fait effort soi-même pour devenir Figure. Maintenant c'est dans le corps que quelque chose se passe: il est source du mouvement. Ce n'est plus le problème du lieu, mais plutôt de l'événement. S'il y a effort, et effort intense, ce n'est pas du tout un effort extraordinaire, comme s'il s'agissait d'une entreprise au-dessus des forces du corps et portant sur un objet distinct. Le corps s'efforce précisément, ou attend précisément de s'échapper. Ce n'est pas moi qui tente d'échapper à mon corps, c'est le corps qui tente de s'échapper lui-même par... Bref un spasme: le corps comme plexus, et son effort ou son attente d'un spasme.
>
> [...]
>
> Toute la série des spasmes chez Bacon est de ce type, amour, vomissement, excrément, toujours le corps qui tente de s'échapper *par* un de ses organes, pour rejoindre l'aplat, la structure matérielle.[27]

The implied walls of *Féerie*'s prison can be seen to act in precisely the same way, and to bring about this same movement in the figure confined within them. For by turning them into isolating, figural devices, the author Céline uses the centripetal force of those walls to his advantage, turning his narrator self into a figure, an icon that by its very nature breaks with illustration and narration, and, most importantly, with Historical representation. Once isolated in this manner, the body (and mind) of the narrator is free to try and escape from itself, but, unlike the figures in Bacon's paintings, the narrator Céline is not able to delight in the excremental spasms that would make this possible.[28] For even when a degree of the prison's centripetal intensity has been channelled into a figural process, the remaining intensity remains too powerful for the centrifugal force of the figure within it to overcome.[29] Hence the tragedy of the work, for all attention is focused on this one figure constantly fighting to exceed, by means of flights of the imagination and excremental spasms, both its own boundaries and those artificial, containing boundaries imposed from the exterior, yet never being able to exceed them, with the result that the processes of reterritorialisation in operation convert the figure's liberated molecular fluxes into pathological conditions:

> Mais je m'amuserais mieux cul pas collé, sans sphacèle, ni croûtes! Je visionnerais comme un Pape! Je le dis! je le dis! Si j'avais pas le boyau non plus noué par la crotte sèche, dysentérique! Si j'avais pas l'ouïe assourdie par les hordes de trains *express*! Ah je serais béat! (*FI*, p.171)[30]

The end of this quotation explains why it is that the isolated figure is not able to exceed the centripetal force. For the cranial noise—and indeed the cries of the other prison inmates—suffered by the narrator Céline throughout the novel, carries the same centripetal force as the walls of the prison (which, as it turns out, are all the more insidious for being invisible). This noise can thus be seen as an internalisation of the molar containing forces of History, as sonic interference that prohibits the direct transmission of Céline's *petite musique*, and so, accordingly, the narration of the novel—and especially the flights of fantasy—are constantly interrupted by noise. In this manner, the walls of the prison—which have been seen to become immaterial, their centripetal force becoming a figural force—are replaced by sonic waves which are, in effect, materialised, imbued with the containing force previously the preserve of the walls. As Cresciucci notes,

> Dans l'espace clos et sombre, infiniment clos et sombre puisque la cellule du narrateur est clôture à l'intérieur de la clôture, obscurité plus profonde à l'intérieur de l'obscurité, les bruits organisent l'espace. Il y a une chronologie et une spatialisation sonores.[31]

Similarly, just as sound is converted into a material mode of containment, so the radio waves—'«Les ondes qui tuent»!' (*FI*, p.7)—carrying the Official word from all the molar capitals of the world, act to reterritorialise the narrator within History by, once again, offering him up as a sacrificial victim:

> Les radios sont contradictoires... c'est pendu! c'est désossé!... écartelé?... En tout cas le châtiment approche... Une question d'heures... De Brazzaville, Berne ou Tobolsk, par toutes les fenêtres du quartier, ça se mugit, beugle, couaque... À la micro des vaillants de Londres c'est «empalé»!... New York l'hallali le plus terrible! *Le monstre de Montmartre sera haché!* (*FI*, p.6)

To thus concretise any wave (or, indeed, to drown out music with noise), however, is to destroy its very nature, to reverse the desubjectifying, dematerialising power of the wave exemplified, in the Célinian universe, by the dancer: 'les danseuses, les vraies, les nées, elles sont faites d'ondes pour ainsi dire!... pas que de chairs, roseurs, pirouettes!...' (*FI*, p.85). For the wave, the medium of emotion, should be that which allows man to escape his materiality, the terrible weight of corporeality, not that which grounds him in that very materiality. In *Féerie pour une autre fois* I, however, this is patently not to be the case, and the narrator's balletic expression will be overcome by this molar aberration, 'cette *furia canto* plein les airs! à tonnerre milliards kilocycles! déluges blablas!' (*FI*, p.28), with the result that every attempt to break out of striated space is foiled, every line of flight cut off by one of the numerous methods of containment molarity has at its disposal.[32] The frustration that this causes can be felt not only in the figure of the narrator, but also in the narrative itself through its frequent metanarrative interruptions and, particularly, through the figure of the imagined reader.

Unlike the photographs or other elements in Bacon's paintings which are used to heighten the movements within the central figure, having 'une fonction de *témoin*', in that they are, 'des témoins, non pas au sens de spectateurs, mais d'élément-repère ou de constante par rapport à quoi s'estime une variation', [33] the recurrent incursion of the voice of the reader in *Féerie pour une autre fois* provides the work with an antagonistic element that contributes to the reterritorialisation of the narrative. For whenever the narrator Céline turns the narrative towards dissolution—be it through an intimate examination of his own corporal disintegration, or flights of fantasy that deterritorialise the strata of History, giving his version of events rather than the Official version—, the imagined reader either attempts to reterritorialise the narrative by citing Historical events, or to discredit the narrator's vision with a barrage of insults or accusations of self-interest. Take the following examples:

> Oh mais je connais les distances! Vous avez les droits du plus fort, lecteur vengeur! Vous dites: «Ca faraud nous induit»! Je vais vous montrer mon derrière! Je vous ai prétendu: je suinte!... Vous avez de meilleurs yeux que moi! même là en l'ombre vous devez voir!... le rouge vif c'est la pellagre... à côté, en sorte de frange ce jaune gris: le lichen! Oh l'affection est peu commune!... éruption torpide papuleuse! Je la remonte de Blaringhem. Là-bas j'en avais au moins quinze... seize cas! des «gales»!... au moins mille! Voilà du derrière occupé! et les coudes donc! et la nuque!
>
> —Eh bien, dites donc alors Augsbourg! c'était pas des plaques papuleuses! c'était l'écharperie totale! toutes les peaux pour lampions d'A.A.! Abat-jour et reliures roustes, mirlitons, Walkyries, sabbats d'Odines et fours à gaz!
>
> Je déclare que j'y suis pour rien! ni de mon derrière, ni d'Augsbourg! J'ai pas déclaré la guerre, j'ai déclaré rien du tout, sauf «Vive la France et Courbevoie! À bas l'Abattoir!» (*FI*, p.31)

> —Faux-fuyeux! Trouilleux! Alibige! mauvaise foi! cochon! (*FI*, p.36)

> L'Enthousiasme, le Dieu en nous! Je suis moi qu'un morceau d'enthousiasme!
>
> —Oh, mais il rodomonte, parole!
>
> Votre réflexion.
>
> —Je me soigne en soignant les autres!
>
> —Son délire est simulé! On l'aurait vu à La Noé! (*FI*, p.72)

> qu'est-ce que je supporte comme maltraitements! pensez l'ophtalmie! et je travaille!... la rétinite!... la pellagre m'attaque les yeux... pas seulement les coudes et le derrière!... le mal des prisons, j'admets, mais encore j'ai des restes d'Afrique!... Si j'ai souffert aussi là-bas!... trois conjonctivites au Cameroun!... Bikobimbo, Rio Cribi, renseignez-vous! mimis sites! ici c'est de pas voir assez clair que je me rends aveugle, là-bas c'était de trop de soleil.
>
> —Ah, le tannant! qu'on le termine! qu'il ramène plus! au marbre le mec! Qu'on le dissèque!
>
> —Je vous conçois! Soit! Prosectez! L'âge! La méchanceté! La personne! vous trouverez tout! L'autopsie? Bravo! et mon névrome! Vive Dupuytren! Ah, et les guerres! Et votre vacherie!
>
> Preuve: ma succession est ouverte!... Vous avez qu'aller au Palais demander les «petites lettres»... «Hors la loi réputé comme mort»... le «Grand Registre»... «Condamné à tout!» plus que tout! Thémis mâche pas l'Iniquité!
>
> —Découpez-le! Bocaux! formol!
>
> Je vous insupporte? m'en fous! J'hurle! J'aboye!

> —Et la dysenterie amibienne? Je l'ai aussi! Kss! kss! vous dire si j'ai vu du pays! si je l'ai suivi le drapeau de la France! au diable! Ah les trois couleurs, cocotte! À moi! À moi! Épopée? Revers? Que me chaut! Bleu! Blanc! Rouge! c'est tout! partout je les ai portées haut! et dans la Gloire! et dans moins de gloire! Je m'en suis enveloppé en défaites! Y a des plis dans les trois couleurs, moi dans ma conscience pas un pli! Sorte du rang qui tique?... où n'ai-je été porter ma foi? ma carne?... mes diplômes?... Sincérité, gentillesse! Haut les cœurs!... Boxon!... Maintenant rigolade *extremis*!... moi mutilé décoré bien avant Pétain je vous emmerde!
>
> —Qu'on le transperce illique! écartle! (*F*I, pp.73–74)

Always reterritorialising the narrative within a Historical/biographical framework, the voice of the reader constantly resists and foils the text's intention to set up a connective synthesis between text and reader.[34] For the antagonistic reader consistently refuses this synthesis, preferring to keep Céline as an abject expiatory other, a practice also adopted by the group of writers who abduct the narrator from his prison cell. This group takes the narrator off in a wheelbarrow to bury him (*F*I, pp.89–96), thereby directing the fluxes of desire liberated in them by his poetic expression (they sing his song (*F*I, p.92)) into the narrator as a scapegoat in order to supress that desire (they frantically rip off their trousers to urinate on him, to give release (*F*I, p.94)), and to put a stop to the narrator's emancipatory expression ('ils veulent plus que je chante' (*F*I, p.89), 'me pisser dessus!... moi dans le bas purin buvant tout!...' (*F*I, p.94)). This kind of antagonistic reader is obviously not the kind sought by the narrator, and so, as a counterpoint, the narrator Céline creates another, fantastic reader more susceptible to the connective synthesis instigated by the text, one who allows the affective aesthetic to act directly on his/her emotional core:

> J'imagine là, j'anticipe, mettons que je meure pas en prison... ça serait la veine extraordinaire, pourri comme je me vois... je sors de tôle... je saute chez vous!... première visite!... votre sourire! comment je vous trouve? sous votre sofa, tout convulsant de rigolade, crispé sur *Féerie*!... arrachant des pages!... fou de plaisir, roulant, étranglant... (FI, p.72)

It is through this second type of imagined reader that the intention of the text can be glimpsed. For by presenting his own emotive deterritorialising version of History, the narrator Céline's wish is that the reader will subsequently carry out the work that he is unable to do for as long as he remains within the centripetal containing structure of the prison (symbolised by his adhesion to his stool by his own running sores), namely, to de-Historicise the name Céline, and bring about the destruction of the dissimulating structures of molarity and History through emotional investment. This intention can be perceived in the following excerpts:

> En somme voyez je vous présente tout!... tout... que vous mourriez pas sans savoir ce que furent les Revues des hautes âmes! la France! et Juillet! et les familles d'enthousiastes agrippés au moulin, aux ailes, aux lierres, hurlantes! Y a des moments sublimes, c'est tout!... le pesage, les diplomates, vous représentez somptuosités!... tout l'État-Major de Paris!... certains souvenirs prennent trop de forces... vous évoquez, vous savez plus, vous chancelez d'émoi!... j'ai le cul collé moi ça va!... j'oscille, je balance! je tombe pas!... tronc en avant!... tronc en arrière!... je peux pas choir!... (*FI*, p.108)

> La révolution du Carreau! et c'est pas fini! Ça que commence!... qu'un saut vous faites! la Bourse, 13 heures! Trois bonds! les marches! Campé je vous vois, beuglant le tonnerre!
>
> —Merde aux valeurs! merde aux «Rios»! merde aux «Tintos»! Commis, crétins, cocus, gogos, vous achetez autre chose vous êtes mort! Épongez la Cote!
>
> Le Temple à merci! La ruée des paumés!... Les colonnes fendent, boulent! fini!... Un énorme nuage monte sur Paris... le ciel s'obscurcit tout noir... c'est les «Valeurs!» c'est les poussières... Vous versez une larme, c'est tout! Vous vous ressaisissez et hop! votre Évangélisation commence! que commence!... les Champs-Élysées!... Une autre foule! Les maradjahs! l'apéritif!... les metteurs en scène... c'est l'heure! Les metteurs, les mises, les soumises! les émetteurs! les mis! Vous attaquez! porto! stout! flip!... sus aux terrasses!... un guéridon!
>
> À vos pieds, ébahis, conquis, les gens les plus fats du monde, les plus vaniteux survoltés... (*FI*, p.112)

There is thus great disparity between the antagonistic reader of *Féerie*—who could be described as phantasmic, being a projection of the narrator's perception of the actual reader-to-be—, and Céline's idealised fantastic reader, so the problem becomes how to convert the former into the latter. In an attempt to do precisely this, the narrator Céline "plays the game"—a common trait in schizophrenics—, employing molar mechanisms to edify the text and to belie its true motives. In this manner, *Féerie* is presented as a quasi-mystical, miraculous object, capable, like any molar icon, of deceptively dissimulating the human condition, offering itself up as, 'le livre qui vous réjuvène l'âme, boyaute le boyau! poudroie les soucis!... humeurs, avaros! avaries!... rosit, dilate, rate! bile! pocondre!' (*FI*, p.111), and, like Jesus with loaves and fishes, as a solution to hunger (*FI*, p.112). Furthermore, imitating the scare tactics of Catholicism, the act of buying *Féerie* becomes the only hope for man's salvation: 'peut-être si vous achetez *Féerie* j'irai d'un petit mot au Diable… qu'il vous épargne vingt… cinquante ans de vous briser le crâne et le rebriser!… Réfléchissez!' (*FI*, p.74).

Still further incentive to buy *Féerie*, is provided by the narrator Céline's feigned aspirations to molar ideals. For he pretends that the only reason he wishes to sell thousands of copies of *Féerie* is in order to reintegrate himself within molar society, to have his name gloriously inscribed in History, and to be able to buy himself bicycles and villas. It is for this reason that many critics consider that Céline, at this point in his career, became genuinely self-interested and mercenary. Take, for instance, this comment from Deleuze and Guattari:

> L'évolution syntaxique de Céline: du *Voyage* à *Mort à crédit*, puis de *Mort à crédit* jusqu'à *Guignol's band* I (ensuite, Céline n'avait plus rien à dire, sauf ses malheurs, c'est-à-dire n'avait plus envie d'écrire, il avait seulement besoin d'argent). Et ça se termine toujours comme ça, les lignes de fuite du langage: le silence, l'interrompu, l'interminable, ou pire encore. Mais quelle création folle entre-temps, quelle machine d'écriture! On félicitait encore Céline pour le *Voyage* qu'il était tellement plus loin, dans *Mort à crédit*, puis dans le prodigieux *Guignol's band*, où la langue n'avait plus que des intensités. Il parlait de la 'petite musique'.[35]

To interpret Céline's *œuvre* in this way, however, is, firstly, to read it selectively, completely ignoring the author's views on the incompatibility of Capitalistic concerns and art, and the sacrilege that the commercialisation of art constitutes:

> Je vous résume donc ce Tome premier, un peu de paroles, un peu de musique... Si ma pauvre tronche dodeline, que je vacille et que je vomis, c'est pas par genre croyez-le! c'est par fatigue matérielle de me rappeler trop de vos choses et d'autres... la *Féerie* c'est joli à dire mais les choses et d'autres! la note du gaz! le téléphone! Fortuné, j'écrirais plus rien!... Je ferais même plus d'économies!... même plus de villa à Saint-Malo! à peine arrivé là-bas, mes deux bonnes, mes portes, à peine achetés mes deux vélos, vous pensez les commentaires! Les «Ainairef» me tarabustent, ils veulent trois... quatre tomes! et musique! de ma pauvre ébréchée caboche! ils veulent en plus un *Digest*!... une *Constellation* croustillante!... cinq cent cinquante pages en trente lignes. (*FI*, p.169)

But to interpret literally Céline's materialistic ravings in his work after *Guignol's band* as do Deleuze and Guattari, is also to miss their schizophrenic nature—how ironic, then, that it should be the authors of *Capitalisme et schizophrénie* who do just that—and their true function. For every time any such comment is introduced into the text, every time that Céline appears to be reterritorialising himself, willingly succumbing to the centripetal force of molarity, that movement is accompanied by a converse centrifugal movement in which either the body of language, or the body of the narrator, enters into a process of dissolution, as these examples demonstrate:

> Oh, mais vivre c'est pas tout fredaine! Je vous entends! Subsister? Prospérer? Tenir? Eh bien vous m'achèterez Lison trois, quatre *Féeries* et ce sera, deux fois plus espiègle que je survive et que vous me payiez! Mais oui! vélo! mon vieux re-vélo! ma villa! tout! Oh! la drôlerie est partout! Je suis atteint, miné au physique, mais je quitterai la plaisanterie qu'après la carcasse! l'ultime souffle! la preuve là en huitième de lueur, suintant du croupion, des aisselles, des coudes aussi, saignant des yeux, du plus humide de ma fosse, sifflotant! vous m'entenderiez! le Merle!... (*FI*, p.26)

> —Achetez-le, vous! et hurlez!... mais regardez un peu les autours si c'est pas trop haineux, jaloux... à tous risques: «Il va crever!» vous ajoutez... «Il est agonique mais marrant!»... «C'est le marrant du Siècle»!... pas du demi!... faible le «demi-siècle»!... c'est comme «demi-dieu»... c'est rien!... parlez pas de génie!... c'est plein les rues les génies!... ça me ferait du tort!... «Achetez-le!» c'est tout... bref! net! ma gratitude vous est acquise... le trèpe se rue sur les «Libraires»... emporte les grossistes d'assaut! Je reboume!... ma fesse cicatrise et mon coude!... *Féerie*!... *Féerie*!... mon névrome?... j'admets... le hic!... mais Tailhefer m'opère... je reprends un «état général»... je revois clair on me sort de ma fosse, on m'adule... je m'achète un vélo, un *cottage*, une bonne pour ouvrir la porte... je pars plus en Sibérie du tout!... je me rétablis praticien sur la côte d'Émeraude! et vous me pouvez tout d'un seul mot: «Il désopile»! tant pis pour Montandon, sa balle, son cancer, Clamart-les-Asies, foultra! Toundras! Fulda! flûte! Zazov! qu'il y reste! (*FI*, p.54)[36]

Céline may claim to want statues made in his image, to have squares, esplanades and cities named after him (*FI*, p.119), he may claim only to be interested in the pecuniary transaction involved in the buying of his book, but he does so only in order to dissimulate his true intention, namely, to invest life positively with death.[37] Accordingly, in *Féerie*, the man who fears and attempts to avoid death with every molar structure available (the Larousse, the family and God, to give the examples from the quotations below), is surely the most ridiculous, repulsive and despicable of all creatures:

> le cancer, mettons, faites pas l'être surpris!... la hantise vous l'avez depuis belle!... combien avez-vous perdu d'heures, déjà, à vous loucher dans le trou du cul?... vous contorsionner à l'envers, miroir devant, miroir derrière, accroupi, disloqué, pleurant, le nez dans vos hémorroïdes, vous humant, rehumant encore?... (*FI*, pp.113–114)

> Et vous voilà rereplié en quatre! en huit! Ah gymnastique à miroir! trois quarts dessous demi devant! Damné Larousse!... Ah divinité d'être gibbon! Si vous en voulez au ciel!... vraiment gibbon! flexibilité infinie!... Le torticolis vous terrasse, abat, acrobate râlant, votre nez pris, en caca et sang! pas d'erreur! plus profond! plus profond encore!... (*FI*, pp.114–115)

> *Vlouf!* vous revoilà replongeant à rebours!... c'est trop Émile! c'est trop de penser!... Votre nez reste au fond du rectum... vous recommenciez à espérer... Las! Las! toutes les horreurs rappliquent!... du tréfonds! étouffant priant...
> —Dieu présent! Dieu toi! Cul! Anu!...
> On vous entend.
> —Pas moi, Dieu bon! Pas moi, cul bon!
> Suppliant! vos cris!
> —Prends tous les culs! moi laisse! moi laisse! ma fille! ma femme! mon gendre! moi laisse! moi laisse! Pimprenelle, ma petite amie, prends-l'y! prends-l'y! moi laisse! moi laisse! mon chien! mon petit André aussi! prends-l'y! prends-l'y! (*FI*, pp.116–117)

If the narrator appropriates a molar discourse, then, claiming to be concerned only with 'les faits' and 'les statistiques' (*FI*, p.117), he does so only to denounce the dissimulating structures of molarity, for the facts and statistics in question concern the inevitable and painful demise of the reader. Céline's intention in *Féerie* is merely to show, then, that, 'le spectacle est à l'intérieur, dans votre péritoine, pas dans les idées du tout!' (*FI*, p.118), as to realise this is to be able to throw off the dissimulating structures of molarity and make way for desiring-production, creation:

> Avec *Féerie* tout est autre!... la circonstance est tragique mais vous êtes plus qu'à la hauteur!... votre moral est extraordinaire!... Sacripant! vous hoquez! fumiste! La Mort? Tudieu!... par le bon bout!...
> —Bénédiction!... Foi d'agonique! le cochon me marre!...
> Voilà ce qu'on raconte, et ce qu'est vrai, comment vous prenez la chose... loustic comme pas!... grâce à *Féerie*!... 2 £ 50! le genre de Socrate que vous muez, pas pompeux du tout, grâce à *Féerie*!... l'agonie chouette!... les

> Antiques meurent emmerdement... la preuve: le bachot, la morale!... tout le monde convient, sauf frère François et Pierre Laval... Ah, du balai! flûte! luth! crééons!... le mort loustic! voilà l'idée! le mort marrateur! (*FI*, p.119)

The readers who understand this, however, remain figments of Céline's imagination, for the catch-22 is that, even though *Féerie* provides the key to its own interpretation for those that need it, it is precisely the reader that needs the key who will not read *Féerie*. In this respect, the text fails in its affective intention, its desire to allow the reader to invest his/her own reality, as the centripetal forces of History are never overcome enough for the text to be converted into a pure, autonomous aesthetic. Whenever a line of flight is initiated, it is immediately grounded by molar forces, or the effects of those forces—constipation, cranial noise, the noise from those driven mad by molarity ('[les] enragés des grilles' (*FI*, p.120)). This is why Céline says,

> À propos faut que vous l'appreniez: la chanson!... *C'est pas ici que je vais vous l'apprendre!...* cul collé comme! Je fredonne, c'est tout... les entrailles nouées par les cacas, durs... quinze jours que je peux pas aller... en plus des fous qui me perturbent!... je veux dire les cellules droite et gauche... les cris des enragés des grilles... ma pauvre nénétte!... en plus de mes bruits personnels... les acouphènes de mes tambours!... tambours, mes oreilles!... tambours et lésions!... mon limaçon microscopique!... des bruits de vingt-cinq fanfares qu'il me donne!... (*FI*, p.120; my italics)

The narrator may, then, attempt to "play the game", to accept the molar strictures placed around him and subvert them from the inside, but the boundaries prove too powerful and, instead, pathologise his molecular being:[38]

> Mes murs seulement!... Voilà!... c'est tout!... Confiance qu'en mes murs!... Oh, je me confine!... Oh je me confine!... et à l'écoute!... et aux visions!... Je capte tout!... en plus de mes bruits personnels, les trains de marchandises... deux... trois!... tout ce qui se manœuvre aux Batignolles... et sous le pont de Flandre et sous trois tunnels adjacents... et pas une confusion de sifflets!... ceux de la prison, ceux du chemin de fer, ceux de mes oreilles... les imaginaires, et les vrais... Jamais la plus petite douterie!... L'exquisité de mon écoute!... Chef d'orchestre en somme!... en plus du putois mal élevé et les beuglements des étages!... tenez, celle du dessus, l'avorteuse, je dirais comme vingt-cinq nouveau-nés!... ces cris!... la «28»! Je me répète?... alors?... J'ai l'oreille, voilà!... (*FI*, p.97)[39]

Having failed to overcome the centripetal forces of History, to conduct an orchestra whose music would be an appeal to desire rather than a pathological and pathologising cry, the narrator Céline, at this point in the text, introduces the character who, in the second volume of *Féerie pour une autre fois*, is to take over this role of 'chef d'orchestre'. Although the music that Jules conducts will have the same affective intent, will spring from the same desire to de-Historicise the aesthetic, however, his symphony will follow an inverse movement to that of the narrator Céline. Portrayed as a thoroughly despicable, hateful character, Jules will not attempt to win the reader over with feigned compliance, to integrate himself into the structures of molarity and submit to their centripetal force. Instead, he will delight in the unleashing of all his pent-up rage, hate and jealousy, in a centrifugal movement so extreme that it will not only exceed the centripetal barriers of molarity, but bring molarity itself to its knees. For Jules, as his name indicates, is pure potential energy,[40] a bomb ready to go off. Indeed, the first time he appears in the text, he is described much like a jack-in-the-box:

> il se renfrongne… il se rentre dans son dedans… sa tête en grimace dans son cou, plus profond, plus profond encore! en ratatinement d'haine de fond… qu'il est plus qu'un rond monstre sans tête… sa tête à l'intérieur du ventre, dans ses propres entrailles, grognant… grognant!… en masse compressé… contre le banc, dans sa gondole… ses fers à pleines mains pour me tuer… ses frondes de cul-de-jatte… (*FI*, p.125)

Having failed in its attempt to surpass the centripetal force of History, *Féerie* I becomes little more than a paranoiac complaint, a self-pitying cry against the injustice of a situation in which attempted compliance is only met with rejection and further condemnation, the textual space it creates being, then, autistic and one from which, once again, no transversal relation can emanate. Not content to wallow in self-pity, however, the narrator will, in *Féerie* II, exact his revenge—and hopefully de-Historicise his name in the same movement. For having been destroyed by the hateful forces of molarity, the well-intentioned narrator Céline will now unleash his secret weapon on the forces of History, a despicable, hateful, alcoholic, erotomanic, crippled Doppelgänger (of sorts) of himself, a figure deserving of the hate bestowed upon Céline, and one who is able to re-direct and accelerate the desire transformed into a hateful line of destruction by the molar apparatus, in an attempt to bring that very apparatus to the ground.[41] Such is the true revolutionary path envisaged by Deleuze and Guattari, who suggest that instead of, 'se retirer du procès'—the retreat for the narrator Céline being into a quasi-autistic condition through submission to the pathologising repressive defence mechanisms of the State—, it might be preferable to, 'aller plus loin, "accélérer le procès", comme disait Nietzsche'.[42] It is just such an acceleration and intensification of the very fluxes of History that will be carried out by Jules/the narrator Céline in the second volume of *Féerie*.

Céline—Jules; Same Difference

It may seem slightly strange to suggest that Jules can be seen as a double of the narrator Céline, since the hate directed towards the former in *Féerie pour une autre fois* II comes almost solely from the latter. For it is he that ceaselessly blames the apocalyptic events depicted in the novel on Jules, taunts him, insults him, exhorts him to jump off the windmill he is perched on, and attempts to convince everyone else of Jules' evil. However, if it is remembered that, at the end of the first volume of *Féerie*, this same narrator was left in what has been termed a pathological state, having succumbed to and internalised the paranoid centripetal forces of molarity, and if, also, it is brought to mind that the main point of contention between the narrator and Jules appears to be over Lili, the relationship between the two may come to be seen as more complex than many critics have assumed to be the case.[43]

It has been suggested here that the struggle at the core of *Féerie pour une autre fois* I is one in which the narrator Céline attempts to de-Historicise his name, to free it from the symbolic capital it has accrued from the publication of his pamphlets, in order that his works may once again be considered as aesthetic artefacts and not as Political tracts. Having failed to do so, the narrator is left trapped within History, and obliged to survive within, if not to accept, the enforced strictures of his situation, hence the pathologisation of both his corporeal and aesthetic fluxes. One of the ways in which he attempts to survive this situation is by using the schizophrenic defence mechanism that has been termed, "to play the game", that is to say, to adopt insincerely the values of molar society, an action which, in its insincerity, implicitly denounces those very values. Considered in the light of this analysis, certain aspects of *Féerie pour une autre fois* II—and, indeed, passages from the latter stages of *Féerie* I—, become clearer. Why, for instance, the narrator who has taken such pleasure in the meticulous description of his own putrid rectum, is suddenly so outraged at Jules' lasciviousness; why, also, someone so obviously distraught at the waves of hate directed against him is so eager to whip up homicidal rage against Jules. If, however, the narrator is merely playing the game, adopting those very attitudes that led to his own condemnation and directing them towards an abject other who is, in fact, merely an exaggerated version of himself, then this apparent disparity will no longer apply. For this theory to hold, it will be necessary, firstly, to consider Jules as a double of Céline.[44]

Jules, like the narrator Céline, is a war hero, mutilated—although to a greater degree than Céline (*F*I, pp.125, 134)—, is constantly complaining (as does the narrator of *Féerie* I for close on two hundred pages), and desires Lili, the narrator's wife. Like Céline in his prison cell, he is described as being in an accelerated state of decomposition because of his art—he constantly licks the paint off his brushes and drinks his solvents (*F*I, p.132) —, both need help to defecate,[45] and, like Céline stuck to his stool, Jules, being a double amputee, is unable to get up from his cart. There are also remarkable similarities in their respective places of work, for even though Céline insists that his work conditions are far worse ('Oh, son taudis était sombre, j'admets, mais pas si sombre qu'où je vous écris!... Fond de fosse!... et comme humidité! minute! Ah! le Julot!...' (*F*I, p.139)), both have walls which are described as being almost fluid, as can be seen in the close coincidence of the following descriptions:

> Ces murs découlent, j'éponge les flaques... (*F*I, p.27)
>
> lui ses murs dégoulinaient... (*F*I, p.139)
>
> Si mes murs, moi, dégoulinent! dix fois comme chez Jules! (*F*I, p.142)

Not only does the vocabulary used in these examples give the necessary impression of degradation and dankness, it also, through repetition, breaks down the solidity of the walls so that they become, like all the walls of the prison, part of an absent materiality. This, in turn, enables the walls to be seen as doors to a passage between the two worlds of the novel,[46] and also, due to the exact coincidence of terminology in the last two examples and the comparison made in the last, sets up an equivalence between the two places, with the effect that they become almost interchangeable, if not one and the same place. Furthermore, whilst the temporally diverse visions that make up much of the narrative of *Féerie I* come to the narrator Céline through the walls of his prison ('J'ai l'air de rien je vois dans mes murs! l'avenir! le passé! les méchants! Je vous transmets! alors? mes propres murs! tout d'avance!' (*FI*, p.91)), the ceiling of Jules' studio is covered with paintings from his various '«Époques»' (*FI*, p.130).[47]

And yet, in spite of the similarities between the narrator Céline and Jules, the former is constantly at great pains to emphasise the difference between them: 'Lui je vous fais remarquer le Jules, puisqu'on parle de ce sale chiard, c'est meurtrir les gens qu'il amuse! la différence de nos natures!... deux caractères!...' (*FI*, p.143). Ironically, it is one of those elements that unites them that drives the narrator to distinguish himself from Jules, for much of the animosity between the two undoubtedly stems from jealousy at their respective relationships with Lili. Even though Lili is Céline's wife, Jules tirelessly attempts to seduce her, to fondle her, to get her to pose for him, to steal away Céline's muse, one might say, for Lili, being a dancer, is the incarnation of the affective aesthetic sought by Céline in his writing. By giving Lili permission to pose for Jules, then, Céline effectively hands over his aesthetic to Jules (*FI*, p.150), relinquishing the only thing that enabled him to survive during his times of trouble (*FI*, pp.84–85), and simultaneously enabling Jules to liberate fully his desire and rid himself of the narrator Céline by reterritorialising him in History:

> —Donne-moi Lili! Donne-moi Lili!
>
> À moi qu'il demande! l'enragé! devant tous les chnocs!... ses fenêtres pleines de ploucs! Ah! Ah!
>
> —Prends-la eh cochon! prends-la!
>
> Il me pousse à bout.
>
> —Boche! Boche! qu'il me chuchote alors, Boche! de dessous le sofa, là comme il est, trempant dans les glaises, la merde! il me montre la porte! (*FI*, pp.150–151)

Indeed, it is as soon as the narrator Céline responds defensively to this charge, leaving the room and, thereby, leaving Lili to Jules, that he gives in to the molar forces of History and to pathological paranoia, as can be seen in the following passages:

> Ce coup-là je sors...

> Et bien, c'est de ce moment... là, je repense... de ce moment-là même... là juste!... et puis la suite... tout ce qu'a suivi... que les horreurs ont commencé... vraiment les horreurs!... qu'on a été de ces traqués, je peux dire traqués si malheureux pires que bêtes!... pas pendant un mois!... dix mois!... dix ans!... (*FI*, p.155)

> —Grouille! Grouille! les flics! Con! les flics! l'alerte!
> J'entendais pas les sirènes... enfin pas assez... Je regarde en l'air... Il me dit l'alerte!... Je vois pas d'avions... Si, un sillage! Ah si! Un sillage!... Un géant V... mais j'entendais pas de sirènes...
> —Grouille! Grouille! Chnok! Grouille!
> Avec mes bourdonnements d'oreille, je doutais... Il m'envoyait au métro. Je me méfie toujours des sirènes... toujours!... Je confonds... l'Avenue était vide c'est certain... plus de flics!... Ah, absolument plus personne!... C'était tout de même peut-être l'alerte?... mais tout le temps y avait des alertes!... des sirènes!... des miauleries hautes!... j'en avais aussi des bruits moi! à moi! des miauleries hautes!... plein les deux oreilles des moments! des miauleries hautes!... pas que des moments... des heures des fois!... de mes propres oreilles!... Tout de même... tout de même... «Au métro! Au métro!»... Je me décide... un pas... un autre pas... je titube... je lâche l'aquarelle, là!... le cadeau... «Au métro! Au métro!» Je lâche la statuette... Je vacille... un pas... un autre... je me rattrape!... et *wouaf!* je dégueule!... Ça me prend là... pas loin... vingt mètres de sa porte... je vois le trottoir, c'est tout... et plus rien... je dégueule plein le trottoir... à quatre pattes alors!... quatre pattes... au ruisseau je veux... parce que c'est l'alerte! Je bourdonne ou je sirène?... C'est l'alerte!... (*FI*, pp.157–158)

Céline thus allows his desire to be captured, ensnared by molarity, and his reaction is one of dissolution, of escape. For as do the central figures of Bacon's paintings, the narrator Céline vomits, such a reaction being, as has been seen, a spasm, 'le corps qui tente de s'échapper lui-même par... Bref un spasme: le corps comme plexus, et son effort ou son attente d'un spasme. [...] le corps qui tente de s'échapper *par* un de ses organes, pour rejoindre l'aplat, la structure matérielle'.[48] Yet the narrator will not cede entirely to this dissolution, holding back from the abyss that is desubjectification, resisting the destratification of molar space, refusing the transference of desire to the reader that such a description would entail:

> Je vomis, oui!... Je vomis!... mais les sirènes? suivant le rebord... le rebord, entendez!... le ruisseau!... C'est énorme un ruisseau des coups!... C'est un gouffre!... un gouffre qui remonte... et qui renfonce!... qui remonte et qui rabaisse!... le vertige!... la tour Eiffel que vous diriez un ruisseau!... tout au fond un petit trou, l'égout!... et puis immense et puis géant!... l'immensité!... tout Paris!... l'égout... au fond de l'égout... moi je sais!... je me cramponne!...

> mille petites lumières!... chandelles!... le rebord!... bravo!... Il m'a pas l'égout... il m'a pas! le précipice m'a pas! bravo!... je dégueule!... je dégueule dedans! je bourdonne!... le vertige! il m'a pas le vertige! vertige de Ménière ça s'appelle!... les maisons tournent! et alors!... s'élèvent! s'enlèvent! et alors! les immeubles en l'air! «Ménière! Ménière!» les trottoirs godent!... je vous entends rire... Non! Non! Non! Je me cramponne et je traverserai! (*FI*, p.158)

Having given away the only thing that enabled him to survive within molarity to Jules, Céline is entirely at the mercy of molarity, his molecular being is territorialised, miraculated by the paranoiac pole, and his dissolution is experienced only as a frightening pathological process.[49] Take the following examples:

> Je vis que par elle [Lili]... j'ai plus de corps!... presque plus d'âme... Le monde a été trop cruel. C'est par les dépeceurs qui manquent! J'ai connu des êtres terribles... (*FI*, p.163)

> Ils m'ont tout pris moi! ma chemise! ma peau! mes années!... ma virilité! je bande plus!... tout est parti à la pellagre! (*FI*, p.160).

Yet it would appear that all is not entirely lost, since, in spite of this pathological dissolution, the narrator Céline has still retained a vestige of his former musical self: 'J'ai plus de peau! J'ai plus de chemises! J'ai plus de dents! mais j'ai des petits airs en mémoire' (*FI*, p.161). However, the short refrains that appear in the text in tablature form, only signal the annihilation of the poetic voice, and, therefore, the text itself ('*feuilles* mortes!'):

> *Faut-il dire à ces potes*
> Que la fête est finie?...
> Au Diable ta sorte!
> Que le vent t'emporte!
> Adieu feuilles mortes!
> (FI, p.162; see also FI, pp.159, 161, 163, 167, 172, 176)

Reterritorialised within molarity, the final pages of *Féerie pour une autre fois* I see the narrator Céline, now capable only of singing a swan song, bemoaning his misfortune and his treatment at the hands of molar society, yet employing molar techniques in order to avenge himself. For instead of denouncing the wrongs he has suffered through a delirious poetic voice that will be transmitted directly to the reader's desire, the narrator Céline professes his wish to use a Historical mechanism of inscription in order to create an eternal monument.[50] This can be clearly observed in the passages that follow:

> Je veux qu'on grave leurs noms ceux-là, en or! en plein granit de Sainte Chapelle! pour l'enseignement des benêts cons trop généreux trop chauds trop francs, pour la preuve ce qui leur arrivera n'importe quelle époque quand ils voleront au canon, au clairon, au sacrifice!... Une autre pierre encore là, gravée, je veux, pour ceux qu'auront vendu des Odes des deux côtés, qu'auront eu sur leurs genoux toute la Cour Ultime... Ça c'est de l'enseignement historique! (*FI*, p.159)

> Je veux leurs noms leurs promotions leurs grades de sadiques, leurs sécurités, leurs tantièmes, tout en lettres d'or, en plein granit, en Sainte Chapelle! (*FI*, p.160)

> Oh, mais j'écrirai moi haineux, je vengerai tout le monde, là cul collé, leurs noms historiques gravés or... en Sainte Chapelle!... le pouvoir d'écrivain si faible! faible poête, plus faible que tout! (*FI*, p.162)

> Ils se surprennent... Ils s'indignent! voilà leurs opinions de moi-même! mais moi j'écrirai leurs noms dans la Sainte Chapelle! leurs noms d'or! ainsi va l'éternité du monde... ils seront attrapés finalement... (*FI*, pp.162–163)

> Je glorifierai leurs noms en or! L'Assesseur aussi de l'Ambassade! et le Ministre! le Romain de l'oignon! J'ai des raisons! Là dans mon roman aussi je glorifie! (*FI*, p.165)

The final pages of *Féerie* I thus describe the conversion of the narrator's poetic voice into a territorialising mechanism as a defence against the containment of that voice by the centripetal forces of History—fighting territorialisation with territorialisation.[51] But these pages also reinforce the role of Jules as an abject other, a despicable being of insatiable desire who has stolen away the narrator's muse/wife (*FI*, pp.162–165, 171–172), deserving only mistrust, hate and violence (*FI*, pp.158, 164, 176). It is, of course, the narrator who brings these charges against Jules, for the narrator is now a molar subject (no matter how sincere his adhesion to the paranoiac pole may or may not be) and considers Jules to be the despised Other, since the molecular/schizophrenic desiring traits the narrator once displayed himself are considered as threatening now that they have been taken on by Jules who, therefore, is in possession of the poetic voice that the narrator has lost. That this is indeed the case can be seen in the examples below, as Jules—the narrator's former duet partner (*FI*, p.168)—adopts the visionary attributes, centrifugal power capable of exceeding a molar centripetal force, and artistic credentials that were previously the preserve of the narrator:

> —On est déjà aux nuages nous autres! la Butte va sauter! tout est miné!... Des Batignolles à Dufayel!
>
> Je vous rapporte les paroles de Jules...
>
> Il savait tout... prévoyait tout... il avait des relations terribles... la Cour des Mises à sa botte! Un mot du Jules ils me font sortir... là même à présent... là d'où je suis!... (*F*I, pp.169–170)

> vous retenez pas un mot sur vingt... vous regardez au loin, fatigués... vous êtes pas artistes comme Jules... lui il retenait ce qu'il voyait! la preuve les cuisses à Arlette, ses nichons, ses reins, ses détentes... ces convulsions de lionne... (*F*I, p.167)

Thus, accompanying the death of the narrator's poetic voice and the text's own metatextual demise, comes a movement that, in the final words of *Féerie* I, hands over that voice to Jules for *Féerie* II: 'J'étais excité comme tout!... C'est tout... excité! client!... la vie passe... le sang passe... il emmène...' (*F*I, p.176).[52]

Talking of Jules in these terms, as the abject other who inherits the poetic voice of Céline, it must not be forgotten, however, that Jules is, in fact, Céline, or rather, the non-territorialised version of the narrator Céline whose own expression has become pathological—hence the vomiting outside of Jules' house which accompanies the handover of the aesthetic (*F*I, p.158). This is made clear at the beginning of *Féerie* II, as the narrator's discourse shows signs of a subjectivity disturbed by the forces of molarity, and one which is consequently unable to distinguish between different events, between memory and reality:[53]

> Raconter tout ça après... c'est vite dit!... c'est vite dit!... On a tout de même l'écho encore... *brroum!...* la tronche vous oscille... même sept ans passés... le trognon!... le temps n'est rien, mais les souvenirs!... et les déflagrations du monde!... les personnes qu'on a perdues... les chagrins... les potes disséminés... gentils... méchants... oublieux... les ailes des moulins... et l'écho encore qui vous secoue... Je serai projeté dans la tombe avec!... Nom de brise! j'en ai plein la tête!... plein le buffet... *Brrroum!...* je ressens... j'accuse... je vibre des os, là dans mon lit... mais je vous perds pas!... je vous rattraperai de ci, de là... tout est là! le caractère!... des loques aux bourrasques! on peut le dire! *broum!...* je vous le dis, ils m'ont remonté là-haut... Je vous disais ils m'ont reporté comme Malborough... vous savez? quand on le porte en terre?... moi, en l'air!... à quatre... à cinq chevaliers et dames d'atour... Lili m'a dit... les

> sept étages!... J'étais tombé sur l'ascenseur par la porte ouverte... non!... plus bas encore... plus bas tombé!... à la cave!... *Brroum!...* en appelant Lili!... en appelant Bébert... appelant tout!... Ils m'avaient ramassé dehors... les quatre chevaliers et les dames, remonté chez moi... c'est pas d'hier que je fais les *braoum!...* depuis 14 à vrai dire... novembre 14... *broum!* je fus envolé par un obus, envolé! soulevé!... un gros déjà! un «107»! en selle sur «Démolition»... ma jument de «serre-fille»! Sabre au clair! nom de zef! Je m'envolais! voilà l'homme! ah les souvenirs me brinqueballent... vous verrez... je les rattraperai tous!... je m'envolerai!... je vous priverai de rien!... loques de 14!... de 18!... 35!... 44!... (*F*II, pp.179–180)

And later,

> j'étais tombé sur les sourcils!.... les arcades fendues! mais rien de cassé d'autre! ah non! je saignais de toute la figure c'est tout... surtout des tempes... je dégoulinais... des horions en somme!... j'aurais pu me tuer un peu plus bas... la cage au premier!... je répète!... ma chance!... mais je m'étais bien sonné le grelot!... les répercussions du vertige!... j'en vomissais dans mon lit... *je déconnais, et je le savais!...* (*F*II, pp.180–181; my italics)

It is thus a pathological narrator who will recount the events of *Féerie* II, a narrator who consciously and deliberately performs a scission of his own self into two in order to deterritorialise his desire; for the desiring half of the narrator—that is to say Jules, 'cette *abjection de demi-être...*' (*F*II, p.192; my italics)—will be 'là-haut', 'en l'air', freed from the materiality of molarity, whilst his pathological half (the narrator/protagonist Céline) will remain firmly grounded in it, 'plus bas encore... plus bas tombé!... à la cave!...'. The fact that this scission can be said to be willed, however, does not necessarily imply that it will be experienced as a felicitous solution; on the contrary, remaining in molarity, pathologised and paranoid, the narrator will suffer from this scission, never knowing whether his own poetic voice—expressed through the projectiles launched by the projection that is Jules—truly emanates from himself or from the outside:[54]

> tout l'horizon est en dentelles... en fines résilles de lumières... projectoires, balles crépitantes... on voit bien les coteaux d'Enghien!... et la trouée vers Mantes, Meulan, l'argent, les voltes de la Seine... maintenant par l'effet des bombes la Seine bouillonne!... jugez l'effet!... et pas de mon oreille!... c'est bien en dehors de moi!... j'ai jamais eu de bruits si forts!... ces *brroum!...* je le dis à Lili...
>
> —C'est pas moi! c'est eux!... (*F*II, p.187)[55]

Displaying symptoms of pathological schizophrenia, the narrator Céline becomes unable to relate to his own creation, and takes on the role of chronicler, rather than that of artist:

> je vous décris tout ce qu'on voit de nos fenêtres... des sortes de petits tableaux d'artistes... mille mille fleurs d'une vivacité!... de ces coloris ardents!... là, sous le ciel de phosphore le resplendissement croît!... croît!... moi-même pas sensible visuel je suis halluciné!... (*F*II, p.188)

One could replace the last words of this quotation with the more Deleuzoguattarian version, 'je suis miraculé', for converted into a 'simple témoin visuel' (*F*II, p.190), the narrator denies his own part in the creative production of the work which, instead, appears like a *socius*, a body on which the narrator's life is (pre-)inscribed (and which thus becomes the quasi-cause for his existence), rather than the product of his desire. Alienated from his own work, the narrator consequently experiences his own externalised thoughts and desiring-flows as persecutory, as an antagonist to be eradicated—hence his exhortations throughout the novel for Jules to jump from the windmill, for, as seen above, he is no longer able to tell whether Jules' projectiles emanate from himself or from the outside. *Féerie* II, in which is recounted the story of the battle between the protagonist Céline and Jules, will thus provide a stage on which to act out the tension between the opposing forces at play in the narrator himself: the centripetal, pathologising force of molarity, and the centrifugal, desiring force of the artist.

Féerie pour une autre fois II: The Centrifugal Force of the Artist

Féerie I has been seen to stage the narrator's struggle to use the confining structures of molarity to his advantage, through the conversion of the centripetal force of History from a means of subjectification to a figural process that would enable the release of deterritorialised desire, a poetic expression freed from the symbolic capital accrued by the name Céline that will not, therefore, be reterritorialised by the reader but act directly on the reader's emotive core. Having failed to do this, however, the centripetal force of History being too powerful, the only flows to emanate from the narrator are pathological—the pathological schizophrenic being created when desire is curtailed.[56] The aim of *Féerie* II (and, indeed, of Céline's entire corpus from *Guignol's band* onwards) is the same as that of *Féerie* I, namely, to attain an auto-objective mode of expression, an affective aesthetic, a collective assemblage of enunciation, but the attempt to do this, in *Féerie* II, will follow the opposite path to that taken by *Féerie* I, reversing those processes already observed. For in *Féerie* II, the centrifugal, poetic expression—embodied by the missiles emanating from the flying war machines at Jules' command—will be employed to wage war on the centripetal forces of molarity, on all those structures erected in order to confer a sense of stability, permanence and purpose on human existence. The first such structure to be exploded, of course, is History itself, for *Féerie* will deliberately contravene the intransigence of linear temporality. As Nettelbeck notes,

> *Féerie* comporte une chronologie et beaucoup de mouvement, mais aucune véritable temporalité. Le seul temps du roman est celui qu'impose le déluge: c'est un "moment" à l'intérieur duquel beaucoup de choses se passent, mais qui ne se rapporte à aucune continuité extérieure à lui-même.[57]

Furthermore, *Féerie* shows little regard for the content of History, for, in spite of the narrator's insistence that we are dealing with Historical Truth, the entire bombardment of Paris depicted in *Féerie* II is radically transposed and distanced from that Truth by the author's imagination.[58] Herein lies a problem, however; for *Féerie* II will wage war primarily on History, yet it is History that, for the narrator of *Féerie* I, operates as an apparatus of capture from which he is unable to extricate his name, and it will not, therefore, be possible for any character bearing the name Céline to appropriate this poetic expression. Instead, Céline will, as has been seen above, project his poetic expression into a pathologically fantasised other, Jules. By doing so, a double deterritorialisation of molarity is practised, for in denouncing Jules' actions from within an enforced molar state, the narrator is merely "playing the game", falsely appropriating a molar discourse with the result that it is that very discourse and its fascistic paranoid mechanisms which are denounced, rather than the supposed target of that discourse, as has already been suggested.[59] The principal attack on molarity, the second and primary deterritorialisation, however, comes from Jules himself.

Already in *Féerie* I, the unleashing of Jules' desire on Lili coincided with a surprising event; for it is at the very same time that Jules sticks his head up Lili's skirt and starts kissing and biting her between her thighs, that aeroplanes appear, making letters in the sky (*FI*, pp.147–148). Postulating that the simultaneity of the unleashing of Jules' desire on Lili and the appearance of the aeroplanes is by no means coincidental, it can be argued that almost the entirety of *Féerie pour une autre fois* II is, essentially, a variation on and an intensification of this event, a description of the effects of desire on molar society. For if, indeed, the coincidence of these two apparently unrelated events is not merely coincidental, it would appear that there is a causal link between Jules' desire and the existence of these calligraphic aeroplanes. If, furthermore, it is remembered that his desire is directed towards Lili, it could be said that the investment of desire in the pure aesthetic incarnate brings about a poetic expression—the letters traced by the planes in the sky. These letters, then, are mere 'trajectoires', poetic intensities—not coded strategic messages (or, to explicitise the metafictional link, Political tracts) as the assembled crowd believes them to be (*FI*, pp.148–149)—, and yet they are nothing compared to the intensified trajectories that fill the sky (and pages) of *Féerie* II once Céline has relinquished Lili to Jules.[60] These poetic trajectories of desire will be seen in the following quotations:

> *Plouaf!* j'y ferais prendre une trajectoire! y en a! y en a des trajectoires! y en a plein le Ciel!... plein la tornade! (*FII*, p.224)

> Et que voilà d'autres artifices! des obus traçants de très loin... des trajectoires originales... spirales!... de canons de plus loin que Poissy!... l'effet comme s'ils cousaient les nuages... les cousaient ensemble... les ourlaient!... en bleu!... mauve! jonquille! (*FII*, p.264)

> Enghien en pleine éruption!... des trajectoires jusqu'à Massy... Joinville... Vincennes, le Château, tout noir sur le fond d'incendies!... (*FII*, p.297)

> une trajectoire de bout en bout, tout le Ciel! s'engouffrer dans la grande crevasse, en même temps au moins que trente avions! (*FII*, p.305)

> toutes les couleurs! à travers le bombardement! à travers mille trajectoires, fusées, dentelles de shrapnells, jusqu'au trou du firmament! passés à travers le trou! et revenus!... (*FII*, p.393)

The 'trajectoires' of *Féerie* II are traced not by the planes themselves, however (although there are still a few instances where this is the case), but rather by the destructive missiles the planes fire. But, as can be seen from the above quotations, although destructive, these 'trajectoires' lose none of their poetic, creative intensity; on the contrary, it could be said that their thematic destruction is inversely proportionate to their heightened poetic and stylistic intensity, for the bigger—or more molar—the building destroyed, the greater the explosion, the more the entire landscape is filled with colour, the stronger the poetic intensity, as is exemplified in these passages:[61]

> Y a du nouveau spectacle dehors!... des géantes chenilles qui crépitent, ondulent... elles cherchent les pinceaux de projecteurs... les stries pâles... je vois! je vois! je m'écarquille bien les deux yeux... je me les tiens ouverts de force...
>
> —Tu vois Lili? Tu vois toi?
>
> Pour m'asseoir, voir mieux encore, je me soulève et puis je me tiens debout, je m'appuie sur elle... je vais à la croisée... côté Gaveneau, l'avenue Gaveneau... par là, alors c'est plus que jour!... un jour jonquille, d'un vif, d'un vif!... tout l'air! tout le ciel!... les toits... tout Paris! si vous seriez éblouis!... rien que les toits! les miroitement des tuiles!... bijoux! diamants!... les bombes éclatent là-dedans en fleurs! rouges! rouges! en œillets!
>
> Voilà ce qu'ils font à la «Passive».
>
> —Regarde les bombes Lili! Regarde! C'est sur Renault!... C'est des avions qui déchargent leurs tonnes d'explosifs!... blancs... blancs papillons d'avions!... un de ces flamboiements sur Renault! la hauteur des nuages! flammes bleues!... oranges!... vertes!... et des géantes chandelles zigzag... elles doivent chercher dans le jaune des points... ah, quels aravions!... (*F*II, p.185)

> elle était pourtant prodigieuse de lumière verte, bleue, orange et de tortillage, la langue!... tout au-dessus de Paris... rouge... verte... orange... crépitante! et plein de petites flammèches aux rebords... ils auraient regardé par la fenêtre ils auraient hurlé: «la merveille!»... qu'elle léchait l'avenue!... des moments!... des moments relevait! voguait... pointait ailleurs!... jusque sous l'Arc de Triomphe!... l'enfilait comme un trou d'aiguille... passait de l'autre côté! entièrement!... vous dire l'effet!... et un autre moment encore! deux coups de liches... l'Opéra!... l'École militaire!... la Salpêtrière!... (*F*II, pp.292–293)

Such is entirely in accordance with Céline's conception of his literary project, in which ideas—the preserve of molarity—are nothing, and style is everything.[62] The lines of destruction aimed at molar targets (homes, factories, cities), then, can be read as metastylistic devices, describing phantasmically the desired effect of the poetic expression, namely, to create a centrifugal force that breaks through the centripetal forces of molarity, to transcend the artificially contained materiality of human society in order to access a spiritual, metaphysical plane that is infinitely irreducible. It is Jules, as the narrator Céline repeatedly points out, who is the conductor of this symphony of destruction, and his podium is a windmill. This, of course, is entirely fitting, since the turning vanes of a windmill—which, according to the narrator, 'avait pas tourné depuis 1813!...' (*F*II, p.293), 'Cent ans et mèche!' (*F*II, p.224)—emit a centrifugal force, as does the schizophrenic/poetic expression of desire (Jules' 'trajectoires') that make them turn. These 'trajectoires' do not only activate the molecular potential of this building, however, for the bombardment sends all of Paris into a state of flux, of material dissolution, and, once again, it would seem that the greater the molar force associated with any building, the more the solidity and stability of that building is threatened. Here are but a few examples:

> Les meubles deviennent des personnes, dandinantes... voguantes... et les murs!... aussi les murs!... (*F*II, p.185)
>
> et il frôle le toit, notre toit!... il nous frise... toute la cabane tremble! il faut des conditions de déluge pour qu'un immeuble de sept étages se trouve secoué de la façon! vous vous rendez compte?... de haut en bas l'immeuble frissonne!... les courants d'air en boutoir lui fripent les murs! alors si l'armoire revadrouille!... je suis pas fou!... (*F*II, p.186)
>
> ils frisent notre toit... *vrrrr! vrrrr!*... ils giclent en flèche du ravin dans un énorme sifflement d'air et tout le tremblement de la maison!... ah c'est infernal!... j'essaye de vous faire comprendre!... et je peux pas quitter la croisée!... les immeubles de l'avenue Gaveneau montent dans les sillages des avions!... parfaitement!... les suivent! s'élancent après eux! toute l'avenue!... tous les petits hôtels cavalent d'ombres en ombres!... c'est miraginant!... les grandes bâtisses aussi s'élèvent!... haussent, s'emportent!... les plus forts immeubles!... certains, quatre fois grands comme le nôtre!... jaunes!... verts!... bleus!... et *broumm!* en l'air! tout vogue!... toute la girandole ondule entre les étoiles... on voit les étoiles dans le jonquille... le ciel est en mer de jonquille... (*F*II, p.186)
>
> Le Ciel crève à gauche, là juste!... *brrrac!* au sud! Drancy par conséquent! Drancy! Drancy qui écope! une cataracte d'or d'en haut... un fleuve des nuages... jaune... et puis vert... c'est pas commun comme masse de feu ce qui cascade, rejaillit, inonde... je vous en ai raconté pourtant... mais là vraiment c'est le ciel entier qu'on dirait qui fond... et puis d'en bas on voit des rues qui s'élèvent... s'enlèvent... montent en serpents de flammes... tourbillonnent... tordent d'un nuage à l'autre... une église entière qui part, se renverse, tout son clocher pointu, brûlant, en espèce de pouce!... c'est extraordinaire! renversé sur nous!... l'église d'Auteuil... je vous l'ai raconté!... à l'envers... mais elle, pas si flambante tout de même... plutôt en reflets... ah vous voyez c'est pas semblable... vogue!... s'envole... (*F*II, p.218)

> Vingt quartiers crépitent! le Luxembourg est plus qu'une rose! une roseraie ardente!... l'Académie fond... en beige... en vert... dégouline au Quai... puis à la Seine... la Coupole flotte un moment... se retourne! coule!... Ah, et la Madeleine et la Chambre!... elles ont l'air de s'envoler... gonflées montgolfières... elles s'élèvent un petit peu... balancent... passent bleu! rouge! blanc! éclatent! (*F*II, p.264)

Following the reversal of movement between the two volumes, then, the centripetal force that the physical confines exerted on the narrator in *Féerie* I, are here exchanged for a centrifugal force, emanating from the abject double of the narrator, and acting upon the physical stability of the molar world. It is not only the buildings themselves that are subjected to the centrifugal force of Jules' molecular 'trajectoires', however, for their inhabitants also undergo a process of dissolution, losing all sense of identity and exterior boundaries, entering into various modes of becoming, including—as will be seen in one of the following quotations—a becoming-animal:

> ah, mais ce nom de Dieu de canon les fait encore se pire compresser! là sous la table! pire sous la table! chiasse partout! bonne mine moi, avec mes appels à l'assaut! *Ouaf! woaouf!* s'ils se recroquevillent!... Pensez l'avenue en enfilade! le vibrement! moi, je rampe à l'envers! c'est fini! je rampe vers l'escalier! au trou!... j'opte pour le trou!... je pars plus au Ciel!... ah, mais attention: ramper?.. ramper, c'est vite dit... la flaque!... le parquet: une flaque!... une flaque, un vrai lac... et qui houle! clapote! (*F*II, pp.276–277)

> j'ouvre les yeux... je veux voir... trop éblouissant, brûlant!... «Piram! Piram!» Piram est là... sa grosse tête... non, c'est pas Piram... c'est une dame... une dame frisotée... je l'attrape... je palpe cette tête... et je change de tête!... une autre... c'est un homme... non! les oreilles, c'est bien Piram!...(*F*II, p.336)

> le Raymond me tombe dessus en fait d'aide!...en plein! et il s'interpelle lui-même! il s'hurle à lui-même! «Raymond! Raymond!» il se cherche encore!...
> Il s'est reperdu!
> —Ta gueule!
> Je le calme... il attrape alors Piram... par la tête!
> —C'est toi, chéri? c'est toi Raymond?
> Il questionne Piram!... il se prend pour Piram!... Piram lui échappe...(*F*II, p.373)

Disabled by the dissolution of the molar structures that allowed them to dissimulate their true molecular condition, the inhabitants of Ferdinand's building take refuge (as do the passengers on board *l'Amiral*

Bragueton in *Voyage au bout de la nuit*) in alcohol and 'vulnéraire': 'Il sait plus qu'il est lui-même!... il se demande à boire sans savoir...' (*F*II, p.320). As is the case in *Voyage au bout de la nuit* also, however, the recourse to alcohol only has the effect of converting these liberated fluxes into an empty body without organs that searches for a new socius (or scapegoat) into which their desire can be channelled as a pure line of destruction. Predictably, a suitable target is found in Ferdinand, who drinks 'que de l'eau!...' (*F*II, p.407), refusing to indulge in the dissimulating apparatus of molarity, and thereby allowing his desire to become pathologised. And so, following the pattern of *Féerie* I in which the persecution and incarceration of Ferdinand is used as a tool to reterritorialise the desire liberated in times of war, Ferdinand is physically assaulted and fettered, his own blood—in a remarkable echo of the prison experiences of *Féerie* I—making him adhere to a wall: 'je peux plus me décoller de la flaque... le sang fait mastic... le sang et l'étoupe du plafond... une gadoue!... y avait de l'étoupe plein les murs en plus des gravats... je suis englué, tête, tronc, jambes...' (*F*II, p.415).

With two thirds of the novel gone, then, *Féerie* II is shown to be a complete and utter failure.[63] For although the centrifugal force produced by the abjectified molecular half of the narrator was intended to exceed the centripetal force of molarity and thereby de-Historicise his name, being the product of an ultra-molecular being totally ruled by instinct and thus removed from the dominant reality,[64] that force proves too excessive, its resultant deterritorialisation of molarity and History being so great that, instead of allowing the subjects of molar society to reinvest their own material reality with desire, it encourages them once again to take refuge in molarity by reterritorialising Ferdinand, turning him into a scapegoat figure.[65]

The text (up until this point), therefore, is entirely self-defeating, for whilst conceived to free Ferdinand from his pathological condition in enforced molarity, his schizophrenic expression has, in fact, merely served as a tool of reterritorialisation that has precipitated his decline. In this respect, the text is exactly like that character who shares his name with the subtitle of the work, Normance.[66] For the body of Normance (both corporeal and textual)—used as a battering ram—offers the tenants (the readers) the opportunity to take advantage of the dissolution of subjectivity they are experiencing, to act effectively as one body, to unite in a common goal, leaving aside their differences for a moment:[67]

> Je ne sais quelle jalousie entre eux...
> C'est pas absolument ignoble? Au lieu de s'unir, s'accroupir et se reformer tous contre la porte!... puisque c'était de sauver Delphine! et qu'il l'avait assez hurlé!... «Vulnéraire! vulnéraire!» alors? alors?... je vais les tancer moi! je vais les battre!
> —Croupissez-vous, fainéants! le mastodonte en avant! que ça se ragglomère!
> Ah, mais le gros de traviole!... faut le remettre! il penche... il oscille!.. faut le reépauler!... et sa tronche, exact, au battant! Mimi, Rodolphe, aident à rien!... fumants qu'ils sont! excités!... je m'en fous!...
> —Allez! à genoux! ici! baroufs!
> Où qu'est Piram? Et Lili?... et Bébert? et tout?
> La veine! la chance! juste à saisir!... je vois venir la houle... je vois le mur!...
> —Et hop! rrah!
> Je râle!...
> Il poussent! ils poussent tous! *crrrac!*
> Ça, c'est unique! à peine placés ils ont poussé comme un seul! quarante comme un seul! crevé la porte! (*F*II, pp.347–348)

This unity is short lived, however, for as soon as they enter Armelle's apartment, they split up into their individual subjectivities again, and, as will be seen in the passages to follow, consequently achieve nothing:

> tout s'engouffre! dix! vingt! trente-six corps! une autre houle! tout dans le local! tous chez Armelle! à la culbute! quelles culbutes!... (*F*II, p.348)

> Ils le cherchaient tous, le vulnéraire! à dix-huit mains! à soixante mains! à tâtons! sous tous les meubles... sous l'armoire! sous les tapis... ils trouvaient rien...
> [...]
> Maintenant ils s'accusent de vol... Plus un qui chante!... c'est de l'altercation ignoble, qu'ils sont des voleurs... ils trouvent rien... moi je suis le pondéré, moi! je raisonne! à quoi ça sert qu'ils rampent tous? et qu'ils s'accusent! Un seul qui chercherait il trouverait! chercherait vraiment! ils trouvent pouic! simagreurs cochons lâches fainéants! pas un seul flacon! (*F*II, p.349)

From this point on in the text, it would appear that such a successful unified formation will only be formed in reaction against an abject other, that is to say, in a fascistic formation which territorialises desire by channelling it into a sacrificial victim. For when Ferdinand declares that he will not help the rest of the group search for the alcohol that acts as a catalyst for such a process, this is their reaction:

Ah, ça suffit qu'ils se ragglomèrent!... mille-pattes! myriapodes!... et rattaquent!... redéfoncent la porte! je m'abrite, moi!... je me retranche!... je me défends contre ces forcenés à coups de talons! *Bing! Ping!* dans leurs gueules!... (*F*II, p.349)[68]

When, on the other hand, Ferdinand attempts to lead them in another 'formation myriapode' for a constructive, productive purpose, in spite of his optimism, the result is far less successful, their collective efforts being consistently foiled by Jules' molarity-destabilising trajectories:

Je les stimule... je connais la manœuvre! saouls pas saouls qu'ils se ressaisissent! ils ont déjà été sublimes! embringués les uns dans les autres ils peuvent réussir des prodiges! je les ai vus pour la porte d'Armelle! pousser le mastodonte à vingt-cinq!... maintenant il s'agit plus de porte... y a plus de porte! il s'agit de sauver Delphine, qu'on passe tous de l'autre côté! il s'agit de franchir la crevasse!... je commence à connaître la tactique!... le bras dessus bras dessous! la formation myriapode!... accroupis les pieds en équerre: le «tous à la fois ou la mort»! la formation invincible! crevasse mouvante, pas mouvante, on passe! le vrai amalgame héroïque!... c'est tout!... si les Lutry étaient là au lieu de baguenauder dans les nuages avec leur coupole!... ça nous ferait six... huit... douze... pieds de plus! je te les fouterais au myriapode!... une autre histoire qu'aller au Ciel!... un peu!... tout le monde peut y aller au ciel!... ils s'étaient fait enlever au Ciel!... personne nous porterait nous, au Ciel! personne! personne nous porterait dans la loge! nous ferait franchir la crevasse! que notre héroïsme! notre élan! et en formation myriapode! un seul élan, quarante pieds! pensez! Je peux pas vous citer tous les noms de ceux qui faisaient partie, mais y avait moi, Rodolphe, Mimi, Toinon qui vomissait plus, Mme Cléot et la crémière... de ceux-là, je suis certain... pas de la compteuse de haricots!... ni de Mme Xantippe!... elles en étaient? en étaient pas?... et quinze... vingt autres... ah, mes deux ganaches par exemple! les deux!... et Piram!... maintenant faut que la phalange s'élance! très à propos!.. à mon commandement! au moment où l'immeuble incline... mais faut pas que la crevasse ouvre trop!... trop large!... parce qu'alors la phalange disloque... bute contre l'autre bord!... c'est l'engloutissement de la phalange!... voyez le risque! Je prends le commandement!... c'est entendu!... le sang-froid, l'à-propos, c'est moi! ils veulent que je sauve la malade? Oui?... non? Mme Toiselle peut rien faire... je la vois de l'autre côté!... elle est impuissante!... elle est penchée sur Delphine, elle essaye de la faire boire... zéro, pour la margoulette! mais elle est pas qu'évanouie Delphine!... les mâchoires fermées à un point! bonjour!... que voilà une vilaine affaire!... moi, j'y ingurgiterais le vulnéraire!... certes! mais faut que j'arrive de l'autre côté!...

—Allez hop là! tous!

Faut qu'ils s'agrippent, s'entrelacent bien... et qu'ils prennent le moment tout juste... que la maison hoque en même temps...

[...]

Voilà qu'un grand roulis se prépare… je le vois au mur… aux lézardes qui ourlent… le moment, nous, de s'agglomérer!… mains, têtes, coudes, tout!… tout l'amalgame passera ou rien! tout l'entremelage!… on oscille et hop!… «Rrraï!» ces cris! quels cris! on a donné contre un écueil!… un écueil dans la crevasse!… en plein milieu de la crevasse! «aïi!… aïi!…» dans la fente!… planté dans la fente! un guéridon en bronze massif!… on l'avait pas vu!… un guéridon de chez Armelle!… coincé… scellé… là!… on est venus s'ouvrir dessus! tout le myriapode! en plein ! *brang!* toute la formation myriapode! ce qu'on a pris! les gnions!… ce naufrage!… on s'était fait renvoyer! Oui! toute la cohorte! éparpiller dans tous les murs! Et que ça piaille! et que ça pleure! si y a de la rage! et y a de quoi!… qu'on était partis au poil!... on aurait sûrement traversé! sans ce malheur du guéridon! eh bien, on recommence!... choc, pas choc, on l'arrachera, le guéridon!... il faut, c'est tout! il faut, voilà!... les enfouis de sous l'ascenseur appellent au secours...

—Venez! venez tous!...

Ils cherchent à crier, ils peuvent pas... trop compressés, et trop émus!... ils font des suprêmes efforts pour s'extirper de sous la cage... un, qu'émerge!... puis deux... puis trois!... c'est la loge qui les attire... c'est pas de nous aider, les salauds!... d'arracher le terrible guéridon... non! ils rampent dans les éclats de verre... ils barbotent... pataugent... ils sont rigolos à regarder... enfin, d'une manière... ils arriveront?... arriveront pas?... faut qu'ils rampent les uns sur les autres... et si ils versent à la crevasse?... ils s'amarrent au gros... ils l'agrippent...

—Jean-Foutres! Jean-Foutres! par ici!

Qu'ils nous aident au moins! l'autre aussi, pourrait nous aider! là-haut! le fléau d'atmosphère! tronc-la-gondole! il pourrait apaiser le Ciel! faire rebrousser les aravions! il pourrait, mais dans des circonstances pareilles y a plus à compter sur personne!... c'est ça l'infect! y a pas de cabalistique qui tienne! y a que les canons, comme sérieux! (*F*II, p.366–369)

In uniting the tenants via Normance, therefore, the narrator Céline has only succeeded in aiding the reterritorialisation of their desire by establishing himself as a sacrificial victim whose destruction will satiate their desire. In effect, then, it is Normance—the text and the character, both being intended to function as a plane of immanence, a surface on which to establish connective syntheses between those engaged in the collective enterprise each allows—that precipitates the narrator's (and the author's) descent back into enforced molarity, into pathology.[69] For having himself been pathologised by the tenant's misuse of him, Normance—who, at this point in the text, bears a striking resemblance to one of the spasmodic isolated figures in Bacon's paintings—joins the ranks of molarity, crying out for alcohol and initiating a series of attacks on the narrator intended to destroy him:

le mari Normance qui s'est relevé! l'énorme!... il s'est décollé du mur!... je vois sa tête!... sa tête entière... elle fait qu'un caillot sa tête, je vous ai déjà dit, un pâté de sang... on lui voit plus du tout les yeux... qu'un trou pour la bouche!... dans son caillot de tête un trou!... il grogne par là... il respire par là...
[...]
il me tord le cou!... et il m'extirpe de sous la table!... par le cou!... et il me monte dessus! il me piétine, il se dandine! il se couche sur moi! je le prends en plein! qu'est-ce qu'il pèse! ah! aaah! de son autre main il me cherche le bras! mon bras qu'est à vif!... il l'a! il le tortille!... j'hurle!... j'hurle!... forcé d'hurler! il hurle avec moi! plus fort que moi! comme je l'ai là contre ma figure, son gros caillot me bouche la bouche! j'étouffe! et c'est lui qui se plaint!

—À boire! à boire!

C'est lui qui réclame!...

—À boire, docteur!

C'est lui qui réclame!...

—À boire, docteur!

Pour ça qu'il s'est jeté sur moi!... pour ça qu'il me garrotte! «À boire!»... s'en fout de sa Delphine!

—J'en ai pas!

Je râle! je crie! j'arrive à crier... il comprend! il se soulève un peu... ah, je respire!... il se met à genoux... à genoux d'abord... «ââh! aah!...» je souffle! et debout! il se remet debout!... qu'il est géant! qu'il est monstre! il grossit encore!... il grossit toujours!... de poitrine! de bide! je bouge pas, moi! je bouge pas!... il recule... il titube à reculons... il dodeline... tout son caillot de tête tremble, oscille... son paquet de tête!... il recule encore!... il va prendre son élan du mur!... il s'appuie... il se lance!... il me charge!... il prend un ballant du pied! il me shoote! sous la table! je me recroqueville... il s'appuie au rebord de la table... et *vrrang!* il m'en remet!... qu'est-ce qu'il me décoche! dans le flanc! en plein!... et encore! *vlof! vlang!* comment qu'il est!... il me cherre!... «rrraa! rrrââ!» je hoque! il recommence!... il veut me finir!... que je lui ai pas donné à boire!... ma tête qu'il vise!... il voudrait me la fendre!... (*F*II, pp.397–399)

These attacks will leave Ferdinand in a petrified state that mirrors exactly that of both Normance and the narrator of *Féerie* I in his prison cell, all three being stuck down by their own pathological flows, as these descriptions show:[70]

J'y rampe, j'y vais, je secoue Normance... il tient collé par la tête... par son turban... son énorme corps vogue au roulis... il fait bouée, il vogue à la houle du couloir... il est amarré au mur... par son turban!... (*F*II, p.362)

le sang me dégouline dans les yeux!... du front!... et des tempes!... elles m'ont pavoisé les coquines! je voudrais m'ouvrir les yeux, de force... mais les caillots

> collent… […] c'est du sang tiède, du sang nouveau que j'avale… du sang à moi, pas de la flaque… (*F*II, pp.410–411)

> j'adhère trop de partout!… je colle par le sang, les loques, le plâtre!… le plâtre me fait carapace… (*F*II, p.428)

Far from deterritorialising, then, the excessive centrifugal force of Jules' molecular bombardment only ends up increasing the pathological, centripetal force exerted on Ferdinand, as the text—Normance—intended to institute a connective synthesis between Ferdinand and the tenants (Céline and the reader) is appropriated by a molar regime and turned against him.[71] Ferdinand will thus have to put an end to Jules' excessive molecular bombardment and rid himself of Normance if he is to be able to de-pathologise/de-Historicise himself. In order to do this, two previously minor characters—in both of whom can be seen allusions to operatic (and musical, therefore) characters—[72] are brought to the fore: Mimi, a dominatrix-like figure who turns Jules into an ignominious figure of ridicule before wheeling him off in his cart (*F*II, pp.397–382, 416–418), and Ottavio, who gets a group of men to throw Normance's corpse into the lift shaft (*F*II, pp.418–422) With Normance and Jules out of the way, Ferdinand is ready to reappropriate his deterritorialising desire, and so, accordingly, his thoughts return to Lili and he is pulled away from the wall (*F*II, p.428–429).

The key figure in these final episodes of the novel is undoubtedly Ottavio, a character who has been mentioned throughout the novel by the narrator as his only possible salvation, the only person capable of putting an end to Jules' bombardment, and who spends the entirety of the novel up until this point manning an air raid siren—an echo of the avowed intention of Céline's pamphlets?[73] For it is Ottavio who organises the disposal of Normance's corpse and the unsticking of Ferdinand from the wall, and who acts as Ferdinand's legs for the remainder of the novel, carrying him everywhere. Furthermore, Ottavio, like the narrator, is accused of Fascism by some of the other characters of the novel, but, unlike the narrator, rather than succumb to the charges, Ottavio flies into such a rage that those who have slandered him beg his forgiveness (*F*II, p.426–427). It would not, therefore, be unreasonable to consider Ottavio as a new kind of double of the narrator, but one totally opposed to the abjectified double that Jules was. For whereas the legless cripple Jules' relationship with Ferdinand was never anything but antagonistic, Ottavio, an awesome physical force with the kind of grace normally only associated (in the Célinian universe) with dancers, displays genuine love and affection for Ferdinand. If Jules was the incarnation of an attempt to create an affective aesthetic infused with desire that fails by being too molecular, too removed from the strata of History to be able to bring about change in the strata, then Ottavio would seem to embody the possibility of a new aesthetic. Indeed, as Nettelbeck points out, 'à travers le personnage d'Ottavio, d'abord, est évoquée l'idée d'un art capable de surmonter les vicissitudes de l'expérience directe et de reconstituer un sentiment de libération et d'unité',[74] an interpretation which is confirmed by a reading of the narrative.

Having carried Ferdinand up to his apartment, Ottavio goes looking for water, breaking a hole in the wall of the neighbouring building with a couple of saucepans, and, as soon as this hole is pierced, Lili and Bébert return to Ferdinand (*F*II, pp.433–434). Once more, the simultaneity of these two events is no coincidence, for it can be said that the act of breaking down this wall with a saucepan is the actualisation of a new aesthetic which is signalled by the return of Lili, the pure aesthetic, and Bébert, the instinctual animal whose mode of communication serves as an aspirational model, to Ferdinand. What they find behind the wall is Norbert, an actor in silent movies, 'en habit de soirée, à table, cravate de la Légion d'honneur!... et qui voulait pas qu'on lui cause' (*F*II, p.452), and who is waiting for, 'le Pape [...] Churchille et Roosewelt!' (*F*II, p.463), that is to say, three figureheads of molar institutions. Even more uncanny is the fact that, apart from the windows, Norbert's apartment hardly seems to have been affected by the bombardment at all, and that there are two dead bodies—one in the bath, one in the kitchen—of which Norbert seems to be completely unaware. Norbert, then, is the epitome of molarity, incapable of communication, an actor, a dissimulator, unwilling to face death and the harsh reality of the world, preferring to shut himself up and place all his faith in illusory structures that give the impression of stability and permanence by being entirely fictional.[75] Céline, with the help of Ottavio, uses saucepans—a symbol of the medical, anti-dissimulating sensibility of his art—[76] to penetrate into that molar space and merely observe Norbert within it, refusing to act or react, instead letting the discourse of molarity crumble by itself. When, for instance, he accuses Ferdinand of being mad for believing that there was any kind of bombardment, Norbert's own discourse and actions are plainly those of a madman:

—T'es à enfermer, Ferdinand!... t'es enragé!...

L'effet que je lui fais!... je l'épouvante!... je le fais reculer!... il se protège de moi!... les mains en avant!... lui qu'avait les yeux en vrille, le voilà les pupilles toutes grandes!... et il recule! il recule!

—Tu retournes au salon, grande tante?

Je lui demande...

Tout ça est mijoté, je suis sûr!... preuve, je le déconcerte pas du tout!... jamais il a gueulé de la sorte!...

—Vous comprenez pas la radio!... *bong! bong! bong!*

Il nous imite *Radio-London*!

—La radio vous tonne dans la tronche! hi! hi! hi! *bong! bong!*

Il se fout de nous! il s'esclaffe!

—Le voilà votre canon! *bong! bong! bong!*

Il imite très bien Radio-Londres...

—Hors d'ici tous! trissez, racailles! *bong! bong! bong! ding! dong! dong!*

Il imite «Big Ben » à présent! l'heure! 10 heures!... 10 heures du matin!... *bong! ben!...*

On l'excède! il nous chasse!... et subit il se calme!... il se ravise!... (*F*II, p.465)

Ferdinand does not rise to the bait, however, and merely asks Ottavio to take him back downstairs. He does not agree to leave Lili behind with Norbert—as he did with Jules—, nor does he let himself feel outrage at Norbert's antics over the balustrade of his stairwell as he did at Jules' antics on the balustrade of the mill:

il se tripote au-dessus de la rampe! voilà l'état du personnage! au-dessus de nous!... en transe!...

—Envoie-moi Lili! envoie-moi Lili! qu'il crie! en même temps!

L'arrogance!...

—Veux-tu cacher ça!...

—Chutt! chutt!

Et c'est lui qui me trouve indécent!... que je crie trop fort! il trouve! il trouve!...

Voilà l'état du Norbert!... je vous fais pas du tout un pastis... je suis juste équitable, voilà tout!... j'observe!... je brode pas!... après des pareilles commotions les natures d'artistes sont terribles!... vous avez observé chez Jules! et bien d'autres!... il faut s'attendre!... et remarquez!... (*F*II, p.470)

Having failed to de-Historicise his name through submission to the centripetal forces of History in *Féerie* I and through the unleashing of an excessive centrifugal force on History in *Féerie* II, then, a new aesthetic—that of the chronicle, but a chronicle for which the narrator, this time, assumes responsibility—[77] is postulated by the end of *Féerie*

II. In taking the form of a chronicle, this aesthetic, which is intended for no other purpose than to transmit emotion, will, of course, radically reformulate the parameters of chronicle, as Robert Llambias points out:

> Les pages de *Normance* dans lesquelles Céline se réclame de Pline prennent alors une signification quasi-surréaliste! Ce n'est plus l'Histoire qui fournit au romancier modèles et matière, mais le récit qui fait fictionner l'Histoire. Par son écriture, le romancier s'élève jusqu'au statut de démiurge et revendique, dans la solitude, la création du monde [...] Le rapport entre l'Histoire et la fiction se renverse et devient extraordinaire. Ce qui fonde l'Histoire authentique, c'est la fiction; et cette fiction n'est autre que l'attirance du romancier vers le chaos, que celui-ci soit déluge ou apocalypse. Ou plutôt qu'il soit en même temps destructeur et créateur. Sans la catastrophe, plus rien n'existe. Le roman n'est alors autre que l'atelier théâtral de l'Histoire et les désastres.[78]

This new aesthetic is not only a rejection of the two aesthetic possibilities posited by *Féerie pour une autre fois*, however, it is a *tabula rasa* (at once destructive and creative, therefore) that wipes the slate clean with a scriptural apocalypse, a paper storm made up of Céline's own manuscripts, described in the following passages:

> je jette un œil, je regarde ces papiers... y a du *Roi Krogold*... *La Volonté du roi Krogold*... œuvre commencée il y a trente ans!... où qu'elle finit!... y avait «des ordonnances» aussi... des «blocs»... et des prospectus... et tout un chapitre de *Casse-pipe!*...(*F*II, p.458)

> plein de papiers en échappent! vire-volent! entre les endroits raplatis... que l'avenue en est comme opaque... on voit plus l'autre côté de l'avenue... c'est pas à croire!... des éclaircies par bourrasques... (*F*II, p.479)

> je vois rien... je vois que des papiers!... toujours des papiers!... tornades sur tornades de papiers!... que toute l'avenue en est opaque... tout l'air!... je vois le Ciel blanc... oui! blanc de papiers!... (*F*II, p.480)

> il tombe des papiers! c'est tout! encore plus de papiers!... par double, triple avalanche! et trombes!... plein l'avenue!... plein le Ciel!... j'ai déjà dit... je voyais plus très clair moi-même... plus bien clair... je voyais opaque... opacité de mes rétines?... peut-être?... peut-être?... (*F*II, pp.481–482)

These papers, then, Céline's previous works—and, indeed, the present work, for the tornado of papers would seem to be a result of the explosion of Normance—,[79] are described as a hindrance to clear sight,[80] an obstacle to the lucid observation required of the chronicler such as Pliny, whose example has served as an inspiration throughout the novel, and whose lucidity Ferdinand is now finally ready to emulate:[81]

> C'est un immeuble qu'a pas souffert!... voilà!... sauf des fenêtres!... je vous le note!... vous remarquerez... l'observation avant tout!... je suis observateur, d'abord! science avant tout!... l'attention directe!... je suis attentif, pas exagéreur, pertinent! même tel quel, la tête à l'envers!... faut observer les phénomènes d'une attention plus que sérieuse, surtout quand ils sont «cataclystes»! qu'on se permette pas de vous contester, dix!... douze siècles plus tard!... personne conteste Pline l'Ancien! il fait toujours autorité!... il en sera de même pour mézigue vers l'an 53–54... 3 000!... il a payé ses «phénomènes» Pline l'Ancien!... moi aussi j'ai payé un peu... y a que ce qu'est payé qui compte!... gratuit, c'est «Jean-Foutre Cie!» blablateurs, charlatans, la clique!... aux chiots! tous! aux chiots!... pas écoutables!... une bande de pets!... je dis!... je dis!... (*F*II, p.469)

There is, of course, considerable irony in the narrator's declaration of his lucidity, for throughout *Féerie pour une autre fois*, he has consistently shown himself to be an unreliable narrator, never sure whether the sounds around him are exterior to him or emanating from his own head, confusing events and chronology, and intermingling levels of reality. This new aesthetic will not attempt to reject such a schizophrenic conception of the world, it will merely depathologise it by accepting the molecular nature of existence and refusing to conform to the illusory stability of the strictly-ordered molar world that is to be observed:

> j'observe... méticuleux, toujours! je regarde... le scrupule, ma force!... je vous rapporte tout!... je veux pas vous omettre un détail... je suis le vétilleux sur l'honnêteté! maniaque, diront mes ennemis... diantre! ce couloir tremble un peu quand même... il se met à trembler je crois! il me semble... je vous note!... heureusement que je m'appuie au mur!... j'oscille... je me rattrape au mur... je lâche le cou d'Ottave... je lâche le bras de Lili... faut que je tienne debout tout seul!... voilà!... que je sorte tout seul dans l'avenue! je veux voir ce qui se passe!... (*F*II, p.473)

It is precisely from the differential between the observer and the observed that this new aesthetic will well, and from which it will draw its deterritorialising force, for within molarity, a molecular expression can only be a cry of pain and suffering: 'c'est ma nature!... j'observe, voilà!... si je les agace!... si elles s'en foutent des destructions! elles!... moi, je suis sensible! moi, je souffre!...' (*F*II, pp.480–481).

In effect, then, the entirety of *Féerie pour une autre fois* is but a pit stop on the journey commenced in *Guignol's band*.[82] For in that work, as was seen in chapter one above, the narrator embarks on a quest for the 'métro émotif', for a mode of expression that brings smooth space into the heart of molarity and that acts directly on the very emotional core of those who experience it, and it is to the *métro* that *Féerie pour une autre fois* leads too:

> Des vrais ouragans d'*oûûû!*... que c'est pas à croire de force! qu'on en est vibré! oui! vibré! pénétré! plus qu'abasourdi! que l'air en tourne comme solide!... exactement l'impression!... que vous ondulez avec! l'*ûûûû* vous rentre complètement dedans!... les ondes!... même moi, le sourd, j'entends l'*ûûûû!*... et je vois les deux, la bignolle, Lili, qui se font des grimaces de douleur!... ça doit drôlement les pénétrer!... ça les crispe! la bignolle agite plus sa cloche... trémousse plus... elle pleure... elle sonne plus... maintenant comme nous sommes, tous les trois, le trottoir en pente devant nous, en descente, on va dévaler au métro!... je crois!... le tunnel!... l'entrée du métro... c'est à tenter!... l'avenue Gaveneau... la rue de la Borne... et puis le coude... le square Fred-Jamais... nous y sommes presque!...(*F*II, p.475)[83]

As an attempt to access the 'métro émotif', *Féerie pour une autre fois* will remain, however, just that, an attempt. For even after undergoing a spasmodic process of desubjectification in which his molecular self is projected into Jules as an abject other in an attempt to get to the *métro* ('«Au métro! Au métro!» Je lâche la statuette... Je vacille... un pas... un autre... je me rattrape!... et *wouaf!* je dégueule!... Ça me prend là... pas loin... vingt mètres de sa porte... [à Jules]' (*F*I, p.158)), the narrator goes nowhere, never managing to arrive, always being grounded by molar forces that frustrate his every turn:

> les flics me l'ont raconté... plus tard!... bien plus tard!... et que j'avais fait grand scandale... moi!... il paraît!... pas beaucoup dans mes habitudes!... l'horreur du scandale!... si j'ai protesté! surtout dans les circonstances!... à peine sorti du cataclysme! pensez, comme c'était vraisemblable!... ragoteries! diffamation! les gens inventent n'importe quoi!... ils sont bourriques que c'est un monde!... *on allait au métro, c'est tout!...* et l'air était bourré de papiers, voilà!... par tornades! des papiers à moi! et des autres! qu'on voyait plus le trottoir en face!... je maintiens!... que c'était du danger extrême!... que les sirènes allaient revenir... non! pas les sirènes, les avions!... et que je devais téléphoner! que j'ai même essayé, au «Poste»... et que les flics ont pas voulu!... voilà les faits, exactement... (*F*II, pp.486–487; my italics)

Ferdinand may be on his way to the *métro* at the end of the novel, but he never reaches it, for, as has been suggested, *Féerie pour une autre fois* is a purely heuristic exercise, constantly searching for a mode of expression instead of actually expressing, just as the destruction wreaked by Jules' 'orages cosmomédiumniques!', 'makes no progress [...but] turns about itself with an unvarying fury that never seems to advance or diminish'.[84] Whence critical comments such as this from Jane Carson:

> The handful of characters are practically indistinguishable one from another, the action can be reduced to an almost uninterrupted climbing up and down of stairs with much screaming of insults, the style is so repetitive that whole pages appear to be more or less interchangeable. For these very reasons it is possible to see the novel as an extended metaphor with Jules playing the role of the artist, the limited scope of the action as a concise picture of the workings of the creative mind, the characters as embodying the writer's fears. Not a single incident is realistic, nor does the novel hold the slightest interest as fantasy; only as an artistic game, a display of the writer's virtuosity, can the reader assimilate these pages, and his attention is more likely to be held by the colorful, evocative language than anything else.[85]

What such an evaluation fails to take into account, is the atomistic nature of the work, for the text is not an undifferentiated chaotic mass, but constituted of two distinct, contrasting parts: the two volumes of *Féerie*, and their respective 'chefs d'orchestre', the narrator Céline and Jules. The fact remains, however, that these constituent parts remain polar opposites, as both the volumes and the characters only ever succeed one another rather than joining together,[86] with the result that the synthesis of the dialectic can only ever be exterior to the text, conjunctive not connective. The entire work, then, in its failure to find a mode of expression able to fuse together the roles of novelist and chronicler, molecular and molar, does not contest the pathologising structures of molarity, but falls prey to them, to their stratifications, apparatus of capture, and pure lines of destruction, itself becoming pathologised, quasi-autistic:

> Éternel forcené, le héros célinien fait figure d'homme transversal, traversé de part en part par les flux et les reflux des agrégats collectifs, et cependant préservé de leur hypnose au sein d'une insolite chambre noire de la conscience individuelle.
>
> Cette nouvelle optique aboutit à une sorte de "monadisme" appliqué: se barricader loin des foules et des meneurs pour advenir au semblant d'autonomie de la monade leibnizienne "sans porte ni fenêtre", puis obturer

> imperceptiblement ce champ clos afin de créer en l'individu un pur point de vue dé-socialisé.[87]

This is not to say, however, that all is lost, for it will be precisely from within such a willed quasi-autistic state that an affective expression will be emitted:

> Là où le despote peut dire: 'connaître l'art d'impressionner l'imagination des foules, c'est connaître l'art de les gouverner', en identifiant le peuple à une plaque daguerréotype sur laquelle on projette des images comme autant de mots d'ordre, le réfractaire opère ses propres *réfractions subversives* en secret et, telle la monade repliée sur elle-même, presque opaque, dévie les rayons lumineux des suggestions politico-sociales vers son ombre singulière pour ne renvoyer au-dehors qu'*un point de vue imperceptible*.[88]

A dance-like mode of expression with the power to penetrate the reader's core, to enable the reader to reinvest his/her own material reality, to exceed the centripetal forces of molarity whilst remaining sufficiently rooted in them to react against them, will be found, then, through an internalisation of the pathologising mechanisms of molarity that will not be re-externalised in a pathological manner. In this way, the collective aggregates' destruction of the individual will be converted into a becoming-imperceptible, and the illogical extreme of molarity's preference for fission over fusion—'Nagasaki' (*F*I, p.99); 'Vriochima' (*F*I, p.119)—[89] will create a war machine, an affective poetic expression that uses molar power for its own ends: '«hirochimiesque»! de la provocation que je suis!...' (*F*II, p.306). In other words, there will be *féerie*, 'cette organisation musicale [qui] se situe de toute évidence, dans le mouvement d'une image en expansion, la transformation d'un microcosme où l'auteur se situe, en un macrocosme qui va bientôt, tout en le comprenant, le dépasser',[90] it will merely be, *pour une autre fois*.

Chapter Three
The Trilogy

Introduction

According to the vast majority of Célinian criticism, it is in Céline's last works, *D'un château l'autre*, *Nord* and *Rigodon*, that the promised *féerie* comes. If this is indeed the case, then these works must be situated, as has been suggested, in *une autre fois*, a time which is both the realisation of the implicit prophecy of the author's previous volumes' title, whilst simultaneously being a time which can never exist, a time which is for ever *autre*. If, in the trilogy, the Célinian aesthetic is to attain its affective, emotive goal of creating an expression capable of passing directly to the reader's emotive core, if it is to become an instance of schizophrenic desiring-production that circumvents the representational modes of Capitalist society, then there must be established a plane of consistency, a zero-intensity coming from the constant injection of anti-production into the process of production, on which can take place connective syntheses. If, in other words, there is to be *féerie*—the highest form of the Célinian aesthetic—in the trilogy, this will only be achieved through the double movement of presence and absence, being and non-being, '«Binotoubi»' (*FI*, p.114), that was never fully achieved in *Féerie pour une autre fois*. As Colin Nettelbeck says of this dichotomy between being and nothingness,

> au fond, dans *Féerie*, Céline cherche surtout à amener le lecteur à une compréhension affective des *termes* de la question d'Hamlet: *To be or not to be* [...]. Certes, en extériorisant et en exorcisant les principaux démons du "*not to be*" [...], il peut orienter son récit, et nous orienter, vers le "*to be*", Lili. Il y a donc, en embryon, la possibilité d'une réponse affirmative. Mais pour que cette possibilité soit réalisable [...] il faudrait qu'elle se situe dans une dimension qui manque au microcosme de *Féerie*: le temps.[1]

It has been suggested that, in *Féerie pour une autre fois*, the passage to a true aesthetic of *féerie* was impeded by the action of Historical centripetal forces that relentlessly overcoded the novels' poetic expression, petrifying that expression in the immutability of Historical time (*Chronos*) and preventing its dissipation into a truly evanescent form, Céline's *petite musique*. As Nettelbeck states, then, it is only once this *petite musique* is situated in time, when it finds the means to effect change in the strata of History, without being pathologised, that this aesthetic will be accomplished. An expression capable of harmonising anti-production and production, the collective and the individual, History and desiring-production, will be governed by style, a style which, according to Gilles Deleuze (referring in all probability to Céline) is not that of a *petite musique*:

> Je voudrais dire ce que c'est qu'un style. C'est la propriété de ceux dont on dit d'habitude "ils n'ont pas de style...". Ce n'est pas une structure signifiante, ni une organisation réfléchie, ni une inspiration spontanée, ni une orchestration, ni une petite musique. C'est un agencement, un agencement d'énonciation. Un style, c'est arriver à bégayer dans sa propre langue. C'est difficile, parce qu'il faut qu'il y ait nécessité d'un tel bégaiement. Non pas être bègue dans sa parole, mais être bègue du langage lui-même. Être comme un étranger dans sa propre langue. Faire une ligne de fuite.[2]

Yet Céline's *petite musique* conforms to just such a definition of style, for true to the double movement of being and non-being necessary for schizophrenic desiring-production which operates through assemblages on a plane of consistency, it is made of, '[des] morceaux de silence et de parole, ce qu'il dit et ce qu'il ne dit pas, [qui] se distribuent dans une fragmentation que le tout vient confirmer, puisqu'il en résulte, et non pas corriger ni dépasser';[3] '[il n'est jamais] de l'homme, il est toujours de l'essence (non-style). Jamais il n'est d'un point de vue, mais est fait de la coexistence dans une même phrase d'une série infinie de points de vue d'après lesquels l'objet se disloque, résonne ou s'amplifie'.[4] Defined thus, style is but a consistency, 'a dynamic holding together or mode of composition',[5] in which, '*les qualités expressives ou matières d'expression entrent, les unes avec les autres, dans des rapports mobiles qui vont "exprimer" le rapport du territoire qu'elles tracent avec le milieu intérieur des impulsions, et avec le milieu extérieur des circonstances*'.[6] It is precisely in this manner that Céline's *petite musique*, his emotive aesthetic, operates, as Alain Cresciucci notes:

> c'est par l'écriture que Céline rend la mort possible, car l'écriture est le mouvement par lequel l'homme devient maître du temps. D'où cette religion du

> style, non un art banal du bien dire, mais un ordre supérieur de structuration capable de dominer le récit de l'horreur par la force de son rythme, par cette qualité si personnelle qu'il désigne du nom de *petite musique* ou *d'émotion*.[7]

Similarly, talking of Céline's 'petit truc', Serge André writes,

> Sur le versant de l'objet, comme cela devient tout à fait manifeste dans ses derniers écrits, Céline laisse de plus en plus la narration s'effilocher au profit de la présence d'une *voix*, dont le rythme et la musicalité commandent la phrase, voire le récit, à la façon dont, dans le *Voyage*... ou dans *Casse-Pipe*, le galop du cheval commande le comportement du soldat. Ainsi, le 'rendu-émotif' qu'il introduit dans l'écrit, c'est ce qui, dans le parlé, n'apparaît pas comme parlé, mais comme causant le mouvement même de parler. C'est quelque chose qui 'vient du trognon de l'être' et dont Céline dit avoir eu la révélation par le métro [...]. Car, si le métro de Céline s'oppose aux illusions de la surface, ce n'est pas seulement parce qu'il y fait trou, mais parce que, sous la surface et sa mascarade agitée, il impose la présence d'un mouvement continu, sans arrêts, sans pertes de temps [...] Ce vide est donc habité par une force que rien n'arrête, ou ne doit arrêter, métaphore de la pulsion à l'état pur.[8]

It is surely Annie Montaut, however, who most clearly links Céline's *petite musique* to a Deleuzoguattarian conception of style as a schizophrenic mode of organisation. She writes,

> Décentrements, ellipses, parodie, texte paragrammatique, dislocation généralisée de la phrase, interjections et obscénités désémantisantes, ambiguïtés, négativisation et pluralisation du langage dans l'hétérogénéité: c'est bien la figure de l'écriture en travail et la réduction de tout langage univoque, comme d'un sens onto-théologique, d'une loi transcendantale. La petite musique est la figure qui consacre la mort du Sens. C'est l'avènement du figural, au sens lyotardien: le texte dans sa "disruption" et ses dischronies, ses heurts rythmiques et sémantiques, la "forme mauvaise" qui "en appelle" au corps, mais au corps disséminé, préunifié, transgressant les limites du corps propre.[9]

Féerie, then, will only be attained when the centripetal and centrifugal forces examined in *Féerie pour une autre fois* resonate together in harmony, when life and any life-affirming expression—such as that of Céline—are positively invested with death, when the two terms of Hamlet's question are connected by an "and" rather than an "or".[10] Thus, although Nettelbeck is undoubtedly right in suggesting that this problematic is overcome through a transcendence (and not a suspension) of time in which, 'la mort elle-même fait partie d'un processus qui la dépasse', those mechanisms which he sees effecting that transcendence in *D'un château l'autre*—namely the creation of an exterior continuity by the inclusion of the metaphoric boat of Caron and recurring passages from the narrative present—[11] serve rather to sustain the problematic of History that provided the narrative impetus of his previous work. Something similar is suggested by Cresciucci when he says, 'si l'on se penche sur le long pré-texte qui ouvre *D'un château l'autre* et qui reprend la situation essentielle de *Féerie* I, on peut y lire l'affirmation réitérée de ce qui constitue l'idéal de la clôture, la prison danoise'.[12] Where the trilogy will differ from *Féerie pour une autre fois*, however, is in its reaction to this problematic, for rather than remaining an insurmountable obstacle, as has been seen to be the case in *Féerie pour une autre fois*, it is this very Historical problematic itself which will, in the course of the trilogy, become one of the means employed to a *féerique* end.

Although a fictional construct, the antagonistic reader of *Féerie pour une autre fois*—the main agent of centripetal reterritorialisation—was phantasmic only according to the Platonic definition of this term; not illusory, but merely transposed by the author's subjectivity, the antagonistic reader was constructed out of a material reality. From a purely empirical perspective, then, there is no reason why the projected reader necessary for the construction of an affective style should differ in any respect, *Féerie pour une autre fois* having been received with much the same underwhelming response as was *Guignol's band*, as is suggested at the beginning of both *D'un château l'autre* and *Nord*: 'Mais un fait est là... mes livres se vendent plus... qu'ils disent!... ou presque plus... que je suis démodé, que je radote! entourloupes! salades!...' (*CA*, p.17); 'les acheteurs me boudent, il paraît...' (*N*, p.303). Thus, the assertion that *D'un château l'autre* marks the point at which Céline's aesthetic comes to fruition, that moment when, 'le temps de la chronique devient une continuité capable de porter l'esprit de la vie',[13] is problematic in the framework of an analysis such as Nettelbeck's in which this continuity comes from the insertion of, 'des passages traitant du "présent" *dans* la narration du passé [qui crée] ainsi une pulsion rythmique qui correspond davantage à la fluidité temporelle de la vie'.[14] For such cannot be the case as long as the reader, be s/he phantasmic or not, continues to reterritorialise the author within History, deflecting the poetic lines of flight into a pre-existing order instead of allowing it to diffract in him/herself, converting Céline the man into a scapegoat to be destroyed, rather than allowing the poetic expression of Céline the author to construct an affective style.

That the former of these two options remains dominant, which is to say that Céline remains overcoded in terms of his Historical reality, is clearly indicated by the opening lines of *D'un château l'autre*:

> Pour parler franc, là entre nous, je finis encore plus mal que j'ai commencé... Oh, j'ai pas très bien commencé... je suis né, je le répète, à Courbevoie, Seine... je le répète pour la millième fois... après bien des aller et retour je termine vraiment au plus mal... (*CA*, p.3)

Nor is it solely the opening lines of *D'un château l'autre* that reiterate this problematic of reterritorialisation; indeed, the first fifty pages of *D'un château l'autre*—if not almost every metanarratival section of the first two volumes of the trilogy—could be said to serve one main purpose, namely, to enumerate the seemingly infinite catalogue of hate accrued against Céline. As will be shown later, this apparent reinforcement of the molar conjunctions of History does (in the third and final volume) come to serve a molecular purpose, preparing the ground for a true plane of immanence both composed of and emanating style, but such is never accomplished in *D'un château l'autre* itself, as can be seen from an examination of the second stylistic device pointed up by Nettelbeck, Caron's boat.

La Barque de Caron

Philippe Bonnefis sees the opening sections of *D'un château l'autre* as a labyrinthine structure in which the reader becomes ensnared to such an extent that the narrator is obliged to, 'se retire[r] soudain du devant de la scène [...] pour céder la place à Charon (il écrit toujours "Caron") et lui confier la tâche de sortir le lecteur de l'impasse dans laquelle il l'avait un peu trop imprudemment fourvoyé'.[15] As Bonnefis goes on to point out, by thus introducing this mythical half-tiger, half-monkey figure who uses an oar to split open the heads of all those wishing to embark upon his boat, 'c'est la mort, et elle seule, qui nous aura permis d'entrer dans le vif du sujet'.[16] Could it be, then, that Caron and his boat achieve the avowed aim of a writing which is truly *féerique*, such a writing being, as has been stated, one in which a life-affirming expression is positively invested with death, one in which the two terms of Hamlet's question are fused into one? The text would seem to suggest that such is precisely the case: 'La façon que Caron va les prendre?… *the question?… vrrang! brang!* je suis sûr!' (*CA*, p.19). Indeed, Caron would seem to be the only one capable of divesting those who attempt to dissimulate their ultimate demise of the molar constructs used to this end, as is made clear in the following quotations:

> Je vous le dis en toute confidence, les amis se doutent pas du tout! bon!... bon!... ils s'amusent du cas Renault... à leur aise! et le cas Caron?... zut!... ils voient rien!... ils nient, ils fument, ils rotent, ils sont tout goguenards satisfaits, à peu près certains de vivre cent ans grâce à de ces petites pilules! Madame!... et ces super-gouttes *Mirador!...* au moins moi une chose, corniaud entendu! mais radar!... je sais par où Caron les piquera!... l'allure qu'ils auront sur sa barque!... je dis fendus! *vrang!* et *brang!* d'une oreille l'autre!... en attendant ils me font liéchem, ils me baratent, ils pérorent, ils se grisent... si sûrs d'eux!... leurs armoires, quinze étagères, pleines de suppositoires et gouttes!... en plus, hein! apéros! quels choix!... sucrés et amers! l'optimisme total!... ah! ah!... un coup de foie gras, une cigarette, deux flûtes de Mumm, vous me direz des nouvelles! le «Relais» chez soi!... l'autoroute chez soi!... (*CA*, p.16)

> je pense à Caron la façon qu'il leur fera passer leur moimoiisme! tous! à la sacrée rame plein le museau! *vrrang!* d'une oreille l'autre!… vous voyez ça! leur décolle presque toute la tronche! oui, leurs yeux pendent!… l'embarquement pour l'outre-là!… ce gringue aux touristes! *vrang! brang!…* d'une oreille à l'autre! (*CA*, p.18)

The narrator Céline's commentary would seem to make clear exactly who it is that he would have brutalised by Caron, namely, all those so-called friends and family who have pilfered his affairs or betrayed him (or who are waiting to do so), as well as all those involved in the publication of his works and the management of his financial affairs:

> Je sais tout ce qu'on m'a secoué, j'ai l'inventaire dans la tronche… «Casse Pipe»… la «Volonté du Roi Krogold»… plus encore deux… trois brouillons!… pas perdus du tout pour tout le monde! certes! je sais aussi! je dis rien… j'écoute les amis… ouai! ouai! moi aussi diable j'attends qu'ils crèvent! eux! eux, d'abord! ils bouffent tous beaucoup plus que moi! qu'une petite artériole leur pète! espoir! espoir!… que je les retrouve tous chez Caron, ennemis, amis, toutes leurs boyasses autour du cou!… Caron leur défonçant la gueule!… bien!… ah, sadique Norbert! servi chaud!… une brutalité que lui, Achille, seront ouverts d'une oreille à l'autre!… j'affirme! que pour leurs narquoises remarques ils auront une sorte d'haut-parleur! chacun! *vrang!* et *brrrang!* comme ça, Caron!… tout est prévu! ah, il pensera plus à ses Suez, Achille! ni à ses de Beers! ni ses croix!… plein la goulette! *vrrang!* ils seront

> mimis dans la barque! et tout le «Brain Trust» bien sûr avec! tronches toutes ouvertes et yeux pendants! le régime des passagers Caron!... je pense la cocasserie que ça sera!... bien plus drôle que Renault à Fresnes!... quand ils viennent un peu m'observer, les vieux amis, si je vais bientôt casser ma pipe, je me dis, je rigole, je les vois au Styx, comment Caron les caressera! *braoum!... vrang!* leur friponnerie! minois! oh, les futés!... déjà le Loukoum, sa bouche en corolle y prête!... sa molle tortueuse... telle qu'il émet plus que des *vuâââ! wâââ!...* cloaque profus de bouche!... il sera chouette d'une oreille à l'autre! marrant Norbert!... et l'Achille! son œil merlan frit lubrique lui pendant derrière l'oreille!... je vois!... je le vois!... ou après sa montre?... ou en sautoir? coquine breloque!... (*CA*, p.15)

Yet, in spite of the obvious contempt in which he holds such people, it would seem that the narrator himself is just as guilty of the molar crime of 'moimoiisme' as the next man:

> Je m'excuse de parler tant de moi-même... je m'appesantis... des déboires?... vous avez les vôtres!... ces gens de lettres sont terribles! si affligés de moimoi-isme!... mais les médecins donc! un beurre!... et les pombiers?... et les coiffeurs? tout kif, allez!... pas un seul bonhomme modeste!... (CA, p.17).

One would think, then, that in his lucidity ('ah, moi l'extra-voyant lucide!...' (*CA*, p.66)) the narrator Céline, 'fanatique des mouvements de ports, de tous trafics de l'eau... de tout ce qui vient vogue accoste', 'tout aussi fasciné... tout aussi féru des mouvements d'eau et des navires que dans ma petite enfance...' (*CA*, p.65), would jump at the opportunity to embark on Caron's boat, *La Publique*, especially since this *bateau-mouche* is not one of the new reproduction models for tourists, but an original such as those that Céline and his school friends used to run riot on before 1900, which is to say, for his generation, pre-Œdipalisation: 'les illusions quant aux instincts sont venues aux familles plus tard, bien plus tard, complexes, inhibitions, tcétéra...' (*CA*, pp.69–70). But when he goes down to the quay to inspect the hallucinated *bateau-mouche* and its mythical oarsman, the narrator Céline does not get on. Instead, he merely observes the stream of people who are having their heads split open to get onto the boat, and talks to La Vigue who is working as a kind of conductor on Caron's boat.

La Vigue, of course, is a character based on Céline's real-life acquaintance, Robert Le Vigan, who has already been seen in transposed form as Norbert, the silent movie actor in *Féerie pour une autre fois*. Nettelbeck, as was seen in the last chapter of this study, considered this

Norbert to be an embodiment of the 'composition nécessaire à la forme artistique, la transposition qu'il faut pour transformer la réalité',[17] a role that is sustained (for Nettelbeck) throughout the trilogy by La Vigue. Talking of the diffraction of the narrating subject into a multiplicity of complementary characters, Nettelbeck states,

> Le centre nerveux de la narration n'est plus le simple chroniqueur: le Je prisonnier du temps cède le pas à un Nous qui est une fusion d'expérience directe (le narrateur), de transposition artistique (Le Vigan), d'instinct (Bébert) et d'esprit vital (Lili), formant ainsi une constellation très forte des valeurs qui constituent "l'être" célinien.[18]

Such an interpretation, however, fails to take account of the fact that those character traits attributed to La Vigue throughout the trilogy—right from his very first appearance here—are both undesirable and disabling for any hoping to attain the *féerique* mode of existence sought by the narrator. For La Vigue is an actor, always playing a role, be it that of a *gaucho*—as is the case in this opening section of *D'un château l'autre*—, of Christ (see *N*, p.342) or an '«homme de nulle part»' (*N*, p.493),[19] an actor who, furthermore, is afflicted by an excessive egotism, an exacerbated 'moimoiisme'. Inauthentic by profession, always assimilating modes of behaviour extraneous to his own emotive core, and self-obsessed to boot, La Vigue is incapable of true communication with others, just as was the other transposed version of Robert Le Vigan, Norbert in *Féerie pour une autre fois*. This is not to say, however, that La Vigue does not constitute one of the elements of the trilogy's narratival Trinity—his constant presence alongside the narrator throughout almost the entire trilogy alone should be enough to indicate that such is the case; but whereas Nettelbeck sees La Vigue as a triumvir complementary to the becoming-*féerique* of the narrative, he is, rather, antagonistic, an obstacle to that mode of communication talked of in *Entretiens avec le professeur Y* that passes, 'direct dans l'émotion!... par l'émotion!' (*EY*, p.536), the 'métro émotif' or, as is the case in *D'un château l'autre*, Caron's boat.[20]

Caron is a mythical monster, half-tiger, half-monkey, a description which could equally apply to the various literary guises of Céline, the mythomaniacal (through transposition) vicious hate-filled buffoon. If Caron is, then, a hallucinated projection of the narrator himself, his boat—a means of transport which operates in smooth space—would be the text. Such an interpretation is lent credence by the fare to be paid by the passengers (*le public*) embarking upon *La Publique*, for although both those with and those without money are allowed passage onto the boat, all must have their heads split open by Caron's oar. To put it another way, all those undertaking this voyage must be killed (have their lives invested with death) by the vessel's means of locomotion, its mode of composition, its style (which, then, operates by feeding anti-production into the process of production). But if this entire scene is indeed metafictional, but an apparition of the *féerique* aesthetic to which the text itself aspires, why is it that the narrator Céline does not climb aboard Caron's boat, but instead shouts insults at La Vigue as the boat leaves the quayside? The answer lies with La Vigue himself.

Certain changes in the text would seem to indicate that, as the narrator Céline approaches the quay where Caron's boat is moored, a gradual shift towards the *féerique* ideal of the Célinian aesthetic is taking place. There is, for instance, an increase in the incidence of points of suspension, litotes, ellipses, digressions and metanarratival commentary, all of which point to a style that rejects the traditional, molar rules according to which should be constructed a linear narrative—indeed, the metanarratival comments themselves point up this distancing from narrative orthodoxy—, instead to create a style which destratifies its own narrative space so as to create a smooth textual space, full of points of rupture, which exists only in the connective synthesis between text and reader.[21] But if the narrative approaches this ideal, it never attains it, for its line of flight is constantly turned back on itself, grounded in the strata of History. It is this very failure to escape the time of *Chronos* ('le temps de la mesure, qui fixe les choses et les personnes, développe une forme et détermine un sujet')[22] in order to attain that of *aiôn* ('le temps indéfini de l'événement, la ligne flottante qui ne connaît que les vitesses, et ne cesse à la fois de diviser ce qui arrive en un déjà-là et un pas-encore-là, un trop-tard et un trop-tôt simultanés, un quelque chose à la fois qui va se passer et vient de se passer')[23] which finds symbolic expression in the narrator Céline's failure to embark upon Caron's boat *because of the antagonism between La Vigue and himself*. For La Vigue, with his excessive moimoiisme, his constant desire and need to be recognised, and his love of the celebrity that accompanies his profession, actively colludes with molarity by facialising himself. As Philip Goodchild notes:

> Œdipalized representation operates by giving people faces; a person is recorded on the socius and participates in society according to the appearance which he or she is given, and by which he or she is recognized. Capitalist

> culture is largely concerned with the investment of desire in the production, recording, and consumption of faces. The capitalist subject wishes to produce a face of his or her own, to be recognized and acclaimed; films, television, newspapers, and magazines operate less as "media" than as machines for the production and recording of faces.[24]

Delighting in the dissemination of his own facial image, La Vigue is miraculated by the paranoiac pole, a fact that would matter little if it were not for the fact that, as mentioned above, he constitutes part of the narratival Trinity of the trilogy. Imbued with the paranoiac traits of faciality that molarity employs to dissimulate organic existence, La Vigue can be said to symbolise that part of the narrator Céline described in *Féerie pour une autre fois* which remains inescapably territorialised in History, the infamy of his name. For as long as La Vigue remains on *La Publique* (in *le public*'s mind), or, indeed, at the narrator Céline's side, therefore, the narrative expression will always be overcoded by molarity, turned to molar ends—in this perspective it is highly significant that La Vigue's position on *La Publique* should be that of fare collector—, never able to convert its own textual space into a smooth space populated only by molecular becomings that appeal to the desire of the reader. Thus, it is only by ridding himself of La Vigue, of that part of himself which has been abstracted from his body and overcoded by perverted desire, that the narrator will be able to board *La Publique*, to attain a mode of expression that appeals to desire by example, having achieved the destiny of all mankind: 'si l'homme a un destin, ce sera plutôt d'échapper au visage, défaire le visage et les visagéifications, devenir imperceptible, devenir clandestin'.[25]

Like *Féerie pour une autre fois*, however, the majority of the trilogy would appear to be a heuristic rather than an algorithmic exercise, for La Vigue remains an ever-present figure for almost the entirety of the trilogy's retrospective narrative.[26] Where the trilogy differs from *Féerie pour une autre fois*, is in the narrator's dealings with that facialised part of himself which finds symbolic expression in the character of La Vigue, namely, Céline, the reviled author of the pamphlets. This facet of the composite narrator is that which appears—in the metanarratival sections—to be narrating the entire trilogy from temporal and geographical situations far removed from those of the true narrative, and which, therefore, would appear to have complete control over the text in both the narrative present and retrospective narratives. This apparent narratival omnipotence would seem to be reinforced by the narrator's narrative strategy in the metanarratival sections, as the text is manipulated so as to allow the reader no autonomous response to it, the phantasmic antagonistic reader present in the metanarrative pre-empting, and thereby annulling, the actual reader's own (expected) response to the text.[27] Critics rooted within a psychoanalytic framework based on a Freudian/Lacanian metaphysics of absence, consider such a strategy (somewhat unsurprisingly) to be indicative of a lack within the author that drives him to create an expression that obliges the reader to seek the author's presence so as to annul a perceived absence within himself.[28] Others see this desire for narrative supremacy as indicative of the retention of Céline's former Fascist tendencies, a suggestion which is lent easy credence by the apparently racist diatribes of the metanarratival sections. Yves de la Quérière, for instance, sees in the oft-quoted ant and iron filings metaphor of *Rigodon* (*R*, p.731) a description of the workings of Céline's adapted Fascist tendencies in his narrative strategy.[29]

Similarly, Ann Murphy has noted how, in the trilogy, two types of discourse inhabit the same textual space, a dialogic, heteroglossic, centrifugal discourse that tends towards polyphony by appropriating the languages and discourses of others in order to create a multiplicity of voices in one, and a second type of discourse that has a centripetal motion, moving towards the inside and marked by a 'suspension of the participation of narrative discourse in the discourse of others'.[30] For Murphy, this coexistence is both inherent to Céline's work—indeed, she states that, 'Céline's writing seems to be shaped by the conflict of opposites'—[31] and problematic for it, since it establishes an irreconcilable contradiction between the texts' polyphonic narration and the Derridean metaphysics of presence that she sees Céline erecting in a quasi-Fascistic attempt to, 'consolidate the plural—[...] the valorized "sémiotique", the affective—into a oneness that would replace the oneness of the Other',[32] that Other, in her analysis, being unbearable for Céline. For Murphy, then, Céline's aesthetic ideology fails—she suggests that the trilogy can be read, on one level, as 'the story of the failure of the solutions it proposes'—,[33] for, as the title of her work implies, it remains always *between* presence and polyphony, claiming to reject all dogma, yet merely superseding the old with a new dogma which itself must fail since emotion, that which is posited as the stable centre of his 'ideological architecture', is by definition a non-centre, a centrifugal force.[34] Although ingenious, Murphy's entire thesis (like that of

Kristeva on which many of Murphy's ideas are based) relies on the same premises as those of Coen and de la Quérière, only to go one step further by establishing a causal relationship between the two, Céline's Fascism being attributed to an Œdipal cry against Jewish monotheism, the latter being equated with the tyranny of the Father.[35]

Far more convincing is the position of (once again) Colin Nettelbeck, who comments that,

> Céline ne chante pas pour le plaisir: au contraire, c'est pour assurer son emprise sur le lecteur et pour le diriger vers les souterrains de l'émotion et du rêve. Le chant est ainsi une espèce de drogue—on pense aux 2 cc de morphine avec lesquels le narrateur traite Mme Niçois—, un moyen de mettre le lecteur dans une position de dépendance à l'égard du narrateur. Plongés d'emblée dans une narration dont le ton et les perspectives sont constamment en train de changer, nous sommes en effet obligés d'accepter cette dépendance, rien que pour suivre le récit à son niveau le plus superficiel. Du coup, nous nous constituons les prisonniers de Céline. Notre propre appareil psychique et affectif devient l'instrument dont le romancier joue, et nous nous identifions, non seulement avec le narrateur ou avec l'un ou l'autre des personnages, mais avec tout le mouvement du récit. Par cette identification, nous pouvons participer au processus de transformation.[36]

However, although Nettelbeck is right to suggest that the process of transformation is handed over to the reader, what he sees as a dictatorial means to make the reader dependant on him, to make the reader his prisoner, is rather an empowering of the reader through an internalisation of the antagonistic reader's perverted desire that abjectifies the narrator to the point of imperceptibility. To put it another way, the narrator Céline deliberately locks himself in the prison created by the antagonistic reader of *Féerie pour une autre fois*, not to expiate his sins, but to destroy that part of him which is rooted in History and thus make way for a pure, *féerique* aesthetic that emanates from a narrative centre which cannot be overcoded, but instead connects directly with the actual reader, thereby allowing, not forcing, both text and reader to sing. So if Céline does, as Ann Murphy suggests, slip into a monologism that subsumes the discourse of the other, thereby constructing a Derridean metaphysics of presence, this is done only to make way for a heteroglossic Bakhtinian dialogism through the conversion of that presence into not an absence, but a becoming-imperceptible through self-abjectification.[37]

Abjec(tifica)tion

Abjection is the term described by Julia Kristeva in her essay on Céline as being like, 'un boomerang indomptable, un pôle d'appel et de répulsion [qui] met celui qui en est habité littéralement hors de lui',[38] and as a,

> surgissement massif et abrupt d'une étrangeté qui, si elle a pu m'être familière dans une vie opaque et oubliée, me harcèle maintenant comme radicalement séparée, répugnante. Pas moi. Pas ça. Mais pas rien non plus. Un "quelque chose" que je ne reconnais pas comme chose. Un poids de non-sens qui n'a rien d'insignifiant et qui m'écrase.[39]

In order to maintain that the aesthetic ideology of the trilogy constructs a new monologic order intended to overcome abjection, then, it is necessary to believe that the tirades against various racial groups contained in the metanarratival sections of the trilogy are properly Fa(s)cistic, intended to bring about the suppression of entire peoples different to one's self. If such were indeed the case, abjection would elicit a facialising response, faciality operating through degrees of divergence from a norm. As Deleuze and Guattari state:

> Si le visage est bien le Christ, c'est-à-dire l'Homme blanc moyen quelconque, les premières déviances, les premiers écarts-types sont raciaux: homme jaune, homme noir, hommes de deuxième ou troisième catégorie. [...] Ils doivent être christianisés, c'est-à-dire visageifiés. Le racisme européen comme prétention de l'homme blanc n'a jamais procédé par exclusion, ni assignation de quelqu'un désigné comme Autre [...]. Le racisme procède par détermination des écarts de déviance, en fonction du visage Homme blanc qui prétend intégrer dans des ondes de plus en plus excentriques et retardées les traits qui ne sont pas conformes, tantôt pour les tolérer à telle place et dans telles conditions, dans tel ghetto, tantôt pour les effacer sur le mur qui ne supporte jamais l'altérité (c'est un juif, c'est un arabe, c'est un nègre, c'est un fou..., etc.). Du point de vue du racisme, il n'y a pas d'extérieur, il n'y a pas de gens du dehors. Il n'y a que des gens qui devraient être comme nous, et dont le crime est de ne pas l'être. La coupure ne passe plus entre un dedans et un dehors, mais à l'intérieur des chaînes signifiantes simultanées et des choix subjectifs successifs. Le racisme ne détecte jamais les particules de l'autre, il propage les ondes du même jusqu'à l'extinction de ce qui ne se laisse pas identifier (ou qui ne se laisse identifier qu'à partir de tel ou tel écart). Sa cruauté n'a d'égale que son incompétence ou sa naïveté.[40]

Whether or not such faciality is in operation in the anti-Semitic pamphlets is a separate question entirely. What should be clear by now, however, is that this cannot be so in the trilogy, for it is precisely that character who practises faciality—La Vigue, the fictional embodiment of Céline's infamy to whom the adjectives incompetent and naïve are applicable throughout the trilogy—who prevents the narrator's passage into his own aesthetic. This being the case, if the fruition of the Célinian aesthetic is found in the trilogy (as Nettelbeck suggests when he notes that, in *Rigodon*, 'le Nord qu'il ne faut pas perdre est la direction qui rapproche de la Vie: c'est encore une métaphore de l'idéal artistique'),[41] if, that is to say, the northbound train journey symbolises the accomplishment of the foiled attempt to embark upon Caron's boat, then the pseudo-racism of the metanarratival sections cannot be truly facialising and must serve another purpose. Indeed, in an inversion of the Kristevan view by which the abject leads to faciality, it is rather the case that, in the apparently monologic diatribes of the metanarratival sections, faciality is deliberately employed to attain the abject:[42]

> «Ne pas fréquenter ces gens-là! réprouvés puants pustuleux...»
> Vu de l'autre bord c'est assez chouette... vous avez plus à bavarder perdre votre temps à être aimable, *le statut de paria a du bon...* (*N*, p.639; my italics)

What is being suggested here, is that in the metanarratives of the first two books of the trilogy, the narrator Céline falsely appropriates a molar, facialising discourse that abjectifies him, which is to say that it places him in that space the abject inhabits, 'à la lisière de l'inexistence et de l'hallucination'.[43] Significantly, this space could be said to be that circumscribed by Caron's boat, the hallucinated embodiment of the *féerique* aesthetic which operates much like a body without organs, affirming existence only by investing it with non-existence in the belief that authentic action can well only from a zero intensity. There is thus an intimate link between the abjectification of the narrator and the attainment of an aesthetic which is properly *féerique*. Indeed, the abjectification of the narrator is but one more way by which to attain a disembodied aesthetic freed from molar constraints, for to inhabit the space that the abject inhabits is necessarily to bring about the dissolution of subjectivity since, as Kristeva goes on to say, by entering into the space of the abject, the subject enters into that reality which, 'si je la reconnais, m'annihile'.[44] Once again, therefore, the construction of what would appear to be a metaphysics of presence is employed only to create what is effectively its opposite, a becoming-imperceptible able to escape the centripetal force of History, since the centre around which that force exerted its power no longer exists. Herein lies the solution to the terrible impasse of *Féerie pour une autre fois*, for rather than struggle against the centripetal forces of History, the narrator of the trilogy internalises those traits falsely attributed him—one of which being, of course, a Fa(s)cism stemming from a horror of the abject—, realising that it is only by doing so, by living up to the readers' expectations of him and accepting the scapegoat role foisted upon him so as to satiate their perverted desire, that he will be able to carry on writing.[45] That this is the case can be seen in these passages:

> Aucune illusion!... soucis personnels... vous me direz... quand même! quand même! que ce soit Gertrut ou Brottin, ou un autre, personne m'avancera plus un flèche pour une histoire genre *Normance!* je le dis!... le lecteur veut rire et c'est tout!... jamais Paris ne fut bombardé!... d'abord!... et d'un!... aucune plaque commémorative!... la preuve!... moi seul, qui me souviens encore de deux, trois familles ensevelies!... *Normance*, question livre, a été qu'un affreux four!... parce que ceci!... parce que cela!... en plus de saboté comme!... par Achille, sa clique, ses critiques, ses haineux «aux ordres», canards enragés!... les gens s'attendaient que je provoque, que je bouffe encore du Palestin, que je refonce au gniouf! et pour le compte!... des «bienfaiteurs», ça s'appelle!... les «hardi-petit»! un de ces sapements! joli Monsieur! vingt ans!... «à vie»!... oh, mais gourrance! bévue! maldonne! moi qu'attends ferme, tout au contraire, qu'on les écroue tous!... flirteurs voyous des échafauds, traves et «recluses»! qu'on rouvre la belle Guyane pour eux! réarme l'Ile du Diable!... plus, prime, chacun quelque chose à la langue... petits épithéliomes... tout choix! entre carotides et pharynx...
>
> Bon!... mais en attendant, Brottin m'avertit: zéro!... «Vous vous vendez de moins en moins!... votre *Normance?* une catastrophe!... rien possible à vous refoutre au trou!... ni pornographe! ni fâchiste! misère de vous!... les critiques pourtant, les crocs hors! prêts! venins! tout!... se la mordent!... vous les écœurez!... leur bœuf alors?... sans cœur!... leurs enveloppes?... leurs familles?...»
>
> «Écrivez plus rien!...» vous me direz... que je vous écoute!... que vous avez bien raison!... mais Lili, les chiens, les chats, les oiseaux, et les «perce-neige»?... avec l'hiver qu'on a eu!... vous avez peut-être une idée?... (*CA*, pp.45–46)

> Mon Dieu, que ce serait agréable de garder tout ceci pour soi!... plus dire un mot, plus rien écrire, qu'on vous foute extrêmement la paix... on irait finir quelque part au bord de la mer... pas la côte d'Azur!... la mer vraie, l'Océan... on parlerait plus à personne, tout à fait tranquille, oublié... mais la croque, Mimile?... trompettes et grosse caisse!... aux agrès, vieux clown! et que ça

> saute! plus haut!... plus haut! vous êtes un petit peu attendu! le public vous demande qu'une seule chose: que vous vous cassiez bien la gueule! (*CA*, p.194)

As can be seen from these quotations, one of the ways in which the narrator will conform to the desires of molarity is by claiming to write solely for molar ends, for the accumulation of capital—hence the incessant tirades against his publishers, those who pillaged his affairs, those with cars, and, in general, all those wealthier than himself. It is these passages, coupled with the discovery in *Rigodon* that the sole reason why the narrator is so keen to reach Denmark is because he has had his royalties placed in an account there,[46] that have led many critics to accept unquestioningly such avowals as the truth, as proof of an obsessive materialistic greed on the part of the author Céline. Take, for instance, Deleuze and Guattari's view that, after *Guignol's band* I, Céline 'n'avait plus rien à dire, sauf ses malheurs, c'est-à-dire n'avait plus envie d'écrire, il avait seulement besoin d'argent'.[47] To believe that such was the true motive behind Céline's post-war novels, however, is to misunderstand the mechanisms of abjectification at work in the trilogy, and blatantly to disregard the text itself. For it seems hard to believe that such a character assessment can be made seriously if the retrospective narrative is taken into consideration, the protagonist Céline/Destouches being consistently portrayed as tirelessly selfless and self-effacing. And even if one examines only those comments in the metanarrative which seem to corroborate the accusations of avarice levelled against Céline, such a judgement remains unjustifiable for all but the most superficial of readings. For, firstly, the narrator explicitly mocks any who may persist in this opinion of him, saying:

> au moins trouillant de ce qu'on va dire!... ouste!... que je sois devenu matérialisse?... hé!... hé!... possible!... mais pas beaucoup!... mes voleurs pillards jaloux le sont sûrement bien plus que moi!... et dans l'état où je me trouve, maladie, mutilé, âge, dèche... il me faudrait la *Chase National*, et un compte comme ça!... pour que je retrouve un peu de souffle... un compte comme Claudel, Thorez, Mauriac, Picasso, Maurois... comme tous les véritables artistes! moi je serai toujours bien inférieur, question forfait ou «à la pièce», à Julien Labase, manœuvre-balai... (*CA*, p.291)

But, more importantly, the narrator also persistently states that the riches he pursues are not for his own good; indeed, he seems to take pride in his frugality: 'le prix d'un complet de «Commissar», en calories, j'aurais de quoi moi subsister, œuvrer, regarder la Seine, aller dans deux trois musées, payer le téléphone, pendant mettons au moins un an!...' (*CA*, p.6). Furthermore, the wealth that he desires is only for the good of Lili and Bébert his cat, the ideal and genuine triumvirs of the narratival Trinity, representing, respectively, a dance-like aesthetic and instinctual animality.[48] The material wealth that the narrator craves, then, is purely for the sustenance of his aesthetic and not his own person which, on the contrary, matters so little to him that his own personal physical and mental degradation appear to be preferable in his eyes, as they render him abject (in the normal sense of the word) in the eyes of his detractors, this, in turn, allowing them an easy means by which to dismiss and abjectify him (in the Kristevan sense):

> moins je mange mieux ça vaut... je titube, certes... on peut dire: voilà! il est saoul!... on le dit... arrangez-vous toujours pour être réputé ivrogne, bon à rien, fainéant, en plus de gâteux... un peu «repris de justice»!... vous êtes méprisé? faites-y-vous!... question moi vieillard, je l'ai dit, moins je mange mieux ça vaut!... mais Lili est pas vieillarde, elle! elle a ses leçons de danse à donner! (*CA*, pp.7–8)

Far from stemming from the integration of a hate complex previously existing only as a 'shadow problem' into the author's own being, as Knapp has suggested,[49] this self-abjectification (again in both senses of the word) is a deliberate act of deterritorialisation which liberates the narrative voice from the centripetal force of molarity by converting the narrator into a becoming-imperceptible, an evanescent, ectoplasmic form, a pure aesthetic that operates according to the negative term of Hamlet's question:

> ah, *not to be! be!* vous êtes coincé par le sort!... pris dans l'étau!... vous avez pas fini de rire!... vous débattre et récriminer! à plus savoir!... *not to be* crotte!... que vous êtes fait!... enfin d'une façon!... rire contraint... rire jaune... je vais vous raconter la suite... s'il se peut!... je suis moi-même, pas besoin de vous dire, l'âge, le crime des hommes, et tout, **bien plus à me faire oublier, finir dans mon coin, qu'à m'évertuer de vous présenter des personnes, branquignols, femmes, choses, peu prou pas croyables!...** le coup de *La Publique* a suffi!... je crois! je vais pas aller encore pour vous dans ces contrées de-ci!... de-là!... peu, prou presque pas avouables... non!... mais si vous êtes pris dans l'étau... pris par le sort... vous vous dégagez prou ou mal!...
>
> À tout prendre et sans prétention le mieux que je vous raconte tel quel!... la malignité publique saura bien sûr tout fripouiller! sacriléger!... tout farcir d'horribles mensonges!... que moi-même, en tout, finalement, je me ferai

> l'effet d'un drôle de piaf!... sorte d'**ectoplasmique ragoteux...** revenant plus sachant... de ci!... de là!... l'attitude!... les mots qu'il doit dire?... lorsque le sort vous a coincé c'est plus que de passer aux aveux... [...] lorsque vous êtes pris dans l'étau, qu'on vous a déchu, à l'os, à la moelle, c'est plus que de passer aux aveux!... et pas que ça traîne! vos heures sont joliment comptées! «bâtir à cet âge!...» et donc, raconter des histoires!... bordel! les jeunes sont tout débiles idiots blablaveux boutonneux tout naves... soit!... les «Incarneurs de la Jeunesse»! évident! pour la raison qu'ils sont pas «faits»... les vieux? **tout suinteux radoteux, inimaginables de haine et d'horreur** pour tout ce qui arrive! et qui va venir!... pour la raison qu'ils le sont de trop, eux, «faits»!... **camemberts verts et vers, coulants puants, vite vite à remettre au frigidaire!...** (*CA*, pp.172–173; my emphasis in bold typeface)

The narrator's apparent racism in the trilogy can also be seen to participate in this same process, for shortly after the above passage from *D'un château l'autre*, there follows a section in which the narrator avows his desire to return to the retrospective narration, protesting that his 'imprécations' are not in the interests of his *œuvre*—a blatant untruth in the light of the present analysis—, only to be retained in the narrative present by his reflections on the problems of inter-racial breeding:

> Mes imprécations avancent pas beaucoup ma belle œuvre! mes petits chichis et misères! vous vous en battez vous aussi! pardi! pardine!... retournons donc au *Löwen*... je vous ai laissé sur le palier... Mme Aïcha von Raumnitz... je lui ramenais sa fille, la jeune belle Hilda... peut-être serez-vous étonné?... mais je vous parle en clinicien, embryologiste et raciste... que ce mariage d'un hobereau si accusé, si Dürer, de stature, nature, et de cette personne Aïcha, si elle, tellement Trébizonde!... Beyrouth!... ondulante, si brune, lascive, bovine, pas Dürer du tout... ait donné une si belle enfant?... oh, les croisements sont pleins de périls... d'aléas... (*CA*, pp.173–174)

Just as was the case with the apparently avaricious Capitalist discourse already examined, passages such as this can be said to be properly facialising only if the text itself is read with pre-conceived notions of the author's political ideologies foremost in mind. For when only the text itself is taken into consideration, it becomes clear that the seemingly unequivocal avowal of the narrator's racism is placed in the middle of a discourse praising the product of a mixed-race marriage, thus, effectively, negating that very racism.[50] In this way, the narrator once again employs an apparently monologic discourse to perform a double deterritorialisation, ridding himself of the centripetal forces of molarity by constructing a phantasmic facialising nucleus around which those forces are accelerated inwards to a point of infinite density, a black hole, whilst simultaneously and deliberately abjectifying the supposedly stable centre of this discourse by positioning it in an abyss of non-sense, of irreconcilable contradiction.

Much the same thing can be seen to operate in other supposedly racist diatribes of the metanarratives with the use of humour. For by directing a quasi-monologic pseudo-Fascist discourse against people or peoples with a lesser symbolic capital than the Jews in the post-Holocaust age, and employing that discourse to a humorous end, the narrator Céline counters his own vitriol and places a centrifugal force at the centre of his monologism—humour being intimately related to emotion.[51] It should not be thought, however, that all of the grievances voiced by the narrator Céline are innocuous, having humorous intent, for, in the first two volumes of the trilogy, he is not always able to diffuse his anger, to convert his own monologic discourse into an expression of desire, to internalise the mechanisms of molarity so as to turn them to his own needs. Significantly, when such genuine rancour is given voice, it is nearly always accompanied by the eruption of a direct quotation within the main text of the metanarrative, as though the sentiment spoken were so anathema and antagonistic to the narrator as to render him incapable of internalising its discourse in the slightest. Somewhat unsurprisingly, this occurs when the narrator's mind turns to his 'comptes à rendre' (*CA*, p.280), to those people and mechanisms that, in the narrative present, persist in overcoding him in terms of his past History, a catalogue of which is provided by the following quotations:

> Je vois que je vous ennuie... autre chose!... autre chose!... tous les bourgeois à la lanterne?... bourgeois de tous les Partis!... absolument total d'accord! bourgeois est fripouille cent pour cent! j'en vois un tout particulier, le Tartre! gratin de cloaque! la façon qu'il m'a diffamé, remué ciel terre qu'on m'écartèle, je lui donne droit à cinq... six néos entre œsophage et pancréas!... priorité!...
>
> Tartre m'a bien volé, diffamé... oh, que oui!... mais pas pire que les parents!... et il est pas drôle comme ma tante!... de loin!... le choc, la syncope de ma tante en me revoyant!... que j'étais pas mort!... qu'ils m'avaient pas exécuté!... «Toi? toi?»... elle doutait... «toi là?»... (CA, pp.46–47)

> Je reviens à nos difficultés... tout résumé, tel quel, sans flan, le dernier manœuvre d'en bas, dans l'île, de chez Renault, travaille moins que moi, mange plus que moi, dort plus que moi... et soixante-trois ans dans deux jours... je spécifie... quant à la considération!... c'est pas à croire le mal que

j'ai de pas être haché, sec! «ordure! stalinien!... naziste! pornographe! charlatan! fléau!...» pas murmurées ces bonnes choses!... noir sur blanc!... plein les panonceaux!... là encore un tort capital: je suis gratuit!... si ma gratuité me fait haïr!... y a que les ordures qui sont gratuites! «ah, il voudrait se faire pardonner! perfide pire que tout! vérole!» (*CA*, p.52)

Vous pensez si je sentais que ça venait à Siegmaringen!... «le mal a des ailes»!... que mon compte était bon!... d'une façon d'une autre!... «Bagatelles» je devais en crever!... c'était aussi entendu à Londres qu'à Rome ou Dakar... et dix fois plus encore chez nous, là! Siegmaringen sur Danube! le refuge des 1 142!... si j'étais pas occis, alors? c'est que je jouais vraiment le double jeu! que j'étais fifi?... agent des juifs?... de toute façon j'y coupais pas! «avec les livres qu'il a écrits»!... en plus que les 1 142 escomptaient bien leur petite veine... que je payerais pour tous!... que tout se passerait très gentiment, grâce à moi! ils rêvaient déjà tous pantoufles, retour dans leurs meubles... grâce à moi!... à moi les supplices gratinés! «avec les livres qu'il a écrits»!... pas eux! pas eux!... eux immuns, pépères, et grigris! moi qu'avais à expier pour tous!... «avec les livres qu'il a écrits»!... moi qui rassasierais Moloch! bien l'avis de tous!... j'y couperais pas! du dernier cloche grabataire crevard fienteux du *Fidelis* au très haut Laval du Château, c'était immanquable... «ah, vous vous n'aimez pas les juifs! vous, Céline!» la parole qui les rassurait!... que c'était moi qu'on allait pendre! sûr!... certain!... mais pas eux! pas eux!... ah, chers eux!... «les livres que vous avez écrits!» ce que j'ai adouci d'agonies, d'agonies de trouilles avec «Bagatelles»! juste ce qu'il fallait, ce qu'on me demandait!... le livre du bouc! celui qu'on égorge, dépèce! mais pas eux!... pas eux du tout! douillets eux! non! jamais!... plus un seul anti-juif d'ailleurs dans les 1 142!... plus un!... pas plus que Morand, Montherlant, Maurois, Latzareff, Laval ou Brinon!... le seul qui restait, ma gueule!... bouc providentiel!... je sauvais tout le monde par *Bagatelles!* les 1 142 mandats!... comme j'ai sauvé de l'autre côté, Morand, Achille, Maurois, Montherlant, Tartre... l'héros providentiel con!... moi!... moi!... moi!... pas que la France, le monde entier, ennemis, alliés, exigent que j'y passe!... bien saignant!... ils ont monté un nouveau mythe!... on éventre pas l'animal?... oui? non? les prêtres sont là! (*CA*, pp.213–214)

je vois mon local, rue Girardon, les épurateurs sont montés, si ivres de patriotique fureur, qu'ils ont pas pu s'empêcher de tout m'embarquer pour la Salle, tout fourguer!... mes amis connaissances aussi, oncles, cousins, nièces, eux aux Puces!... ils m'auraient empalé en plus, c'eût été vraiment la Jouissance! presque tout le monde m'a oublié... pas eux!... pas eux!... vos voleurs vous oublient jamais!... vos copieurs non plus!... pensez!... la vie, qu'ils vous doivent!... Tartre va pas un jour se mettre à table «Moi, plagiaire et bourrique à gages, j'avoue! je suis son trou d'anu!...» vous pouvez vraiment pas compter!... (*CA*, p.292)

> là-haut à Zornhof, chez les Prussiens en état de guerre, que cette folle m'accuse de tout c'était pas à être étonné... plus la douleur de ses deux fils... mais maintenant, vingt-cinq ans plus tard, et dans ma propre famille c'est un peu plus rigolo... et pas de petits crimes qu'on m'accuse!... «assassin de ma mère!»... si je disais: non! ça irait mal!... je sais ce que ça cache... ils ont tout volé chez ma vieille... très sûrs d'eux! «il reviendra jamais!»... pareil de mes bois à Montmartre, que j'aille les réclamer!... si je serais étendu! la loi du milieu!... et par les quatre Commandeurs!... voleurs et déménageurs! «hardi l'hallali! il reviendra jamais!» même ribouldingue sur mes belles œuvres... «hardi petit! satanés ratés tapez dedans!... il reviendra jamais!... pillez-lui tout, bons à lape! à l'assaut!... hardi! clan-culs! ça se verra pas!... on saura rien! il reviendra jamais!» (*N*, p.602)

Ironically, however, although such diatribes protest against the molar mechanisms which prevent the conversion of the narrative into a pure aesthetic, they only serve to reterritorialise the narrative—or, rather, to help sustain the mechanisms of territorialisation already in place—, for, by directing the poetic expression towards a definable, stable target, the text operates as a monologism with a centripetal motion which converts the supposedly poetic expression into the opposite of the emotive, affective aesthetic intended. Such would seem to be explicitly recognised by the narrator, for such passages, which deal with subjects affecting only the narrator in the narrative present, are often described as deviations from or hindrances to the true intent of the narration, the avowed intent of which, as is exemplified in the passages below, is to free itself from molar constraints in order to establish connective syntheses between poetic expression and reader:

> Que je vous perde pas dans les vétilles!... j'en étais à Gertrut Morny... ce vif intérêt qu'il me portait!... Tartuffe... que je plaque l'Achille, saboteur conjuré dessous de tout, pour les Éditions Bérengères!... que je me perdais chez Achille!... que c'était sa joie, lui, Loukoum et toute sa tribu, de me réduire à rien! au profond de leur cave!... moi, mes ours!... (*CA*, p.48)

> Encore mes rancœurs!... vous m'excuserez d'un peu de gâtisme... mais pas tellement que je vous lasse!... moi et mes trois points!... un peu de discrétion!... mon style, soi-disant original!... tous les véritables écrivains vous diront ce qu'il faut en penser!... et ce qu'en pense Brottin!... et ce qu'en pense Gertrut! mais l'épicier ce qu'il en pense?... voilà l'important!... voilà ce qui me fait réfléchir!... Hamlet du poireau... je réfléchis d'en haut de mon jardin... l'endroit du vraiment grand point de vue... l'endroit vraiment admirable si vous avez les «moyens»... mais si vous êtes juste l'angoissé nerveux anxieux de tout!... pour tout!... tout le temps!... pour les poireaux... les Contribu-

> tions… et le reste!… alors au diable les points de vue! vous avez pas à rêvasser!… merde, panoramas! délinquant le fauché qui rêve! (*CA*, pp.292–293)

By far the most striking and revealing example of such an admission comes after one of the monologic passages from *D'un château l'autre* quoted above, as the narrator says, 'J'épilogue… je vous laisse en pantaine… j'allais enfin pouvoir sortir…' (*CA*, p.214). Not only does this indicate that such passages which contribute to the mechanisms of molar reterritorialisation are accessory to the main text, merely an epilogue, however, it also confirms that, in order for his aesthetic quest to come to its fruition, the narrator will have to abandon all of those rigid, constraining, molar boundaries which prevent his expression from 'sortir'.

The narrator has already been seen to rid himself of molar boundaries through an internalisation of the territorialising mechanism which subsequently participates in an abjectification of the narrator which, in turn, initiates a becoming-imperceptible that liberates his poetic expression. To internalise the perverted desire that remains external to the narrator, however, will be, effectively, to commit suicide, for the molar desire which still torments the narrator and prompts a monologic response from him, calls for his annihilation: 'les pirates de la Butte Montmartre voulaient me saigner que mes tripes dégoulinent la rue Lepic… les pirates baltiques eux voulaient m'avoir au scorbut… que je laisse mes os en leur prison la «Venstre»…' (*CA*, p.5). That the possibility of literary suicide exists should not surprise the reader of Céline, for, as Nicole Debrie points out,

> Dès *Voyage*, commence pour Céline une sorte de course contre tout ce qui se cristallise, se fige, conçu comme un obstacle à la communication, à la subjectivation. Véritable course à "contre-courant", peut-on dire, de l'existence. Vivre en faisant abstraction de son individualité biologique? De son identité? Ce n'est pas sans raison que notre auteur qualifiera l'effort de l'écriture et de toute création comme un genre de 'suicide'.[52]

It is Debrie also who suggests—in language far more poetic than the machinic Deleuzian vocabulary employed here—that to do so, to 'mourir de poésie', remains a 'fantasme latent' throughout Céline's *œuvre*.[53] Such is undoubtedly the case up until the last instalment of the trilogy, but in *Rigodon*, Céline's last work, the trajectory of his entire career is brought to its apotheosis as this phantasm is actualised in the production of the pure aesthetic sought for so long, the becoming-imperceptible of the narrator, the creation of a disembodied voice able to deterritorialise itself and connect with the reader.

Becoming-intense, Becoming-imperceptible

In both *D'un château l'autre* and *Nord*, there is an unwillingness on the part of the narrator who speaks directly to the reader in the metanarratives to internalise that perverted desire which calls for his destruction or re-imprisonment—which, no doubt, would have amounted to the same thing for the author Céline—, with the result that the antagonised narrator's reaction becomes monologic and contributes to his own overcoding. The narrator presented at the beginning of *Rigodon*, however, seems to display no such open hostility towards those who insist on reterritorialising him in terms of his past History. His reaction may, at first sight, seem to be one of tired resignation as he waits to die, turning to the obituaries in the *Figaro* for amusement (*R*, pp.717–718), but it is rather a lucid awareness that, whatever he may do or say, however hard he may kick against certain molar factions, nothing will change the opinions of the closed-minded. An antagonistic reaction serves no purpose, therefore, for not only does it construct a monologism, as has been seen, but it attempts to combat that very thing which constitutes the essence of a great writer, namely, opposition, abjectification. Such is precisely what is suggested by the Barjavel text quoted in the novel:

> «Pour moi, le vingtième siècle ne compte jusqu'à présent qu'un novateur, c'est Ferdinand. Et je dirai même qu'un seul écrivain. J'espère que tu n'en seras pas froissé. Il est tellement au-dessus de nous. Qu'il soit torturé et persécuté est normal. C'est affreux d'écrire cela quand on pense que c'est un homme vivant, mais en même temps, à cause de sa grandeur, on ne peut s'empêcher de le considérer en dehors du temps et des contingences qui l'écrasent. Je crois profondément que plus un homme est grand, plus il s'expose à être blessé par tous. La tranquillité n'est que pour les médiocres, ceux dont la tête disparaît dans la foule. Céline voudrait revenir à Paris ou en France, et tu fais tout ce que tu peux pour l'aider, mais dis-toi bien ceci: où qu'il soit, il sera persécuté. Son désir de trouver la paix ailleurs qu'à l'endroit où il est, n'est qu'un rêve. Il ne trouvera la paix nulle part. Il sera persécuté jusqu'à la mort; où qu'il aille. Et il le sait bien. Et il n'y peut rien, ni nous non plus. Nous pouvons seulement proclamer, à chaque occasion, qu'il est le plus grand, et encore en faisant cela nous attirons sur lui les haines décuplées des petits, des médiocres, des châtrés,

de tous ceux qui crèvent de haine jalouse dès qu'on leur relève la tête pour leur montrer les sommets. Ils sont la multitude.» (*R*, pp.716–717)

The attainment of a pure aesthetic, therefore, can only come—albeit in a number of ways—from an internalisation and intensification of the perverted molar fluxes of desire; an examination of the narrator's conversation with the journalists who come to interview him at the beginning of *Rigodon* seems to indicate that such is precisely what he intends to do:

«Vous venez de *L'Espoir?*

—Parfaitement Céline! Nous étions à nous demander, et nous demandons encore, nous et nos amis, si vous êtes vraiment si immonde qu'on l'affirme partout?... nous venons vous demander.

—Qui sont vos amis?

—Ah tout d'abord l'immense Cousteau!

—Une belle ordure pour ce qui me concerne!... d'où sort cet individu?

—De *Je Suis Partout.*

—Donc un employé de Lesca et de la *Propagandastaffel.*

—Il a écrit que c'était vous qu'étiez à la solde des Allemands, il l'a affirmé, noir sur blanc, avec son immense courage, dans notre *Rivarol!* un *Rivarol* vaut dix *Huma!* sachez-le! savez-vous?... que nous répondez-vous Céline?

—Très ennuyeux puceaux sachez! que si je devais répondre à toutes les conneries, les billevesées des gazettes, et les lettrres, tout ce qui me reste de vie y passerait!... j'ai ma chronique à finir, et mes dettes énormes à payer!... Cousteau était un petit jaloux, député raté, bien fait pour fanatiser les turlupins de votre espèce...»

[...]

«Céline nous l'avons dit au téléphone, nous vous le demandons encore, jusqu'où vous pourrez aller dans l'égoïsme, la trahison, la lâcheté?

—Oh, je vais très loin mes chers amis! (*R*, pp.714–715)

Nettelbeck is thus right in noting a change in the prologue of *Rigodon* as opposed to those of the first two books of the trilogy, but the tonal shift is the polar opposite of that which he suggests. He states, 'even in the prologue [of *Rigodon*], where the narrator indulges in his customary attacks on his publisher and predicts the imminent destruction of the white race, the angry tone is gone, replaced by a constant sparkling humor',[54] but such does not tally with the text of the prologue of *Rigodon* itself, where the angry, virulent discourse of the narrator achieves its apotheosis. Indeed, one need only examine the opening pages of *Rigodon*—the dedication to which (‘*Aux animaux*’) alone indicates utter contempt for mankind—, to see that this is the case:

> Je vois bien que Poulet me boude... Poulet Robert condamné à mort... il parle plus de moi dans ses rubriques... autrefois j’étais le grand ceci... l’incomparable cela... maintenant à peine un petit mot accidentel assez méprisant. Je sais d’où ça vient, qu’on s’est engueulé... à la fin il m’emmerdait à tourner autour du pot!... vous êtes sûr que vos convictions ne vous ramènent pas à Dieu!
>
> «Putain que non!... je suis bien sûr! je suis de l’avis de Ninon de Lenclos! le bon Dieu, invention des curés! absolument antireligieux!... voilà ma foi une fois pour toutes!
>
> —Une autorité votre Ninon!... c’est tout, Céline? hum! hum!
>
> —Si! si Poulet! mieux encore!
>
> —Ah!... j’attends! je veux savoir!
>
> —Toutes les religions à “petit Jésus”, catholiques, protestantes ou juives, dans le même sac! je les fous toutes au pas! que ce soit pour le mettre en croix ou le faire avaler en hosties, même farine! même imposture! racontars! escroquerie!
>
> —Alors?
>
> —Alors, je prétends encore mieux! essayez de me suivre très cher abruti.
>
> —Allez! Allez!
>
> —Il n’y a qu’une seule religion: catholique, protestante ou juive... succursales de la boutique “au petit Jésus”... qu’elles se chamaillent s’entretripent?... vétilles!... corridas saignantes pour badauds! le grand boulot le seul le vrai leur profond accord... abrutir, détruire la race blanche.
>
> —Comment Céline? vous?
>
> —Pur métissage, mariage pardi! avec tous les sacrements! Amen!
>
> —Je vous comprends mal Céline...
>
> —Comprenez, condamné à mort! tous les sangs des races de couleurs sont “dominants”, jaunes rouges ou parme... le sang des blancs est “dominé”... toujours! les enfants des belles unions mixtes seront jaunes, noirs, rouges, jamais blancs, jamais plus blancs!... passez muscade! avec toutes les bénédictions!
>
> —La civilisation chrétienne!
>
> —Création, Poulet! l’imagination! escroquerie! l’imposture!
>
> —Tout de même! création du grand.
>
> —Métissage! destruction de vingt siècles, Poulet! rien d’autre! faite pour! créée pour! chaque création porte en elle-même, avec elle, avec sa naissance, sa propre fin, son assassinat!
>
> —L’Église assassine, Céline?
>
> —Et comment! et vous avec! elle ne fait que ça votre Église! cul béni!
>
> —Vous aimez trop les paradoxes! Céline! les Chinois sont antiracistes!... les noirs aussi!

—Cette fouterie! qu'ils viennent ici seulement un an ils baisent tout le monde! le tour est joué! plus un blanc! cette race n'a jamais existé... un "fond de teint" c'est tout! l'homme vrai de vrai est noir et jaune! l'homme blanc religion métisseuse! des religions! juives catholiques protestantes, le blanc est mort! il n'existe plus! qui croire?

—Céline vous me faites rire...»

Je n'ai jamais revu Poulet... j'ai lu ses articles de temps en temps... des petites allusions... pas plus... je l'ai un peu vexé... (*R*, pp.711–712)[55]

As can be seen in this passage, the narrator's virulence is channelled primarily into a racist/facialising diatribe, a diatribe which, however,—and this is of the utmost importance—is expressed *not for a Fa(s)cistic end, but only for the abjectification and becoming-imperceptible of the narrator*. For the narrator no longer tempers his anger, no longer holds back from what he wants to say, and welcomes the consequences that his words may entail:

—Vous désespérez la jeunesse! Maaaître! vous mésestimez la France et ses prodigieuses ressources et l'Algérie, l'Académie, et les participes!

—Aux chiottes, je vous dis! tout! tout ça! un pays qui n'existe plus, n'a plus que des Ordonnateurs!... pompes et funèbres... cent langues plus fortes que la nôtre, n'existent plus! Allez-vous parler l'hittite? l'araméen!

—Alors très décidément cher Maître nous irons vous voir! Nous bousculerons vos domestiques, nous tuerons vos chiens, et nous foutrons vos tripes à l'air! et votre cervelle dingue et pourrie! allô! allô! vous nous entendez? vous nous comprenez?

—Eh, bigre que oui! je prends mon pied! l'interview féroce! j'en suis! face aux fauves! le colloque romain! j'éructe!

—Oh oui! oh, Maître!

—Venez! Venez vite chers garçons! que je vous étreigne! je vous baise!...

—*Mgam! Mgam!*» (*R*, p.714)

It should not be thought, however, that at the end of his life Céline indulged a properly Fascist discourse, for, as can be seen in the very subject matter of the above and later diatribes, his discourse, which if truly facialising would castigate all deviation from the norm of White Male, in fact serves only to tell of the ultimate and inevitable eradication of that very norm. Take the following examples:

Cher *Figaro*, mon scoubidou!... pas que sa nécrologie! une autre gaieté!... les nouvelles des ex-colonies... comment les récents électeurs s'entendent à décapiter, rissoler les attardés blancs... oh, sans du tout penser à mal, ni racisme! croque au sel!... pas de svastikas à Tombouctou! (*R*, p.718) je pense à ce curé, ce culot!... je l'ai viré... certes, il méritait, cent fois! mille fois! il aurait été rabbin, anabaptiste, pasteur de l'Église réformée, orthodoxe, je l'aurais éconduit la même chose, tous militants du petit Jésus, absolument dans le même sac!... leurs bisbilles, zizanies me trompent pas, tous issus de la Bible, absolument total d'accord qu'on est que blancs, viandes à métissages, tournés noirs, jaunes et puis esclaves, et puis soldouilles et puis charniers... je vous apprends rien... Bible le livre le plus lu du monde... plus cochon, plus raciste, plus sadique que vingt siècles d'arènes, Byzance et Petiot mélangés!... de ces racismes, capilotades, génocides, boucheries des vaincus que nos plus pires grands guignolades tournent pâles et rosâtres en rapport, «suspenses» pour écoles maternelles... après la Bible, Racine ou pas, Sophocle ou non, tout est guimauve... un peu de plus ou moins roudoudou, c'est tout... (*R*, p.721)

—"Les hommes blancs avaient inventé la bombe atomique, peu après ils ont disparu." Tu veux que je te dise comment?»

Il hausse les épaules... il baisse les paupières, demi-baissées, genre croco...

«Ça sera long?

—Non! tiens tu vois, à peine deux pages!... tu peux écouter, pâle inepte!... plusieurs thèses: ils sont disparus dans les guerres, et par l'alcoolisme, l'automobile, et le trop manger... d'autres auteurs sont plutôt d'avis qu'ils ont succombé aux religions et fanatismes succédanés, politiques, familiaux, sportifs, mondains, toutes leurs religions, catholique, hébraïque, réformée, franc-maçonne... avant tout, par-dessus tout, Rome ou rue Cadet! même credo: métissez! credo absolu! tu saisis, ignare?

—Oui... pas grand-chose!...

—Écoute la fin! le sang des blancs ne résiste pas au métissage!... il tourne noir, jaune!... et c'est fini! le blanc est né dans le métissage, il fut créé pour disparaître! sang dominé! Azincourt, Verdun, Stalingrad, la ligne Maginot, l'Algérie, simples hachis!... viandes blanches! toi tu peux aller déjeuner!

—Tu m'as engueulé, t'es content?

—Toi t'as assez voulu qu'on me pende!

—Non, jamais!

—Oh, qu'on me fusille! et comment!... taille, Tartuffe!»

—Hi!... hi!... il rit le torve! en somme nous étions fâchés... notre brouille a duré quinze jours... (*R*, p.729)

ils parleront encore de moi, de mes horreurs de livres, que les Français existeront plus... traduit en mali je serai, ce petit cap d'Asie absolument effacé! les gens de là, d'autrefois blancs... blonds, bruns, noirs, invraisemblables!... blague de l'Histoire!... déchiffré entre les langues mortes, j'aurai ma petite chance... enfin! (*R*, p.731)

Although the narrator belongs to this race destined for non-existence, however, in order to be able to give voice to a pure, smooth aesthetic, in order to resume his retrospective narration which, this time, might accomplish its aim, he must first fully internalise these processes of abjectification and becoming-imperceptible, directing his discourse towards himself, for only once this has been done will a connective synthesis between reader and text be established. This synthesis might be termed a becoming-reader/text, for it signals that moment at which the text becomes auto-objective, fusing with the reader in a single subject pronoun:

☆

«Allons Céline!... vos lecteurs ont un petit peu le droit que vous cessiez de faire le pitre... vous aussi! vos histoires de Chinois à Brest peuvent amuser un moment... pas plus! toutes vos Églises, métisseuses, antiblanches, hum! hum! facéties vraiment douteuses!... votre public veut autre chose!... vous ne le savez pas?... des opérations "plein crâne", vivisections en couleurs, des accouchements à trois forceps, et des fabrications de "génies" dans les usines chromoplastiques de la Cordillère, par 4 000 mètres d'altitude...

—Zut! "peau blanche" que je suis, monsieur! et buté comme tel!

—Les "peaux-rouges" ont bien disparu!

—L'alcool les a beaucoup aidés, je ne bois que de l'eau... les "peaux-rouges" ont eu leurs "réserves" et leurs privilèges... leur conquérant les protégeait... ici moi "peau blanche" le conquérant ne pense qu'une chose, m'avilir encore toujours plus! me tout voler, m'humilier à mort... qu'à fond d'égout, tel flic du "grand autolysat" s'avise, me détecte, Fréjus n'est rien à côté de ce qui m'échoit, les torrents d'acide sulfurique! Buffalo Bill avait le cœur western, bien placé!... très raciste certes, mais loyal... le Sioux avait sa chance!... au galop! *ptaff!*... nous là aux égouts, zéro!... nous ne passerons jamais au Châtelet... espèce à biffer, hontes c'est tout... rampants d'épandages...»

Que j'ai du mal à m'y mettre!... j'ai promis, il faut!... l'âge? demain ne peut être que pire baderne, assez réfléchi!

☆

Nous voici!... hommage au lecteur!... révérence!... **nous nous retrouvons** à l'endroit même... (*R*, pp.732–733; my emphasis in bold typeface)[56]

Everything in this prologue points towards this analysis, especially the pseudo-Bergsonian philosophy which precedes the above passage and serves as, 'a metaphor of the novelist's art':[57]

Bergson nous le dit! vous remplissez une boîte en bois, une grande boîte, de toute petite limaille de fer, et vous donnez un coup de poing dedans, un fort coup de poing... qu'observez-vous? vous avez fait un entonnoir... juste de la

> forme de votre poing!... pour comprendre ce qui s'est passé, ce phénomène, deux intelligences, deux explications... l'intelligence de la fourmi tout éberluée, qui se demande par quel miracle un autre insecte, fourmi comme elle, a pu faire tenir tant de limaille, brin par brin, en tel équilibre, en forme d'entonnoir... et l'autre intelligence, géniale, la vôtre, la mienne, une explication, qu'un simple coup de poing a suffi... (*R*, p.731)

Adopting the perspective of the ant faced with this spectacle, the narrator merely informs the reader that, as 'chroniqueur', it will be his aim to recount the war (symbolically represented by the 'coup de poing', an act of pure destruction) not using the objectifying intellect of the human mind which converts the past into History—*Chronos*, the strict molar ordering of past events into a regimented hierarchy with hermeneutic relations of cause and effect between events—, but that of the ant, an almost-imperceptible animal whose reaction, formed by a subjective appreciation of the scene of the event, is one of wonder and questioning that revitalises, reactualises the past event, reinvesting it with desire:[58]

> moi chroniqueur j'ai à choisir, le genre fourmi, je peux vous amuser... aller et venir dans la limaille... avec l'explication coup de poing je peux encore vous divertir, mais beaucoup moins... les Chinois à Brest... toutes les Églises dans le même sac... Anéantissantes C°... Hébraïque, Rome, Réforme, *tutti frutti!* «Ligue des Métissages»! pour le peu qui me reste à vivre, mieux que je vous vexe pas trop... vous traite de titubants ivrognes... Byzance a très bien tenu dix siècles à bluffer le monde... le monde a rien vu que conjurations, doubles et triples courses de chars et troufignoleries, et puis les Turcs... et puis rideau... que ça se passera pareil ici? possible! vous demandez pas mieux... moi chroniqueur des Grands Guignols, je peux très honnêtement vous faire voir le très beau spectacle que ce fut, la mise à feu des forts bastions... les contorsions et mimiques... que beaucoup ont réchappé! (*R*, pp.731–732)

It is thus by rendering himself imperceptible, living life in terms of its end (yet positively nonetheless) rather than attempting to dissimulate that end ('pour le peu qui me reste à vivre') in order to re-inject the past with desire, that the narrator's aesthetic will achieve its true goal of establishing a connective synthesis between text and reader that will not be reterritorialised, but allow the text to operate like a 'lanterne magique' which illuminates that past in such a way that it is, 'comme si vous y étiez!' (*R*, p.731). Yet, in spite of all this, those truly intent on overcoding the narrator with the History of the author, still find a means by which to do so, seeing behind the text's avowed intent an ulterior motive. Take, for instance, Yves de la Quérière's comments on the narrator's ant philosophy:

> *Amuser, divertir*: pour affirmer, contre les 'furies de l'opinion' la primauté du biologique sur la politique et l'Histoire et annoncer la dissolution prochaine du 'sang dominé' dans le 'sang dominant', le raciste impénitent chercherait peut-être à esquiver par des manœuvres de diversion l'hostilité possible du public à l'égard d'une prophétie qui vient aujourd'hui, par trop à contre-courant. D'où l'oscillation, d'un bout à l'autre du texte, d'une part entre ces allées et venues de 'fourmi' qui seraient destinées à *amuser* en limitant la vision pour ainsi dire au ras du sol—effet de perspective rapprochée, au niveau de la péripétie, qui masque la perspective historique en suspendant le lecteur au fil narratif, et, d'autre part, ces soi-disant "digressions" où "l'explication coup de poing" se camoufle tant bien que mal sous les dehors ambigus d'un radotage incoercible, certes moins *divertissant*.[59]

This analysis will only stand up to closer scrutiny, however, if it can be proven that there is a fundamental antinomy between the two textual levels of metanarrative and retrospective narrative. Whilst it is undeniable that the text of *Rigodon* does disturb at the same time as it entertains, this affective duality wells not so much from a fundamental antinomy between the metanarrative and the retrospective narrative—on the contrary, as will be shown, there is concordance between these two levels in all of the volumes of the trilogy—, however, as from a radical reassessment of the meaning of the verb 'amuser'. For if 'amuser' is to create a connective synthesis between text and reader through a reinvestment of desire into events of the past which converts History into *chronique*, *Chronos* into *aiôn*, then it is by nature molecular, anti-molar, and must cast off all of those dissimulating mechanisms which attempt to overcode in an almost infinite variety of ways the one ineluctable truth of the human condition.[60] As is made clear in the following lines, lucidity and instinctuality are accessible to man only when life is positively invested with death:

> rien ne vaut que d'être soi-même condamné à mort, pour que presque plus rien vous gêne... (*CA*, p.95).

> dans les conditions très sensibles que vous y êtes total de votre vie, et pas au «pour», illico sonnant!... vous avez l'intuition directe, vous savez avant que tout arrive, implacable, que c'est pour vous pas pour un autre... la certitude animale... la connerie de l'homme dialectise tout, brouillaminise... (*CA*, p.96)[61]

If the emotive aesthetic aims to 'amuser', then, it will necessarily entail something 'moins divertissant', since the reader's capacity for *jouissance* will depend solely on a *petite mort*.

Becoming-death

Rejecting all of those molar techniques invented as a futile attempt to postpone death *ad infinitum*, *Mort à crédit*, the narrator Céline inevitably problematises the role of the protagonist Céline/Destouches. For the lucidity of the former contravenes the fundamental ethos of the latter whose very *raison d'être*, being a medical doctor, should be to aid in the prolonging of life, the suspension of man's *pourriture*. For as long as the protagonist Céline/Destouches remains unwilling to abandon the Hippocratic oath, then—and this will be the case for the first two volumes of the trilogy—, he will be a hypocrite, an implicit accomplice to that which he detests. Indeed, how else could one describe a medical practitioner who informs his patients of a health problem only when it suits him, and who carries on practising medicine against his better judgement?:

> En attendant j'ai plus de «Pachon»... je me suis fait prêter un Pachon pour liquider les ennuyeux, pas mieux!... vous les faites asseoir, vous leur prenez leur «tension»... comme ils bouffent trop, boivent trop, fument trop, c'est rare qu'ils se tapent pas leur 22... 23... *maxima*... la vie pour eux c'est un pneu... que de leur *maxima* qu'ils ont peur... l'éclatement! la mort!... 25!... là, ils s'arrêtent d'être loustics! sceptiques! vous leur annoncez leur 23!... vous les revoyez plus! ce regard qu'ils vous jettent en partant! la haine!... le sadique assassin que vous êtes! «au revoir! au revoir!»
>
> Bon!... moi toujours avec mon Pachon je prends soin des amis... ils venaient pour se marrer de ma misère... 22!... 23! je les revois plus!... mais tout résumé, sans broderie, je voudrais bien ne plus pratiquer... (*CA*, p.4)

Further aiding molar dissimulation by prescribing pills he knows serve no purpose ('ils voient rien!... ils nient, ils fument, ils rotent, ils sont tout goguenards satisfaits, à peu près certains de vivre cent ans grâce à de ces petites pilules! Madame!... et ces super-gouttes *Mirador!...*' (*CA*, p.16)), handing out alcohol, cigarettes and culinary delicacies from Harras' cupboard as though there were no tomorrow, the Dr. Céline/Destouches of *D'un château l'autre* and *Nord* panders to molarity—just as the narrator Céline's antagonistic reactions have been seen to do in the metanarratives. The retrospective narrative can thus be considered as a symbolic representation of the struggle to attain a pure aesthetic recounted in the metanarrative, the way in which, in attempting to bypass molarity by pacifying it, the narrator only succeeds in further hindering his passage to that aesthetic, his actions being diametrically opposed to those prescribed by its allegorical embodiment:

> Je les vois venir… entendu… ils sont! Madeleine, Schweitzer et l'Abbé, je les reçois… oh, pas du tout méthode Caron… je leur redéfoncerais pas le couvercle! je les ferais pas re-re-remourir! non!… vous allez voir moi! tout le contraire!… tout douceur!…. tendresse thébaïque!… morphine 2 c.c.!… que bigre!… (*CA*, pp.99–100)

The prologue to *Rigodon*, however, presents a new kind of doctor, as the narrator Céline, in a delirious bout of paludism, has a vision of his old colleague, Vaudremer. It is this figure who will serve as an example for the protagonist Céline/Destouches as he, in the retrospective narrative, attempts to follow the same trajectory as that of the metanarrative towards a pure aesthetic, for Vaudremer is a doctor who prescribes medicines intended to accelerate rather than suspend his patients' decomposition, who prefers to liberate man's biological fluxes than to contain them:

> Il ne bouge pas… je vois pas sa figure… mais! c'est lui… nous consultions là-bas ensemble… lui médecin-chef… il se faisait drôlement insulter d'une baraque l'autre… l'esprit était détestable… tous les ménages se plaignaient qu'ils avaient froid, qu'ils avaient faim, qu'ils avaient soif, tout le personnel S.N.C.A.S.O., campé en baraques Adrian! ouvriers, maîtrise, ingénieurs, et les infirmiers… que c'était la honte!… que nous médecins étions criminels, ennemis du peuple, réactionnaires, que nous avions tout préparé, les *stukas*, la cinquième colonne, le trust des denrées, que les pauvres gens meurent de faim et d'épidémies.. que nos soi-disant médicaments étaient bel et bien des poisons… la preuve que personne pouvait plus aller aux gogs (trois enfants noyés) tellement les feuillées débordaient, que c'était la brune inondation, par les coliques, pisseries, dues à nos soi-disant remèdes… que la diarrhée générale submergerait tout… que les boches de Saint-Jean-d'Angély avaient leur tactique, tous leurs tanks en position pour nous refouler tous dans la merde qu'on meure tous, bouge plus, sous au moins un mètre d'excrément, si on faisait mine d'échapper… (*R*, pp.722–723)

Vaudremer, then, serves to illustrate the new bidding of the protagonist Céline/Destouches of the retrospective narrative—the similarities between them and the use of the first person plural indicate that this is so—, which, in turn, brings the retrospective narrative into harmony with the metanarrative.[62] For Vaudremer serves not only as an indication of the protagonist's new role, he also illustrates the dual affectivity of the Célinian aesthetic intended to 'amuser', and it is fitting, therefore, that he should be described in such a way that he becomes the resurrected Mille-Pattes of *Guignol's band*, the first fictional embodiment of the 'métro émotif'.[63] These similarities between Vaudremer and Mille-Pattes can be easily observed in the following passages:

> en tout cas dans le coin là, quelqu'un... je vais pas y aller... je tremble et transpire... quelqu'un?... quelque chose?... assez à faire!... l'esprit demeure, remarquez... je considère... oui! mieux! *verdâtre ce quelqu'un, assis... une lumière de ver luisant...* j'ai bien fait d'attendre... ces apparitions ne durent pas... je le vois maintenant presque... c'est un militaire... il vient me parler? qu'il parle... j'attends... il parle pas, il bouge pas... assis... *verdâtre...*
>
> «Alors?... alors?»
>
> Je questionne... je tremble... Oh! il me fait peur!... bigre mais c'est lui!... je le connais... je le connais! là, *verdâtre... luisant... plus ou moins...*
>
> «Vaudremer!»
>
> Je l'appelle!... il répond rien... il est là pourquoi? pour Noël?... comme le ratichon?... il est passé par la grille?... à travers?... *les chiens n'ont pas aboyé...* bizarre frasque!... ce Vaudremer je l'ai connu médecin quatre galons... c'était où?... vous pensez un peu la mémoire dans mon état de fièvre, sudations, saccades de tout le page... j'ai le droit de pas être sûr... surtout qu'il ne m'aidait pas du tout... je hausse le ton... je me force, vous remarquez...
>
> «Vaudremer! *semi-lumineux!...* je vous somme!... qu'est-ce que vous me voulez?... vous êtes là?... oui?... non?... revenant d'où?...»
>
> Il ne bouge pas... *je vois pas sa figure...* mais! c'est lui... (*R*, p.722; my italics)

> Je n'ai jamais revu Vaudremer... pourtant n'est-ce pas c'était bien lui, il était là, assis, ne disant mot... *et fluorescent*!... je vais l'interpeller à la fin!... non!... je ne peux pas... une chose, j'oublie!... je vous ai dit je m'embarquais avec joie pour *Londres*... vous direz il nous affirme ça pour les besoins de la circonstance, pour avoir l'air résistant... que non! mais non! j'ai des raisons et pas d'hier, d'être anglophile... bien plus que ceux qui y ont été! je pense à ce général qui m'offrait... *je pense à ce fantôme de Vaudremer là, fluorescent, assis... enfin l'espèce de fantôme... et je sais que je m'en vais... oh pas n'importe où*!... ici même l'espèce de Vaudremer s'éteint... (*R*, p.724; my italics)

In saying that it is only in *Rigodon* that the retrospective narrative and the metanarrative achieve this harmonious relationship, it should not be thought that in the first two volumes of the trilogy the two levels are mutually exclusive. On the contrary, the progression of the protagonists in the retrospective narratives of *D'un château l'autre* and *Nord* mirrors this study's analysis of the (non-) progression of the metanarrative's foiled attempts to escape the mechanisms of reterritorialisation that constantly ground the poetic expression tending towards polyphony/a becoming-imperceptible in a monologic metaphysics of presence. To put this simply, the geographical spaces and trajectories described in the retrospective narratives of all three volumes mirror the textual space created by the metanarrative—and, more generally, the narration—, but it is only in *Rigodon* that the geographical spaces described in the retrospective narrative will coincide with the schizophrenic/nomadic space sought after by the Célinian aesthetic, with the result that the stylistic problematic posed in the (metafictional) thematic level is resolved by the novel's very style. As Philip Stephen Day observes, '*D'un château l'autre* donne l'idée d'un mouvement compris quelque part entre des lieux; *Nord* est un lieu, mais dans le vide et sans mouvement; tandis que *Rigodon* est un mouvement dans le vide sans lieu'.[64] In other words, the space in which the protagonists of *D'un château l'autre* find themselves is a sedentary space, the trajectory being subordinated to the points—as is indicated by the ellipsis formed by the omission of the preposition of place in the title—,[65] just as, in the metanarrative, the poetic expression is inevitably subordinated to the strata of History; likewise, in *Nord*, the protagonists' movements take place within a strictly delimited boundary defined by the radius around a stable, regimented centre, just as the narrator, in the metanarrative, seems constrained by the expectations of his era, whilst in *Rigodon* there comes a nomadic trajectory taking place not exactly, 'dans le vide', but in smooth space, that space in which the points are subordinated to the trajectory, and which is defined only by the trajectory passing through it.[66]

It should, of course, come as no surprise that events from the *récit* can be seen to have metanarratival symbolic significance, for, as has already been pointed out, it is La Vigue's presence that prevents the narrator from embarking upon Caron's boat, from attaining a pure life-affirming poetic expression invested with death that cannot be reterritorialised by the centripetal forces of molarity. This event, however, although explicitly more narratival than metanarratival, is situated in the narrative present, so it is perhaps natural that it should have such symbolic importance. A textual analysis of the retrospective narratives of all three volumes of the trilogy, however, will reveal that, in addition to the customary transposition of History and deformation of biography taking place, the texts once again provide the possibility for a metafictional reading in which the events taking place in the *récit* proper have symbolic import for the very production of the work, which is itself recounted in the metanarrative and is governed, therefore, according to a schizophrenic conception of style.

Before passing to a textual analysis of the retrospective narratives in which will be highlighted their metafictionality, however, it will be useful briefly to examine precisely how the texts describe the aesthetic whose creation is to be recounted (metafictionally) in their retrospective narratives. A clue as to the construction of the new aesthetic to be attempted in the retrospective narrative of *D'un château l'autre*, comes in the narrator's delirious episode following his quayside experiences with Caron and La Vigue:

> Voilà!... voilà!... je batifole! je vise l'effet! je vais vous perdre... [i] et le pansement de Mme Niçois?... où ai-je la tête? ce qu'il me reste de nénette!... la fièvre! la fièvre, entendu!... mais le pansement de Mme Niçois la nuit!... tout à la nuit!... grelotte! grelotte! mais que s'effondre ce foutu page! je le branle assez! craque!... je dis!... je le secoue de paludisme!... [vi] plein accès!... la colère avec!... [ii] et ce qu'ils m'ont dit, hurlé d'en bas!... «glaïeul!» de leur pourri bateau de voyous!... ils ont osé!... «trouillard!» aussi! et «viens-y-donc!» bien sûr, j'irai!... dix fois plutôt qu'une!... et tout seul!... ils me reverront!... l'indignation que je bouille! [iii] je me sens en fusion!... [vii] je le brûlerai ce page! [vi] j'ai attrapé la «fusion» au Cameroun 1917!... ils verront voir ce qu'ils verront! je prends mon pouls!... la fièvre monte encore! à 40° je rassemblerai!... le moment des idées!... blablafouilleries?... peut-être?... [iv] je m'emmêle... mêle... le Bas-Meudon... Siegmaringen... oui!... [v] (CA, pp.91–92)

L'effet visé by the narrator, then, will be to lose the reader [i] through a process of becoming-imperceptible by internalising the molar enmity that prevented him access to his own aesthetic (Caron's boat) [ii], this, in turn, making possible his passage towards that pure aesthetic [iii] which will operate by reinvesting History with desire/delirium [iv], juxtaposing contiguous events to disrupt *Chronos* and relive the past in terms of an *aiônic* temporality [v]. The aesthetic constructed according to these means will be capable of exceeding the boundaries of the written text [vi] —the deliberate and repeated use of the slang term 'page' for 'lit', which itself occurs a number of times in the conjugation of the verb 'lire', invites this metatextual reading—, indeed, it will be its *raison d'être* to do so, for it is only by so doing that the text will be able to transmit its aesthetic directly to the reader [vii], thereby avoiding the threat of reterritorialisation which occurs when the reader objectifies the aesthetic experience, converting the text from a poetic expression into a concrete artefact overcodable in terms of its Historical author. To summarise, then, the pure aesthetic sought will be an instance of schizophrenic desiring-production whose very existence deterritorialises the strata of molarity, for it will create a smooth textual space which, by definition, does not emanate from a stable narrating centre, and which exceeds its own boundary with every move: 'Je voudrais que le lit croule!... que j'y ouvre une brèche! une voie d'eau!... que je m'enfonce avec sous les ondes! je transpire... ruisselle' (*CA*, p.92).

As the above passage itself illustrates, all of the volumes of the trilogy will contain elements of this pure aesthetic which "amuses" by investing the dead with life and vice versa ('je vous amuse, je sors plus des défunts!... où je me tourne... défunts!... défunts!...' (*CA*, p.92)), but it will not be until *Rigodon* that this aesthetic finds the means to sustain itself throughout the work. It is this movement towards that moment—which itself will signal the dissolution and becoming-imperceptible of the text—that is recounted in the retrospective narratives of the trilogy.

The Retrospective Narratives

D'un château l'autre

It has been suggested that all movement in *D'un château l'autre* is governed by the principle according to which a trajectory in striated space, being a line drawn 'entre deux lieux', is always subordinated to its points and is itself, therefore, effectively annulled, a movement encapsulated by the symbol of the castle at Siegmaringen, as analysed by Luc Rasson: 'Paradoxe enfin de l'édifice fortifié inséré dans un cycle romanesque qui ne désigne que les flux que met en circulation la guerre'.[67] This principle of movement, although ultimately rejecting the trajectory in favour of its illusory stable points, nonetheless allows for an intuition of the ideal trajectory—as is illustrated in the metanarrative by the narrator's vision of Caron's boat (the embodiment of the pure aesthetic/trajectory) and his subsequent failure to embark upon it—, a movement which can equally be said to describe the retrospective narrative of *D'un château l'autre*. For the protagonist Céline/Destouches may repeatedly intuit the authentic path to an instinctive, animalistic mode of expression, he may repeatedly find himself in situations overflowing with unbridled fluxes, and yet, unwilling to abandon entirely the illusory stability of those molar forces he is attempting to assuage, his actions ultimately go against the grain of desire, rejecting a schizophrenic mode of organisation in favour of pre-defined paranoiac structures.

The main protagonist of *D'un château l'autre* often dwells jealously on the question of animal and female intuition, yet seems woefully incapable of accessing this mode of existence which does not rely on the strict hierarchical orderliness of molarity:[68]

> D'un tournant l'autre, je me paumais!... je vous le dis, j'avoue... Lili ou Bébert me retrouvaient... les femmes ont l'instinct des dédales, des torts et travers, elles s'y retrouvent... le sens animal!... c'est l'ordre qui les interloque... l'absurde leur va... le biscornu leur est normal!... la Mode!... pour les chats: greniers, tohus-bohus, vieilles granges... les demeures en «Contes fantastiques», les attirent, irrésistible... où nous nous avons rien à foutre!... l'Embryogénie leur drôlerie, pirouettes, virevoltes de gamètes... la perversité des atomes... les bêtes, pareil!... tenez Bébert!... il me faisait «coucou» par les lucarnes... *brrt!... brrt!...* la niche!... je le voyais plus!... il se foutait de moi!... les chats, enfants, dames, sont d'un monde à eux... Lili allait où elle voulait dans tout l'Hohenzollern-Château... d'un dédale de couloirs à l'autre... du beffroi de tout en l'air, des cloches, à la salle d'armes, à fleur du fleuve... un itinéraire que d'instinct!... à la raison, vous travioliez tout!... (*CA*, pp.111–112)

Unable to orientate himself in non-molar spaces, the narrator of *D'un château l'autre* is equally unable to operate outside of a molar linguistic system. Consequently, his every utterance must pass through an intellectual process of objectification that kills desire, the expression functioning according to a synthesis which is conjunctive—passing through a system external to the expression itself—and not connective, as can be the case for women and animals. Céline writes,

> La tête est une espèce d'usine qui marche pas très bien comme on veut... pensez! deux mille milliards de neurones absolument en plein mystère... vous voilà frais! neurones livrés à eux-mêmes! le moindre accès, votre crâne vous bat la campagne, vous rattrapez plus une idée!... vous avez honte... moi là comme je suis, sur le flanc, je voudrais vous parler encore... tableaux, blasons, coulisses, tentures!... mais je ne sais plus... je retrouve plus! la tête me

> tourne... oh, mais attendez!... je vous retrouverai!... vous et mon Château... et ma tête!... plus tard... plus tard... je me souviens d'un mot!... j'ai dit!... le sens animal! de Bébert!... je retrouve le fil!... Bébert notre chat... ah, m'y revoici!... que Bébert était comme chez lui dans l'immense Château du haut des tourelles aux caves... ils se rencontraient Lili lui d'un couloir l'autre... ils se parlaient pas... ils avaient l'air s'être jamais vus... chacun pour soi! les ondes animales sont de sorte, un quart de milli à côté, vous êtes plus vous... vous existez plus... un autre monde!... le même mystère avec Bessy, ma chienne, plus tard, dans les bois, au Danemark... elle foutait le camp... je l'appelais... vas-y!... elle entendait pas!... elle était en fugue... et c'est tout!... elle passait nous frôlait tout contre... dix fois!... vingt fois!... une flèche!... et à la charge autour des arbres!... si vite vous lui voyiez plus les pattes! bolide! ce qu'elle pouvait de vitesse!... je pouvais l'appeler! j'existais plus!... (*CA*, p.114)

And later,

> ce qu'est beau dans le monde animal c'est qu'ils savent sans se dire, tout et tout!... et de très loin! à vitesse-lumière!... nous avec la tête pleine de mots, effrayant le mal qu'on se donne pour s'emberlifiquer en pire! plus rien savoir!... tout barafouiller, rien saisir!... si on se l'agite! la grosse nénette!... dégueule!... peut plus!... plus rien passe!... pas un milli d'onde!... tout nous frise!... file!... (*CA*, p.128)

The protagonist Céline/Destouches, like the narrator Céline, then, intuits the possibility of a mode of communication 'capable de passer direct dans l'émotion!... par l'émotion!' (*EY*, p.536), by means of a becoming-woman/becoming-animal, that minor linguistic usage in which, as Deleuze and Guattari write,

> Il n'y a plus sens propre ni sens figuré, mais distribution d'états dans l'éventail du mot. La chose et les autres choses ne sont plus que des intensités parcourues par les sons ou les mots déterritorialisés suivant leur ligne de fuite. Il ne s'agit pas d'une ressemblance entre le comportement d'un animal et celui de l'homme, encore moins d'un jeu de mots. Il n'y a plus ni homme ni animal, puisque chacun déterritorialise l'autre, dans une conjonction de flux, dans un continuum d'intensités réversible. Il s'agit d'un devenir qui comprend au contraire le maximum de différence comme différence d'intensité, franchissement d'un seuil, hausse ou chute, baisse ou érection, accent de mot. [...] Faire vibrer des séquences, ouvrir le mot sur des intensités intérieures inouïes, bref un *usage intensif* asignifiant de la langue.[69]

But just as a becoming-imperceptible eluded the narrator in the metanarrative of *D'un château l'autre*, so the protagonist Céline/Destouches—as can be seen in the above quotations—fails to become-Bébert/Lili, and thus to attain this intensive usage of language.

It is not only through a becoming-Bébert/becoming-Lili that the protagonist Céline/Destouches has the opportunity to access a mode of communication which operates not according to a molar representational/signifying system, however; he witnesses other scenes of unbridled fluxes and non-verbal communication, yet always remains removed from them, colluding with molarity in order to bring about the end of such behaviour. In a very significant inversion of the Vaudremer scene from the prologue to *Rigodon*, for instance, the protagonist Céline/Destouches of *D'un château l'autre* enlists the help of von Raumnitz, his wife Aïcha and their dogs,[70] to reterritorialise—in 'le 36', the only striated space in the smooth space of the *Löwen*—the young drunk Germans whose free-flowing biological fluxes inundate the corridors of the *Löwen* and who, their desire unrestrained, bay for sex and blood from, respectively, two young female opera singers and a madman pretending to be a surgeon:

> les jeunes [...] bien plus déchaînés que nous du *Löwen*... d'abord le *Stam* en bas, la bière... et hop on monte pisser, et la colique! casser la porte et les verrous, s'enfourner aux gogs!... à six... dix... casser la lunette!... la sonnette!... emporter la couronne, le siège!... victoire! victoire! de vive force!... repisser compisser encore plein le vestibule, l'escalier!... que tout déborde! mais... ah, tenez-vous! à l'instant même en position! en plein la pisse! deux Allemandes s'épeluchent!... en position!... acharnées! reniflantes! retroussées comme ça! là... et hop! et toute la jeunesse autour! trépignante, folle de rigolade! ça bat plein des mains!... stimule!... et pisse avec! en peut plus!... deux très belles filles qui sont aux prises... des réfugiées de Dresde... la «ville des artistes»... de Dresde qu'elles venaient toutes les artistes... la ville-abri!... refuge des arts!... les deux là, embrasseuses terribles, chanteuses, d'Opéra, il paraît!... et devant les gogs et devant Frucht et devant tout le monde!... toute la cohue du palier... hurrah! ils hurlaient!... «hurrah Fraulein!» une brune et une rousse... l'orgie, c'était pas choisi comme endroit... je peux pas vous dire plus... aux prises, en plein étang de tout!... moi je voyais, c'était impossible que même je pousse la porte... la nôtre, le 11... ils sont je ne sais combien maintenant là-dedans autour de mon lit... autour du maboul et l'opéré dessous... dingues aussi, autour... qui stimulent!.... «vas-y! vas-y! coupe-z-y l'oreille!»... ceux-là c'est du sang qu'ils veulent! «vas-y! vas-y!»...
>
> [...]
>
> «Alors, Docteur? alors?
>
> —Je viens de la part de Brinon vous demander...

—Je sais… je sais… il me coupe la parole… vous avez un fou chez vous… et plein de fous encore plein le couloir… je sais!… Aïcha!… Aïcha!… veux-tu!»

Pas beaucoup le temps de réflexion…

Il lui passe un trousseau de clefs…

«Prends les chiens!…»

Les deux dogues… il fait signe aux dogues… un bond, ils sont aux pieds de sa femme… enfin, à sa botte!… elle porte bottes… bottes cuir rouge… elle fait cavalière orientale, toujours à tapoter ses bottes… et une très grosse cravache jaune…

«Allons Docteur!…»

J'ai plus qu'à la suivre… avec elle je sais que tout s'arrange… les dogues savent aussi… ils se mettent à grogner et ils montrent les crocs… crocs comme ça!… ils cessent pas de grogner… ils mordent pas!… ils suivent Madame dans les talons!… ils sont prêts à déchirer celui qu'elle fera signe… c'est tout!… oh, des bêtes dressées, admirable!… […] tous les dégoûtants se reculottent… les braillards pisseurs… tout refoule vers la rue… la brune et la rousse aussi, elles se rafistolent… et hop!… sautent!… stupre pas stupre!… les pires faunesses se touchent plus!… hurlent plus!… personne rugit plus de rien… même du supplice d'envie de caca!… chez moi… chez moi, ma porte, le 11, sitot entrevue Aïcha, panique! affolerie! ils nous renversent calter plus vite! ils se montent dessus, qui qui passera!… […] ils veulent tous passer à la fois… en même temps! oh, mais pardon ça va plus!… Aïcha a l'œil!… elle est langoureuse mais précise!… «stop! stop!» qu'elle fait… aux trois!… qu'ils bougent plus! qu'ils restent là!… pile! le dingue, l'infirmière, et l'hagard! tous là! sur place!… et le nez contre le mur!… elle leur montre!… bien debout! bien contre!… les dogues leur grognent fort aux fesses… les crocs, je vous ai dit!… il s'agit plus de remuer du tout!… ils remuent plus… tout le palier est dégagé et le grand couloir, ma chambre, plus personne!… le vide!… ah, les pisseurs qui se tenaient plus! et les deux artistes!… tout ces effrénés! clic et clac! un charme!… mais c'est pas tout!… Aïcha avait son idée… *Komm!* un coup, elle leur parle en allemand… aux trois, nez au mur… qu'ils viennent qu'ils la suivent!… je la suis aussi moi! je veux voir aussi… tout à l'autre bout du vestibule, un petit passage et puis deux marches… le 36!… […] c'était la seule chambre solide de tout le *Löwen*… comme fortifiée vous auriez dit, les murs béton, porte de fer, fenêtres à barreaux… pas petits barreaux! des «super-prison», je connais… toutes les autres piaules du *Löwen* étaient comme flottantes, ondulantes, jeux de briques et de fissures… tout débinait! les plâtras, le plafond, les lits, tout! pas un lit qu'avait ses quatre pieds!… trois, au plus! beaucoup, qu'un! (*CA*, pp.148–151)

It is also the protagonist Céline/Destouches who is sent by the von Raumnitzs to retrieve their adolescent—and thus, by definition, desiring ('l'âge enragé 14… 17… surtout les filles!…' (*CA*, p.154), 'elle ma foutue Hilda la garce, c'était que de fiévreuse puberté' (*CA*, p.159))—

daughter from the train station, a haven of non-verbal communication and desiring-production that Céline soon puts a stop to by pretending to be von Raumnitz himself:

> question Hilda, et sa bande, sûr, je les retrouvais à la gare!... fatal! espionnes, troubades, ministresses, gardes-barrières, mélimélo!... aux salles d'attente! l'attirance viande fraîche et trains de troupes, plus le piano et les «roulantes», vous représentez ces scènes d'orgies! un petit peu autre chose de bandant que les pauvres petites branlettes verbeuses des Dix-sept Magots et Neuilly!... il faut la faim et les phosphores pour que ça se donne et rute et sperme sans regarder! total aux anges! famine, cancers, blennorragies existent plus!... l'éternité plein la gare!... les avions croisant bien au-dessus!... tout bourrés de foudres! et que toute la salle et la buvette se passent entre-passent poux, gale, vérole et les amours! fillettes, sucettes, femmes enceintes, filles mères, grand-mères, tourlourous! toutes les armes, toutes les armées, des cinquante trains en attente... toute la buvette entonne en chœur! *Marlène! la! la! sol dièse!* à trois... quatre voix! passionnément! et enlacés!... (*CA*, p.155)

> moi l'instant, c'était pas la grande stratégie, c'était qu'Hilda rentre chez son père! je l'avais appelée vingt fois! Hilda! je pouvais y aller! le mieux, la résolution: les S.A.!... tout le monde à la route! vider les plates-formes, la buvette, les rails! après, on verrait! oh mais tout de suite ça se rebiffe! crie! «S.A., faites sortir tout le monde»! je vous ai raconté les S.A... de ces énormes armoires à muscles, et méchants butés, fronts de gorilles et des pristis de Mausers comme ça! modèle «canon de poche»!
>
> «Franzose? franzose?»
>
> Ils me demandent.
>
> «*Nein!... nein!* Obersturmführer von Raumnitz.» (*CA*, p.167)

By thus falsely appropriating a Fascist discourse not as a means to abjectify himself in a becoming-imperceptible, but as an egotistical defence against a perceived molar threat, however, the protagonist Céline/Destouches—like the monologic sections of the metanarrative—defeats his own purpose, for he ends up colluding with those very paranoiac, fascistic forces he intended to assuage, thus aggravating his own reterritorialisation:

> Tout de même là, buvettes et plates-formes, les S.A. forcent que ça déblaye! à la Marlène et d'autres chansons!... piano joue plus!... bureaucrates... grand-mères et troubades, bras dessus, bras dessous, puisqu'on les tarabuste! salut! monôme! et en ville!... et les ménagères fritz aussi! du bourg! qu'étaient venues elles voir en curieuses!... bras dessus bras dessous!... je me consolais: ça ira! j'avais l'Hilda et les copines!... les S.A. faisaient bien leur boulot, s'il y avait pas eu l'incident! mais tout d'un coup *ptaf!* je me dis:

> ils ont tiré! ça y est!... c'était les S.A., les douze, qui séparaient les femmes des hommes!... scindaient leur monôme! vous pensez! refoulaient les hommes vers la gare, les femmes vers le bourg!... là fatal! bang!... vlang!... les gamelles volent! je me dis: Ferdinand t'es cuit!... (*CA*, p.168)

The one episode of *D'un château l'autre* in which the protagonist Céline/Destouches does exist harmoniously in a truly molecular space, is the last of this volume, namely the train journey to and from the burial of Bichelonne. For at the start of the outbound journey towards Hohenlynchen, the ministers desperately try to retain those molar trappings which imbue their mission with the sense of importance and grandiosity that should accompany such an official delegation: they suffer the cold and hunger in silence, and take consolation in their map and compass—even though such instruments serve no purpose in the smooth space they are traversing, this landscape in which all stratification (including the rail tracks that may or may not be guiding their trajectory) has been obliterated by the snow—whenever they appear to be heading east rather than north (*CA*, pp.274–275). Such molar concerns are quickly abandoned, however, the lack of pomp and ceremony *en route* and the train driver's diffidence to them, debunking any delusions of grandeur they might have harboured, delusions which, furthermore, become less and less attractive the further north they travel, as the mercury in the thermometer drops lower and lower. Thus begins the debunking of molarity, for to keep warm the ministers wrap themselves in the finery that adorned their regal carriage, reducing both their own respectability and that of their regal carriage to rags (*CA*, p.275–276). As anti-molar as their actions may be, however, the delegates, at this point, remain in molarity, for they are united only in their opposition to an abject other, and justify their actions according to a facialising metaphysics of presence:

> ah, le Shah!... ornementeries Wilhelminiennes!... ah, turqueries! bazar arabe!... un autre Boukhara! merde, la revanche! puisque personne veut nous parler! «saloperies boches! bourreaux!... vampires! affameurs! cons!» voilà ce qui se crie, s'hurle! toute la Délégation d'obsèques absolument unanime! puisqu'ils veulent rien nous expliquer!... on leur en foutera du Guillaume! I! III! IV! où qu'ils nous mènent d'abord? et d'un! au Pôle Nord?... en Russie?... pas à Hohenlynchen du tout, ces salauds sont capables!... traîtres aux moelles!... en leur lacérant tout, on l'hurle! «boches! saxons! cochons!» arrachant tout, on s'est mis tout! on s'est formidablement recouverts! ah, les capitons! à nous, capitons! ils nous foutent rien à bouffer, ils le font exprès! les

> cahots aussi, exprès!... au moins que tout le wagon y passe! toutes leurs fanfreluches! (*CA*, pp.275–276)

Any remnant of molar grandeur that the delegates might have retained during the journey to Hohenlynchen, is soon stripped away by the farcical, humiliating sequence of events at the burial ceremony they have travelled so far to witness (*CA*, pp.289–281), and there thus arises the possibility of establishing a mode of unification which would operate according to connective, not conjunctive syntheses. It is precisely this kind of communication which is brought about by the hordes of children and pregnant women who invade their carriage in Berlin, rendering the delegates themselves as though non-existent, imperceptible: 'nos deux wagons s'arrêtent juste, d'autor on est envahis!... *on existe plus!* submergés sous mômes et rombières!... un flot, la façon qu'ils déversent, nous passent dessus, nous écrabouillent! écrasent...' (*CA*, p.282; my italics). These children and pregnant women care nothing for molar hierarchies or codes of behaviour, they are creatures of desire, interested only in eating, defecating, keeping warm, drinking beer and sleeping, so in order to survive amongst them, the delegates must do as their new travelling companions. In this task they succeed admirably, becoming as one with these beings of desire to the extent that they no longer resemble themselves at all:

> grâce à la Croix-Rouge, et ses mômes, et ses femmes enceintes, qu'on avait pu tenir!... ça valait une reconnaissance! sans les mômes et les femmes enceintes, et les caisses suédoises, amerloques, cubaines, on faisait bien tintin!... la preuve toute la Délégation ronflait, cahot pas cahot, gavés, entremêlés, sous les mômes et les femmes enceintes, réchauffés!... ils avaient plus de loques, les mômes avaient tout! mais pardon, ce qu'ils avaient boustiffé, pinté, depuis Berlin-Anhalt!... au moins cinquante caisses! et de tout!... et que du «très bon»! les mômes question des costumes leur avaient tout pris!... les avaient plumés, positif!... mousselines, velours, satins, et leurs vestons et pantalons!... ils s'étaient attifés pareil!... vous parlez d'un divertissement!... l'ouragan comme dévastation, cinquante mômes en boîte! si on était arrivés de jour, on aurait dû attendre la nuit, on pouvait pas se montrer tels quels, surtout les Ministres!... (*CA*, p.287)

This train journey, however, does not signal the end of the protagonist's quest for the North, nor, therefore, the narrator's quest for a pure aesthetic. For although this return journey may be an intuition of what is to come, it is still directed southbound, the protagonist Céline/

Destouches having failed to achieve what he had hoped on this voyage, namely, to procure for himself a passage to Denmark—the North incarnate—from Gebhardt (*CA*, p.290). So it is that the Ministers have to hide under cover of night in order to be able to resume their molar positions the following day, the children and pregnant women continue their journey alone, and Memel, the one pregnant woman who stays in Siegmaringen with the protagonist Céline/Destouches, remains, at the end of the novel *and like the novel itself*, only '*presque* «à terme»' (*CA*, p.291; my italics), not quite ready to bring her creation to fruition.[71] Memel's condition does not signal the failure of the Célinian aesthetic, then, but its postponement, the renewed promise of *féerie pour une autre fois*.[72]

Much the same thing is promised by the final metanarrative with which *D'un château l'autre* ends, as the narrator Céline's facialising diatribe is silenced by Mme Armandine, 'personnage vigoureux, souple, gai, et surtout pas prêt à mourir',[73] an exemplary figure who personifies all that the Célinian aesthetic ideal strives towards, but will not attain just yet, this being the end of the novel.

Nord

It might be expected that, with the title *Nord*, the second volume of Céline's trilogy would be that in which the narrator finally fulfils his aesthetic quest. Ultimately, however, *Nord* will progress no further than *D'un château l'autre*, for the north of *Nord* is not an end in itself, but merely an end towards which to aspire, a pole exerting a constant pull which will not be reached. It should not be thought that this Sisyphic movement signals the failure of the Célinian aesthetic, however. On the contrary, the disrupted Historical chronology according to which the events of *Nord* are anterior to those of *D'un château l'autre*, the first volume of the sequence, is, by the narrator's own admission in the following passages, a deliberate stylistic ploy:[74]

> m'en veuillez pas si je vous raconte tout en désordre... la fin avant le commencement!... belle histoire! la vérité seule importe!... vous vous y retrouverez! je m'y retrouve bien!... un peu de bonne volonté, c'est tout!... vous regardez un tableau moderne vous vous donnez un peu plus de mal!... (*N*, p.310)

> Vous n'avez pas à être surpris, lecteur... au moment de cet attentat les faits incidents quiproquos s'entremêlèrent, que maintenant encore vous vous retrouvez souvent en mésententes parallèles... conjurations contradictoires... le mieux je crois, imaginez une tapisserie, haut, bas, travers, tous les sujets à la fois et toutes les couleurs... tous les motifs!... tout sens dessus dessous!... prétendre vous les présenter à plat, debout, ou couchés, serait mentir... la vérité: plus aucun ordre en rien du tout à partir de cet attentat...
>
> Ils l'auraient tué, réussi, c'était un ordre! maintenant voyez où nous en sommes qu'il est échappé! entrés dans le désordre pour toujours!... donc trouvez assez naturel que je vous raconte l'hôtel Brenner, Baden-Baden, après le «*Löwen*», Sigmaringen... où nous ne fûmes que bien après!... faites votre possible pour vous retrouver!... le temps! l'espace! Chronique, comme je peux!... je dis!... peintres, musiciens, font ce qu'ils veulent!... d'autant fêtés, couverts de milliards et d'honneurs... cinémas, jeux de boules!... moi là, historique, il me serait dénié de coudre tout de traviole?... foudroyé suis lors?... Zabus!... folle honte!... me sauve en loques et lambeaux!... la meute aux chausses!... pitié à pendre!... je vous salue, Messieurs Mesdames... les jeux sont faits? tant pis!... larguez!... retrouvez-vous!... la roulette cahote?... bonne mine!... la boule dingue?... contrition!... sottise!... la faute de cet attentat mou!... (*N*, pp.318–319)

> pourvu que vous ne vous perdiez pas, avec mes façons d'avancer trop tôt... de plus savoir... sens dessus dessous... d'autres avatars en oublis!... *pflof!* cette titubation dans les heures, les personnes, les années... je crois, en fait, ce bric et broc, la conséquence des galopades et mauvais traitements... trop d'ébranlements... coup sur coup... (*N*, p.330)

This notion of movement without progress is fully in accordance with Day's analysis of *Nord* as, 'un lieu, mais dans le vide et sans mouvement',[75] and it is according to such a spatial itinerary that both the metanarratives and the retrospective narratives of *Nord* are governed.

Some of the metanarratival sections of *Nord* follow the same pattern and slip into the same kind of monologism as those of *D'un château l'autre* already analysed. Far more abundant in *Nord* than in the previous book, however, are comments expressing anxiety about the work's eventual reception, concerns as to whether or not the work in progress is in tune with its time. Here are but a few examples of such anxiety:

> les acheteurs me boudent, il paraît... ils n'aiment et n'achètent que les auteurs presque comme eux, avec juste en plus, le petit liseré à la couleur... chef-loufiat, chef torche-chose, lèche-machin, fuites, bénitiers, poteaux, bidets, couperets, enveloppes... que le lecteur se retrouve, se sente un semblable, un frère, bien compréhensif, prêt à tout... (*N*, p.303)

La classe 12 date, c'est entendu… mais je vais vous dire une bonne chose c'est de cent ans avant J.-C. qu'il faudrait être!... tout ce que nous racontons ennuie!... les pièces de théâtre, mêmes bâillements! et les cinés et télévises... calamité! ce que veulent populo et l'élite: du Cirque!... des mises à mort dégoulinantes!... des vrais râles, tortures, tripes plein l'arène!... plus de semi-bas de soie, faux nichons, soupirs et moustaches, Roméos, Camélias, Cocus... non!... du Stalingrad!... tombereaux de têtes coupées! héros, verges en bouche! qu'on revienne avec sa brouette d'yeux des grands festivals... plus de petit programme tranche dorée! du sérieux, du sanguinolent... plus de frimes pancraces «répétés», non!... le Cirque fera fermer tous les théâtres... la mode oubliée fera fureur... la trois cents ans avant Jésus! «enfin! enfin!» vous pensez le roman! je me dépêche!... la tenue de soirée est de rigueur? mais non! mais non! «la vivisection des blessés»!... voilà! tant d'art, des siècles de soi-disant chefs-d'œuvre pour rien! escroqueries! crimes! (*N*, p.304)

tous les auteurs vous le diront, qu'ont tant de mal que le trèpe arrive... à se faire applaudir par trois rangs d'orchestre... et n'est-ce pas après quels tapages!... partouses, placards à la une, *strip-tease* d'ouvreuses, pancraces de grooms!... nib!... vous pouvez rien faire venir qu'au sang, boyaux hors... à la vérité!... vivisection!... tripes plein le plateau!... l'agonie, voilà! qui qu'est pas gladiateur ennuie! et gladiateur éventré!... au spasme!... (*N*, p.402)

«Si il avait pas ses trois points, son style, qu'il dit, oh là! là! on le lirait peut-être un peu plus!... depuis le "Voyage" il est illisible!... le "Voyage" et encore! maintenant il est si abruti, il a l'air, que même à la Télévision, il est pas regardable, la preuve M. Petzareff vient de lui faire sauter, juste à temps, "une heure d'entretien"... c'était fait!... la France était encore perdue!... Juanovici est en prison, mais Petzareff, œil à la brèche, perd pas un geste des anti-tout!... et sans certificat d'études!... réseau "Honneurs, Bénéfices"...»

Ce sont là aimables propos... mais sur cette route de Moorsburg nous n'avons pas à giberner... (*N*, pp.563–564)

Là je voyais où j'en étais, presque à la page 2 500... à cet endroit où j'ai trois morts, trois assassinés, je dois dire... qui cela peut intéresser?

Juste Mlle Marie vient me voir, ma secrétaire... je lui demande ce qu'elle croit...

«Oh, vous savez... vos livres... depuis le *Voyage*...

—Le *Voyage* quoi?

—Vous ne pouvez plus attendre grand-chose...

—Que je n'attendrais rien du tout, je vous jure, Mademoiselle Marie, si ils ne m'avaient pas tout volé!... moi qui vis de si peu, qui tiens si peu de place, et ne demande à voir personne...

—Donc?

—J'irai finir sous un autre nom... dans un endroit où on ne va pas... dans les dunes, tenez... quelque part...» (*N*, pp.649–650)

> Oh, bien sûr je suis averti... combien de fois ils m'ont répété: vos livres ne se vendent plus!... d'ailleurs pas que vos livres, tous les livres! les gens n'achètent plus! ils ont n'est-ce pas les impôts! la télévision, les vacances, l'apéritif, plus la voiture, les assurances!... ils n'ont même plus le temps!... encore un plus, à vrai dire, on a jamais acheté de livres, on se les faisait prêter et on les gardait... on les volait chez des amis ou aux étalages... un sport! mais à présent, le golf, le strip-tease, les blousons! les têtes sont ailleurs! (*N*, p.650)

In this respect also, then, the work can be said to obey Day's spatial conception of the novel, for, by hypothesising about the wishes of a Historical readership, the narrator's expression wells not solely from an aesthetic imperative whose course would be determined only by the act of creation itself, but is, to a certain extent, constrained by a strictly delimited boundary defined by public taste and expectations. The apotheosis of this prostitution of the aesthetic comes with Roger's suggestion that the narrator Céline try his hand at comics, a new art form more likely to succeed at a time when the book buying public is as good as extinct:

> —Avez-vous pensé aux *comics*?»
> J'avoue j'étais mal au courant...
> «*Comics*, voyons!... plus important que la bombe d'atomes!... la sensa-super de l'époque!... Renaissance ah!... Quattrocento enfoncé! pfoui!... *comics! comics!* pas dix ans que tout sera aux *comics!*... sens unique!... Sorbonne, communales, normales!... y avez-vous pensé? (*N*, pp.507–508)

At first the narrator rejects this suggestion out of hand, realising that it is not by conforming to public taste in this way that he will be able to convey his aesthetic, for those who do still read will nonetheless persist in overcoding his expression regardless of its form:

> *Comics?... Comics?...* dessinateur?... je crois pas beaucoup... il trouvera pas... «revenants obligeants» ceux que je connais sont d'un hostile!... m'ont dénoncé de tous les côtés, acharnés la trouille!... question *comics*, je les ai connus dans ma jeunesse, et en sept couleurs... les *Belles Images* 0 fr. 10... à l'heure actuelle je vois pas beaucoup, même tout contractant mon histoire, comment elle pourrait un peu se vendre dans l'état des kiosques et des gares et des librairies, que tout ça dégueule d'invendus... que le public, si pressé, blasé, si alcoolique, si fatigué, veut plus rien lire, ni entendre, peut-être un petit truc pédé?... une pouponnière en folie? confidences de nurses roses ardentes?... alors là moi je me présente mal avec nos avatars aux flammes, phosphores, séismes... (*N*, pp.508–509)

And yet, later on in the text, frustrated at his consistent failure to deterritorialise his expression, the narrator seems to give the idea serious consideration:

> zut! un peu plus de patience, j'aurais pu parler à Nimier peut-être?... de son projet de *comics?* je me demande s'il y pense toujours?... sérieusement?... je me permettrai la prochaine fois... la prochaine fois, dans quelques années... de lui dire un mot... (*N*, p.654)

The metanarratives of *Nord* are thus primarily concerned with recounting the persistent temptation for the narrator to convert his emotive aesthetic (which must create and operate within smooth space) into a bastardised product for mass-consumption to be integrated into the strata of society (any mass consumable being a constituent part of the apparatus of capture in the civilised Capitalist machine), an artificial striated space in which free expression, or any non-predefined trajectory, is impossible, 'un lieu, mais dans le vide et sans mouvement'. To give in to this temptation, of course, would be to destroy rather than accomplish the desired aesthetic, for conformity to exigencies exterior to the work itself would abandon the tenets of the emotive aesthetic. Furthermore, the narrator, in his lucidity, knows that if he does deform his aesthetic, he will be doing so only for an audience who will never read his work, to please people who will never be pleased, to appeal to those whose opinion of Céline the author/collaborator/Fascist will never change.[76] Take the following examples in which the narrator's perception of the public awaiting him is made clear:

> un moment les complications s'enchevêtrent… tant de balourdises! vous seriez si hébété?… pas Dieu possible!… mais si!… que si!… vous osez plus rien vous demander, personne cherche à vous comprendre! lecteurs, spectateurs, vrai de vrai, exigent qu'une chose, qu'on vous suspende! et vite! haut, court! en quel style vous vous balancerez? compliquez pas les Écritures! le génie de cette Civilisation c'est d'avoir trouvé des raisons aux pires paranoïaques boucheries... le sens de l'Histoire!... *new look*, assurés sociaux sanguinolents, foies en marmelade, méninges en loques, sadiques fainéants motorisés, télévisés, ravis!... béats... et plus... et plus!.... un verre! deux!... roter! (*N*, pp.492–493)

> Roger est un homme tout de finesse, amitié, élégance de cœur et d'esprit… subtil, sensible, l'ambre!… en tant que felcher, loin de vouloir lui, la mort du rat, il fait tout pour le dépanner… vous pensez qu'une telle mansuétude est prise plutôt mal en haut lieu et qu'on en jase, et foutrement, à travers

rédactions, loges, radios, sacristies, librairies de choc... il a pas fini d'en entendre, felcher sans conscience!... bamboula et tamtam des haines suis! y a qu'à me taper dessus que ça résonne! moustille, gambade, érecte fol! jacule, pâme! (*N*, p.506)

And yet, *Nord* is arguably that book of the trilogy which does give in to this temptation, which, regardless of the ambient tendency towards dissolution and disorder, does pander to the desire of a hostile public by attempting to imbue the *récit* with as much order, coherence and humour as possible.[77] For, in spite of the explicit avowal that the conditions in which the events of the *récit* take place are such that no order (and, by the very nature of those events, no humour) is possible, throughout the novel there is a concerted effort on the part of the narrator to guide and amuse the reader, not to disrupt the *récit* too often with comments from the narrative present and to justify such interruptions when they do come, as will be seen in these quotations:

quand je pense que je suis encore là à essayer de vous distraire!... que de très vaillants Européens en pourraient plus, poseraient la chique sous tant d'avanies, tels torrents d'outrages... (*N*, p.442)

je vois pour mon compte ce qu'ils m'ont gâté les uns comme les autres... toutim! tout squelette j'en parlerai encore, qu'ils sont foutus le camp en 40, qu'ils sont revenus pour me voler, me condamner à tout, et eux s'ériger des statues... passez muscade! jamais ils retourneront d'où ils sortent, gardes-charniers! je raconterai tout dans mes Mémoires...

«Où ça vos Mémoires?»

Attendez!... ceux qu'iront me les secouer, mille fois plus marles que mes voyous de la Butte, et de Saint-Malo Ille-et-Vilaine... pas peu dire!... je vous raconte ces tout petits riens!... j'ose!... je vous sais en sympathie!.... (*N*, p.451)

Tout ceci pour vous amuser, petits à-côtés... le seul récit de nos avatars peut vous paraître monotone... quand vous avez tant de choses à faire ou simplement à vous asseoir, boire... vedettes, télévisions, pancraces, chirurgie du cœur, des nichons, des entre-fesses, des chiens à deux têtes, l'Abbé et ses spasmes homicides, whisky et longues vies, les joies du volant, l'alcôve de la Grande-Duchesse, basculeuse de Trônes... que je vienne moi en plus vous demander de vous procurer mon pensum d'une façon d'une autre!... je vois mal!... arrive que pourra!... tant pis!... la suite! (*N*, p.454)

Mais je vous promène tort et travers, je me laisse entraîner moi aussi!... deviendrais-je jean-foutre?... présent, passé, je me permets tout!... si vieux, je me dis: zut! tant pis! je pourrai pas écrire toujours, si j'en omets?... Nimier me promettait l'autre jour: quand on vous passera en «comics» on vous coupera ceci!... cela!... «tout finira par la canaille!» Nietzsche... parbleu, nous y sommes!... connaissez-vous rien de plus voyou que la Télévision françoise? impossible?... pas un mercredi que ne surgisse un affreux quelconque incapable qui me plagie éhontément et qui hurle, culot! que je n'existe pas!...

Vous pensez, j'ai pas l'appareil, mais Lili l'a!

Bien!... que je vous reprenne au Brandebourg, où nous étions, devant la plaine... (*N*, p.580)

mais là-nous-mêmes?... où suis-je? où sommes?... la tête ébranlée... je vous perds encore!... certes quelques excuses, mais enfin... vous perdre est grave!... mon dernier lecteur, peut-être?... allons! allons! où nous étions! ne flânons plus!... d'autres soucis!... (*N*, p.654)[78]

The narrative is thus constructed so as deliberately to resist its instinctive tendency towards a dissipated, evanescent form, which would allow it to become truly emotive, and it is this very same movement which also provides the framework for the events of the *récit* itself. For the world in which the protagonists of *Nord* find themselves, is one in which all order, all stratification is being obliterated, not only because of the attempt on Hitler's life, but because of the war machine (described in the passages below) which has escaped the control of the State to revert to its natural nomadic, multiplicitous state, thereby becoming unstoppable:

Dans les très vieilles chroniques on appelle les guerres autrement: voyages des peuples... terme encore parfaitement exact, ainsi prenons juin 40 le peuple et les armées françaises ne firent qu'un voyage de Berg-op-Zoom aux Pyrénées... les derrières bien en cacas, peuple et armées... aux Pyrénées se rejoignirent, tous!... Fritz et François!... ne se battirent, burent, firent sisite, s'endormirent... voyage terminé!... (*N*, p.311)

de notre point de vue épidémique... plus rien virulait!... la vérité! la guerre par massacres, c'est une chose, elle fait du bruit, mais résout rien!... les microbes se désintéressent? pitié de vos pauvres bataillons! infinis conflits, eaux de boudins... même «l'atomique» je vous garantis, finira jamais sans microbes... le virus, du fond du silence, vous attaque la terrible armée, que vous avez plus un bonze debout, deux trois semaines, tous à dégueuler, fauchés! âmes, boyaux, bramer à la Paix! voilà du décisif, sérieux! ça, qu'ils attendaient à Lisbonne... comment cette affaire finirait?... napalm, gaz, soufre, méchantes foutaises! la vraie de vraie peste prenait plus! comment la nôtre allait finir, saleté, guerre de guerre, 44?... tous les virus millénaires faisaient faux bond! les maréchaux peuvent bien des choses, déchaîner foudres et cataclysmes, mais pas réveiller un microbe... les grands empereurs peuvent s'entendre, s'entr'offrir tellement de tonnes de viandes, troufions, tellement de villes, provinces, berceaux, hôpitaux, personnes déplacées, charniers, que c'est la nouveauté totale, nouvelles frimousses, nouvelles boucheries, mais la guerre arrête pas pour ça! microbes fainéants, guerre continue! millions et millions sous les armes, prêts à tout... milliards de puces inutiles! deux typhoïdes à Zagreb!... une varicelle à Chicago!... de quoi abattre bien des courages! même dans la vallée du Vardar, où pourtant depuis douze siècles aucun conquérant n'avait tenu, maintenant impeccable, pas un rat mort!... ni un comitadji fiévreux... l'humanité dans de beaux draps... pas les maréchaux, ni les diplomates, qui dictent la paix, les puces, et les rats... maintenant, zéro!... (*N*, pp.380–381)

The war machine raging in *Nord*, then, is of the kind analysed by Deleuze and Guattari, a nomadic assemblage that, having escaped the reterritorialising mechanisms of the State, turns to destroying that State and its various manifestations. Deleuze and Guattari write,

Bref, chaque fois que l'on confond l'irruption de la puissance de guerre avec la lignée de domination d'État, tout se brouille, et l'on ne peut plus comprendre la machine de guerre que sous les espèces du négatif, puisqu'on ne laisse rien subsister d'extérieur à l'État lui-même. Mais, replacée dans son milieu d'extériorité, la machine de guerre apparaît d'une autre espèce, d'une autre nature, d'une autre origine. On dirait qu'elle s'installe entre les deux têtes de l'État, entre les deux articulations, et qu'elle est nécessaire pour passer de l'une à l'autre. Mais justement, "entre" les deux, elle affirme dans l'instant, même éphémère, même fulgurant, son irréductibilité. *L'État n'a pas par lui-même de machine de guerre*; il se l'appropriera seulement sous forme d'institution militaire, et celle-ci ne cessera pas de lui poser des problèmes.[79]

And later,

C'est pourquoi, en repoussant la question, on demande si la guerre elle-même est l'objet de la machine de guerre. Ce n'est pas du tout évident. Dans la mesure où la guerre (avec ou sans bataille) se propose l'anéantissement ou la capitulation de forces ennemies, la machine de guerre n'a pas nécessairement pour objet la guerre [...]. Mais, plus généralement, nous avons vu que la machine de guerre était l'invention nomade, parce qu'elle était dans son essence l'élément constituant de l'espace lisse, de l'occupation de cet espace, du déplacement dans cet espace, et de la composition correspondante des hommes: c'est là son seul et véritable objet positif (*nomos*). Faire croître le désert, la steppe, non pas les dépeupler, bien au contraire. Si la guerre en découle nécessairement, c'est parce que la machine de guerre se heurte aux États et aux villes, comme aux forces (de striage) qui s'opposent à l'objet positif: dès lors, la machine de guerre a pour ennemi l'État, la ville, le phénomène étatique et urbain, et prend pour objectif de les anéantir. C'est là qu'elle devient guerre: anéantir les forces de l'État, détruire la forme-État.[80]

One need only turn to some of the descriptions of the various cities and buildings in *Nord* (and especially those dealing with Berlin) to see that the war machine that serves as a backdrop to all of the action taking place in the *récit*, is but such a creator of smooth space:

> Vraiment l'imposant édifice!... bien huit étages... mais quel état! des étages entiers s'en vont par les fenêtres... pendent... en ferrailles... camelotes, verreries... cascades... par lambeaux... aux coups de vent... je vois pas ce qu'ils peuvent avoir à vendre! nous profitons de la poussière... une rafale... et nous nous jetons dans l'intérieur!... les bombes ont fait une salade! vous voyez plus rien des rayons... ni des escaliers... vitrines... ascenseurs... tout ça en vrac mélimélo vers le sous-sol... (*N*, p.332)

> mais je connais le décor des façades, vous croyez qu'une rue existe, elle existe plus... tout son intérieur, poutres, briques, escaliers, lui pend par les fenêtres... ou se trouve en tas devant les portes... si vous voyez de loin, une certaine hauteur de briques, c'est tout le souvenir de l'immeuble.. vous acquérez l'habitude... le trottoir est plus qu'un petit boyau juste à passer pour une personne... entre le haut mur des ordures et les soi-disant maisons... là du «Thüringer» à cette rue Schinkel, au bout de deux minutes c'était plus que des bouts de devantures qui voguaient, s'effilochaient... et des persiennes... vous auriez ri! à chaque bourrasque, il vente beaucoup dans une ville qui n'a plus d'immeubles... (*N*, p.340)

Even when the action moves away form Berlin to Zornhof, the topographical backdrop to the protagonists' adventures is still nomadic, for the mock grandeur of Zornhof is set against the plains, a truly grand space being smooth and irreducible: 'Il nous fait faire le tour des massifs, du petit étang... en effet, Versailles, d'un côté, si on veut... le semi-grand escalier de marbre... avec deux lions de bronze... de l'autre côté, la plaine... la steppe, comme il dit... vraiment infiniment la plaine...' (*N*, p.404).[81]

This last quotation neatly surmises the uneasy antinomy of human existence in which order and grandeur are employed to dissimulate the human condition, order and grandeur which, in a world of accelerated deterritorialisation such as that described in *Nord*, can only appear futile and ridiculous. Hence the Berliners' 'ménage des bombardements' and their 'débris numérotés!...' (*N*, p.333), Doctor Pretorius' gravity-defying apartment (*N*, p.350) and his grandiose delusional visions outside the Chancellerie (*N*, pp.353–354), the pseudo-aristocratic pretensions of the families in Zornhof and Moorsburg, and the code of mistrust and untruth that all who live there abide by. Too lucid to conform to such a way of life, the protagonist Céline/Destouches does, nonetheless, seem content to comply with the molar structures he comes across in order to survive, to lead an easy life. All too often, however, he is prevented from doing so by his two instinctual travelling companions, Lili and Bébert. It is because of Bébert, for instance, that the main protagonists are turned away from the grand (although somewhat precarious) *Thüringer Hof*, and instead have to make do with the Zenith Hotel (*N*, pp.339–341)—a hotel which is, in reality, more hole than hotel.[82] Likewise, it is because of Lili and Bébert's 'manie de [...] s'en foutre que ce soit défendu, sortir coûte que coûte...' (*N*, p.375), that the protagonist Céline/Destouches is awoken from his contented slumber in Harras' underground bunkers at Grünwald, whilst Lili's instinctive reaction to von Simmer's threats against Bébert during a dinner party in Céline/Destouches' honour, endangers their integration into the Zornhof community (*N*, p.544).

Lili and Bébert, then, are that which prevent the group of main protagonists from taking the easiest option and slipping into a life of molarity. This is not to say, however, that the group (who, it should be remembered, constitute a symbolic narratival Trinity) automatically takes the obverse path to molecularity and a becoming-imperceptible, for the subjectivity beloved of humankind cannot be cast off easily. On the contrary, the possible dissolution of subjectivity is a terrifying prospect against which the unconscious pits a whole range of defence mechanisms. Hence, when faced with a multiplicity or any situation that threatens their dissolution, it is La Vigue—who is, in many respects, the very opposite of Lili, being petrified by animals (*N*, p.457)—who comes to the fore. When a German official refuses to believe that the photos given him do indeed belong to Céline/Destouches and company, for instance, La Vigue finds it outrageous that he has not been recognised (*N*, pp.335–336), whilst when a group of *Hitlerjügend* and an enraged crowd are on the verge of ripping them apart, it is La Vigue's fame which rescues them, as their new-found friend Picpus turns the crowd's feeling to their favour by explaining who La Vigue is (*N*, pp.362–365).

Superficially, then, La Vigue would appear to save the main protagonists from catastrophe; on a metanarratival level, however, his character can be seen to perform the same function as in *D'un château l'autre*, namely, to symbolise the territorialising infamy of the overcoded proper noun Céline that prevents the narrator's expression from attaining the pure emotive aesthetic sought. This territorialisation of the poetic expression can be seen most clearly in a similar incident later in the novel in which La Vigue's fame fails to have any effect upon another crowd and mass of *Hitlerjügend*, for, although the apparent danger is eventually averted with the help of Harras, the specificity of the details described as the narrator recalls the last such incident can but recall an important episode from *Guignol's band*:

> Et que ça y est!... nos canadiennes! le même coup qu'à Berlin, bien le trio de foutus saboteurs, recherchés par toutes les polices!... *au fait à Berlin sans Picpus nous y passions! sous le métro!* où il pouvait être à présent, Picpus?... lui avait reconnu La Vigue!... pas un seul de ces morveux pouvait reconnaître le grand acteur!... mais bon Dieu qu'ils nous accrochaient!... et qu'ils nous forçaient d'avancer!... à dix!... à vingt! garçons, filles, à nous trépigner... vers où? que j'avais beau leur hurler qu'on était de Zornhof!... de chez les von Leiden! où ils voulaient nous emmener?... au Poste?... (*N*, p.568; my italics)

Far from saving the protagonists led by Céline/Destouches, then, La Vigue's fame has, in fact, merely prevented the narrator's expression from achieving what Mille-Pattes did, to become the *métro émotif* and communicate via connective syntheses. Indeed, if one re-examines *Nord* retrospectively with this in mind, it can be seen that, throughout the novel, La Vigue serves only to reverse the general trend towards dissolution and a becoming-imperceptible, as is the case in the incident mentioned above, when a passport official refuses to believe that the photos they present are indeed of themselves. For La Vigue, this constitutes a terrible affront and insult to his pride and excessive vanity:

> «Pensez Monsieur! pas reconnaissable, moi!... moi!... ma photo sur tous les murs! toute l'Europe a ma photo! hélas! hélas!... et l'Amérique! cet ahuri ne me reconnaît pas! il sort d'où, je demande, ce crétin?... voilà leur police!... jolie clique d'emmerdeurs planqués!... il aurait mieux fait d'être dans le train, notre train!... moi j'étais dans le train, moi, Monsieur!... le dernier train de la gare de l'Est... regardez ma valise!» (*N*, p.336)

The protagonist Céline/Destouches, on the other hand, once away from the influence of La Vigue, admits that they no longer resemble themselves ('là, on a le temps... on se regarde... et regarde encore... Lili, moi, La Vigue, on a changé de tronches!...' (*N*, p.348)), even if he cannot quite get used to the idea:

> j'étais pas encore habitué à être identique et moi-même et cependant méconnaissable... plus tard je m'y suis fait, très bien fait, promener un double, un espèce de mort, un mort avec cannes et soucis... (*N*, p.349)

This physical dissolution of the protagonist Céline/Destouches is also conveyed by the steady deterioration of his health, especially his ability to walk and his increasing reliance on his walking sticks, but whereas for the protagonist Céline/Destouches himself this physical condition is merely an inevitable fact of the later years of life, the very idea of such decrepitude is anathema to La Vigue:

> «Tu peux plus marcher sans cannes?»
> Il me demande.
> «Si! je pourrais, mais je suis mieux avec!
> —Tu te vieillis!»
> Sa terreur lui, vioquir! vioquir!…
> «Mais dis donc fils, t'as dix ans de moins! tu verras un peu dans dix piges!…»
> Normal que je titube, lui droit comme un I… (*N*, pp.338–339)

By implying that Céline/Destouches should do away with his sticks, La Vigue can once again be seen to go against the general trend towards dissolution and a becoming-imperceptible, for the protagonist Céline/Destouches' physical condition is explicitly likened to that of the molar structures under attack by the nomadic war machine: 'là dans la rue je vois vraiment que j'ai besoin de cannes, je me ramassais tous les trois pas... *je suis comme les maisons... j'ondule...*' (*N*, p.347; my italics).

It should come as no surprise, then, that the protagonist Céline/Destouches and La Vigue grow apart, for La Vigue consistently attempts to explain his dissolution in terms of theatrical roles,[83] whilst the protagonist Céline/Destouches gives in gracefully to this process of becoming-animal/becoming-imperceptible with the result that he becomes unbearable for La Vigue:

> «Toi!... toi!... un rat!... un rat!...
> Tu déconnes La Vigue!... je suis pas un rat, je suis moi! je te dis de t'asseoir!... tu me fatigues!»
> Il est tout debout sur sa paillasse, il fait des gestes avec ses bras que je suis terrible que je l'épouvante! que je vais le bouffer! (*N*, p.574)

La Vigue's discourse, from this point in the novel, is essentially that of a madman, and it is thus through a kind of reverse pathologisation that La Vigue is definitively separated from Céline/Destouches. For whereas pathological discourse would normally be created by the forced internalisation of a molar model by an excessively molecular being, here, an excessively molar being—La Vigue—is rendered mad by the all-pervading molecularity, the nomadic war machine which is, appropriately, described in the most poetic language possible:

> C'est un peu moins bruyant là-bas, Berlin... mais toujours en lumière, aux nuages... rose d'incendies et jaune de soufre...
> «Ce que je suis heureux!...»
> Il répète...
> «Je t'ai dit, aux anges!... nous sommes bénis!...»
> Pour des mouettes, y en a!... par grands envols... et encore d'autres!... elles planent... s'abattent... les corbeaux se sauvent...
> «La Vigue tu vois une plaine comme ça... c'est infini!
> —Infini?
> —Non!... pas infini!... de la Somme à l'Oural!...»
> Je veux le faire réfléchir...
> «Oui! oui!... t'as raison!... mais Ferdine est-ce que t'es heureux?»
> Que ça qui le tracasse... le temps passe... (*N*, p.635)

In *Nord*, then, the way out of paranoia towards desire and true communication can only be attained by accepting and internalising the mechanisms of the nomadic war machine.[84] For those still pre-Œdipalisation, this poses no problem at all, indeed, to do so is instinctual:

> surtout des mômes russes je crois... qui nous connaissent... qui nous tirent la langue et nous appellent de tous les noms... sûrement des gros mots... et que ça rigole!... filles et garçons... chacun à présent porte une brique... et chacune... ils tombent les uns sur les autres... les briques avec!... et que ça se ramasse!... hop! et se bat, s'empoigne! *boum!... braoum!* même les tout-petits font *broum!...* imitent! font les bombes comme sur Berlin! là-bas! et *zzzz!* comme les avions!... aussi, ils savent!... *braoum!* et *zzzz!...* que tout culbute! mômes et les briques!... *zzz!* et en avant!... le plus fou rire, la bombe?... la brique?... l'âge où tout est drôle!... aucune importance... qu'une autre culbute! et *ptaf!* la gifle!... et *zzz* là-haut! l'avion qu'arrête pas!... la brique qui bascule... trop lourde!... on y va tous!... l'extirpe... du trou de neige... jamais tant ri!... *ptaf!* une autre beigne!... (*N*, pp.675–676)

For the Œdipalised, however, to do so risks pathology, as is the case for La Vigue:

> Je lui indique.
> «Par là Berlin!... t'entends? *broum!...* t'entends Berlin? ils pilonnent!
> —Ah c'est vrai, fils!... t'as raison!»
> Il répète comme moi: *braoum!*
> «Ils arrêtent pas!... tu te souviens! la Chancellerie?

> —Tu crois, vraiment?»
>
> C'est pas grave qu'il doute… de la Chancellerie et des bombes… ce qu'est grave c'est qu'il nous refasse son scandale… une fois ça avait passé, les gens d'ici le connaissaient… mais ailleurs?…
>
> «T'as qu'à faire *braoum!* La Vigue, c'est tout!… (*N*, pp.673–674)

With La Vigue reduced to an infantile, quasi-autistic state, however, the protagonist Céline/Destouches, who desires to be left alone above all else, requires a new example if he is ever to escape the stagnant and increasingly paranoid community of Zornhof. This example is provided by the German commanders Kracht, Harras and Göring, who are of the opinion that, 'les psychoses s'enveniment dans un lieu, s'évaporent ailleurs, en route… tel est parti assassin s'arrête au pont, pêche à la ligne.. pense désormais très calmenent!... autrement!...' (*N*, p.704). As proof of this theory, Harras cites the case of Nikolas, a free man who, due to the shock of confinement, was incited to murder:

> et Nikolas!... mon prisonnier Nikolas!... *oooah!...* vous savez je vous ai raconté... je l'avais donné au cul-de-jatte... il a jeté le cul-de-jatte au purin... son bon maître!... *oooah!* normal!... normal! inhibition, libération, choc!... vous savez!... choc en retour, normal! (*N*, p.693)

Believing that it is only stagnation that leads to this kind of homicidal behaviour, however, Harras rejects the disciplinary methods of the past, preferring what he terms a, 'philosophique accélérée!' (*N*, pp.690, 693), which essentially consists of mobilising people, of placing them on a trajectory in order to liberate them or, it might be said, deterritorialise them, for although all points on the trajectory are meticulously planned (just as the author Céline's prose is painstakingly crafted), it is the trajectory itself which forms the new territory.[85] It is in the interests of this 'philosophique accélérée' that the Kretzers and Tulff-Tcheppe are sent on a journey, even if (for the time being) it is only Cillie who is affected by the voyage ('la petite Cillie était pas gaie, je l'ai jamais vue gaie à la ferme, là y a de la joie!… voyage! elle nous fait encore des *heil!* toute seule! personne nous a répondu qu'elle…' (*N*, p.706)), and it is also thanks to this 'philosophique accélérée' that Göring grants the protagonist Céline/Destouchcs the visa necessary for his passage north. This being the end of *Nord*, however, that northbound journey will only come in *Rigodon*.

Rigodon

If it is indeed true that, spatially, '*Rigodon* est un mouvement dans le vide sans lieu',[86] if, in other words, *Rigodon* marks the point at which the Célinian aesthetic finally achieves its apogee, its expression becoming nomadic, a trajectory taking place in and defining in its very creation a smooth space, then it is only appropriate that the first event recounted in the retrospective narrative of *Rigodon* should tell of the separation of La Vigue from the protagonist Céline/Destouches and Lili. For La Vigue, the symbolic incarnation of the territorialising infamy accrued by the proper noun Céline, who has clung to the protagonist Céline/Destouches like a leech up until this point in the trilogy, preventing him from embarking upon Caron's boat and from heading north, must be got rid of if the Célinian expression is to be able to deterritorialise itself, and if the protagonist Céline/Destouches is to be able to travel north.[87] It is for this reason that the protagonist Céline/Destouches decides to leave La Vigue behind whilst Lili and himself—this being the first time that they act alone in the trilogy—[88] go to make plans for their eventual route north:

> Il me laisse décider... voilà, La Vigue lui, restera ici... avec Bébert... nous on ira à Warnemünde, voir... il nous attendra, pas plus de deux, trois jours... si vraiment le ferry marche encore?... si c'est possible d'embarquer?... *et en clandestins*? (*R*, p.733; my italics)

With La Vigue out of the way, then, the action of the retrospective narrative of *Rigodon* will once again mirror the progression of the narrative quest recounted in the metanarrative: for the latter, as has been suggested, actualises the latent phantasm of suicide present throughout Céline's career as he abjectifies himself to the point of imperceptibility, whilst the former will see the protagonist Céline/Destouches accomplishing the destiny of mankind: 'si l'homme a un destin, ce sera plutôt d'échapper au visage, défaire le visage et les visagéifications, devenir imperceptible, *devenir clandestin*'.[89]

The time for this becoming-clandestine/becoming-imperceptible does not come immediately in *Rigodon*, of course, as the narratival Trinity cannot embark upon the pure aesthetic—symbolised by the boats in Warnemünde harbour, the *Danemark* (the epitome of the Célinian north) and the boat with no name, only the number '149' (the page number of the manuscript?) (*R*, p.747)—[90] being incomplete, Bébert having been left with La Vigue. Once reunited with La Vigue, however, the protagonist Céline/Destouches does not revert to his old conformist ways, always taking the path of least resistance; on the contrary, so preoccupied is he by his eventual passage north that he grants little time to anything which threatens to ground him or distract him from that goal, as the following excerpts show:

> «Il ne vous a pas expliqué? technique nietzschéenne... l'Oberartz Haupt est nietzschéen... la sélection naturelle!... les forts survivent! le froid, la neige, la nudité, les fortifient... surtout les blessés!... les faibles succombent, on les enterre... technique de l'Oberartz Haupt, on vide les wagons, tous, on pose tous les corps à même la prairie... tels quels... on les laisse là... deux jours... trois jours... au froid, à la neige, tout nus... ceux qui peuvent se lever font l'effort... on les voit, même sur une jambe... ils vont vers Rostock... là on sépare!... ceux qui vont à l'hôpital, en chirurgie... et ceux qui restent aux terrassements... qui creusent les fosses... pour les morts, ceux qui ne bougent plus après deux... trois jours...»
>
> Proseïdon avait été médecin de service... à la prairie et aux fosses...
>
> «Il va vous y mettre peut-être?»
>
> Je comprenais qu'il y ait tant de main-d'œuvre, que j'aie vu tant de loqueteux autour des wagons... la méthode n'étais pas sotte... mais moi le Danemark mon intérêt! pas la sélection nietzschéenne... j'avais un but... qu'il me parle d'Haupt, de ses manies... et surtout si nous avions le droit d'aller voir la mer? (*R*, p.743)

> je pense à ce capitaine du Génie... à son message pour Lemmelrich... que j'irais lui dire dans l'oreille que sa fille patati! ta! ta! pas plus à ce Lemmelrich qu'au Pape! celui qui se tait pas, en tout et partout, est qu'un cabotin, vil quelque chose, député, bourrique, viande à fuir... bien!... (*R*, p.778)

> je lui prends le pouls... très tendu... temporales de même... il me fait penser à l'Hôtel-Dieu, Rennes... au père Follet, "au lit du malade"... le rite... la clinique... le père Leduc de Nantes... il vous monte des bouffées de souvenirs drôles et moins drôles, vous avez le choix, un petit instant, complaisant, un certain âge, vieillesse acquise... [...] je voudrais redescendre... sûrement la police va venir... je ne sais laquelle?... mais une!... fritz, russe, english?... peut-être deux!... je voudrais parler à Lili... pas à La Vigue!... rien à La Vigue!... (*R*, p.780)

The protagonist Céline/Destouches is right, of course, to want to distance himself from La Vigue, for at the same time as he is telling Lili of his intention not to do what Hoffmann has asked of him in order to avoid any further complications and not to attract attention to himself ('«Dis, Lili... tu parles que je vais pas chercher des relations autour de ce Rundstedt… s'il existe! si il va à cet enterrement… je vais pas pousser des "*Heil*"*!* comme le Pretorius de Berlin…[»]' (*R*, p.787)), La Vigue is busy doing the opposite, drawing attention to himself, revelling in his fame (*R*, pp.789–790), and jumping out in front of the procession from which the becoming-clandestine protagonist Céline/Destouches was trying to hide:

> je reste bien fixe debout contre la borne… un banc de motos!… *rrrrrt!*… une formation… là pas d'erreur!… je tourne un peu la tête… ce sont des gendarmes!… je vois, ils ont encore de l'essence… je vois aussi l'autre côté de la route… La Vigue et son admiratrice, tout de leur long dans l'herbe… ils me cherchent, ils me voient pas, debout contre ma borne… moi je les vois! et d'un coup là je vois quelque chose! La Vigue se lève… se secoue… sort de l'herbe, descend du trottoir… juste un gros peloton de motos… *rrrrrt!*… il passe, il profite… il saute au milieu de l'avenue!… je vous raconte exact… là il se campe!… comme ça!… le bras droit en l'air!… je me dis, ça y est!… il défie!… j'aurais dû rester pas remarqué, plaqué contre la borne… va foutre!… je bondis!… (*R*, p.792)

Although incarceration following this incident is averted thanks to Bébert (*R*, pp.794–795), it is obvious that the protagonist Céline/Destouches and La Vigue can stay together no longer, having grown apart irreconcilably. For whilst the protagonist Céline/Destouches has his eyes fixed on the north and is willing to undergo the process of de-individuation through "blackening" necessary for his goal ('ce qu'est bien dans la crasse, la poussière, c'est que vous remarquez plus… vos yeux sont faits… gens impeccables et à la mode… snobs, quel trou allez-vous?' (*R*, p.780), 'y a à rire comme nous sommes sales, gluants noirs!…' (*R*, p.770), 'nous serons tout noirs au terminus…' (*R*, p.799)),[91] La Vigue longs for the sunny climes of Rome and peaceful celebrity (a form of hyper-individuation) that faciality brings—hence his adoption of the Christ pose as he announces his departure (*R*, pp.801–802).[92]

This definitive break between La Vigue and the protagonist Céline/Destouches in the *récit*, of course, will necessarily have profound consequences for the narrative itself, signalling, as it does, the liberation of the narrator's expression through a process of becoming-imperceptible via self-abjectification (*noircissement*). It is only appropriate, then, that directly preceding this farewell scene comes the trilogy's most virulent and violently personal monologic diatribe, in which the narrator, who describes himself as 'si effacé […] miteux pacifique' (*R*, p.796), rants against 'le tænia' Sartre (*R*, pp.796–798), and reiterates his predictions concerning the extinction of the white race through a "blackening" of blood:

> «Non! biologiste! j'ai dit, c'est tout!... seule la biologie existe, le reste est blabla!... tout le reste!... je maintiens, au "Bal des Gametes", la grande ronde du monde, les noirs, les jaunes gagnent toujours!... les blancs sont toujours perdants, "fonds de teint", recouverts, effacés!... politiques, discours, fariboles!... qu'une vérité: biologique!... dans un demi-siècle, peut-être avant, la France sera jaune, noire sur les bords...
>
> —Les blancs?
>
> —Les blancs au folklore, strip-tease et pousse-pousse... (*R*, pp.797–798)

This passage follows the same pattern as the trilogy's previous diatribes in that, once more, a monologic discourse which constructs a metaphysics of presence is utilised only for the narrator's own self-abjectification in his becoming-imperceptible. Yet this passage differs considerably from its predecessors in one important regard, namely, in its explicit avowal of this fact. For upon further questioning, the narrator Céline seems to imply that it is through an intensification of the territorialising fluxes of molarity that he has escaped molarity itself, that it is by internalising and intensifying the madness attributed him that he has entered into a becoming-clandestine/imperceptible, his schizophrenic desiring-production—like himself—able to escape the reterritorialising paranoiac pole since almost evanescent:

> —On vous a dit que vous étiez dingue, Maître?
>
> —Dix fois par jour depuis trente ans!
>
> —Et pendu?
>
> —Il est trop tard, je tiendrais pas, je tomberais par morceaux!... (*R*, p.798)

La Vigue's departure, then, heralds a new start, for it is the moment in the trilogy when the narratival Trinity of Céline/Destouches, Lili and Bébert will finally travel directly north, and that moment when the Célinian aesthetic will come to its fruition, a becoming-(*petite*) music:

> tout de même ça faisait des mois que nous nous promenions, si j'ose dire... Est... Nord... et zigzag d'un aiguillage l'autre et voies coupées et tortillards et trains spéciaux... nous pourrions être un peu faits... pour le moins!... cependant j'avais à apprendre que nous n'en étions qu'au début... que nous aurions bien des surprises, encore... des comiques et des très sérieuses... même des musicales, je vous raconterai... (*R*, p.799)

Becoming-music

The becoming-imperceptible of the narrator—which is itself but a different intensity of a becoming-animal/becoming-woman/becoming-child—and the becoming-music of the Célinian aesthetic are, essentially, one and the same thing, 'l'expression musicale [étant] inséparable d'un devenir-femme, d'un devenir-enfant, d'un devenir-animal qui constituent son contenu'.[93] As the aesthetic enters into a becoming-music, then, there will no longer merely be concordance between the events of the retrospective narratives and the pattern of the metanarratives, there will be equivalence between them. For true to Céline's style which, as has been shown, is but a consistency, a mode of composition that operates according to a double movement of being and non-being, and in which, '*les qualités expressives ou matières d'expression entrent, les unes avec les autres, dans des rapports mobiles qui vont «exprimer» le rapport du territoire qu'elles tracent avec le milieu intérieur des impulsions, et avec le milieu extérieur des circonstances*',[94] the accomplishment of that style, the becoming-(*petite*) music of the poetic expression will necessarily entail the rejection of the punctual system according to which the narrative has, up until this point, been constructed, in favour of a multilinear system. As Deleuze and Guattari state,

> *Un système sera dit ponctuel* tant que les lignes y seront ainsi considérées comme des coordonnées, ou comme des liaisons localisables: par exemple, les systèmes d'arborescence, ou les systèmes molaires et mémoriels en général, sont ponctuels. La Mémoire a une organisation ponctuelle parce que tout présent renvoie à la fois à la ligne horizontale du *cours* du temps (cinématique), qui va d'un ancien présent à l'actuel, et à une ligne verticale de l'*ordre* du temps (stratigraphique), qui va du présent au passé ou à la représentation de l'ancien présent.[95]

Such is how the trilogy can be said to have been constructed up until this point, there being a definite temporal separation between the levels of narrative, as the narrator Céline recalls from the narrative present events from the past, the metanarratival interruptions being seen as distractions from the text's primary content, the *chronique*. Now deterritorialised, however, a becoming-music, such a mode of structuration becomes impossible, the diatribes of the metanarrative being an essential element of the becoming-music of the entire text ('Il faut dans l'état où je me trouve, et à mon âge, rien vous omettre... *je vous dois des comptes, tant pis si je digresse un peu!...*' (*R*, p.848; my italics)), and the text must thus be composed instead as a multilinear system:

> Tout se fait à la fois, dans un système multilinéaire: la ligne se libére [sic.] du point comme origine; la diagonale se libère de la verticale et de l'horizontale comme coordonnées; aussi bien la transversale se libère de la diagonale comme liaison localisable d'un point à un autre; bref, une ligne-bloc passe au milieu des sons, et pousse elle-même par son propre milieu non localisable. Le bloc sonore est *l'intermezzo*. Corps sans organes, anti-mémoire, qui passe à travers l'organisation musicale, et d'autant plus sonore.[96]

Composed as an anti-mnemonic multilinear system in which the levels of retrospective narrative and metanarrative become concomitant (neither being epistemologically prior to the other), the narrator will lose control over his own text—any degree of control or omniscience presupposing a fixed centre of narration—, for not only will events in the narrative present affect the narration of the past, but events from the retrospective narrative (which is, strictly speaking, no longer retrospective as the rules of stratigraphy no longer apply) will be able to affect the apparent centre of narration in the supposed narrative present. So it is that, just as the protagonist Céline/Destouches and Lili's line of flight is about to be reterritorialised ('ils nous insultaient... ils s'étaient relevés, couraient... ils cherchaient d'autres chariots comme nous, faire comme nous, traverser Hanovre... sûr, si on se magnait pas, qu'on se laisse rattraper... qu'ils nous agrafent ils nous finissent!... (*R*, p.822)), the protagonist Céline/Destouches is hit on the head by a brick—liberated from its molar structure as a result of the action of the war machine—, an incident which, in turn, confounds the two temporalities and disrupts the narrative capacities of the narrator Céline:

> À partir de cet instant, je vous préviens, ma chronique est un peu hachée, moi-même là qui ai vécu ce que je vous raconte, je m'y retrouve avec peine... je vous parlais de «comics» vous ne pourriez pas même en «comics» vous faire une idée de cette rupture, de fil, d'aiguille, et de personnages... du si brutal net événement... tel quel, hélas!... un de ces empapaoutages que subit plus rien n'exista... et que moi-même là vous racontant, vingt-cinq ans plus tard, j'ergote, je m'y retrouve mal... bric et broc! vous me pardonnerez...
>
> «Mais précisez!... bafouillez pas!»
>
> Certes! **figurez-vous qu'à ce moment nous nous rejoignîmes!...** les poursuivants en pleine colère et leurs quatre... cinq chariots bourrés!... et nous les fuyards... à cause d'un balcon, tombé au beau milieu de la rue, obstruant

> tout... d'une maison encore debout, pas entièrement, que la façade!... mais quel balcon! fer forgé!... je l'avais pas vue de loin cette maison... beaucoup dire: maison! la façade et les murs d'une cour... au moment juste je disais: ça y est nous sommes faits, ils nous dépècent!... *vlac!* une bombe!... pas une petite, une énorme à éclaboussures et *raoumb!*... une autre plus près... panique sans doute... chez nous, les nôtres, et chez les autres, les poursuivants... je dis: je crois... je ne sais pas, je suis forcé d'imaginer... je ne sais plus... défaillir? pas beaucoup mon genre, mais là endormi je dirais, un peu mal et du sang... au cou... je dégouline, oui, le sang du cerveau... non! du cervelet, je crois... enfin de la région, je précise... je peux dire, j'ai fait tout ce que j'ai pu pour rester lucide... j'ai encore pensé à Lili... et à Bébert... mais comme s'ils étaient partis ailleurs... déjà loin... moi aussi, encore plus loin... un autre côté! tout ce que je peux honnêtement me souvenir... de cette bombe aussi, tombée où? cette rue obstruée... ces fondrières et toute cette ferraille... y a bientôt vingt-sept ans... (*R*, pp.823–824; my emphasis in bold typeface)[97]

Far from destroying the narrative, however, it is this very incident, this internalisation of the war machine, which provides the necessary conditions for a becoming-imperceptible and thus acts as a catalyst for the production of the Célinian aesthetic, the true expression of his style. That it is this event which brings the Célinian aesthetic to its fruition, that brings about a dissolution of subjectivity in the narrator and awakens the text's music, intensifying, then, both his own and the text's schizophrenic intensity, is explicitly recognised by the following quotations:

> depuis le moment des briques, sauf que j'ai bien mal à la tête, je serais porté à rire!... et de tout... ainsi de cette plate-forme où nous sommes... et de la fraîcheur du matin... fraîcheur?... je suis modéré... il fait froid... mais je peux pas me plaindre!... «Lili j'ai la fièvre!... et toi?... et vous Felipe?» y a de la tremblote, je ne sais pas de qui, mais d'un de nous... pour mon cas y a du paludisme en plus de la circonstance... plus tard... un peu plus tard j'approfondirai... l'aspect clinique... mais... mais... cette plate-forme bouge!... oui!... je me disais... nous étions partis... sans du tout nous être aperçus... démarrés bel et bien!... nous roulions!... ah le paysage charmant!... enfin, un peu flou... je dirais: poétique... (*R*, p.831)

> ce coup de brique m'a pas arrangé... soit! mais nullement déprimé... du tout!... je dirais même, au contraire!... porté à une certaine gaieté!... un peu spéciale... ainsi les chaumières me semblent devenues assez artistes... des deux côtés du paysage... je dirais elles font tableaux, elles penchent et gondolent... surtout les cheminées... c'est une vision, c'est un style... oh, ma tête y est pour quelque chose certainement!... la brique.... (*R*, p.832)

> je me sentais moi-même je dirais «abstrait»... l'effet pas tellement de la fatigue, mais sûrement du choc, du coup de brique... (*R*, p.850)

This style, of course, will be characterised by a different mode of composition, a consistency that breaks with the strict temporal regimentation of *Chronos* to enter into the time of *aiôn*, 'le temps indéfini de l'événement', that temporality in which the 'confusion des lieux, des temps' promised in *Féerie pour une autre fois* (*F*I, p.15) will become possible, and lead to a total conflation of the two levels of narrative:

> Maintenant nous sommes devant Hambourg, nous allons chercher fortune... beaucoup dire!... du haut de ce remblai il nous arrive certains bruits... des explosions un peu sourdes... après les bombardements, des mines qui se décident... souvent après des délais de mois... d'années... «suspense» je devrais dire, «Modern-style»!... Mais notre Felipe?... je le voyais pas il était pas des fois reparti?... non! mais comme caché dans les replis d'une énorme bâche... mieux, il était dessous, je ne pouvais pas le voir... zut! je pense encore au tænia! je peux pas vous raconter dans l'ordre, voici! la brique et ma tête... Mais *alas too late poor Tænia!* vous m'excuserez!... si vous m'excusez pas tant pis! une petite fugue!... la première fois tout est tragique, la seconde fois tout est grotesque... *alas! alas!* je vous parlais de ces mines à retardement... c'était mieux d'envisager le pire... je suivais Felipe, sa bâche en paquet sur sa tête... les petits crétins avaient pas compris mon français mais ils demandaient pas mieux que de me suivre... tituber plutôt... buter... nous étions aussi crétins qu'eux... ils en savaient autant que nous... eux au moins sortaient d'un asile, nous de je ne sais où... aussi vacillants, baveux qu'eux d'un caniveau l'autre vers là-bas la ville, enfin les fumées les décombres... le temps quand même de réfléchir... réfléchissons!... pas en geignant pleurant non! je demande pas à être pleuré! foutre tous ces gens doléants qu'on les pende! et hop!... qu'ils ne pleurent plus! crocodilars!... souvenirs qu'il me faut... et je peux pas me souvenir de tout... choses et personnes... je m'y retrouve plus... comme Felipe là sous sa bâche... écrasé, perdu... je vous le retrouverai... mes souvenirs d'abord!... méli-mélo... Baden-Baden... La Vigue... Restif... Harras... Moorsburg... Zornhof... je suis certain de ceux-ci... les autres il faudrait que je dorme ils me reviendraient... la preuve, par bribes... tant bien que mal...
>
> «Il n'a ni syntaxe, ni style! il n'écrit plus rien! il n'ose plus!»
>
> Ah, turpitude! menterie éhontée!... plein de style que je suis! que oui! et pire!... bien plus! que je les rendrai tous illisibles!... tous les autres! flétrides impuissants! pourris des prix et manifesses! que je peux comploter bien tranquille, l'époque est à moi! je suis le béni des Lettres! qui m'imite pas existe pas!... simple!... allons! que je regarde où nous sommes! (*R*, pp.854–856)

The passage into this style, this new mode of composition, will inevitably lead to many other changes in the novel, for, once freed from the strictures of *Chronos* and other such rigid forms of organisation, the stagnant molar concept of a being is a fallacy; in the time of *aiôn*, only a becoming is possible, a constantly shifting mode of existence governed solely by differing levels of intensity, differentials of speed, and so it is that there comes in the text (once the narrator/protagonist Céline/ Destouches has been reunited with Lili) a becoming-music of the narrative voice, a becoming-imperceptible of Céline the narrator and protagonist (involving the release of biological fluxes), and the arrival and subsequent departure of a train—an agent of speed—which can only be Céline's style incarnate, the *métro émotif*, all of which is, of course, set to a backdrop provided by the nomadic war machine. All of this is found in a remarkable passage, filled with mentions of colour, laughter and *féerie*, and which concludes in the following manner:

> depuis le moment des briques, sauf que j'ai bien mal à la tête, je serais porté à rire!... et de tout... ainsi de cette plate-forme où nous sommes... et de la fraîcheur du matin... fraîcheur?... je suis modéré... il fait froid... mais je peux pas me plaindre!... «Lili j'ai la fièvre!... et toi?... et vous Felipe?» y a de la tremblote, je ne sais pas de qui, mais d'un de nous... pour mon cas y a du paludisme en plus de la circonstance... plus tard... un peu plus tard j'approfondirai... l'aspect clinique... mais... mais... cette plate-forme bouge!... oui!... je me disais... nous étions partis... sans du tout nous être aperçus... démarrés bel et bien!... nous roulions!... ah le paysage charmant!... enfin, un peu flou... je dirais: poétique... (*R*., pp. 830-831; see also the pages preceding this passage, *R*, p.824 et passim)

The aim of the Célinian aesthetic, then—as can be seen in the passage quoted in the appendix to this study as well as in numerous other poetic descriptions of the war-torn landscape of Germany—, will be to inject desire (or poetry or music, depending on one's preferred terminology) into the petrified temporal strata of History, into a life infected with its own demise, with death, but a death which, 'is no longer a reason for sterile fear, but a promise of renewed life and a stimulus for creation',[98] for it is only once the molar mechanisms of dissimulation are cast aside that a true transference of the aesthetic through a connective synthesis can take place. Such is entirely in accordance with Deleuze and Guattari's concept of becoming-music:[99]

> La musique n'est jamais tragique, la musique est joie. Mais il arrive nécessairement qu'elle nous donne le goût de mourir, moins de bonheur que mourir avec bonheur, s'éteindre. Non pas en vertu d'un instinct de mort qu'elle

> soulèverait en nous, mais d'une dimension propre à son agencement sonore, à sa machine sonore, le moment qu'il faut affronter, où la transversale tourne en ligne d'abolition. Paix *et* exaspération. La musique a soif de destruction, tous les genres de destruction, extinction, cassage, dislocation. N'est-ce pas son "fascisme" potentiel? Mais chaque fois qu'un musicien écrit *In memoriam*, il s'agit non pas d'un motif d'inspiration, non pas d'un souvenir, mais au contraire d'un devenir qui n'a fait qu'affronter son propre danger, quitte à tomber pour en renaître: un devenir-enfant, un devenir-femme, un devenir-animal, en tant qu'ils sont le contenu même de la musique et vont jusqu'à la mort.[100]

The action of the Célinian aesthetic will thus be cancerous, invading the molar organism and proliferating within it, coexisting inside of it, becoming-reader just as the reader is becoming-music:

> nous sommes là à bringuebaler sur ces plates-formes avec plein de personnes invisibles... coexistence se dit maintenant... en avant donc, coexistants!... que nous roulions, l'essentiel!... même avec ces dissimulés nous arriverons à Hambourg, à moins que ce train saute!... ce qu'on ne voit pas qui compte dans la vie, ce qui se voit s'entend n'est que mascarade, coups de gueule, théâtre!... ce qui se passe au fond de votre prostate qu'est intéressant, ce millionième de gamète qui décide qu'il en a assez, qu'il obéit plus aux ordres, qu'il va travailler pour son compte, foutre des marquises et du petit ami! qu'il va proliférer et hop! vite, pour lui, lui-même! vous à la fosse! hop! vous le verrez jamais ce millionième d'anarchiste gamète crasseux cancéreux!... vous sauriez même pas qu'il a existé!... hé là! si je prolifère je vous perds de vue... oh là! acré!... battre la campagne?... je vous ai prévenu, certes!... ma tête!... ma tête fait aussi des siennes... oh, que je refuse!... et vous ramène à notre plate-forme... roulante... (*R*, p.832)

The problem with this becoming-music that obeys the double movement of being and non-being, to be and not to be, is that the fundamental positivity of music risks being engulfed by its accompanying morbid 'goût de mourir'. In order to counter this negativity and ensure that it is the text's life-affirming qualities which ultimately triumph over death, a further complementary becoming is introduced into the narrative, a becoming-child.[101] This becoming-child is allowed for, of course, by the introduction of the (uncountable) group of retarded (apparently sexless) children who join the narratival Trinity (or is it the other way around?), and who, as Nettelbeck remarks, 'save the group from starvation by finding food, and, later, [...] become Céline's passport to Denmark'.[102] These children, then, are that which make possible the protagonist Céline/Destouches' passage to the north, and, consequently, the text's passage into the style announced at the beginning of *Rigodon*. For the children's foray into the 'géante cloche en glaise fragile... cloche... en somme une cloque... une soufflure géante en terre glaise...' (*R*, pp.865–866), can but recall the image of an (almost-imperceptible) ant faced with the 'entonnoir' of the impression of a fist in a box of iron filings, which is used as an allegory by the narrator to describe the way in which his art is to revitalise the past through the retention of a (childish) sense of wonder and infinite possibility. By following the children (and Bébert and Lili) into the holey space of this 'butte [... avec] des trous partout' (*R*, p.865), in which there is an all-pervading stench of death, then, the protagonist Céline/Destouches enters into a becoming-child/animal/woman, actualising the virtuality of his molecular self, making possible that which his logical, molar, objectifying intellect would have deemed impossible:

> Lili me dit: «le mieux tu vois c'est de laisser aller Bébert!...» comme ça un trou Bébert irait, c'était sûr, lui était pire que les mômes, question de disparaître... il fonçait... et puis il trouvait, il miaulait... «lâche-le!...» Lili le pose à terre... comment les mômes ont pu passer?... je me demande... Bébert entre facile, il va... Lili l'appelle... il miaule... un miaulement tranquille... Lili me demande pas, elle va aussi, pas le temps de faire ouf... à genoux elle y va, elle peut se risquer, elle est acrobate... moi, je pourrais pas... ah si!... je peux!... à genoux!... de même... hardi petit!... arrive ce qu'arrivera!... (*R*, pp.864–865)

Nor is it only during this episode that the protagonist Céline/Destouches enters into this kind of assemblage with the children, as the becoming-imperceptible of the protagonist Céline/Destouches—signalled by his general physical degradation throughout the course of the trilogy—[103] can be seen to be intimately linked to this becoming-child, as he likens his own physical failings to those of the 'mômes baveux', as will be seen in the examples to follow:

> on voit très bien le port, les bateaux, etc... au moins vingt fois que je vous raconte... les hélices en l'air... je vais sur mes soixante-dix ans... que je bave pas tant que mes petits crétins est déjà bien extraordinaire... surtout travaillant ma façon, acharné, je peux le dire, m'y reprenant des dix fois, vingt fois... (*R*, pp.850–851)

> «Suivez-moi!... suivez mes batons!»
>
> Ceux que Felipe m'avait fabriqués, en gros bois blanc... oh, les mômes demandent pas mieux, même ceux-ci ci débiles avortons baveux... a l'aventure!... titubants, flanchants, pire que moi... se ramassent d'un rien, tous

> les pas, d'un caillou de travers… et pas à piailler, *à rire!…* (*R*, p.852; my italics)

Becoming-imperceptible, becoming-child, these, then, are the means by which the Célinian expression is deterritorialised and liberated, the way in which Céline's aesthetic, territorialised and overcoded in terms of a Political History he never intended, finally returns to that po(i)nt at the end of *Guignol's band*, pre-territorialisation, when the key to an expression of desire from within the strata of molarity was found in a joyous *danse macabre* on a bridge, a quasi-suicidal ballet delighting in the threat of dissipation. One need only compare the following passages to realise the close coincidence of situation:

> Ça les amusait au possible, tout farceurs maintenant, des démons, ils faisaient semblant de s'envoler, d'être soulevés au vide, que je coure après, que je les raccroche...
>
> Deux petits fous...
>
> «Allez! que je me fâche... ça suffit!»
>
> Ils faisaient semblant de lâcher la rampe. C'est le vieux qu'était le plus turbulent. (*GB*II, p.758)

> Je m'égare encore! au fait!… au fait!… je vous disais ce pont tremblotait, gigotait même!… pourtant pas un pont fragile, une géante armature de poutres et d'arcs… vous auriez dit impossible… si! et rien qu'aux souffles des explosions… le genre de rigodon que c'était! et nous à nous amuser à regarder l'éclosion des mines!… violettes! rouges!… jaunes!… au fond du gouffre… sûr, dans le canal! les sous-marins devaient écoper!… vous parlez de remous d'air… de quoi bien valser nous aussi!… mais nos mômes baveux?… on pourrait un peu être inquiets! ils pouvaient être partis dans un souffle, planer au gouffre… ils pouvaient avoir passé le pont, bien s'amuser de l'autre côté, l'autre rive… ce qui était grave chez ces gniards c'est pas seulement qu'ils étaient sourds mais qu'ils avaient peur de rien, qu'ils étaient faits aux bombes et tonnerres… que ça avait dû leur arriver pas une fois, cent fois… eh bien non!… ils étaient pas passés en face! ils étaient là sur cette passerelle, je les voyais, ils s'attrapaient, ils se rattrapaient… ils jouaient à s'envoyer au vide… les explosions les gênaient pas, au contraire on aurait dit… je les avais jamais vus si gais… ils se faisaient des niches… moi je pouvais plus avancer, ni Lili… aussi fallait voir le pont se soulever et les rails et nos plates-formes… et *proum!…* tout retomber!… mieux dire, tout ondule… (*R*, pp.882–883)

Alain Cresciucci is thus perfectly correct when he asserts that, 'si la vision-restitution du monde est perturbée, c'est que le narrateur l'est lui-même. […] Au-delà des explications extra-textuelles, la perturbation de la vision du monde répond dans le texte à l'effondrement du moi'.[104] Where he is wrong (according to the thesis proposed by the present study) is in reading this movement towards dissolution in negative terms—he talks of 'cette **déprécation** constante des interventions: le *je raconte* ou *je dis* se voyant **dévalué** en un "je délire" ou plus brutalement en un "je déconne"'—,[105] for it is precisely as a result of this quasi-schizophrenic dissolution that the Célinian aesthetic fulfils its aim of bypassing the Capitalist axiomatics and modes of representation, to pass, 'direct dans l'émotion par l'émotion'. Alain Cresciucci (perhaps unwittingly) makes this very point, for, when talking of the ramifications of this dissolution of subjectivity for the text, he writes,

> L'univers romanesque ne se lit *qu'à partir de l'ici-maintenant du narrateur*, non pas, selon lui, par décision consciente mais par une impulsion incoercible. Le monde morcelé n'est plus comme dans *Voyage* un monde fait de lieux juxtaposés, mais *un univers dont la cohérence ne peut s'affirmer que dans son rapport au sujet énonciateur.*[106]

Dependant on a narrative centre which no longer exists, then, the work achieves a non-transcendental unity from which a transversal relation can emanate, a connective synthesis able to transmit desire directly to the reader in a collective assemblage of enunciation. And so it is that the reader embarks upon the 'métro émotif' which, like the train in which the protagonist Céline/Destouches finds himself, 'allait à la perfection, roulait, un charme' (*R*, p.903). That these trains manage to run at all is itself remarkable, for, in times of war, it would be only too easy for them to end up like the train that the protagonist Céline/Destouches sees from his carriage window:

> une locomotive à l'envers... perchée... et pas une petite je vous dis, une à douze roues!... en l'air à l'envers les douze roues!... je les compte, je les recompte... ça devait être une explosion, je dirais volcanique, qui l'avait envoyée à dache, perchée, telle quelle, sur le dos! soufflée! au sommet!... (*R*, p.833–834)[107]

What is even more extraordinary, however, is that these trains run so smoothly that the passengers are hardly aware of the device, the mode of composition used to keep them on course. For although one might expect the train tracks in this war-torn landscape to be broken and twisted out of place—as indeed they have been throughout the course of *Rigodon*—or, even, to be completely obliterated ('une telle hâte il paraît, que cette ligne n'existe plus!... hi!... hi!...' (*R*, p.831)), it is, rather, as though there had never been a war, as though Céline's poetic expression had never been subjected to Historical reterritorialisation and overcoding: 'je reviens à notre train, plutôt à notre wagon-cuisine... je vous dis: question suspension et confort, *comme avant la guerre, vous sentiez pas du tout les rails...*' (*R*, p.905).

D'un po(i)nt l'autre

The final sections of *Rigodon* take on a new meaning in the light of the above analysis, for if, at the end of *Rigodon*, the Célinian aesthetic has finally found the means to operate within the strata of History, to re-inject the past with desire without falling into the kind of pathological remove found in *Féerie pour une autre fois* II, then the treasured objects that the protagonist Céline/Destouches and Lili go to a park to inspect—and, indeed, the exotic birds that flock around them—must be symbols of this achievement, their passports and marriage certificate symbolising their ability to move as one in molar society, the cyanide and pistol a model of death, the latent phantasm of suicide so vital to their, and thus the text's, becoming-music symbolised by the songbirds, inherently musical creatures capable of flight.[108]

To be and not to be, this, in the final analysis, is the double movement according to which *Rigodon*, '[qui] se danse sur un air à deux temps, sur place, sans avancer ni reculer, ni aller de côté',[109] strikes the bull's-eye, passes 'direct dans l'émotion':[110]

> Et c'est alors le texte de Céline dans son état final. *Braoum!...* D'abord l'onomatopée, la semence de l'onomatopée, semence de foudre; et après, après seulement, la musique, ce que Céline appelle sa petite musique, tout en broderie d'ondes et dentelle de silence. Et derechef, *braoum!...* et de nouveau la musique. Ainsi de suite sans discontinuer. Ça éclate, puis ça musique. Oreille gauche, oreille droite. Céline boite d'une oreille (comme un cheval). Mais enfin il avance; à son pas, à son rythme. Au rythme du pendule qui fait la phrase aller et la phrase s'élancer, pont volant, de cette oreille de gauche à l'oreille de droite. Entre les deux oreilles, la phrase comme un pont.[111]

The apparent contradiction on which the Célinian aesthetic is founded does not, then, as Denise Aebersold suggests, lead to Fascism,[112] an empty body without organs, for it is precisely from this contradiction that desiring-production is made possible, that connective syntheses well from a full body without organs. Such is made apparent by Deleuze and Guattari in the following passages:

> Le corps sans organes n'est pas le témoin d'un néant original, pas plus que le reste d'une totalité perdue. Il n'est surtout pas une projection; rien à voir avec le corps propre, ou avec une image du corps. C'est le corps sans image. Lui, l'improductif, il existe là où il est produit, au troisième temps de la série binaire-linéraire [sic]. Il est perpétuellement réinjecté dans la production. Le corps catatonique est produit dans l'eau du bain. Le corps plein sans organes est de l'anti-production; mais c'est encore un caractère de la synthèse connective ou productive, de coupler la production à l'anti-production, à un élément d'anti-production.[113]

> Un CsO est fait de telle manière qu'il ne peut être occupé, peuplé que par des intensités. Seules les intensités passent et circulent. Encore le CsO n'est-il pas une scène, un lieu, ni même un support où se passerait quelque chose. Rien à voir avec un fantasme, rien à interpréter. Le CsO fait passer des intensités, il les produit et les distribue dans un *spatium* lui-même intensif, inétendu. Il n'est pas espace ni dans l'espace, il est matière qui occupera l'espace à tel ou tel degré—au degré qui correspond aux intensités produites. Il est la matière intense et non formée, non stratifiée, la matrice intensive, l'intensité = 0, mais il n'y a rien de négatif dans ce zéro-là, il n'y a pas d'intensités négatives ni contraires. Matière égale énergie. Production du réel comme grandeur intensive à partir du zéro.[114]

And so it is that the Célinian phrase serves merely to distribute intensities, 'comme un pont'. But not any old bridge, for the body without organs, feeding anti-production into the process of production, is constituted only by the interruption of desire, a 'moment of suspension'.[115] 'La phrase comme un pont', yes, but a *pont suspendu*, for like human existence, 'pourriture en suspens', the success of each phrase depends on the zero intensity at its core, the *points de suspension*:[116] '*mes trois points d'abord... soi-disant renouveau du style...*' (*R*, p.848; my italics).[117]

D'un ... l'autre. This, then, is the schizophrenic trajectory of the Célinian expression, the essence of his style, the content proper to his music, his refrain, that '*ensemble de matières d'expression qui trace un territoire, et qui se développe en motifs territoriaux, en paysages territoriaux*'.[118] His is not a fascistic territory, however (pseudo-Fascist, maybe), for it opposes the fixity of all strata, all of those pre-defined patterns and pre-assigned meanings employed by Capitalist society to recontain desire within its own artificial boundaries. Furthermore, whereas a fascistic territory is built around an apparently stable despotic centre, Céline's territory depends on its own becoming-imperceptible for its fruition, on a feedback loop of its own processes and ultimate demise into its very production. The Célinian territory is, then, one of, 'des motifs et des contre-points, qui expriment le rapport du territoire avec des impulsions intérieures ou des circonstances extérieures [...]. Non plus des signatures, mais un style'.[119] Given its consistency only by the *points de suspension*—as is lace by its holes and champagne by its bubbles—[120] Céline's art is a plane of *délire* with no pre-givens, composed only of points of rupture that allow his territorial assemblage to pass into other assemblages in a process of mutual becoming:

> «Mon cher balzacien les choses en resteront pas là!...
> —Pourquoi?
> —Pourquoi? voici!... je suis informé! les Chinois, les vrais, les Chinois de choc, ceux qui viendront nous occuper, bivouaquent déjà en Silésie... Breslau et les environs... mines et hauts fourneaux... il en viendra d'autres! bien d'autres d'à travers les steppes... de ces hordes!... kirghizes, moldo-finnois, balto-ruthènes, teutons... vous les verrez à Pantin, à la porte que vous connaissez, accueillis je ne vous dis que ça par de ces foules! hurlantes au pinard, au bonheur, à la liberté!
> —Bravo! bravo! quand voyez-vous les jaunes ici?...
> —Bientôt... mettons deux-trois ans.
> —Tout ce monde communiste?
> —Il va de soi! détail!... l'important le sang!... le sang seul est sérieux! tous "sang dominant"... n'oubliez pas!...»
> Je lui fais remarquer qu'à Byzance ils s'occupaient du sexe des anges au moment où déjà les Turcs secouaient les remparts... foutaient le feu aux bas quartiers, comme chez nous maintenant l'Algérie... nos Grands-Transitaires vont pas s'en occuper du sexe des anges!... ni de péril jaune! manger qui les intéresse... toujours mieux!... et vins assortis... de ces cartes! de ces menus! ils sont ou sont pas les maîtres du peuple le plus gourmand du monde? et le mieux imbibé?... qu'ils viennent, qu'ils osent les Chinois, ils iront pas plus loin que Cognac! il finira tout saoul heureux, dans les caves, le fameux péril jaune! encore Cognac est bien loin... millards par milliards il auront déjà eu leur compte en passant par où vous savez... Reims... Épernay... de ces profondeurs pétillantes que plus rien existe... (*R*, pp.926–927)

To write a schizophrenic style is, of course, to reject the normalised representational mode of the traditional molar novel, the easy recognition of Capitalist faciality, and it is also, therefore, to disallow all normal modes of interpretation. For this reason it would be futile to attempt to impose a definitive meaning on this final passage of Céline's *œuvre*, for to do so would destroy the affectivity (becoming) that has been said to exist in the text at this point. As Robert Llambias writes, 'la narration logique perturbée, le récit élime l'effet de représentation pour permettre l'accession immédiate à une émotion extrêmement proche de celle que peut provoquer la musique'.[121] Although Llambias is right to point out the similarity of these pages to the final pages of *Les Beaux draps*, however, to conclude from this comparison that, in both works, it is, 'comme si, au bout d'un certain nombre de lignes enfantées dans la douleur, extorquées, le romancier, dans l'impossibilité de terminer, éparpillait son texte, le faisait éclater musicalement',[122] to qualify the becoming-music of the text as an 'évasion musicale',[123] is to attempt (and necessarily fail) to understand this new aesthetic, the text's becoming-music, instead of allowing it to pass into one's emotive core. For in valorising *délire* as the foundation for an aesthetic, converting it into a plane composed of and emanating style, the becoming-music of Céline's aesthetic allows his assemblage to pass into that of the reader who must not, cannot provide a reading, but must instead *dé-lire*.

Conclusion

In the introduction to this study, it was suggested that, in the later novels of Louis-Ferdinand Céline, starting with *Guignol's band*, the thematic level of the text is put to the service of the stylistic level, that thematic level being—as well as a denunciation of the dehumanising mechanisms of Capitalist society—a self-reflective account of the very process of production by which the work of art comes into being, its style. Due to the nature of this style—which has been termed schizophrenic—it was suggested, furthermore, that this style comes to behave like a body, resolving the problematic posed in the texts' thematic level, namely, how to achieve an affective mode of communication, an emotive aesthetic, within the axiomatics of Capitalist society. Chapter one has seen the blueprint for such an expression drawn up in *Guignol's band*, a blueprint which could not be put to immediate use for the aesthetic construction of *Féerie pour une autre fois* due to the excessive centripetal, territorialising force of History inside of which the author Céline found himself at that time. Chapter two has, consequently, analysed *Féerie pour une autre fois* in terms of that work's negotiations with this centripetal force, its attempt to establish an emotive, centrifugal aesthetic within this excessive centripetality by, firstly, denunciation of that centripetality through subjugation to it, and then, in the second volume, the unleashing of an excessively centripetal force to counter it. Chapter three, meanwhile, has seen this emotive aesthetic gradually to be attained throughout the course of the trilogy, through a process of self-abjectification leading, in the trilogy's final volume, *Rigodon*, to a becoming-imperceptible of both the narrator (the thematic level) and the aesthetic (the stylistic level). Being constructed according to a schizophrenic mode of composition, this aesthetic has been seen to provide the solution to the problematic posed in the thematic level, since the style proposed in the exposition of that aesthetic, is precisely the auto-objective, direct, affective mode of communication sought after by the various guises of the narrator throughout the narratives of the Célinian corpus. More than this, however, being inseparable from a way of life, a mode of existence, the fruition of the Célinian aesthetic, the attainment of a truly schizophrenic style conceived as a mode of composition, has been said to allow the reader subsequently to reinvest his/her material reality with desire.

Two objections might be raised to this analysis. Firstly, it might be asked how a metastylistic/metafictional reading can be said to affect anything but its own processes, how a transversal relation can possibly emanate from a space whose unity is constituted only by its own construction and demise? Secondly, if a transversal relation does emanate from this aesthetic, if, in other words, Céline's aesthetic can be said to be an instance of schizophrenic desiring-production, if it is indeed constructed according to a schizophrenic conception of style in which the mode of composition is inseparable from a mode of existence, one might wonder how the recipient of the desire passing from the work via a transversal relation is subsequently to reinvest his/her material reality, since the affect created by this aesthetic is a direct intensive sensation, a pure emotion, and by definition, then, anti-ideological, anti-pragmatic?

The first of the above questions is essentially that posed rhetorically by Michel Foucault in his post-Kantian reflection on the transcendental thought systems of modern western society, what he calls '*épistémès*'. According to Foucault, inherent in the modern *épistémè*'s desire for a unified, transcendental thought system, is a fundamental failure to recognise the impossibilities that it creates for itself. For if consciousness (or, for the purposes of this study, the work of art) can be empirically considered as an object, and, at the same time, as an epistemological subject, then consciousness can no more know the truth about its own nature (as an object), than it can know the limits that it is supposed to constitute as a subject creating a transcendental unity, an absolute knowledge.[1] Louis Sass has likened this Foucauldian problematic to a (pathologically) schizophrenic and modernist conception of the mind. He writes,

> Foucault's discussion of the modern episteme suggests a way of understanding the profound interdependence of these two ways of experiencing one's mind—these two visions that function like the systole and diastole of the same reflexive process. It seems that the reflexive move, the turning inward, has the potential of bringing on the condition and contradictions of the doublet: insofar as I focus on the world, it will seem like *my* world; but insofar as I focus more directly on thoughts or feelings, these will seem to exist out there and apart. And so, in the realm of madness, as in modernism, we find, tightly intertwined, a solipsism that would elevate the mind and derealize the world and a self-

> objectification that would rob the subject of its transcendental role as a center of power and knowledge. This parallelism of paradoxes is no mere coincidence; what we are discovering in both domains are the characteristic paradoxes of the reflexive—contradictions generated by the alienation and hyper-self-consciousness that are central both to schizophrenia and to the modern episteme.[2]

In privileging the self-reflective (metafictional/metastylistic) mode of his work, indulging this solipsism that elevates the mind and derealises the world (the a-Historical artifice of the pure aesthetic), whilst simultaneously diffracting (in a becoming-imperceptible) the supposedly stable centre of power and knowledge (or narration and language), then, Céline imbues his work with a non-transcendental unity from which can emanate an auto-objective expression, a transversal relation. In so doing, Céline's aesthetic, his music, might be said to breach the apparent aporia presented by both the schizophrenic and modernist conditions, as outlined by Sass, for in writing a hyper-reflexive style from an imperceptible centre, Céline both de-pathologises this schizophrenic space—as it is no longer an enclosed space, autistically removed from reality, but capable of affect in reality—at the same time as he resolves the paradox that Sass sees at the heart of the modernist project. Even in its darkest moments, then, Céline's music is eminently positive, as Michael Donley understands well:

> Céline a horreur du figé, symbole de l'anti-musique, de la mort. Avec ses branles, ses *com-motions* de toute sorte—mentales aussi bien que physiques—ses 'danses du sens dessus dessous', il ne nous mène pourtant pas vers le chaos. Son goût pour la mobilité, l'efferverscence et l'ébullition, sa capacité de discerner partout de l'énergie potentielle 'en suspens', fait que son œuvre devient une corne d'abondance joyeuse et vitale.
>
> Qui plus est, cette 'matière mouvante' est organisée, à l'instar pour ainsi dire de Hanslick, en formes oscillatoires. Il ne faut pas se laisser prendre au piège comme le fait Julia Kristeva lorsqu'elle parle d'un 'trop-plein d'émotion'. Que la musique dépasse l'intelligence, il faut comprendre cela du point de vue de l'auditeur. Tout l'art dépend pourtant de cette autre intelligence—celle du créateur. Seule une critique superficielle de la musique peut prétendre qu'il s'agit d'un déversoir incontrôlé d'émotion. Il en est de même avec les textes de Céline musicien. 'Travaillant en tension transposée musicale extrême du premier mot au dernier', il *compose* soigneusement des dentelles de tension et de relâchement, de mouvements centrifuges et centripètes, d'expansion et de contraction, de diastole et systole. Peut-il en être autrement, s'il veut, comme il le dit, 'transposer *directement*'—voilà encore ce mot—'la vie'?[3]

The way in which Céline achieves this transversal relation from within an apparently solipsistic space, might be better understood if posited in different terms. It was suggested in the introduction to the present study, that this very study might be termed a feedback loop, for it was to aim to interpret its chosen body of work solely according to precepts perceived in that body of work itself, to come into being only through a constantly renewed contact with the text that feeds back into the text itself. In the course of this analysis, it has become apparent that the Célinian aesthetic might be said to operate in precisely the same way, for the text's thematics constantly feed back into the text's stylistics, that is to say, into that very aspect of the work which brings those very thematics to life in the first place. This process may appear to provide a perfect circle from which no affect, no transversal relation could ever emanate, the space created being, much like that inhabited by a dog chasing its own tail, entirely solipsistic. The lack of a stable centre within that solipsistic space, however, denies a transcendental unity, destabilises the normalised centre of authority, and thus allows a transversal relation to come into being. For, just as in sonic feedback a high intensity sound is produced by the loop created when a part of a loudspeaker's output is returned to the input source, so the imperceptible part of the Célinian aesthetic, the silence at its core, its anti-production, by constantly feeding back into its own production, d'un … l'autre, produces an affective intensity, a pure intensive affect. Sonic feedback is sometimes described as the passage of a whisper to a scream. The same might be said of the Célinian aesthetic, for, like the paintings of Bacon, its affect comes not from a mimetic representation of the world's horror, but from a piercing cry of intense pain and pleasure (for the one necessarily implicates the other) in the midst of that horror.[4]

Conceived of in this way, one might better be able to provide a response to the second of the above objections concerning the reinvestment of the text's desire in the recipient's material reality. For if the Célinian aesthetic, in the final analysis, can be likened to a cry, a spontaneous response to external stimulus, then whomsoever hears that cry, that *petite musique*, will respond in kind, not according to a pre-defined plan of action, not according to perceived ideological tenets, but according to the internal stimulus provoked by that cry. It is at that moment when one hears a cry, be it a squeal of pleasure, the yelp of an animal, or a scream of pain or terror, that one is able to intuit what Deleuze and Guattari mean when they talk of subjectivity in terms of an assemblage, for traversed by the pure sensation of the cry, the boundaries of subjectivity and the egotism so despised by Bardamu, crumble and cede to an emotive, centrifugal empathic response, a becoming. Such an instinctive response is, in Céline's eyes, far preferable to man's normal mode of communication:

> Quand vous chatouillez une amibe, elle se rétracte, elle a de l'émotion; elle parle pas, mais elle a de l'émotion. Le bébé pleure, le cheval galope, à l'un, à l'autre, il faut apprendre à parler, à trotter. Seulement nous on nous a donné le verbe. Ça donne l'homme politique, l'écrivain, le prophète. Le verbe, c'est horrible, c'est pas sentable.[5]

Like Deleuze and Guattari's *Capitalisme et schizophrénie*, then, Céline's aesthetic is eminently pragmatic, which is not to say that it is ideological. For, as Brian Massumi points out in his translator's foreword to the English version of *Mille plateaux*,

> [Deleuze] calls his kind of philosophy "pragmatics" because its goal is the invention of concepts that do not add up to a system or belief or an architecture of propositions that you either enter or you don't, but instead pack a potential in the way a crowbar in a willing hand envelops an energy of prying.[6]

To this end, *Mille plateaux*, as Massumi also points out, 'is conceived as an open system. It does not pretend to have the final word. The authors' hope, however, is that elements of it will stay with a certain number of its readers and will weave into the melody of their everyday lives'.[7] For Deleuze and Guattari, as for Céline, this affectivity of the text is accomplished through the very nature of the text itself—its style as a mode of composition—, since each section is conceived of not as a chapter, but as a plateau, that point reached,

> when circumstances combine to bring an activity to a pitch of intensity that is not automatically dissipated in a climax. The heightening of energies is sustained long enough to leave a kind of afterimage of its dynamism that can be reactivated or injected into other activities, creating a fabric of intensive states between which any number of connecting routes could exist.[8]

The Célinian aesthetic brought to its fruition arrives at just such a plateau, for the harmonious resolution of style and form, being and non-being, creates a deafening silence, a plane of consistency, a point at which 'plus rien existe' (*R*, p.927), and from which anything can exist.

As might be expected of such an aesthetic which delights in the paradoxical, however, the infinite potential opened up by Céline's aesthetic is both its greatest achievement and its biggest failing, for being a molecular agent of deterritorialisation, it is particularly prone to reterritorialisation. Hence, even though the entire Célinian corpus can be said to progress towards this zero-intensity of absolute *délire*, it appears to get stuck, for a time, in a *délire* not of its own making, a *délire* from which, furthermore, few have been willing to extricate it.[9] Céline's emotive aesthetic may, then, be considered as another instance of "pragmatics" (in the sense that Deleuze conceives of this term with regards to his own philosophy); it is, nonetheless, not at all suited to the Historical world in which its cry resonates—his *délire*, one might say, is *not* coextensive with the social field constituted by the unequal oscillation between the potential schizophrenic pole and the actual paranoiac pole.[10] For Céline's music to pass directly into one's emotive core, then, it is *vital* to close one's eyes,[11] and it is not true, nor should it be, that 'tout le monde peut en faire autant'.

NOTES

Notes to the Introduction

1 Nicholas Hewitt, *The Golden Age of Louis-Ferdinand Céline* (Leamington Spa: Berg Publishers, 1987).
2 Ian Noble's *Language and Narration in Celine's Writings: The Challenge of Disorder* (Atlantic Highlands, N.J.: Humanities Press International, 1987) falls prey to this claim to a lesser extent than some others, but the ultimate failure that he sees at the heart of the Célinian aesthetic can nonetheless still be attributed to the failure of his study to grasp the total conflation of the stylistic and thematic elements of the novels.
3 See Julia Kristeva, *Pouvoirs de l'horreur: essai sur l'abjection*, coll. Points Essais (Paris: Éditions du Seuil, 1980), Paul A. Fortier, *'Voyage au bout de la nuit': étude du fonctionnement des structures thématiques: le "métro émotif" de L.-F. Céline*, Bibliothèque des Lettres Modernes, 33 (Paris: Minard, 1981), and Bettina L. Knapp, *Céline: Man of Hate* (Alabama: The University of Alabama Press, 1974).
4 See Philip Goodchild, *Deleuze and Guattari: An Introduction to the Politics of Desire* (Sage Publications: London, 1996), p.82.
5 Ian Buchanan in his introduction to *The South Atlantic Quarterly*, 96.3 (1996), 381–391 (p.383).
6 J.H. Matthews, *The Inner Dream: Céline as Novelist* (Syracuse, NY: Syracuse University Press, 1978), p.6.
7 *Ibid.*, p.9.
8 Philip Stephen Day, *Le Miroir allégorique de Louis-Ferdinand Céline* (Paris: Klincksieck, 1974), p.17.
9 Buchanan in his introduction to *The South Atlantic Quarterly*, p.384.
10 *Cahiers Céline* 2, *Céline et l'actualité littéraire, 1957–1961*, ed. by Jean-Pierre Dauphin and Henri Godard (Paris: Gallimard, 1976), pp.175–176. See also the interview with Madeleine Chapsal in her, *Les Écrivains en personne* (Paris: Julliard, 1960). If the present study appears at times to rely somewhat heavily on the ideas of Colin W. Nettelbeck, this is because (in some of his studies) he is one of the very few Célinian commentators who, whilst never neglecting the importance of the Historical context of the texts, are willing also to consider such an a-Historical, pan-stylistic reading. Take, for instance, the following comments of his:

> En vérité, si paradoxal que cela puisse paraître, plus le décalage apparent entre la biographie et la fiction se réduit, plus le rôle de la transposition s'agrandit. Et si Proust et Céline insistent tant là-dessus, n'est-ce pas précisément pour avertir le lecteur que leur œuvre *n'est pas* leur vie?
>
> L'important, c'est de remarquer comment des différences absolues de tempérament et d'expérience, une fois passées par le processus de la création, et en

> particulier par cette transposition en musique, tendent à converger vers un but esthétique commun: à savoir la transmission, à travers cette incarnation unique et toute relative qu'est leur monde imaginaire, du principe même de la créativité. (Colin W. Nettelbeck, 'Notion et fonction de la "transposition" chez Céline et Proust', *Actes du colloque international de Paris, juillet 1976*, *Bulletin de la Société des Études céliniennes*, 1 (1978), 7–26 (pp.15 & 22–23 respectively))

This attitude is not entirely consistent, however, as can be seen from the following quotation in which Nettelbeck implicitly suggests that, in certain texts, a Political thematic dominates this aesthetic principle:

> If the real-life Céline was too much of an active collaborator to be identified with mainstream behavior and reaction, as novelist he is wily enough to "marginalize" the extreme deeds and attitudes of his autobiography, so that readers are left with a historical vision that is both plausible in itself and subversive of the synthetic history constructed by the alliance of Gaullian and communist politicians, who posited the rebirth of France on the notion of wide-spread Resistance. By couching that vision in a self-deprecatory and comic mode, he renders his vision disarmingly powerful: in laughing, we allow ourselves to think that perhaps, indeed, things happened more in the way he describes than as recounted in the more official histories. (Colin W. Nettelbeck, 'Historical Vision in Céline's Last Novels', in *Critical Essays on Louis-Ferdinand Céline*, ed. by William K. Buckley (Boston: G.K. Hall, 1989), pp.268–278 (p.277))

11 In this respect, the present study sets out with much the same goal as Stanley J. Coen who writes, 'If literature is not reduced to a compromise formation, then the task is not necessarily to discern a central conflict or unconscious fantasy within (or behind) it' (Stanley J. Coen, *Between Author and Reader: A Psychoanalytic Approach to Writing and Reading* (New York: Columbia University Press, 1994), p.24). However, although Coen's study adheres to its stated intention of not using the literary text as a means to construct a psychobiography of the real-life author, his analysis nonetheless remains a dogmatic and reductive example of psychoanalytic interpretation since, rather than construct an image of the author, he constructs an image of the reader (a reader who, for all of Coen's apparent hostility to Lacan, is erected on a fundamental lack) whose response to the text is used to determine the mechanisms behind an image of the literary author/narrator. Coen states, 'I will argue in this work of Céline's [*D'un château l'autre*] that the readers' need to create his fantasy of the author-narrator has been shaped (consciously and unconsciously) by this "author-narrator" so that the reader will attend to the author's craft and presence. It should be borne in mind that this does not attribute artistic or psychological *intentions* to the "flesh-and-blood author' (*ibid.*, p.49). In other words, Coen maintains that the narrator's holey language, rife with lack, creates in the reader the need to seek out the author (a kind of *à la recherche de l'auteur perdu*), a need which originates not in a constructed psychobiographical figure of the author, but in the

reader's projection of his own fantasies (*ibid.*, p.61). Such an analysis, however, is surely more an examination of Coen's own projected fantasies than it is a literary analysis of a Célinian text.

12 It is important for this claim to be made so as to avoid the accusation of a certain conception of 'la lecture immanente' in which, as Danièle Racelle-Latin points out, the corporeal author in the empirical universe is conveniently and systematically denied. See Danièle Racelle-Latin, 'Création littéraire et économie de la libido dans *Voyage au bout de la nuit* de L.-F. Céline', *Actes du colloque international de Paris, juillet 1976, Bulletin de la Société des Études céliniennes*, 1 (1978), 259–280 (p.259). This study will not indulge such a vulgar phenomenology, but will address or reject the Historical as appears fitting in the *con*-text, the reading proposed herein being produced only from contact with the text.

13 Letter to Milton Hindus dated May 15th 1957, in *L.-F. Céline*, ed. by Dominique de Roux, Michel Beaujour and Michel Thélia, *Les Cahiers de l'Herne*, 3 & 5 ([n.p.]: l'Herne, 1972), p.112 (henceforth, *L'Herne*). For a survey of this antagonistic relationship with the figure of the intellectual in Céline's writing, see Denise Aebersold, 'Céline et les intellectuels', *Actes du colloque international de Paris, juillet 1976, Bulletin de la Société des Études céliniennes*, 1 (1978), 185–196.

14 See especially Paul A. Fortier, *'Voyage au bout de la nuit': étude du fonctionnement des structures thématiques: le "métro émotif" de L.-F. Céline.* J.H. Matthews also consistently notes the careful aesthetic construction that the apparently chaotic surface of the texts belies (see Matthews, *The Inner Dream*), and Ian Noble writes, 'clearly, a written text can never *be* spoken language. Even leaving aside the problem of the graphic signifiers which replace the acoustic signifiers of speech, the two systems are bound by completely different contexts in terms of which their messages are constituted. In particular, the spoken work presupposes intonation and (usually) a whole array of gestures, facial expressions and other visual signs which are absent from the written text. What the written text can do, however, is to use a number of artifices in order to reproduce some of the characteristics of the spoken work—above all, [a] sense of incompleteness' (Noble, *Language and Narration in Céline's Writings*, p.7). Éric Mazet, on the other hand, unequivocally dispels the common misconception regarding Céline's 'langage parlé' as he writes:

> La prose de Céline est image et musique, donc haute poésie, s'entend derrière le masque, chante à l'intérieur de l'oreille. En découvrant ce langage où l'artifice et le naturel s'entrelacent, et oubliant souvent leur difficulté à entrer dans le rythme, nombre de lecteurs croient lire du 'langage parlé', donc fait pour être lu à haute voix. La plupart des livres scolaires répètent à l'envi cette erreur initiale. Si l'écrivain s'est bien procuré le parler de la rue, rien n'est plus éloigné de la prose orale, du discours, que la '*petite musique*' de Céline, qui avait ainsi précisé sa recherche à Robert Sadoul: '*Je suis un homme qui fait des trucs pour des gens qui sont chez eux et qui veulent lire [...] Tout le travail [...] quand ils me lisent à voix basse: avoir quelqu'un qui leur parle dedans. À l'intérieur [...] Et qui parle à eux, à leurs nerfs directement, et non pas à leur*

> *oreille, mais par les yeux, que la chimie se fasse dans leur tête, et directement [...] Pas besoin de lire tout haut. Je suis un bonhomme fait pour l'intimité*'. On ne peut être plus net. (Éric Mazet, 'D'un masque l'autre', in *L'Année Céline 1993: Revue d'actualité célinienne* (Tusson & Paris: Du Lérot/IMEC, 1994), pp.211–222 (pp.214–215))

15 Allen Thiher, 'Le "je" célinien: ouverture, extase et clôture', *Australian Journal of French Studies*, 13.1–2 (1976), 47–54 (p.51). Thiher's subsequent comments are irreconcilable with the stance of the present study (for reasons which will become clear in chapter 3), and seem also somewhat to contradict this affirmation of Céline's *délire* as 'jubilant'. He states,

> Le moment de la plénitude positive est toujours de courte durée chez Céline. La révélation qui devrait aboutir à une rédemption se mue en fascination avec le mal et la folie. L'ouverture extatique se trouve minée de l'intérieur, car elle n'ouvre finalement que sur l'omniprésence des maléfices qui, comme dans *Normance*, envoûtent inlassablement le narrateur célinien. Et la parole célinienne, abolissant la temporalité, finit donc par offrir une sorte de parodie de la révélation extatique en créant sa négation absolue. D'un point de vue moderniste ceci est le paradoxe intenable de l'écriture célinienne: cette écriture rétablit l'essence de la présence, mais cette présence s'avère aussi dévastatrice que le temps dont l'écriture a cherché à triompher. (*ibid.*, pp.52–53)

16 See Deleuze and Guattari, *L'Anti-Œdipe*, p.11 and *passim*. This process of the pathologisation of schizophrenia, the creation of an autistic space through the curtailing of desire is described with regards to the Œdipal mechanism of repression in the following manner:

> [Œdipe] ce n'est pas une opération abstraite: on impose au psychotique une "organisation" œdipienne, serait-ce pour en assigner le *manque* en lui, chez lui. C'est un exercice en pleine chair, en pleine âme. Il réagit par l'autisme et la perte de réalité. Se peut-il que la perte de réalité ne soit pas l'effet du processus schizophrénique, mais l'effet de son œdipianisation forcée, c'est-à-dire de son interruption? Faut-il corriger ce que nous disions tout à l'heure, et supposer que certains tolèrent moins bien l'œdipianisation que d'autres? Le schizo ne serait pas malade en Œdipe, d'un Œdipe qui surgirait d'autant plus dans sa conscience hallucinée qu'il en manquerait dans l'organisation symbolique de "son" inconscient. Au contraire, il serait malade de l'œdipianisation qu'on lui fait subir (la plus sombre organisation) et qu'il ne peut plus supporter, parti pour un lointain voyage, comme si l'on ramenait sans cesse à Bécon celui qui dérive les continents et les cultures. Il ne souffre pas d'un moi divisé, d'un Œdipe éclaté, mais au contraire d'être ramené à tout cela qu'il a quitté. Chute d'intensité jusqu'au corps sans organes = 0, autisme: il n'a pas d'autre moyen de réagir au barrage de tous ses investissements de réalité, barrage que lui oppose le système œdipien répression-refoulement. Comme dit Laing, on les

> interrompt dans le voyage. Ils ont perdu la réalité. Mais quand l'ont-ils perdue? dans le voyage ou dans l'interruption du voyage? (*ibid.*, p.147)

17 *Ibid.*, pp.9–10.
18 In the present context, Robert Llambias' comment regarding Céline's conception of the novel takes on a whole new dimension. He writes,

> Le roman fonctionne comme une analyse sauvage, débarrassée par l'explosion narrée dans *Mort à crédit* de tous les concepts liés au triangle œdipien. Elle explore, de l'intérieur, par un supplice au cours duquel le romancier s'offre en victime expiatoire et théâtrale, les mille et une ruses de notre pulsion de mort. (Robert Llambias, 'Guerre, histoire et langage dans le récit célinien', *Revue des Sciences Humaines*, 75. 204 (1986), 89–105 (p.102))

19 In the light of this statement, it should be noted that, in the title of the present study, the words Capitalism and Schizophrenia are not italicised and do not, therefore, refer simply to the title uniting Deleuze and Guattari's *L'Anti-Œdipe* and *Mille plateaux*.
20 Deleuze and Guattari, *L'Anti-Œdipe*, pp.11–12.
21 See Roland Barthes, *Mythologies* (Paris: Éditions du Seuil, 1957), p.187.
22 This is not say that this study has no definite thesis to propose, however, far from it; this stylistic tactic is merely an (perhaps vain) attempt to avoid the didactic, dictatorial, ideologically-biased methodology of much Célinian criticism—examples of which will be examined throughout the course of the present study—, because, as Charles Krance has pointed out, '[Céline's] works resist the traditional approaches of critics whose esthetic and ethical systems are hermetic in inverse proportion to the expansive quality of the scrutinized works' (Charles Krance, 'Céline and the Literature of Extasis: The Virtuosity of "Non-Genre"', *Language and Style: An International Journal*, 6 (1973), 176–184 (p.179)). Krance sees this resistance as an integral part of the works' 'plea to reinstate man at the hub of the human experience, rather than to dehumanize him by subjecting him to a system based on abstract truths, whether they are expressed in Judeo-Christian terms or Marxist terms' (*ibid.*), a plea which, in spite of their machinic vocabulary, can also be heard throughout the works of Deleuze and Guattari.
23 Deleuze and Guattari, *L'Anti-Œdipe*, pp.163–164.
24 Nick Heffernan, 'Œdipus Wrecks? Or, Whatever Happened to Deleuze and Guattari: Rereading *Capitalism and Schizophrenia*', in *Redirections in Critical Theory: Truth, Self, Action, History*, ed. by Bernard McGuirk (London & New York: Routledge, 1994), pp.110–165 (p.117).
25 Deleuze and Guattari, *L'Anti-Œdipe*, p.12. In spite of the above comments, many valiant attempts at precisely such an explication of Deleuze and Guattari's thought have been made. These works, although obviously problematic, are nonetheless extremely useful for the reader attempting to come to terms with the immensely complex and elusive thought of Deleuze and Guattari. Of particular note are: Nick Heffernan's study cited above, 'Œdipus Wrecks?'—an excellent synthesis of the principal concepts and theoretical contexts of *Capitalisme et schizophrénie* that resumes many concepts in such

a succinct way that the present study will borrow much from it rather than attempt to surpass it; Ronald Bogue, *Deleuze and Guattari* (London and New York: Routledge, 1989)—of note mainly for its exposition of the progression of thought in the respective and joint careers of Deleuze and Guattari; Philip Goodchild, *Deleuze and Guattari: An Introduction to the Politics of Desire*—an examination of the concepts of knowledge, power and desire in Deleuze and Guattari's works which is both too categorical and too vague, too accessible and too hermetic, and perhaps brilliant precisely because of this. By far the most useful book of this kind, however, one which, furthermore, avoids the charge of being an exercise in self-defeat by its explanation of thought via the application of that thought, is Brian Massumi's *A User's Guide to 'Capitalism and Schizophrenia': Deviations from Deleuze and Guattari* (Cambridge, MA: MIT Press, 1992).

26 See Deleuze and Guattari, *L'Anti-Œdipe*, p.11.

27

> Le capitalisme est bien la limite de toute société, en tant qu'il opère le décodage des flux que les autres formations sociales codaient et surcodaient. Toutefois il en est la limite ou coupures *relatives*, parce qu'il substitue aux codes une axiomatique extrêmement rigoureuse qui maintient l'énergie des flux dans un état lié sur le corps du capital comme socius déterritorialisé, mais aussi et même plus impitoyable que tout autre socius. La schizophrénie au contraire est bien la limite *absolue*, qui fait passer les flux à l'état libre sur un corps sans organes désocialisé. On peut donc dire que la schizophrénie est la limite *extérieure* du capitalisme lui-même ou le terme de sa plus profonde tendance, mais que le capitalisme ne fonctionne qu'à condition d'inhiber cette tendance, ou de repousser et de déplacer cette limite, en y substituant ses propres limites relatives *immanentes* qu'il ne cesse de reproduire à une échelle élargie. Ce qu'il décode d'une main, il l'axiomatise de l'autre. (Deleuze and Guattari, *L'Anti-Œdipe*, p.292)

28 Nick Heffernan notes that in *Mille plateaux*, the rhizome comes to replace the notion of schizophrenia as a politically positive organising principle for the mobilisation of desire; he states,

> the rhizome—a kind of horizontal subterranean stem by which certain plants proliferate—is important because it is a structure *without* a structure, with no transcendent law of development, which can assume 'very diverse forms, from ramified surface extension in all directions to concretion into bulbs and tubers'. A rhizome is thus that *decentred* structure least likely to reduce multiplicity or difference by subordinating it to some higher developmental unity, and most likely to produce it [...]. As such, the rhizome is the model for a new kind of thought, of writing, ultimately of a whole new spatio-temporality, which Deleuze and Guattari counterpose favourably to the prevailing "arborescent" model of thought derived from the more orthodox (botanically speaking) root-radicle structure. (Heffernan, 'Œdipus Wrecks?', p.130)

29 Fredric Jameson, *Fables of Aggression: Wyndham Lewis, the Modernist as Fascist* (Berkeley: University of California Press, 1979), p.8. Although it is necessary to grasp the idea of the essential antinomy inherent in existence as viewed by Deleuze and Guattari, it must nonetheless be borne in mind at all times that this antinomy can never be absolute, that, even when one of these modes is in a position of dominance, the molar levels and the molecular levels are in a constant state of oscillation and reciprocal exchange. Nowhere is this clearer than in Deleuze and Guattari's analysis of Capitalism examined in note 27 above.

30 Deleuze and Guattari, *L'Anti-Œdipe*, p.451. It is in Capitalist societies that this oscillation can be seen most clearly, for, as Ronald Bogue notes, 'the preservation of despotic signs and the despotic state within capitalist societies [...] is evidence of an exacerbated oscillation in such societies between the two fundamental poles of desire, paranoia and schizophrenia' (Bogue, *Deleuze and Guattari*, p.102).

31 Heffernan, 'Œdipus Wrecks?', p.121.

32 *Ibid.*

33 Deleuze and Guattari, *L'Anti-Œdipe*, pp.14–15. Later in this same work they state,

> le corps sans organes est le modèle de la mort. Comme l'ont bien compris les auteurs de terreur, ce n'est pas la mort qui sert de modèle à la catatonie, c'est la schizophrénie catatonique qui donne son modèle à la mort. Intensité-zéro. Le modèle de la mort apparaît quand le corps sans organes repousse et dépose les organes—pas de bouche, pas de langue, pas de dents... jusqu'à l'auto-mutilation, jusqu'au suicide. (*ibid.*, p.393)

For a remarkable explanation of the concept of the body without organs, see Brian Massumi, *A User's Guide to 'Capitalism and Schizophrenia'*, pp.70–71, where he uses the analogies of an infant and the universe to describe this elusive concept.

34 Deleuze and Guattari also invoke the term "nomadologie" to describe this means of existence, the nomads inhabiting, in their account, not the sedentary striated space of molarity, but a smooth space, a space which is created only by the trajectories passing through it:

> l'espace sédentaire est strié, par des murs, des clôtures et des chemins entre les clôtures, tandis que l'espace nomade est lisse, seulement marqué par des "traits" qui s'effacent et se déplacent avec le trajet. Même les lamelles du désert glissent les unes sur les autres en produisant un son inimitable. Le nomade se distribue dans un espace lisse, il occupe, il habite, il tient cet espace, et c'est là son principe territorial. (Deleuze and Guattari, *Mille plateaux: capitalisme et schizophrénie 2* (Paris: Les Éditions de Minuit, 1980), p.472)

35 Deleuze et Guattari, *Mille plateaux*, p.199.

36 Heffernan, 'Œdipus Wrecks?', p.126.

37 Goodchild, *Deleuze and Guattari*, p.6.

38 Denise Aebersold, *Céline: un démystificateur mythomane*, Archives des Lettres Modernes, 185: Archives L.-F. Céline, 3 (Paris: Lettres Modernes, Minard, 1979), p.38.
39 'Conversation avec Louis-Ferdinand Céline', in Marc Hanrez, *Céline*, coll. Pour une bibliothèque idéale (Paris: Gallimard, 1961), p.227. Commenting on this statement, J.H. Matthews has stated that, 'for Louis-Ferdinand Céline [...] eschatology was less the anticipation of death than the invalidation of human activity, measured by the scale of death' (Matthews, *The Inner Dream*, p.3). In the light of the present analysis, Matthews' analysis of this comment can only be a blatant misunderstanding of the Célinian conception of death.
40 André Smith has suggested that death and Céline's obsession with death forms the only true unifying trait of his thought system (André Smith, *La Nuit de Louis-Ferdinand Céline* (Paris: Grasset, 1973), p.158), Erika Ostrovsky has noted that, although the eschatological phase is the most evident of Céline's subversive mythology, his *eschaton* is nonetheless invariably followed by cosmogony (Erika Ostrovsky, 'Louis-Ferdinand Céline: Creator and Destroyer of Myths', in *Critical Essays on Louis-Ferdinand Céline*, ed. by William K. Buckley (Boston: G.K. Hall, 1989), pp.92–100 (pp.96–98)), and Pierre-Marie Miroux writes,

> Écrire pour transposer l'atroce réalité en féerie de l'écriture, mourir pour passer de notre condition d'être déjà pourrissant à l'état de fantôme léger et dansant, voilà en fin de compte un même geste, celui qui consiste à dépasser le réel qui s'incarnerait en particulier dans le corps d'une mère boiteuse et engluée dans la matérialité du monde, et au-delà de laquelle il faudrait passer. (Pierre-Marie Miroux, 'Féerie de la mort', in *Actes du colloque international de Toulouse, juillet 1990* (Tusson & Paris: Du Lérot/Société des Études céliniennes, 1991), pp.183–193 (p.183))

It is surely Denise Aebersold who has expressed these ideas in the most fitting manner, however. She writes,

> Vermine potentielle prédestinée à devenir 'poussière', le corps et la matière sont perçus comme une prison physique, une geôle moléculaire que seule la mort pourra transgresser. Il est remarquable que la mort soit, dans l'imagerie céliniene, un éclatement biologique qui permettra aux cellules de remonter, en feu d'artifice, vers les étoiles, dans le mouvement contraire de celui qui fit leur déchéance. (Aebersold, *Céline: un démystificateur mythomane*, p.41)

It is precisely this positivity which is to be found in the notions of death and madness that is somewhat lacking in Isabelle Blondiaux's book, *Une Écriture psychotique: Louis-Ferdinand Céline* (Paris: A.G. Nizet, 1985), which, in many other respects, finds resonance in the present study. Blondiaux employs Deleuze's notion of the 'procédé linguistique' which is inseparable from the psychotic and his/her language (*ibid.*, p.14), for instance, and understands the psychotic in extremely schizophrenic terms, quoting from Resnik's *Personne et psychose*:

> le psychotique 'est "la multitude où règne la discorde, un troupeau dont le berger est souvent absent, l'homme qui est sorti de sa peau", qui ne perçoit pas ou qui dépasse les limites de son corps, celui qui erre entre le dedans et le dehors parfois sans savoir où se place ce qui lui est étranger, ce qui est extérieur à sa personne'. (Blondiaux, *Une Écriture psychotique*, p.15, quoting S. Resnik, *Personne et psychose*, coll. Sciences de l'homme ([n.p.]: Payot, 1973), p.23, quoting Nietzsche)

However, in spite of Blondiaux's claim that, 'L'univers du psychotique étant par définition celui du ressassement et de l'intrication, tout discours qui tend à l'organiser en un projet cohérent s'expose à en fausser complètement le mouvement' (Blondiaux, *Une Écriture psychotique*, p.15)—the very same claim made by the present study, albeit couched in slightly different terminology—her own analysis is, to a certain extent, guilty of the ideological methodology she warns against, being premised on certain normalised psychoanalytic (and often Œdipal) conceptions of death and madness, Céline's writing being for her an incessant confrontation against death and madness (see *ibid.*, p.117), rather than an expression built upon death and madness as a plane of immanence.

41 Allen Thiher, *Céline: The Novel as Delirium* (New Brunswick, NJ: Rutgers University Press, 1972), p.4.

42 Michel Beaujour, 'La Quête du délire', in *l'Herne*, pp.285–302 (p.287).

43 Yannic Mancel, 'Sémiotiques de la folie et de l'écriture dans *Féerie pour une autre fois*', in *L.-F. Céline 4: Lectures (2) de 'Féerie pour une autre fois'*, La Revue des Lettres Modernes, 560–564 (Paris: Minard, 1979), pp.123–147. Mancel's comments on this matter will be examined in more detail in Chapter 2 of the present study. Thiher also suggests that Céline emulates a state of pathological madness so as to negate time past. See Thiher, *Céline: The Novel as Delirium*, especially pp.199–203.

44 George Steiner, 'Cry Havoc', in *Critical Essays on Louis-Ferdinand Céline*, ed. by William K. Buckley (Boston: G.K. Hall, 1989), pp.198–204 [first publ. in *Extraterritorial* ([n.p.]: Atheneum Publishers & Faber and Faber, 1971)]; Patrick McCarthy, *Céline* (Harmondsworth: Allen Lane, 1975); Alain Ferrant, 'D'une compulsion l'autre: écriture et rhétorique de la confusion chez L.-F. Céline', *Revue Française de Psychanalyse*, 58 (1994), 483–492; Knapp, *op. cit.*.

45 Ferrant, 'D'une compulsion l'autre', p.484.

46 Knapp, *Céline: Man of Hate*, pp.147–148. Knapp is not the only critic to talk of schizophrenic traits in Céline's fiction. Denise Aebersold, for instance, writes, 'L' "amour-haine" que Céline voue à ses personnages témoigne à coup sûr d'un conflit profond chez l'auteur. Ces doubles que sont Ferdinand, Bardamu, Robinson, symbolisent tous un Moi tiraillé, schizoïde, oscillant entre des directions extrêmes et incompatibles, et qui visent à sa propre destruction afin de mettre un terme à ses conflits internes' (Aebersold, *Céline: un démystificateur mythomane*, p.70), but again, her comments attempt to uncover psychopathological traits in the author rather than processes in the texts.

47 This is understood by Isabelle Blondiaux when she writes, 'Mais, Céline n'est pas un banal psychotique, c'est un écrivain qui *négocie* avec la psychose pour construire son

écriture. Cette écriture, c'est indissolublement une certaine représentation du monde et des hommes et une manière de dire, un style, ces deux aspects étant soumis à une même logique' (Blondiaux, *Une Écriture psychotique*, p.14). In spite of the present study's divergence from some of the key concepts of Blondiaux's thought (expounded in note 40 above), her study should not, then, be thought of in the same terms as other psychoanalytic studies such as Willy Szafran's *Louis-Ferdinand Céline: Essai psychanalytique* (Bruxelles: Éditions de l'Université de Bruxelles, [n.d.]), and Albert Chesneau's *Essai de psychocritique de Louis-Ferdinand Céline*, Archives des Lettres Modernes, 129 (Paris: Minard, 1971) in which, as has been seen to be the case in a number of critical works, it is the author himself rather than the literary creation who is taken as the analysand.

48 Pierre Verdaguer, 'Tendances fantastiques et merveilleux raciste chez Louis-Ferdinand Céline', *Symposium: A Quarterly Journal in Modern Literatures*, 39.4 (1985–6), 284–300 (p.289).

49 *Ibid.*, p.287. One should perhaps substitute the term hyperreal for supernatural in the last of these quotations. See also Pierre Verdaguer, *L'Univers de la cruauté: une lecture de Céline* (Genève: Librairie Droz, 1988) where Verdaguer highlights the similarity between certain aspects of the thought of Céline and that of Artaud, the originator of the Deleuzoguattarian concept of the body without organs.

50 See Deleuze and Guattari, '1227—Traité de nomadologie: la machine de guerre', in *Mille plateaux*, pp.434–527.

51 Llambias, 'Guerre, histoire et langage dans le récit célinien', p.99.

52 *Ibid.*, p.100.

53 Henri Godard, 'Un Art poétique', in *L.-F. Céline 1: pour une poétique célinienne*, ed. Jean-Pierre Dauphin, *La Revue des Lettres Modernes*, 398–402 (Paris: Minard, 1974), pp.7–40 (p.16).

54 Llambias, 'Guerre, histoire et langage dans le récit célinien', p.102.

55 This statement is particularly significant in the light of the following comments from Philip Stephen Day concerning the *féerique* nature of Céline's ballets:

> Répondant à la définition de Roger Caillois, cet univers féerique ne s'oppose pas au réel parce qu'il est privé de réalité, mais parce que les tableaux sont situés 'où l'on voudra'. Le monde imaginaire des *Ballets* étant un paysage métaphysique, le réel ne possède ni consistence, ni permanence; le désir de l'écrivain est capable à lui seul de créer des personnages et des objets, de réduire les espaces et de télescoper le temps. Aussi, dans la mesure où ce monde parfait se fait proche du nôtre pour le hanter et l'attirer vers lui, aucune déformation sur la réalité n'est nécessaire: au contraire des romans, il n'y a pas de conflit ici entre l'aventure fantastique et un rétablissement éventuel de la réalité. Les *Ballets* sont donc soumis à une sorte de logique circulaire qui répond aux besoins de la féerie. Dans un cosmos imaginé, il est normal que seule l'imagination soit réelle et créatrice; cela fait que cette nature tourne dans son propre cercle et qu'elle paraît à la fois vraisemblable, cohérente et inexistente. (Day, *Le Miroir allégorique de Louis-Ferdinand Céline*, pp.197–198)

The present study will aim to show to what extent this concept of *féerie* can be said to govern the entire Célinian aesthetic project, not only that of the ballets.

56 Capitalisation is used in this list of molar institutions, and, indeed, throughout this study, to highlight the self-perpetuating mock grandeur and seemingly unquestionable authority of these institutions. Céline himself often uses capitalisation in precisely the same way.

57

> Si nous invoquons le désir comme instance révolutionnaire, c'est parce que nous croyons que la société capitaliste peut supporter beaucoup de manifestations d'intérêt, mais aucune manifestation de désir, qui suffirait à faire sauter ses structures de base, même au niveau de l'école maternelle. Nous croyons au désir comme à l'irrationnel de toute rationalité, et non pas parce qu'il est manque, soif ou aspiration, mais parce qu'il est production de désir et désir qui produit, réel-désir ou réel en lui-même. (Deleuze and Guattari, *L'Anti-Œdipe*, p.455)

58 See especially Bardamu's flight from Africa during a particularly severe bout of delirious fever brought on by paludism (*V*, pp.172–183).

59 See Ferdinand's experiences at the fair on his arrival in England (*MC*, pp.704–719), the reversed Œdipality of his life with Nora and Jonkind at Meanwell College (*MC*, pp.721–773), the picnic incident in the Tuileries (*MC*, pp.813–816), and his life with Courtial des Pereires both at the *Génitron* and *Blême-le-Petit* (*MC*, pp.831–993, 994–1088).

60 Henri Godard, 'Les Références au travail narratif dans le roman célinien', *Actes du Colloque international d'Oxford, septembre 1975*, *Australian Journal of French Studies*, 13.1–2 (1976), 7–17 (p.7). Godard goes on to remark that,

> d'une part cette présence indiscrète et cette allure passablement chaotique sont ce qui frappe d'abord, parfois ce qui arrête, les nouveaux lecteurs de Céline; d'autre part on peut penser que ce travail imprimé à la forme du roman est un des apports importants de Céline à ce genre littéraire que son ancienneté et son succès même ont usé, que l'on dit depuis longtemps déjà en crise, et qui ne peut plus vivre qu'en se renouvelant. Céline effectivement pose en termes nouveaux les choix narratifs que fait nécessairement tout romancier: choix entre différents rythmes temporels, entre différents types de regards jetés sur l'histoire et sur les personnages, entre une plus ou moins grande présence ou absence du narrateur dans son récit. Son originalité, ses innovations dans ce domaine du langage romanesque sont tout aussi sensibles que celles qui touchent au langage proprement dit. (*ibid.*)

It is surely to such aspects of the Célinian text that Xavier Tallon is referring when he suggests that,

> il n'est pas facile de lire un roman de Céline comme un récit, une configuration du temps particulière, pour reprendre les termes de Paul Ricœur. Le critique

> devra trouver un langage qui rend compte de l'incohérence, de la digression, de la fragmentation... Et il n'est pas sûr que l'appareil conceptuel de la narratologie soit parfaitement efficace en la matière. (Xavier Tallon, 'Thames and time: temps et narration dans *Guignol's band*', in *L'Année Céline 1990: Revue d'Actualité Célinienne*, ed. by André Derval, Henri Godard, Jean-Paul Louis et Éric Mazet (Tusson & Paris: Du Lérot/IMEC, 1991), pp.173–194 (pp.174–175))

It is hoped that the Deleuzoguattarian vocabulary to be used in this study will suffice as precisely such a language.

61 That there should exist such common ground between the notions of a supermolecular desiring/delirious mode and the anarchist attitude outlined by many critics is perhaps not surprising in the light of the following statements from Brian Massumi and Alain Cresciucci: 'Becoming-other is "anarchy". Since it undermines identity, its process can be considered schizophrenic' (Massumi, *A User's Guide to 'Capitalism and Schizophrenia'*, p.116); 'Céline met en évidence deux notions: l'anarchie et l'hystérie qui sont, au fond, une seule et même chose présentant les mêmes symptômes de perte de mesure' (Alain Cresciucci, *Les Territoires céliniens: expression dans l'espace et expérience du monde dans les romans de L.-F. Céline* (Paris: Éditions aux Amateurs de Livres (diff. Klincksieck), 1990), p.23).

62 Erika Ostrovsky, *Céline and his Vision* (London: University of London Press, 1967), p.31, quoting Suarès, 'A propos de Céline', *La Nouvelle Revue Française*, 9, 104, p.329. See also Yves Pagès, *Les Fictions du politique chez L.-F. Céline* (Paris: Éditions du Seuil, 1994). Pagès writes, 'L'apport limité que nous espérons apporter à la compréhension de l'œuvre célinienne tiendra surtout à l'étude minutieuse des sources et du destin de l'influence d'une sensibilité anarchiste sur l'ensemble de ses écrits, influence toujours vaguement évoquée, jamais analysée en profondeur' (*ibid.*, p.17).

63 Throughout this study, Céline (or the author Céline as distinct from the narrator Céline) will be taken to mean the literary voice that can be perceived through Céline's texts, not a real-life writer. This will remain true even when it is stated that situations in the Historical world can be seen to affect the Célinian aesthetic, for even though the material conditions of le Docteur Destouches will inevitably have repercussions for the art of Céline, it does not necessarily follow from this that the voice by which that art comes into being can be attributed to Destouches, the man behind the mask.

64 As Henri Godard has noted,

> le primat de l'émotion est d'abord pour Céline une vérité d'ordre général: l'homme est émotion avant d'être raison et langage; le chant précède le logos; il est en nous le plus "nature", donc le plus précieux, ce qu'il faut à toute force essayer de ressaisir. C'est cette vision qui commande la plupart des choix de Céline dans le domaine de la création romanesque. (Godard, 'Un Art poétique', p.14)

See also *ibid.*, p.23 where Godard says, 'L'émotion est pour lui à l'œuvre littéraire ce que le cœur est au corps; ce grâce à quoi il se tient debout, respire—vit'.

65 Something similar is suggested by Allen Thiher who, having proposed Céline's works as the culmination of a certain modernist project, states,

> Qu'il s'agisse de l'œuvre de Proust, de Joyce, ou de Virginia Woolf (et dans un autre sens de celle de Mallarmé, de Yeats, ou de Rilke), la recherche essentielle du modernisme est un espace de révélation qui propose une forme de rédemption. Dans ces œuvres, révélation et rédemption se trouvent reliées dans un espace narratif d'où on cherche à expulser la temporalité, car la rédemption est conçue d'abord comme un triomphe sur les ravages absurdes du temps. [...] Seule l'œuvre d'art, en rétablissant le présent dans toute sa plénitude ontologique, peut triompher de l'absurde et apporter une forme de salut. La révélation de cette plénitude statique, qui refuse tout dynamisme temporel, constitue l'essence même du modernisme européen. (Thiher, 'Le "je" célinien: ouverture, extase et clôture', p.47)

This position also finds resonance in Julia Kristeva's study, *Pouvoirs de l'horreur*, where it is suggested that literature is able to perform the task previously reserved for religion of providing the means to confront abjection, transcending horror and supplying meaning where there is none. The present study will use many of Kristeva's ideas on abjection, but in a modified form, for her study, in its determination to overcode Céline in terms of a Political, Historical reality, is often too reductionist and guilty of the psychobiographical fallacy that flaws nearly all studies on Céline premised on a psycho-analytic foundation. See also Julia Kristeva, 'Actualité de Céline', *Tel Quel*, 71–73 (1977), 45–52, where she writes, for instance,

> Et c'est là, dans cette annihilation de la transcendance pour autant qu'elle soutient toute identité subjective et institutionnelle, que le délire s'énonce positivement comme rationalisation défaillante (fictionnelle) du non-sens. La seule positivité vivable après l'effondrement de la transcendance serait-elle la positivité analytique—dissolvant le non-sens, le délire aussi bien que la rationalité totalisante? Céline, au contraire, n'analyse pas: sa positivité dans le délire (outre la "*forme*" où il laisse loin derrière lui tout recours psychana-lytique) consiste, pour ce qui est de la *signification*, à imposer, à confirmer le délire par des identifications partielles qui se prennent pour un tout. *Contre l'analyse, il a joué cette partialisation totalisante qui se nomme la politique.* (*ibid.*, p.51)

66 Gilles Deleuze, *Proust et les signes* (Paris: Quadridge/Presses Universitaires de France, 1996) pp.201–202. Although this concept of the work of art's totality cannot be understood in overly simplistic terms, it is nonetheless because of the incompleteness of *Casse-pipe* that this work will not be analysed in the present study for which the transversal dimension coming from the unity and totality of the work of art will be of paramount importance.

67 Philippe Bonnefis seems to intuit the existence of this transversality when he notes that Céline, 'renon[ce] progressivement à l'idée du beau style, pour l'idée, elle-même un peu tordue, d'un style qui irait tout de travers' (Philippe Bonnefis, 'De l'âme. L'hypothèse du ballon dans l'œuvre de Céline', *Revue des Sciences Humaines*, 71.200 (1985), 93–155, (p.119)).
68 J. H. Matthews has rightly suggested that in *Entretiens avec le professeur Y*, 'Céline's intention was to offer practice more than precept' (Matthews, *The Inner Dream*, p.228).
69 Céline's aesthetic will thus be seen to employ a mode of transmission more normally associated with music. As Michael Donley writes,

> Céline prend ce métro métaphorique parce qu'il veut aller 'directement à son but', 'au cœur droit', 'à l'âme', 'en plein système nerveux', tout en évitant les 'encombrements' de la surface—c'est-à-dire les habitudes de tri, classement, et de médiation de nos procédés de raisonnements qui ralentissent tout et nous placent à distance du plus riche de la vie émotive. Or, cette idée-clé de communication, *immédiate* parce que *sans médiation*, est déjà contenue au sein de l'analogie plus englobante qui donne forme, selon notre thèse, à l'ensemble de la production de Céline, c'est-à-dire *la musique*. Il est bien conscient de ce pouvoir qu'elle possède. N'écrit-il pas à plusieurs reprises que la musique est 'un message *direct* au système nerveux'? Il précise encore à Poulet qu'il voudrait bien imiter cette capacité de la musique d'être 'en prise directe sur les sentiments—sans intermédiaires'. 'Ce qui fait la force de la musique', selon Bourguès et Denéréaz, auteurs d'une étude sur *La Musique et la vie intérieure*, 'c'est qu'elle peut atteindre l'être sans passer par l'intelligence; elle n'exige ni concept ni idée pour être comprise'. Cette réflexion résume l'essentiel de tout l'*ars poetica* de Céline. (Michael Donley, 'Céline musicien', in *Actes du colloque international de Paris, juillet 1994* (Tusson & Paris: Du Lérot / Société d'Études céliniennes, 1996), pp.71–79 (pp.75–76))

The present study will go beyond this musical analogy, however, to analyse Céline's aesthetic construction in terms of Deleuze and Guattari's concept of a becoming-music, as this will be seen to have the advantage of introducing death into the score.
70 On this subject, see also Michael Donley, 'L'Identification cosmique', in *l'Herne*, pp.327–334, (p.331):

> En encourageant cet état de flux sur le plan mental, l'homme obtiendra la même satisfaction qu'en satisfaisant à ses besoins naturels. Ceci veut dire, en effet, que toute identité individuelle est un mythe. C'est l'orgueil pourtant, ou l'amour-propre, qui exige une telle identité et qui essaie d'arrêter le flux. Il est bien vrai que '*c'est tenir ensemble qui est difficile*', mais l'orgueil s'obstine à nier quand même le vœu fondamental de notre substance.

71 Goodchild, *Deleuze and Guattari*, p.6, quoted *infra*, p.12.

Notes to Chapter One

1 In the *Notice* and Preface to *Guignol's band*, Henri Godard notes how three or four volumes were originally envisaged for *Guignol's band* (indeed, he even provides evidence as to their projected plot lines) and considers the number of mistakes and illegible passages in the manuscripts to be indicative of the incomplete nature of the work, Céline normally being such a precise revisionist. See *Romans* III, ed. by Henri Godard, coll. La Pléiade (Paris: Gallimard, 1988), pp.ix & 934. Jill Forbes notes that this has also been remarked upon by Kenneth Ross Mullins in his doctoral thesis *Délire et création littéraire dans les romans londoniens de Céline* (Bordeaux III, 1974), where he suggests, like Forbes, that the second volume of *Guignol's band* may be either the second or third volume of the trilogy Céline intended to write, or else the first draught of two eventual volumes. See Jill Forbes, 'Symbolique de l'espace: le "Londres" célinien', *Actes du colloque international de Paris, juillet 1976, Bulletin de la Société des Études céliniennes*, 1 (1978), 27–40 (p.28). Such considerations will essentially be considered of little importance for the present study, however, for which *Guignol's band* I and II in themselves present a unified, coherent body of work which can be studied in its own right.

2 This choice of title was not Céline's own, but Robert Poulet's, the editor who undertook the posthumous publication of this volume, and is considered by Henri Godard, for instance, to rob the work of the unity that the title *Guignol's band* II would have provided (Godard, in *Romans* III, pp.x-xi). It should not be inferred from the present study's defence of Poulet's title that *Le Pont de Londres* is preferable to *Guignol's band* II—which itself highlights the importance of the *foule* in these novels, an aspect analysed by Yves Pagès in his *Les Fictions du politique chez Louis-Ferdinand Céline*, p.345—merely that it is an apt choice which highlights the importance of the bridge not only in this cycle of novels, but in Céline's entire career. This is in contrast to Alain Cresciucci's remarks that,

> Le pont, dont l'association avec l'eau vient immédiatement à l'esprit, est un peu le symétrique du passage. Mais le pont est découvert et sa valeur de lieu de passage paraît sans ambiguïté. Il est le lieu privilégié de l'éveil de la rêverie d'évasion. Il ne peut que faire rêver à l'évasion, car passer sur le pont ce n'est pas pour autant s'évader. Le pont est rivé à la terre, il n'a pas la capacité du navire ou même du train. Peut-être faut-il dire, aussi, que tout lecteur de Céline est porté à accorder au pont une place prépondérante à cause du titre que Robert Poulet a donné à *Guignol's band* II, *Le pont de Londres* et, effectivement, de l'importance de cet élément du paysage dans les romans du cycle londonien. (Cresciucci, *Les Territoires céliniens*, p.137)

This study's divergence from Cresciucci's opinion on this matter will become apparent throughout this chapter.

3 Philippe Bonnefis, 'Passage Céline', *Revue des Sciences Humaines*, 69.198 (1985), 141–167 (p.141).
4 *Ibid.*, p.143.
5 *Ibid.*, p.143.
6 *Ibid.*, p.145.
7 It should be remembered that, in a passage from *Voyage au bout de la nuit*, Ferdinand is drawn to a bridge from which some of his fellow *puceux* are urinating (*s'oublient*), using their own biological fluxes to create a connection with smooth space. On this subject, Michael Donley writes,

> Nous avons parlé de l'impression de soulagement qu'apporte tout flux. Or, l'écoulement de l'eau dans une rivière semble produire un tel état d'âme chez l'homme qui le regarde qu'il se laisse aller aussi à son propre flot. La coordination entre le flot microcosmique et macrocosmique—ce qui se passe lorsqu'un homme urine dans une rivière par exemple, ces '*artères*' du monde—suscite ce sentiment pour le temps cosmique. (Donley, 'L'Identification cosmique', p.333)

8 Bonnefis, 'Passage Céline', p.146. This statement should be contrasted with Alain Cresciucci's comments examined in note 2 above.
9 Interestingly, this last phrase echoes the vocabulary most often used to provide a layman's explanation of the creation of a closed system attaining a state of spontaneous self-organisation through the introduction of a simple attractor. See, for instance, Massumi, *A User's Guide to 'Capitalism and Schizophrenia'*, pp.58–59.
10 Note the coincidence of imagery between this passage and that from *Mort à crédit* to which it can be likened; in both cases the music seems to be an emanation from within the 'ventre'. See *MC*, p.815.
11 It is possible to talk of the action of the Imperial War Formation as being a function of Capitalism, since the former is one of the increasingly fascistic and paranoid mechanisms employed to recontain the liberated fluxes on which the Capitalist system is founded:

> Désirs décodés, désirs de décodage, il y en eut toujours, l'histoire en est pleine. Mais voilà que les flux décodés ne forment un désir, désir qui produit au lieu de rêver ou de manquer, machine désirante, sociale et technique à la fois, que par leur rencontre en un lieu, leur conjonction dans un espace qui prend du temps. C'est pourquoi le capitalisme et sa coupure ne se définissent pas simplement par des flux décodés, mais par le décodage généralisé des flux, la nouvelle déterritorialisation massive, la conjonction des flux déterritorialisés. (Deleuze and Guattari, *L'Anti-Œdipe*, pp.265–266)

12 The italicised words are those which are most relevant to the present analysis of this passage. What is particularly remarkable is the specificity of the vocabulary used. A

dictionary definition of *hébétude*, for instance, defines this term as an, 'état morbide marqué par une obnubilation des fonctions intellectuelles', a definition which is in complete accordance with the phenomenon proposed by the present discussion. As an aside, it should be noted that Brigitte is pregnant, as Virginie's pregnancy will later be seen as the physical manifestation of the fulfilment of schizophrenic desiring-production.

13 This vision has been analysed in a manner similar to that of the present study by Daniel Frizot, who writes,

> The hand is the hand of the artist who has been severed from the body, perhaps as a punishment for stealing the truth about man, and is still suffering of life. The birds are feeding on the hand, as poetry is the blood-thirsty creation feeding on a tortured artist. Poetry drinks the blood of the creator as the Christian drinks the blood of the Savior which brings the association of the artist as Christlike clown. Literature which is produced by suffering is the great soother that rocks the universe gently ('berçant les mondes') and creates the dream. The chapter ends in a poetic soaring which is immediately contradicted in the next chapter which starts ironically, 'rien ne s'affirme, rien ne luit!...'. (Daniel Frizot, 'The Clown Figure in Louis-Ferdinand Céline and Nathanael West or the Tragi-Comic in Modern Fiction' (unpublished doctoral dissertation, Purdue University, 1973), p.131)

See also his 'Céline's *Guignol's band* I and II, Puppet Show and Grotesque', *Synthesis: Bulletin du Comité National de Littérature Comparée de la Republique Socialiste de Roumanie*, 6 (1979), 263–268.)

14

> *Voyager c'est bien utile, ça fait travailler l'imagination. Tout le reste n'est que déceptions et fatigues. Notre voyage à nous est entièrement imaginaire. Voilà sa force.*
>
> *Il va de la vie à la mort. Hommes, bêtes, villes et choses, tout est imaginé. C'est un roman, rien qu'une histoire fictive. Littré le dit, qui ne se trompe jamais.*
>
> *Et puis d'abord tout le monde peut en faire autant. Il suffit de fermer les yeux.*
>
> *C'est de l'autre côté de la vie.* (*V*, p.5)

15 Godard, in *Romans* III, p.1017.

16 This metanarratival stratagem by which various possible readings of the text are presented by the text itself is, in itself, a means to highlight the metafictionality—which is to say the autonomy, or smoothness—of the text. As Peter Stoicheff notes:

> If language is recognized not as a neutral occasion for the direct transferral of meaning, but as a chaotic generator of significance whose interpretations are multiple, then the determinacy of the text it

> occasions becomes somewhat troubled. In effect, the text ceases to transmit the exterior world, and interrogates its own medium of transmission instead. This self-reflexive moment is a characteristic indicator of a metafictional text: it is a moment at which the subject under investigation is neither the ontological nor the phenomenal worlds external to it, but the complex margin of language strategy that separates the text from them. (Peter Stoicheff, 'The Chaos of Metafiction', in *Chaos and Order: Complex Dynamics in Literature and Science*, ed. by Katherine N. Hayles (Chicago: The University of Chicago Press, 1991), pp.85–99 (p.86))

Metafiction, when considered in the light of this analysis, can be seen to demonstrate specifically schizophrenic traits; for schizophrenics have a tendency to concentrate on the signifier itself rather than the signifier's signifying value, with the result that in a Rorschach test, for instance, the schizophrenic will be unable to see anything but an ink blot (see Louis Sass, *Madness and Modernism: Insanity in the Light of Modern Art, Literature, and Thought* (Cambridge, MA: Harvard University Press, 1992), pp.164–170). However, in light of Sass' subsequent comments that, '[this] tendency to focus on the *medium* of representation [...] has often been seen as a sign of a concretistic mentality, as showing an inability to transcend the literal, physical presence of a stimulus-object by perceiving it as representative of some meaning or some hypothetical world existing beyond itself' (*ibid.*, p.157), it is important to stress, once again, that by imbuing Céline's metafictional devices with schizophrenic traits, no suggestion regarding Céline's own mental state is being made. Even though his narrative can be said to destroy the standard signifying function of the signifier, it does this through a conscious process of *transposition*, not an unwilled symptom of pathology.

17 Godard talks of the polemic being 'repouss[ée] au second plan', (Godard, in *Romans* III, p.xx), and Dunwoodie highlights as one of the goals of *Guignol's band*'s anti-realism, 'une distanciation protectrice qui sert d'écran entre l'écrivain et les réactions du lecteur au contenu polémique et satirique souvent violent' (P. Dunwoodie, 'Merveilleux, étrange et fantastique dans les romans de Louis-Ferdinand Céline', *Les Lettres Romanes*, 37.1–2 (1983), 82–111 (p.84)). Although Dunwoodie's comments here are undoubtedly pertinent with regards to this specific aspect of the text, his attempt to try and pinpoint the exact way in which normal perception is transformed to create an effect of *merveilleux*, *étrange* or *fantastique*, seems somewhat problematic, for to do so necessitates a search for 'des indications concrètes *extérieures*' (*ibid.*, p.107), whereas the metafictional space that Dunwoodie is describing is that aspect of the text produced and transmitted heterogenetically, with no recourse to a pre-existing exterior reality.

18 '*Notre vie est un voyage / Dans l'Hiver et dans la Nuit, / Nous cherchons notre passage / Dans le Ciel où rien ne luit*' (*V*, p.3). The footnote to the Pléiade edition of *Guignol's band* also points out this similarity.

19 One need only recall the three most famous anniversaries which are based primarily on a fireworks display to see that this is the case: Bastille day in France, Guy Fawkes's in Great Britain, and Independence day in the United States. Isabelle Blondiaux also talks of

Céline's use of the *feu d'artifice*, but although she points out its "spectacular" qualities, she seems to relegate this interpretation in favour of one that sees in it precisely the Historical metaphor that the present discussion refutes. See Blondiaux, *Une Écriture psychotique*, pp.85–88.

20 Godard talks of the style of these sections in terms of 'un effet cinématographique de flou' (Godard, in *Romans* III, p.xx).

21 For a discussion of these terms, which are originally Genette's, see Shlomith Rimmon-Kenan, *Narrative Fiction: Contemporary Poetics* (London: Methuen, 1983; repr. London and New York: Routledge, 1989), pp.3, 46–51.

22 Thiher, *Céline: The Novel as Delirium*, p.88.

23 Dunwoodie sees this self-referential character of the novel in its fantastic elements, the incertitude created by the irreal being, for him, 'bien moins un renvoi *hors* du texte qu'un jeu infini, l'arbitraire et l'incohérence *dans* le texte' (Dunwoodie, 'Merveilleux, étrange et fantastique', p.109).

24 Hewitt, *The Golden Age of Louis-Ferdinand Céline*, p.203. See also: Nicholas Hewitt, 'Londres, la Capitale du vingtième siècle: esquisse d'une topographie de *Guignol's band*', *Actes du colloque international de Paris, juillet 1979, Bulletin de la Société des Études céliniennes*, 3 (1980), 31–44; Forbes, 'Symbolique de l'espace: le "Londres" célinien': Peter Dunwoodie, 'L'Espace londonien: *Guignol's band* I et II', *Australian Journal of French Studies*, 19.2, (1982), 158–184; Godard, in *Romans* III, pp.968–969.

25 The narrator's assurance at the beginning of this passage that he is guiding the reader can, of course, only be highly ironic, for by the very nature of this space, he is no more able to know it before entering into it than is the reader.

26 See, for instance, footnote 1 to p.497, *Romans* III, p.1127.

27 Godard, in *Romans* III, p.954. Pantin is also, of course, a district of Paris.

28 Colin W. Nettelbeck, 'Journey to the End of Art', *PMLA*, 87.1 (1972), 80–89 (p.84); and, Colin W. Nettelbeck, 'The Antisemite and the Artist: Céline's Pamphlets and *Guignol's band*', *Australian Journal of French Studies*, 9 (1974), 180–189, (p.185).

29 This metafictional interpretation of these scenes is lent credence by the explicit intertextual reference to the prologue of *Voyage au bout de la nuit* indicated by the italicised passage.

30 In the introduction to this study, it was suggested that Bardamu undertakes a similar quest. In stating that any character seeks an inter-polar mode of existence, it should not be thought that it is possible to attain a state of stability in-between the two poles of existence. All that it is possible to achieve is a balanced oscillation between the two poles, as opposed to the wild oscillation of pathological desire, or the subdued oscillation of the molar-subsumed subject who cannot escape the dominant pull of the molar pole.

31 It should, of course, be remembered that in every such oscillation, there is always the potential for imbalance; if there were not, the stylistic struggle being played out in the narrative of *Guignol's band* would never need arise.

32 Being an agent of the reterritorialising tendencies of Capitalist society, it is not unreasonable to see in the choice of name for this character a reference to Matthew the apostle, who was, of course, a tax-collector.

33 See *infra*, p.29. The implication of this parallel scene should be apparent, for if the opening sections can be said to be metanarratival, then this echo supports the thesis that the main body of the novels can be read as metafictional, Ferdinand's travails being an allegory for the author's search for a particular mode of expression that will sing an individual music in harmony with the collective.
34 See also *GB*I, p.254, *GB*II, pp.339, 342, 450, 536, 587, 589. To render explicit the metafictional reading, Matthew could thus be said to represent the ever-present spectre of "good", "traditional", "classic" literature.
35 Nettelbeck, 'Journey to the End of Art', p.84. Nettelbeck's comments on Ferdinand's attempted murder of Mille-Pattes have been omitted here, due to a divergence of opinion on the significance of this episode and the character of Mille-Pattes. This divergence will be examined later in this chapter, during the section dealing with Mille-Pattes.
36 *Ibid.*
37 The somewhat awkward term, 'the author Céline', is used so as to further emphasise the aesthetic nature of this quest, for to try and attribute Political intentions or goals to the man Céline from his writing—as do, to a certain extent, Nettelbeck's comments—is an infinitely complex and problematic task.
38 This character also appears as le colonel des Entrayes, of course, in the project for *Casse-pipe*.
39 Reference is being made, of course, to his frequenting the 'souteneurs' frowned upon by Matthew, and especially the murder of Van Claben and the burning down of the latter's house in Greenwich.
40 This phenomenon of the noise in Ferdinand's head will be examined shortly.
41 See the footnotes to the Pléiade edition for precisions on these points. It is also significant that, whilst in the Major's office, the smooth space outside seems to be calling to him, never letting him truly believe that the army will provide him with the oblivion he seeks therein:

> Moi je regarde les buées là-dehors... les buées qui passent devant la fenêtre... qui dansent... grands falbalas... le ballet des brumes!... pendant qu'il examine mes fafs... J'en fredonne un petit air!... [...] Ah! moi je rêve facilement!... Je me laisse aller comme ça tout de suite... je déconne pour un rien... je veux qu'il sache l'autre là... je le préviens le major... je l'avertis bien poliment...
> «Y a de la féerie dans l'atmosphère...» (*GB*I, p.261)

42 See, for instance, *GB*I, p.121.
43 *Mort à crédit*'s Courtial des Pereires could be considered as an earlier instance of such a figure in Céline's work.
44 As might be expected, this particular realisation is said to come 'Au moment où montent les ombres, où bientôt il faudra partir' (*GB*I, p.177), that is to say, at a time when the molar-governed subject is entering into a smooth or nomadic space.
45 Dunwoodie, 'Merveilleux, étrange et fantastique', p.90. To this list of Sosthène's counterfeit attributes could be added the fact that he hates the rain and fog, that is to say,

the elements' version of smooth space (*GB*I, p.284), that he talks of the primal energy he wishes to harness as a business venture, 'Le commerce des Ondes' (*GB*I, p.278), that his forays into 'la magie morte' merely turn into a sadistic enterprise that gives the illusion of death with cosmetics (*GBI*, p.298–300), and, finally, that Sosthène is seen to be a complete misogynist, saying to Ferdinand '«Attention aux femmes! Elles embrouillent tout! elles emmêlent nos moindres effluves! Elles affolent notre Destin! Je vais enfermer la mienne! Dès son retour!... Quelle garce!...»' (*GB*I, p.307). This last point may seem somewhat of an anomaly in this list, but, as will be seen later in this chapter, an inter-polar mode is only attained through communion with a woman.

46 The desubjectification intended as a result of Sosthène's dances has been expertly contrasted with that of the ballet dancer by Jean-Marie Guinebert, who writes,

> La danseuse ne renvoie qu'à elle-même. On retrouve ici la distinction majeure qui était faite entre la danse de ballet et la danse orientale incarnée par Sosthène. Dans cette dernière, tournée en ridicule par Céline, le danseur est à interpréter comme une figure symbolique. Par le jeu de son corps, il renvoie à une réalité supérieure. Mais ce ne peut être qu'un échec, une 'évasion manquée vers un sens évanescent'. Le corps est toujours amené à reprendre ses droits et Sosthène finit toujours par retomber 'seul subsistant, nu comme un ver, pâle et grisâtre…'. À vouloir fuir le corps, on s'explose à le voir revenir sous sa forme la plus misérable, dans la mollesse du 'ver'. La danseuse de ballet, tout au contraire, ne fait référence qu'au corps lui-même et c'est en cela que sa danse peut être une réussite, dans sa dimension a-symbolique. (Jean-Marie Guinebert, 'Présences de la danse dans *Guignol's band* et *Féerie pour une autre fois*', in *L'Année Céline 1991* (Tusson & Paris: Du Lérot/IMEC, 1992), pp.181–198 (p.190))

47 Knapp, *Céline: Man of Hate*, p.173. Yves Pagès also talks of this phoney Orientalism of Sosthène's as 'une relecture personnelle des "sciences orientales" [qui] aboutit au *double transport* de l'ésotériste néophyte; transport comme voyage de l'esprit mystique et transport comme apprentissage itinérant, parmi les "jolies vignettes" des Écritures bouddhiques' (Pagès, *Les Fictions du politique*, p.90). Pagès also suggests an intertextual precursor for the inverted Oriental symbolism of *Guignol's band* in *Le Singe et le Pourceau: Aventures magiques chinoises du XIIIe siècle*, which was published by Les Éditions La Sirène where Fernand Destouches was employed for a time. See Pagès, *Les Fictions du politique*, p.90.

48 Knapp, *Céline: Man of Hate*, p.174.

49 Henri Godard, in his footnotes to the Pléiade edition, makes a similar point and, furthermore, explicitises the implications of this consideration of jazz with regards to Céline's own style.

50 Bettina Knapp actually appears to believe that the whole of *Guignol's band* is constructed according to this model, likening Céline's novelistic project to the Nazi's

reversal of the swastika, converting cosmic order into desire for annihilation (Knapp, *Céline: Man of Hate*, pp.133–134). As will be seen, however, *Guignol's band* ends with, and is thus a quest for, creation.

51 As was mentioned in the introduction to the present study, anti-production injected into the process of production and a model of death in the unconscious are two of the various ways in which Deleuze and Guattari describe the body without organs.

52 Heffernan, 'Œdipus Wrecks?' pp.134–135. The sentence that Heffernan quotes at the end of this passage can be found on p.199 of the original French version of Deleuze and Guattari's *Mille plateaux*.

53 Hewitt, *The Golden Age of Louis-Ferdinand Céline*, p.218.

54 See Deleuze and Guattari, *L'Anti-Œdipe*, p.451.

55 Pagès, *Les Fictions du politique*, p.323.

56 Pagès, *Les Fictions du politique*, pp.323–333.

57 *Ibid.*, p.332.

58 Pagès (p.332) quoting Deleuze, *Présentation de Sacher-Masoch*, p.86, and paraphrasing Deleuze, *Présentation de Sacher-Masoch*, pp.85–90.

59 Letter to Milton Hindus, in *l'Herne*, p.110.

60 See *infra*, p.31.

61 Much the same thing is suggested with regards to the Borokrom of the pamphlets by Colin Nettelbeck, who draws this same comparison between Boro and Céline, pamphleteer. See Nettelbeck, 'The Antisemite and the Artist', p.184.

62 Deleuze and Guattari, *Mille plateaux*, pp.334–336.

63 For examples of the acute head pains that follow the vehement return of the molar paranoiac pole and reinstatement of Ferdinand's paranoid persecution complex, see *GB*II, pp.339–340, 342, 373, 397–399, 428–430.

64 It should be pointed out that, even though Virginie at this point in the novel is both removed from the world and supermolecular, her condition has nothing to do with the autism Ferdinand experienced in *Voyage au bout de la nuit* since she has not undergone the process of Œdipalisation and cannot, therefore, suffer from pathological schizophrenia. Her condition is, rather, one similar to that sought by the Sadian (as analysed by Pagès above, see *infra* p.52), that is to say, a state of primordial chaos anterior to all morals.

65 Thiher, *The Novel as Delirium*, pp.98–99.

66 Nettelbeck, 'Journey to the End of Art', p.84.

67 Even in *Guignol's band* II when Mille-Pattes comes back to haunt Ferdinand, he is not acting as an agent of the molar paranoiac pole that causes Ferdinand's persecution complex, for it is not Mille-Pattes himself, only the fact that Ferdinand has murdered him that risks a breach of molar codes.

68 Nettelbeck, 'The Antisemite and Artist', p.186.

69 'Impossible de faire comprendre à une famille qu'un homme, parent ou pas, ce n'est rien après tout que de la pourriture en suspens...' (*V*, p.426).

70 Cresciucci, *Les Territoires céliniens*, p.77. Cresciucci continues,

On notera la progression qui va de l'expression la plus abstraite, qui est comme le point de départ théorique du processus, au résultat le plus concret et cependant invisible, la puanteur. On reconnaît là le mouvement centrifuge de l'étalement—identique pour le monde: du cœur de la ville à la périphérie—qui est cette propension à échapper à toute tenue, à mal se tenir. C'est le pourrissement interne qui s'exprime par l'excrétion et l'odeur. (*ibid.*)

See also Michael Donley, 'L'Identification cosmique', p.328:

Nous avons vu que la matière, de par sa nature, tend à pourrir et à se désagréger. Or Céline, ayant souligné le fait que l'homme n'est que matière, conclut logiquement que sa destinée n'est autre que la désintégration; l'homme n'étant que '*de la pourriture en suspens*', il existe pour se désagréger, ceci constituant pour ainsi dire sa '*raison d'être*'. De plus, sa désagrégation, étant une force centrifuge, procède du dedans. De là, la réalisation que '*tout l'horrible de la mort*' vienne non pas du '*dehors*'—comme le croit Mme Henrouille, et beaucoup d'autres aussi—mais '*du dedans*'.

71 It should be pointed out that even though Ferdinand is fleeing through the night, he is still at the mercy of the molar paranoiac pole, hearing in the distance—as he did at the end of *Voyage au bout de la nuit* when in a similarly paranoid state—, 'une sirène de très loin... c'est du fleuve, c'est d'un navire...' (*GB*II, p.495), that is to say, a molecular vessel that he cannot reach.

72 Dunwoodie, 'Merveilleux, étrange et fantastique', p.105.

73 One could even see in this description of the dancer who is 'désossé de tous les membres' a literal description of a body without organs in the making.

74 Le professeur Y spends the entirety of the interview trying to suppress a dreadful need to urinate, reluctant to give in to the emotive style to which he is being subjected in the very explanation of the workings of that style.

75 This analysis differs from that of Nettelbeck's purely insofar as the interpretation of Mille-Pattes is concerned. For whereas Nettelbeck also sees Virginie's pregnancy as an aesthetic principle turned into a creative act, he goes on to state that, 'it is only with the incursion of Cascade's band into the idyllic life of Virginia's house, and particularly with the return of Mille-Pattes, that he is able to seduce her and release her potential fertility. In other words, if the esthetic principle is perceived initially as a spiritual value, it is only within the cultural context that creation—symbolized by Virginia's pregnancy—becomes possible' (Nettelbeck, 'Journey to the End of Art', p.84; see also his 'The Antisemite and the Artist', pp.186–187).

76 See *infra*, p.42. It should be pointed out that Virginie is already pregnant at this point.

77 The metafictional implications of this phenomenon have been examined above. See *infra*, p.36.

78 Nettelbeck, 'The Antisemite and Artist', p.185.

79 See *infra*, p.26.
80 Stoicheff, 'The Chaos of Metafiction', p.86, previously quoted *infra*, note 16 to Chapter One.
81 Quoted in Thiher, *The Novel as Delirium*, pp.113–114.
82 Colin Nettelbeck has noted how Kenneth Ross Mullins' thesis, *Délire et création littéraire dans les romans londoniens de L.-F. Céline*, also points up the significance of the bridge and the structuring role that it plays in the novel. Nettelbeck goes on to suggest from this, however, that, 'le pont détruit qu'on ne peut pas passer est remplacé par un pont intact dont le passage ouvre sur un avenir possible', this being, according to Nettelbeck, 'un exemple de la manière dont Céline cherche, par les moyens de l'art, à transformer le réel' (Colin Nettelbeck, 'Céline devant l'an 40: *Les Beaux draps* et le début de *Guignol's band*', *Actes du colloque international d'Oxford, juillet 1981*, *Bulletin de la Bibliothèque L.-F. Céline de l'Université de Paris VII et de la Société des Études céliniennes*, 5 (1981), 67–80 (pp.73–74)). Although Nettelbeck's comments are appropriate to his reading of the novels' first bridge, however—a bridge whose name, as Nettelbeck notes, carries a profound Historical significance (*ibid.*, pp.74–75)—, progressing ever onwards to 'Le Pont de Londres', the transformation of the real becomes, in the main body of the novel, the transformation of artifice by artifice, a *mise en abyme*, hence the autistic space that the novel creates between these bridges, the *mise en abyme*, as Louis Sass remarks, 'ha[ving] been described as a paradoxical combination of self-constitution and self-cancellation, a process in which categories are "torn apart" by their own self-referentiality' (Sass, *Madness and Modernism*, p.238). This progression towards a self-referential space of artifice is, of course, implicitly recognised even in the opening bombardment scene, by the direct allusion to the Pont d'Avignon commented upon above.
83 Nettelbeck, 'Céline devant l'an 40', p.76. Philip Stephen Day sees the differing degrees of integration of these bridges into the narrative as indicative of this very disjunction. He writes, 'dans *Guignol's band*, un des phénomènes les plus remarquables est la disjonction entre les "ouvertures" et le reste du texte. Le premier pont, celui d'Orléans pendant le "*bombardement*", est en fait le seul nettement présent dans le récit' (Philip Stephen Day, 'Ponts et creux dans les premiers chapitres de *Guignol's band*: passages, plongées, émergences, inversions, réversibilités', *Actes du colloque international d'Oxford, juillet 1981*, *Bulletin de la Bibliothèque L.-F. Céline de l'Université de Paris VII et de la Société des Études céliniennes*, 5 (1981), 243–251 (p.243)).
84 The following comment from Charles Krance forms an interesting counterpoint to this argument. He writes, 'le thème que vise la rhétorique de tout *Guignol's band*: à savoir, la détoxication de tous ceux de la bande (y compris Céline lui-même) qui ne cessent de prendre les mots pour des choses et les choses pour des mots' (Charles Krance, '*Guignol's band* et la rhétorique du geste célinien', *Actes du colloque international de Paris, juillet 1976*, *Bulletin de la Société des Études céliniennes*, 1 (1978), 123–140 (p.138)).
85 Deleuze and Guattari, *L'Anti-Œdipe*, p.16.

86 Cresciucci would appear to disagree with the present analysis, implying that there is, in *Guignol's band*, 'une logique sensuelle', a phrase which can only recall the title of Gilles Deleuze's work on Bacon, *Francis Bacon: logique de la sensation*, 2 vols (Paris: Éditions de la Différence, 1981), in which Deleuze proposes that Bacon's paintings can be seen as an attempt to attain precisely that kind of emotive aesthetic affect that this study sees at the heart of the Célinian project. (Deleuze's work on Bacon will be examined in more detail in chapter two of this study.) Cresciucci writes,

> Le féerique ne s'oppose pas au réel en ce qu'il n'introduit pas un deuxième récit à côté du premier. Dans *Guignol's band*, point d'interruption comme on en trouve au début de *Mort à crédit* lorsque le narrateur se met à raconter des légendes. La féerie est une dimension du récit lui-même qui met en avant une logique sensuelle. Dans les premiers romans, les lieux appelaient des images composant un univers sensible mais souvent rapportées à une interprétation idéologique. Nous ne disons pas que la vision célinienne du monde est complètement transformée dans *Guignol's* [...], mais les lieux font surgir des images possédant une dynamique autonome, donc capables de se développer et d'éclairer, enretour, le monde d'où elles proviennent. Cette liberté totale ouvrant la possibilité d'un monde onirique fait la différence avec *Voyage* ou *Mort à crédit*. [...] L'espace est le terrain de la rêverie ou, même, la rêverie est créatrice d'espace. (Alain Cresciucci, *Les Territoires céliniens*, p.186)

87 Dunwoodie sees this as yet another characteristic of the fantastical elements of the text. He writes, 'L'incertitude reste donc entière, signe de l'auto-référentialité du texte fantastique qui, en dernière analyse, est bien moins un renvoi *hors* du texte qu'un jeu infini, l'arbitraire et l'incohérence *dans* le texte' (Dunwoodie, 'Merveilleux, étrange et fantastique dans les romans de Louis-Ferdinand Céline', p.109).

88 Charles Krance's comments concerning 'parole' and 'geste' in *Guignol's band* are, then, entirely appropriate, if not as paradoxical as he suggests, for it is precisely through the positing of a subjectivity engaged in a becoming-imperceptible that an auto-objective expression, a collective assemblage of enunciation becomes possible. Krance writes,

> la différence majeure entre geste et parole en tant que signes qui *démontrent* tout en *se désignant* réside en ceci: c'est que d'après la tradition rhétorique le geste, surtout quand il accompagne la parole, démontre une virtualité dont la durée à la fois spatiale et temporelle dépasse celle de la parole. (Par analogie musicale, le geste serait l'accord qui résonne à travers l'espace de plusieurs mesures à l'intérieur desquelles se suit toute une série de notes.) Or, *Guignol's band* est le premier texte célinien à réunir geste et parole dans une corrélation actantielle immédiate (ce qui prête à ce roman sa qualité à la fois statique et dynamique). Toutefois, des les '*Braoum! Vraoum!*', ces phonèmes fricatifs qui explosent dans l'Ouverture, tout s'y

> annonce comme anti-durée. En nous rappelant, dans sa préface, que c'est '*le Jazz [qui] a renversé la valse [et que c'est] l'Impressionisme [qui] a tué le "faux-jour"*' et que par conséquent '*vous écrirez "télégraphique" ou vous écrirez plus du tout*', Céline semble surtout viser les syncopes dans lesquelles s'abîment, à la fois, les gestes et paroles du récitant. Pourtant—et nous voulons insister sur ce fait paradoxal—c'est à partir de *Guignol's band* que justement la présence de celui-ci se fait de plus en plus sensible. En d'autres termes, la présence de Ferdinand, voire sa lisibilité même, se fait d'autant plus remarquable que les signes qu'il agite, et dont il est lui-même agité, s'inscrivent selon une certaine réversibilité du code gestuel. (Krance, '*Guignol's band* et la rhétorique du geste célinien', pp.125–126)

89 Although his study concentrates on different aspects of the text, Philip Stephen Day also considers the diptych composed of *Guignol's band* and *Le Pont de Londres* to be a transitional work. See Day, *Le Miroir allégorique de Louis-Ferdinand Céline*, p.203.
90 Bonnefis, 'Passage Céline', p.142.
91 Thiher, 'Le "je" célinien: ouverture, extase et clôture', p.51.
92 John Updike has suggested that Céline's *points de suspension* are, 'driven with maniacal monotony toward a single point of deafness, of nothingness, of futility' (John Updike, 'The Strange Case of Dr. Destouches and M. Céline', in *Critical Essays on Louis-Ferdinand Céline*, ed. by William K. Buckley (Boston: G.K. Hall, 1989), pp.334–339 (p.337)), but to interpret them in this way is to negate all of their positivity, the fact that, if they themselves are an instance of anti-production, it is only by the constant feedback of anti-production into the process of production, as in the functioning of the body without organs, that production itself becomes possible. Some of the negativity of Updike's comments can also be felt in Charles Krance's study where—inferring a metafictional reading similar to that of this study, but one in which Ferdinand would look dumbly on whilst language crumbled around him—he writes,

> c'est précisément dans une telle rencontre entre geste et parole que se déclenche le fameux procédé des trois points. Car en plus du fait que l'aposiopèse traduit une certaine hésitation devant la parole dont dépend l'émotion pour se faire lisible, chez Céline elle annonce aussi bien l'efffondrement de tout point de repère qui permettrait de fixer la parole dans une cohérence discursive quelconque, si ce n'était pour le geste qui en fait partie intégrante. Ainsi, en *subvertissant* la fonction du discours proprement dit, Céline met dans un même abîme geste et parole, ces signes démonstratifs qui, en fin de compte, ne dé-montrent, ni dé-signent autre chose que leur écroulement partagé, tandis que Ferdinand, lui, le pitre châtié de ses propres tentatives d'essor parlant et gesticulant, reste toujours sur scène derrière le grand alibi du récit. (Krance, '*Guignol's band* et la rhétorique du geste célinien', p.131)

Notes to Chapter Two

1 See Deleuze and Guattari, *Mille Plateaux*, p.472.
2 Hewitt, *The Golden Age of Louis-Ferdinand Céline*, p.221.
3 Nicole Debrie, *Il était une fois... Céline* (Paris: Aubier, 1990), p.45.
4 In this respect, *Féerie pour une autre fois* can be considered a precursor to the trilogy on an aesthetic level, as well as, as Colin Nettelbeck suggests,

> la base même de la dernière entreprise romanesque de Céline [... car] sur le plan de l'anecdote, en expliquant les raisons de l'exode des protagonistes et en annonçant leur itinéraire, il s'impose comme un point de départ [... et] permet [aussi] d'établir la structure générale de l'ensemble, et fournit les données fondamentales de sa symbolique. (Colin W. Nettelbeck, 'Un Art conscient: structures, symboles et significations dans les derniers romans', in *Louis-Ferdinand Céline 2: écriture et esthétique*, ed. by Jean-Pierre Dauphin, La Revue des Lettres Modernes, 462–467 (Paris: Minard, 1976), pp.99–119 (p.100)).

5 Céline writes to Milton Hindus, 'Délirez si vous le voulez, mais délirez JUSTE attention. Pour délirer *juste* il faut que cela prenne au trognon de l'Homme de son âme, pas de *sa tête*' (letter dated 12 June, 1947, in *L'Herne*, p.116).
6 Frédéric Grover, 'Le Romancier et l'histoire: le cas Céline', *L'Esprit-Créateur*, 15, (1975), 332–342 (p.333).
7 Charles Krance, *L.-F. Céline: The I of the Storm*, French Forum Monographs, 75, (Lexington, Kentucky: French Forum Publishers, 1992), p.132.
8 Yannic Mancel, 'Sémiotiques de la folie et de l'écriture dans *Féerie pour une autre fois*', p.145.
9 Christine Sautermeister, 'Pitreries et dérobades dans *Féerie pour une autre fois*', in *Louis-Ferdinand Céline 4: lectures (2) de 'Féerie pour une autre fois'*, La Revue des Lettres Modernes, 560–564 (Paris: Minard, 1979), pp.93–105 (pp.103–104).
10 Thus, unlike *Guignol's band*, the retention of the same title for both volumes is vital, for to replace the title of the second volume with its subtitle—*Normance*—would break the already obscure unity of the work. In spite of this, the title and subtitle of *Féerie pour une autre fois*, *Normance*, were originally switched for publication (on the history of this title, see note 66 to Chapter Two below). Even when *Féerie* II is retained as the main title (as is the case in the Pléiade edition of the novels), some critics fail to reconcile the two volumes into a whole, as Allen Thiher notes when he says, 'Avant d'aborder une interprétation globale, le premier problème auquel le critique doit faire face lorsqu'il parcourt cette féerie ironique est de découvrir pourquoi Céline aurait donné le même titre à deux tomes qui se ressemblent assez peu' (Allen Thiher, '*Féerie pour une autre fois*: mythe et modernisme', in *Louis-Ferdinand Céline 4: lectures (2) de 'Féerie pour une autre fois'*, ed. by Jean-Pierre Dauphin, La Revue des Lettres Modernes, 560–564 (Paris: Minard, 1979), pp.107–121 (p.108)).

11 Although Henri Godard's painstaking work on the successive versions and genesis of *Féerie pour une autre fois* will not influence this study's interpretation of the novels in any way, his work in this field nonetheless brings a fascinating extra dimension to these novels which is vital to a full appreciation of them. See Godard, in *Romans* IV, ed. by Henri Godard, coll. La Pléiade (Paris: Gallimard, 1993), pp.1112–1177.
12 André Colombat and Ann L. Murphy provide good explanations of this terminology. The former states:

> Le molaire caractérise alors, pour la schizoanalyse, toutes les forces réactives qui forment des structures à partir d'une multiplicité quelconque, de flux libres et d'émissions de singularités, d'affects, pour former des masses signifiantes, des organismes, des figures, des symboles, des métaphores, des fantasmes, des ensembles, des sujets, des groupes assujettis avec leurs origines et leurs buts. Son mouvement sera décrit comme centripète puisqu'il part du multiple pour organiser des unités signifiantes autour de l'identité du "je" et de la structure qui garantit sa cohésion. (André Colombat, *Deleuze et la littérature*, American University Studies, Series II: Romance Languages and Literature, 132 (New York: Peter Lang, 1990), p.201).

Talking of Céline's valorisation of emotion, on the other hand, Murphy says,

> at the origin of this metaphysics is not a fixed or stable center, but rather the potential for the proliferation of centers, since it is the intrinsic quality of emotion to be precisely this movement away from the center and toward the outside, emotion by definition signifying a "moving away or out of". (Ann L. Murphy, 'Célinian Esthetics and Narrative Polyphony', *French Forum*, 16.1 (Jan 1991), 67–79 (p.73))

13

> L'axiomatique sociale des sociétés modernes est prise entre deux pôles, et ne cesse d'osciller d'un pôle à l'autre. Nées du décodage et de la déterritorialisation, sur les ruines de la machine despotique, ces sociétés sont prises entre l'Urstaat qu'elles voudraient bien ressusciter comme unité surcodante et re-territorialisante, et les flux déchaînés qui les entraînent vers un seuil absolu. Elle recodent à tour de bras, à coups de dictature mondiale, de dictateurs locaux et de police toute-puissante, tandis qu'elles décodent ou laissent décoder les quantités fluentes de leurs capitaux et de leurs populations. Elles sont prises entre deux directions: archaïsme et futurisme, néo-archaïsme et ex-futurisme, paranoïa et schizophrénie. Elles vacillent entre deux pôles: le signe despotique paranoïaque, le signe-signifiant du despote qu'elles tentent de réanimer comme unité de code; le signe-figure du schizo comme unité de flux décodé, schize, point-

> signe ou coupure-flux. (Deleuze and Guattari, *L'Anti-Œdipe*, pp.309–310)

14 Deleuze and Guattari, *L'Anti-Œdipe*, pp.263–285, 16–17.

15 At the risk of clumsiness, the narrator of *Féerie* will be referred to as the narrator Céline, so as to distinguish textual expression from authorial intent whilst pointing up the inseparability of the two.

16 Rosemarie Scullion, 'Social Spaces of Excluded Madness in the Writings of Louis-Ferdinand Céline' (unpublished doctoral dissertation, University of Wisconsin-Madison, 1987), p.35. Scullion uses Ostrovsky as an example of this movement, but by far the most worrying instance of such criticism comes from Bettina Knapp, who claims that, 'this [*Féerie* I] is the work of a man fighting for his sanity, a man trying to extricate the pain, anger, resentment, and unassimilated feelings that have built up within him and curdled in his subliminal world' (Knapp, *Céline: Man of Hate*, p.147), and that *Féerie* II sees the author sinking 'even more deeply into the morass of his subliminal world [...] no longer aware of the fact [...] that writing is an art and not a release mechanism' (*ibid.*, p.157). This is precisely the kind of reading warned against by J.H. Matthews when he says, 'No greater error could be made than that of taking this work of fiction [...] for the regrettable product of an undisciplined mind, floundering about at the whim of uncontrollable emotions'. Matthews goes onto to point out to what extent the narrator's apparent 'surrender of lucidity [... is] not the loss of professional competence but the intentional effect of a conscious esthetic decision' (Matthews, *The Inner Dream*, p.138), although he does later suggest that the misinterpretation the work tempts may be willed on the author's part (*ibid.*, p.149).

17 There is a subtle but important difference between this view and that of Mancel already discussed (see *infra*, p.78), who sees in *Féerie* a deliberately feigned schizophrenic discourse intended to procure a pardon for the author, to make possible the reintegration of Louis Destouches back into society.

18 The one instance of a material wall, that Cresciucci neglects to mention, is the cell wall against which Le Putois constantly attempts to break open his head.

19 Cresciucci, *Les Territoires céliniens*, pp.219–220. Yannic Mancel talks of the,

> fonction actantielle de la prison qui "transforme" le texte dans le sens du négatif et du néant (celui, précisément, du non-texte) [qui] nous amène tout naturellement (compte tenu des significations ambivalentes, à la fois très matérialistes et très métaphysiques, que revêt chez Céline ce type de structuration sémiotique) à nous interroger sur la nature de l'investissement que le narrateur-sujet aurait pu éventuellement placer dans sa pratique de l'écriture. (Mancel, 'Sémiotiques de la folie et de l'écriture', p.143)

20 Cresciucci, *Les Territoires céliniens*, p.220.

21 Massumi's definition of the apparatus of capture highlights the insidious, impersonal nature of this concept particularly well. He writes, 'There is fundamentally NEITHER BASE

NOR SUPERSTRUCTURE in a society. There are, however, STRATIFICATIONS: statistical accumulations of regularized functions of many kinds which interlink to form a self-reproducing mechanism preserving and disseminating certain balances of forces (an apparatus of capture)' (*A User's Guide to 'Capitalism and Schizophrenia'*, p.194, note 51).

22 Ian Noble astutely comments that this phrase, 'could [...] stand as an epigraph to that tendency of *Féerie* I which seeks to dissolve into a disconcerting flux all the fixed points in a system based on the norms of representational narrative' (Noble, *Language and Narration in Céline's Writings*, p.77).

23 Noble, *Language and Narration in Céline's Writings*, p.72.

24 For a discussion of Deleuze's theories on Bacon's work, see Mireille Buydens, *Sahara: l'esthétique de Gilles Deleuze* (Paris: Librairie Philosophique J. Vrin, 1990).

25 Deleuze, *Francis Bacon: logique de la sensation*, p.10.

26 *Ibid.*, p.9.

27 *Ibid.*, pp.16–17.

28 It is significant, therefore, that when the narrator does finally vomit, he does so in front of Jules' house (*FI*, p.158), for—as will be shown—the process of desubjectification the narrator undergoes involves the projection of his molecular self into Jules as an abject other. On vomit as a double movement of expulsion and retention symbolising man's ambivalence towards the death drive, see Vincent Mahé, 'Les deux temps du rigodon: répétition et destruction dans l'œuvre de Louis-Ferdinand Céline', in *L'Année Céline 1990* (Tusson & Paris: Du Lérot/IMEC, 1991), pp.157–172 (p.170).

29 It is thus the end to which the artistic expression is employed that acts to reterritorialise, rather than the expression itself as Noble suggests when he writes, 'for the narrator of *Féerie* I, imprisonment is at one and the same time the confinement within which a liberating form of writing is produced and a metaphor for the constraints of language' (Noble, *Language and Narration in Céline's Writings*, p.71).

30 Ian Noble also talks of the disintegrating body as a 'symptom [...] of the centrifugal, destabilising tendency of this novel', but sees 'the fragmentation of the body which frequently occurs in the text [as] analogous to that fragmentation of dispersal which the process of writing necessarily entails' (Noble, *Language and Narration in Céline's Writings*, pp.86, 88).

31 Cresciucci, *Les Territoires céliniens*, p.220. If the prison is said to be constituted by its inmates and their noises as well, it can be said, directly contradicting Nicole Debrie, that, *la prison est la folie* (see Debrie, *Il était une fois... Céline*, pp.27–28).

32 Thus, although Rosemarie Scullion grasps the intent of the narrator when she asserts that the prison in *Féerie*—one of 'three social spaces [...] through which power and its effects are disseminated'—becomes a 'textual space [...] through which madness is disseminated, [and in which a] dispersion of disorder functions as a form of resistance to and subversion of the normalizing strategies and effects of power' (Scullion, 'Social Spaces of Excluded Madness', pp.68–69), she is mistaken in believing that this is achieved in *Féerie*. She writes,

> through his writing of madness, Céline transgresses the laws of rational discourse and of the symbolic order. In his effort to catapult himself beyond the boundaries of the criminal code of the French Republic, he resorts to writing a "féerie". By means of this verbal enchantment, he will overtly defy the law and challenge the juridico-political norms of the state justifying his imprisonment. (*ibid.*, p.225; see also pp.220–221)

As has been seen, however, the denunciation of the normalising structures of the prison comes, on the contrary, from an internalisation of those structures that renders the narrator's expression as pathological as his neighbours' cries.
33 Deleuze, *Francis Bacon: logique de la sensation*, p.15.
34 It is, therefore, this antagonistic reader that prevents *Féerie* from achieving the double immediacy seen in the paintings of Bacon, in which are found,

> *immédiateté de l'œuvre à elle-même* en ce que l'œuvre n'est creusée d'aucune ambition représentative (pas de spectateur intérieur au tableau, pas d'intervalle séparant une forme d'un fond, pas de profondeur chromatique); *immédiateté de l'œuvre à non sens*, puisque les forces présentées sont censée influer directement sur notre système nerveux. (Buydens, *Sahara*, p.96)

35 Gilles Deleuze and Félix Guattari, *Kafka: pour une littérature mineure* (Paris: Les Éditions de Minuit, 1975), p.49.
36 See also *FI*, pp.71, 122–123.
37 To recapitulate, any true instance of desiring-production taking place on a plane of consistency, continually feeds anti-production into the process of production, so a truly emotive aesthetic intended to allow its recipient to re-invest reality, must, either implicitly or explicitly, foreground the finite nature of human existence, its zero-intensity.
38 Noble's analysis of the distortions of the signifier in *Féerie I* are highly significant for an understanding of how this analysis of the pathologisation of the narrator operates on a linguistic level, but only when his comments are freed from the psychobiographical trap they fall into. For although Noble is justified in stating, as has this study, that, 'the journalist's [(antagonistic reader's)] remarks are frequently concerned more or less directly with the placing of the narrator in the history of the Occupation', to use this statement to justify retroactively his own pseudo-psychoanalysis that sees *Féerie*'s linguistic disturbances as, 'a symptom of a repressed allusion to Céline's past, to the accusations of collaboration with the Germans', seems ill-advised (Noble, *Language and Narration in Céline's Writings*, p.108). Instead, it can be stated that the territorialising remarks highlighted by Noble act to reterritorialise the narrator's expression, which thus becomes pathologised or, in Noble's terminology, disturbed.
39 It could be argued that, in this passage, the return to molarity, the acceptance of the walls as a shielding device, enables the narrator to distinguish between his internal

sounds and the sounds external to him. However, in light of the doubt thrown on the reliability of the narrator's account by the question 'Je me répète?', it seems far more likely that his assurances serve rather to convince himself of the therapeutic value of molarity than to provide proof of it.

40 Potential energy is measured in joules.

41 The projection of the narrator's molecular self into another character, then, is a continuation of the attempt to find a pure aesthetic expression within molarity, not, as Noble suggests, 'a kind of symptom of the narrator's failure fully to realise an evident desire to conduct a pure monologue' (Noble, *Language and Narration in Céline's Writings*, p.81).

42 Deleuze and Guattari, *L'Anti-Œdipe*, p.285.

43 See, for instance, Jane Carson who sees the narrator and Jules sitting one at each end of a see-saw (Jane Carson, *Céline's Imaginative Space*, American University Studies, Series II: Romance Languages and Literature, 42 (New York, Paris: Peter Lang, 1987), p.64), later talking of, 'an epic battle between his [the doctor's] paranoid self and his aggressive shadow' (*ibid.*, p.73), and, 'a nightmare in which he (as Jules) seeks to destroy himself (as doctor)' (*ibid.*, p.74). Patrick McCarthy, on the other hand, sees the predicament of the artist in *Féerie* split into a trio of artist figures, 'Lili, who personifies the artist's triumph, Jules, who is his guilt, and Ferdinand, who bears his pain' (McCarthy, *Céline*, p.251). Closest to the stance of the present study is that of Jean-Marie Guinebert, who sees the fight over Lili as an aesthetic struggle, but a struggle not so much over appropriation of the aesthetic, rather than the form in which that aesthetic can most suitably be conveyed (Guinebert, 'Présences de la danse' pp.187–188). For her part, Isabelle Blondiaux suggests that, 'dans *Normance* narration et explosion sont placées sur le même plan' (Blondiaux, *Une Écriture psychotique*, p.80), and that, 'Jules n'est qu'une figure "projetée" de Ferdinand' (*ibid.*, p.85), 'une défense de type psychotique [...qui] consiste en un mécanisme de projection à l'extérieur du sujet du danger qui le menace à l'intérieur' (*ibid.*, p.63), only to enclose her analysis in an Œdipal framework in which, 'la parole maternelle meurtrière correspond en premier lieu au bruit des déflagrations. Concert apocalyptique orchestré de main de maître par Jules, le cul-de-jatte lubrique, celui-là même qui a osé porter la main sur Lili, l'épouse' (*ibid.*, p.83). As a result, Blondiaux's study fails to see the productive potential of the split subject, and thus sees the bombardment merely as a painful symptom of the, 'morcellement de l'être du sujet' (*ibid.*, p.59), a reading which does not correspond with the aesthetic *jouissance* conveyed in the bombardment scenes.

44 Godard, in the footnotes to the Pléiade edition of the novels, carefully documents the similarities of the character Jules to the painter Gen Paul, the character Jules being a consciously transposed and deformed version of the latter, and the deformation of Paris in Jules' apocalyptic symphony being inspired by Gen Paul's paintings. Indeed, Céline wrote in a letter to Lucette Destouches,

> J'ai commencé notre récit des Maudits—par le bombardement de la Butte—Comme c'est drôle à remémorer—Je place Gen Paul en chef

> d'orchestre du Bombardement—il dirige tout sur la haute plate-forme du Moulin avec sa canne—l'esprit du mal que tout le paysage gondole, enfle, gonfle, les maisons perdent leurs formes—Tout chahute—C'est l'esprit de ses tableaux qui se réalise—C'est le Sabbath à Popol. (letter to Lucette Destouches dated 28 March 1946, quoted by Godard, in *Romans* IV, p.1116)

The similarities to be found between Jules and Gen Paul are not denied by the present study's assertion that Jules can be considered as a double of Céline. On the contrary, these similarities only support this proposition, Céline and Gen Paul being (until 1944) close friends.

45 See *FI*, pp.38, 128.

46 It should be remembered that Céline's fantastical prison visitors, most notably his literary persecutors, arrive through the walls of his cell (see *FI*, p.89; see also *FI*, p.64).

47 David O'Connell points up some of the above similarities in his article, 'Jules, l'*alter ego* de Céline dans *Féerie* I', *Actes du colloque international de Paris, juillet 1976, Bulletin de la Société des Études céliniennes*, 1 (1978), 157–165, but uses his observations in an autobiographical reading which attempts to ascertain authorial intentions and ultimately perceives *Féerie pour une autre fois* to be a kind of self-help manual for Céline.

48 Deleuze, *Francis Bacon: logique de la sensation*, pp.16–17.

49 For this reason, McCarthy's assertions on this matter seem untenable, even if he sees the eventual result of Jules' appropriation of Lili in the same light as the present study. He states,

> Si Ferdinand ne renie pas Jules, s'il lui prête Lili, c'est parce qu'il sait que Jules est nécessaire. Il *collabore* avec lui. Jules séduit Lili qui, en tant que danseuse, incarne la beauté. La séduction, sexuellement incomplète selon la conception que Céline se fait des rapports entre la sexualité et la beauté esthétique, permet à Jules d'imposer sa vision: de transformer le Paris ordinaire en un Paris de rêve, Paris atroce mais beau. (Patrick McCarthy, 'La Multiplicité des narrateurs dans *Féerie pour une autre fois*', *Actes du colloque international de Paris, juillet 1976, Bulletin de la Société des Études céliniennes*, 1 (1978), 231–246 (p.239))

50 It is for this reason that the 'feuilles' are 'mortes', being petrified and devoid of desire.

51 It should be noted that the majority of the examples given to describe this process are to be found in the final pages of the novel.

52 In his footnotes to the Pléiade edition of the novel, Henri Godard notes Céline's disdain for the figure of the 'client' (Godard, in *Romans* IV, p.1301). In the present analysis, this term, apparently referring to the narrator himself, would therefore seem to express his disgust at his own integration into molarity. This interpretation may also

explain why it is that one of the highest insults repeatedly directed against Jules by the narrator is 'artiste', for it is both what the narrator no longer is, and precisely what he still desires to be.

53 Godard notes that,

> À deux lignes d'intervalle, Céline donne deux indications contradictoires, disant d'abord être tombé dans la cage de l'ascenseur, ensuite avoir été ramassé dehors. C'est qu'il mêle, avec un parfait mépris de ce genre d'incohérences, deux scénarios différents de l'épisode. [...] Le récit continuera à osciller entre les deux dans les pages suivantes. (Godard, in *Romans* IV, p.1303)

For this study, however, the ambiguity of this apparent contradiction is far more willed than Godard implies, resulting not merely from indifference, but a conscious choice.

54 The inability to distinguish between interior and exterior with the result that thoughts can come to behave like bodies has, of course, been highlighted as a specifically schizophrenic characteristic.

55 Although at this point in the text, Jules has not been spotted on the windmill, his absence from the building has already been noted, the narrator remarking, on p.182, 'Je m'enquière de ce qu'il est devenu?...'.

56 On this subject, Brian Massumi notes,

> A SCHIZOPHRENIC in the clinical sense is someone who attempted an escape from identity-undifferentiation, but was thwarted by society or otherwise failed. "SCHIZOPHRENIA" in Deleuze and Guattari's [sic] is not a malady; it is a process (that of becoming). A diagnosed "schizophrenic" is produced when the process ends in an abrupt impasse'. (Massumi, *A User's Guide to 'Capitalism and Schizophrenia'*, p.179, note 76)

See also Deleuze and Guattari, *L'Anti-Œdipe*, p.147, quoted in note 16 of the introduction to this study.

57 Nettelbeck, 'Un Art conscient', p.106. Nettelbeck's analysis of *Féerie*'s temporality, here, describes what can be called an aeonic temporality ('le temps d'*aiôn*'), a time described by Deleuze and Guattari as, 'le temps indéfini de l'événement, la ligne flottante qui ne connaît que les vitesses, et ne cesse à la fois de diviser ce qui arrive en un déjà-là et un pas-encore-là, un trop-tard et un trop-tôt simultanés, un quelque chose à la fois qui va se passer et vient de se passer' (Deleuze and Guattari, *Mille plateaux*, p.320). Such a time can only, of course, be described in the moment that it is experienced, which is why Nettelbeck's approach to this exploded temporality seems far more advisable than that of Allen Thiher who, whilst recognising the ever-present nature of the temporality, nonetheless attempts a classification of the levels of temporality between the two volumes. He writes,

> Malgré [les] différences entre les deux tomes, on peut voir que chacun est écrit par un Je perdu dans le flux du temps présent, par un Je qui affiche le masque du collaborateur bien connu et qui, opprimé par des forces extérieures, n'est pas capable de prévoir la fin de sa propre narration. Chaque narrateur existe donc selon la fiction de la parole directe, branchée sans médiation sur le déroulement même de la temporalité, ou, plus précisément, branchée sur la présence débordante du moment présent. Pourtant le narrateur de *Féerie* I peut se souvenir, et le surgissement du passé dans le présent, surtout le souvenir de Jules, l'artiste démoniaque, indique que dans l'esprit de Céline il existe entre les deux tomes un rapport de séquence. *Féerie* I, lieu où le souvenir peut exister, est une sorte de prélude qui présente la nécessité d'aller à la recherche du temps perdu, de déterrer le temps passé qui peut expliquer les catastrophes présentes, en l'occurrence, cet emprisonnement incompréhensible dans un pays étranger. *Normance*, lieu mythique où le mal se déploie, est donc ce passé, mais narré comme un délire présent. (Thiher, '*Féerie pour une autre fois*: mythe et modernisme', pp.110–111)

The reason why Thiher attempts the impossible becomes clear later in his article, as he attempts to attribute the author's choice of narrative temporality to an exculpatory intention, as Mancel has been seen to do with regard to Céline's schizophrenic discourse. Thiher writes,

> Pour créer le mythe de sa chute, Céline est obligé d'annuler le temps historique dans sa linéarité; un simple enchaînement causal d'événements dans le temps ne suffirait pas à tenir compte des maléfices dont il est victime. *Normance* propose donc un mythe fondé sur un temps cyclique, temps dont la structure est destinée à démontrer l'éternel retour du délire. En effet cette épopée tourne en rond. Le bombardement progresse sans jamais faire de progrès, et à la fin du roman le mouvement narratif ne peut aboutir qu'à son point de départ. (Thiher, '*Féerie pour une autre fois*: mythe et modernisme, p.116)

58 See Godard, in *Romans* IV, pp.1178–1179.
59 Ann Murphy also talks of this process, drawing on Bakhtin's theories on the 'hetero-directed double-voiced word' to make her point. See Murphy, 'Célinian Esthetics and Narrative Polyphony', p.74 and accompanying footnote.
60 The narrator Céline only gives Lili permission to pose for Jules on p.151, that is to say, after the first appearance of the aeroplanes in *Féerie* I, this section of the story following a linear chronology. Jules does not wait for permission to unleash his desire on Lili, but it is only once the narrator Céline has handed Lili over to Jules that the desire of the latter can find its full expression. It could be argued, of course, that, in the second volume of *Féerie*, Lili spends most of her time with the narrator Céline and not with

Jules. However, until the time of her disappearance, Lili's sympathies always lie with Jules, and she constantly defends him against her husband's verbal attacks.

61 The present analysis would therefore seem to be in agreement with Colin Nettelbeck who suggests that, 'il serait possible de démontrer que non seulement le bombardement de Montmartre, mais les grands épisodes de tous les derniers romans sont le produit d'une imagination profondément pénétrée par un esprit chorégraphique' (Colin W. Nettelbeck, 'Coordonnées musicales de l'esthétique romanesque de Céline', *Actes du Colloque international d'Oxford, septembre 1975*, *Australian Journal of French Studies*, 13.1–2 (1976), 80–87 (p.86)).

62

> Tous ces admirables auteurs ne jouent pas assez près du nerf à mon sens... en un mot je hais la prose... je suis poète et musicien raté—c'est le message direct au système nerveux, qui m'intéresse ce babillage m'assomme—Vive Aristide Bruant, Villon, Shakespeare, Joachim du Bellay, Barbusse (du *Feu*) HORREUR de ce qui *explique*... Proust explique beaucoup pour mon goût—300 pages pour nous faire comprendre que Tutur encule Tatave c'est trop. (letter to Milton Hindus, dated 11 June 1947, in *L'Herne*, p.114)

On the nature of style, see *Bagatelles pour un massacre* (Paris: Éditions Denoël, 1937), p.164: 'Un style c'est une émotion, d'abord, avant tout, par-dessus tout...'. According to Matthews, 'We can only misjudge *Féerie pour une autre fois* if unwilling to evaluate this novel in the light of Céline's statement of [this] esthetic principle in *Bagatelles pour un massacre*' (Matthews, *The Inner Dream*, p.155).

63 Such would seem inevitable for Blondiaux, who sees the failure of communication, especially between a subject and his double, as 'l'impossibilité de reconstituer l'unité de l'être clivé du sujet psychotique' (Blondiaux, *Une Écriture psychotique*, p.71). Using the terminology of the present study, however, this can be said to be true only if the schizophrenic subject is pathological, for, as will be seen later, it is only through the schizophrenic/l'être clivé, that Céline will achieve true communication.

64 Knapp actually sees Jules' disability as indicative of his inability to have a normal relationship with reality (Knapp, *Céline: Man of Hate*, p.153).

65 On the molar mechanisms involved in the creation of a scapegoat, see *infra*, p.80.

66 Some might find this metafictional reading a little far-fetched in view of the fact that *Normance* was not Céline's original choice of title. As Henri Godard notes,

> Le manuscrit qui avait été remis à l'éditeur le 2 avril 1954 portait encore, peut-on supposer, le titre sous lequel Céline l'annonçait dans sa lettre du 26 février, soit *Féerie* II. Est-ce ce jour-là que Gaston Gallimard fit admettre à Céline la nécessité d'un sous-titre qui distingue le nouveau livre plus nettement qu'un simple numéro de tome? Sa lettre à Céline du 21 avril nous apprend que celui-ci avait accepté la suggestion et proposé *Normance* pour ce sous-titre. En suggérant dans la même lettre une interversion du titre et du sous-

> titre, Gaston Gallimard donnait un second coup de pouce destiné dans son esprit à favoriser la destinée éditoriale du livre. Dès le lendemain, Céline accepte, avec un esprit de conciliation rare chez lui, dont témoignait aussi la dédicace du livre à Gaston Gallimard, tout équilibrée qu'elle était par une autre dédicace à Pline l'Ancien. (Godard, in *Romans* IV, p.1203)

The interpretation proposed by this study in which the protagonist Normance is a metafictional representation of the text *Normance*, stands up to this accusation, however, for, save one excess consonant, NORMANCE is an anagram of CE ROMAN.
67 On this subject, Pierre-Marie Miroux writes,

> De même que la tête de Normance a éclaté libérant des gerbes d'étincelles semblables au feu féerique, n'est-ce pas, symboliquement, l'écrivain qui explose dans cette œuvre qu'est *Féerie* II où l'écriture de Céline n'a jamais été aussi éclatée, même s'il s'agit bien sûr d'un délire totalement maîtrisé par le travail destiné à produire cette émotion, qui est la visée de Céline en tant qu'écrivain? C'est à l'ensemble des *Entretiens avec le professeur Y* qu'il conviendrait ici de se reporter pour y trouver cette théorie du "rendu émotif" qui caractérise les livres de Céline. Mais ce qui nous importe ici, c'est d'indiquer que dans cet éclatement se produit un renversement des forces de la mort en forces de production d'une féerie, au sens propre du terme, c'est-à-dire d'un spectacle extraordinaire, analogue à ceux que Céline pouvait voir dans sa jeunesse, comme la Prise de Pékin par les Boxers, mais qui les dépasse encore en merveilleux. (Pierre-Marie Miroux, 'S'Éclater la tête', in *Actes du colloque international de Paris, juillet 1994* (Tusson & Paris: Du Lérot/Société d'Études céliniennes, 1996), pp.183–188 (pp.187–188))

68 The metafictional parallel is reinforced here with an intertextual reference to that character who, in *Guignol's band*, has been seen to constitute a metafictional representation of the 'métro émotif'.
69 This analysis of the self-referential metafictional devices in Normance is given further credence by Llambias' highlighting of the 'théâtralisation' of the text via the operatic parallels found throughout (see Llambias, 'Guerre, histoire et langage dans le récit célinien', p.98. On this subject, see also Marie-Christine Bellosta, '*Féerie pour une autre fois* I et II: un spectacle et son prologue', in *Louis-Ferdinand Céline 3: lectures de 'Féerie pour une autre fois'*, ed. by Jean-Pierre Dauphin, Revue des lettres modernes, 462–467 (Paris: Minard, 1978), pp.31–62 (p.61)).
70 For the pathologised biological flows of the narrator of *Féerie* I, see *infra*, pp.85.
71 This is the very same movement practised by critics such as Knapp, who points out the schizophrenic nature of certain aspects of the text only to use them as charges against the author, as proof of, as she says, 'a mutilated psyche [...] a manifestation of the

physical and psychological distortions experienced by the author in his twisted and tormented world' (Knapp, *Céline: Man of Hate*, p.148).

72 For the allusions to Opera in the text, see the articles cited in note 69 above.

73 Talking of the motives behind his pamphlets, Céline would claim that they were only written to prevent the war: 'Je ne me suis lancé, (comme un con) dans cette effroyable aventure et quelle misère! que dans un but = un seul UNIQUE: éviter une *autre guerre*—Que le sang français *ne coule plus*—Hélas! Voyez comme j'ai réussi!' (letter to Milton Hindus dated 2 September 1947, in *L'Herne*, p.124). 'Une seule fois, à propos de cette guerre, j'ai dit: merde! faut faire quelque chose. Ces pauvres Français vont se faire embarquer dans un truc dont ils ne sont pas sortis. Mais c'est un fait qu'ils sont entrés dans un truc dont ils ne sont pas sortis. Ils n'en sortiront jamais. Mais ça, ça m'a valu un surcroît d'emmerdements' (from an interview with André Parinaud, in *Cahiers Céline*, 2, p.192). On this subject, François Gibault has written,

> Il estima dès lors qu'il fallait éviter à tout prix un nouveau conflit entre la France et l'Allemagne et foudroya tous ceux qui jetaient de l'huile sur le feu et poussaient à la guerre.
>
> Céline s'est précipité seul dans un combat mené principalement contre les Juifs, ennemis naturels du nazisme dont ils avaient été les premières victimes, et aussi contre tous ceux qu'il jugeait responsables de la décadence française: le Front Populaire, les communistes, les francs-maçons, qu'il fustigeait entre autres avec l'Église, les intellectuels en général, les alcooliques, les responsables de l'instruction publique et les Anglais.
>
> Animé au départ d'une intention qui n'était pas reprochable, Céline a voulu forcer le ton, pour être sûr d'être bien entendu, passant délibérément la mesure et se jetant lui-même dans un étau qui ne pouvait que le broyer. (François Gibault, *Céline 2: 1932–1944 délires et persécutions* (Paris: Mercure de France, 1985), p.10)

74 Nettelbeck, 'Un Art conscient', p.105.

75 Norbert's faith in the molar figureheads is fictional as they never arrive (*F*II, p.483), and the building that remains virtually untouched by the bombardment is described in such a way as to make it seem fantastical: 'la maison jumelle de la nôtre! la maison à l'envers de la nôtre!... pas à croire!...' (*F*II, p.472). In this respect, this analysis differs from that of Nettelbeck who sees Norbert as an indicator of, 'la composition nécessaire à la forme artistique, la transposition qu'il faut pour transformer la réalité' (Nettelbeck, 'Un Art conscient', p.105). This discrepancy stems from a fundamental difference between the present study and that of Nettelbeck in which the chaos of the bombardment is seen as reality, and the calm at the end of the novel as reality ordered by art (*ibid.*).

76

> —Ah les casseroles, c'est sa manie!
>
> —Mais non! mais non! c'est mon art! bouillir les seringues! (*F*I, p.63)

77 For a contrast to this kind of chronicle, see *infra*, p.103, where it is suggested that, at the beginning of *Féerie* II, in switching into the mode of chronicle, the narrator's existence is miraculated by the narrative.
78 Llambias, 'Guerre, histoire et langage dans le récit célinien', p.101. Llambias' insistence on the coexistence of the destructive with the creative are entirely in agreement with the present study's analysis of the ideal Célinian aesthetic as a plane of immanence on which anti-production is fed into the process of production.
79 See note 66 above.
80 Hindering clear sight, these events are apocalyptic, but do not constitute a true apocalypse which, as Kristeva points out, etymologically signifies, 'déchirement, enlèvement d'un voile' and thus constitutes 'une énonciation *visionnaire* [...] condensant au maximum le discours pour faire passer en marques sémiotiques cette innommable pulsion dans laquelle se loge, sans cela, la transcendance [...] Un texte donc où le récit s'est résorbé en syntagmes, ou en mots épars qui virent leur sens au rythme, à la couleur' (Kristeva, 'Actualité de Céline', p.49).
81 It is Pliny who serves as an example for this new aesthetic in which observation, not chronologicisation as the term chronicle might imply, is all important. For previous mentions of Pliny, see *F*II, pp.177 (*dédicace*), 190, 346, 352, 361, 447.
82 This is not to say by any means, however, that *Féerie pour une autre fois* should be attributed a lesser importance in the progression of Céline's *œuvre*, for Nettelbeck is absolutely right in asserting that, 'sans nier leur valeur individuelle, nous considérons les derniers romans de Céline comme un tout, dans lequel les deux volumes de *Féerie pour une autre fois* ont une place essentielle. [...] En fait, ce roman est la base même de la dernière entreprise romanesque de Céline' (Nettelbeck, 'Un Art conscient', p.100).
83 Some will object to this interpretation, saying that, in *Féerie*, the *métro* is repeatedly said to be being used as a shelter. This only adds weight to the present interpretation, however, for the use of the *métro* as a shelter provides a direct parallel with the appropriation of the poetic expression for molar ends talked of above.
84 Thiher, *Céline: The Novel as Delirium*, p.158. In the light of this analysis, Krance's lucid evaluation of *Féerie* would thus concern only the text's intentions and not its actual effects. He writes,

> Underlying Céline's subversive strategies is his concerted effort to revalorize his narrative in such a way as to make *explicit* the *implicit* capacity of the creative process to represent its own activity: in other words to turn the confined word inside out, 'sens dessus dessous' (*F*II, p.259), in order to create, for the narrating voice, a new space in which to reinvest itself—a space for another time. As a result of this subversion, the reader experiences a kind of double vision: as his eye shuttles along the erratic, disarticulated, fragmentary enunciations, he begins to develop a sense of the presence of the narrative I, whose whole purpose of being in this text is to draw attention to itself as an invalidated mouthpiece for the unjustly silenced author. (Krance, *L.-F. Céline: The I of the Storm*, p.149)

85 Carson, *Céline's Imaginative Space*, p.12.

86 *Féerie pour une autre fois* is rarely referred to as a whole, most critical works—this study included, to a certain extent—treating each volume as an individual entity or even, as is the case in Noble's study, entirely neglecting one volume and thus, in effect, only getting half the story. It is perhaps for this reason that Noble sees, in *Féerie* I, 'insistent opposition to the plural, dispersive tendency of Céline's novels [...] in the strident, obsessive, dictatorial tone of the narrator and [...] other forms of monolithic sameness' which, for him 'resemble[..] a desperate defence mechanism against the forces of dispersal' (Noble, *Language and Narration in Céline's Writings*, pp.109–110).

87 Yves Pagès, *Les Fictions du politique chez L.-F. Céline*, p.364.

88 *Ibid.*; my italics.

89 In spite of the apparent insignificance of these two proper nouns, Pagès points out that, 'écrit du temps des "petites autos atomiques", après Hiroshima, depuis que "plus rien" n'existe "que pour l'atome" (*F*II, p.268), selon le leimotiv rétroactif du livre, *Normance* est tout entier impregné de cette figure atomique: le souffle d'une explosion à partir d'un noyau de particules en extrême turbulence' (Pagès, *Les Fictions du politique chez L.-F. Céline*, p.165).

90 Debrie, *Il était une fois... Céline*, p.144.

Notes to Chapter Three

1 Nettelbeck, 'Un Art conscient', p.106.

2 Gilles Deleuze and Claire Parnet, *Dialogues*, coll. Champs (Paris: Flammarion, 1996), p.10.

3 Deleuze, *Proust et les signes*, p.198.

4 *Ibid.*, pp.200–201. As André Colombat points out, however, in such definitions,

> Il faut cependant faire attention à ne pas se laisser abuser par les termes employés par Deleuze. Le non-style et le pôle schizoïde ne "s'opposent" pas vraiment au style classique et au pôle paranoïaque. Tout au contraire, on doit affirmer le primat du non-style sur le style et du schizoïde sur le paranoïaque, des forces et des flux sur les formes et les ensembles grégaires ou moléculaires, le primat de la différence sur la répétition. En un sens, c'est le non-style qui est premier et le style qui crée des formes signifiantes et les ordonnent, mais, dans l'expérience, les deux ne sont jamais dissociables, actif *et* réactif, schizoïde *et* paranoïaque, différence *et* répétition. (Colombat, *Deleuze et la littérature*, pp.212–213)

5 Massumi, *A User's Guide to 'Capitalism and Schizophrenia'*, p.7.

6 Deleuze and Guattari, *Mille Plateaux*, p.390.

7 Cresciucci, *Les Territoires Céliniens*, p.453.

8 Serge André, *L'Imposture perverse*, Coll. Champ Freudien (Paris: Éditions du Seuil, 1993), pp.413–414.

9 Annie Montaut, 'Médecine, théorie du "style" et antisémitisme chez Céline', *Littérature*, 58 (1985), 42–59 (p.50). The affinity between this article and the present study soon turns into enmity, for Montaut goes on to suggest that there is a contradiction between the Célinian conception of style and the ideological thought system behind that style, that, in other words, the thematic and stylistic levels of the narrative remain irreconcilably divided.

10 Serge André is thus mistaken when he states that Céline's *petite musique* is a way for Céline to, 'introduire la danse dans la langue maternelle, de façon à la sauver de l'infirmité de la mort', for it is precisely by investing it with death—which is not to say that language thus becomes petrified—that the maternal language is saved (André, *L'Imposture perverse*, p.390). It is for this reason that André fails to see the concordance of form and content in the trilogy; he states, 'Le style de l'œuvre aurait donc chez Céline un sens diamétralement opposé à son contenu: le premier le sauverait de la pourriture et de la mort qui règnent à la surface et auxquelles le second le ramène inéluctablement' (*ibid.*, p.408). Michael Donley, on the other hand, well understands the importance of death in the process of dissolution necessary for the direct transmission of the Célinian aesthetic, and likens it to Bardamu's quest to rid himself of his egotistical pride. He writes,

> Néanmoins, la solution [que Céline] propose reste peu pratique et ne peut exister que sous la forme d'un état d'esprit. Pour son application totale il faut attendre la mort. De là, des remarques comme la suivante aui apparaît au premier paragraphe de *Mort à crédit* (titre qui illustre, lui aussi, l'obsession de la mort): '*Bientôt je serai vieux et ce sera enfin fini*'. Ce mot '*enfin*' implique le caractère désirable de la mort et de la détente qu'elle amène. La dissolution totale et l'harmonie entre microcosme et macrocosme ne proviendront que d'une coordination du rythme de celui-là avec le rythme de celui-ci. (Donley, 'L'Identification cosmique', p.332)

11 Nettelbeck, 'Un Art conscient', p.107.

12 Cresciucci, *Les Territoires Céliniens*, p.301. Although the beginning of *D'un château l'autre* is indeed a reiteration of *Féerie pour une autre fois*, it should be pointed out that one major element absent from *Féerie* is present and, as will be seen, of tantamount importance in *D'un château l'autre*, namely, Caron.

13 Nettelbeck, 'Un Art conscient', p.106.

14 *Ibid.*, p.107.

15 Philippe Bonnefis, *Céline: le rappel des oiseaux* (Paris: Galilée, 1997), p.39. See also Bonnefis, 'Passage Céline', p.151.

16 Bonnefis, *Céline: le rappel des oiseaux*, p.39.

17 Nettelbeck, 'Un Art conscient', p.105.

18 *Ibid.*, p.114.

19 It should not be thought that in playing this role of the '«homme de nulle part»', La Vigue enters into a becoming-imperceptible, for, as will become clear later, to play a role, to imitate, is not to enter into a becoming. As Deleuze and Guattari say of a becoming-animal, 'non pas imiter le chien, mais composer son organisme avec *autre chose*, de telle manière qu'on fasse sortir, de l'ensemble ainsi composé, des particules qui seront canines en fonction du rapport de mouvement et de repos, ou du voisinage moléculaire dans lequel elles entrent' (Deleuze and Guattari, *Mille plateaux*, p.336).

20 Philippe Muray also notes this link between Caron's boat, the trilogy's trains and the *métro émotif*. He writes:

> Le moyen de transport, le train, a une importance énorme. Il joue ici un double rôle. Il est à la fois l'équivalent sur sol ferme de la barque de Caron, et la généralisation du 'métro émotif' de l'écriture, l'application romancée de sa conversion au gouffre de négativité du métro. Il est l'image même de la fusion d'un sens et d'une forme. (Philippe Muray, *Céline* (Paris: Éditions du Seuil, 1981), p.214)

21 A litote, for instance, has no meaning in and of itself, it can only ever be imbued with a meaning by the engagement of the reader.

22 Deleuze and Guattari, *Mille plateaux*, p.320.

23 *Ibid.*

24 Goodchild, *Deleuze and Guattari*, p.107. La Vigue's faciality is never more accentuated than when he feigns his Christ role, for, as Deleuze and Guattari state, 'Le visage, c'est le Christ' (Deleuze and Guattari, *Mille plateaux*, p.216).

25 Deleuze and Guattari, *Mille plateaux*, p.209.

26 Retrospective narrative is here used to designate those passages describing events taking place in the supposed narrative past anterior to the supposed present time of narration, the narrative proper as opposed to the metanarrative, the level of focalisation as opposed to that of narration.

27 For an analysis of this strategy, see Yves de la Quérière, 'L'Écriture et le contre-courant: *Rigodon* de Céline', *Australian Journal of French Studies*, 19.2 (1982), 25–35 (pp.31–32).

28 See, for instance, Stanley Coen, *Between Author and Reader*, discussed in note 11 of the introduction to the present study.

29 See de la Quérière, 'L'Écriture et le contre-courant', p.35. These ideas of de la Quérière's will be examined in more detail later in this chapter. See *infra*. p.152.

30 Ann Murphy, 'Louis-Ferdinand Céline: Between Presence and Polyphony' (unpublished doctoral dissertation, Brown University, 1988), p.228.

31 *Ibid.*, p.16.

32 *Ibid.*, p.14.

33 *Ibid.*, p.65.

34 *Ibid.*, p.120. See also *ibid.*, pp.100–105 where Murphy demonstrates how, according to her analysis, this replacing of one monologism with another monologism infected with

the trace of the other it is intended to erase can be seen at work in Céline's theories on Rabelais and his dismissal of Aymot. See also Murphy, 'Célinian Esthetics and Narrative Polyphony', p.73.

35 *Ibid.*, pp.184–185. See also Kristeva, *Pouvoirs de l'horreur*.

36 Nettelbeck, 'Un Art conscient', p.102.

37 The metaphysics of presence being transitional towards polyphony rather than oppositional to it, the trilogy is situated, then, not *between* these two terms, but moves away from the former towards the latter.

38 Kristeva, *Pouvoirs de l'horreur*, p.9.

39 *Ibid.*, p.10.

40 Deleuze and Guattari, *Mille plateaux*, p.218.

41 Nettelbeck, 'Un Art conscient', p.116.

42 Denise Aebersold is thus perhaps correct in her suggestion that, in the pamphlets, Céline, by predicting what will happen to him and continuing on the same path regardless, effectively places himself in the position of the Jew, sewing a yellow star onto his own 'chemise brune' (Aebersold, *Céline: un démystificateur mythomane*, pp.89–90). This view is shared by Serge André who unfortunately, however, sees Céline's self-abjectification (he actually uses the word 'infâme', not abject) as a deliberate ploy to gain forgiveness for his anti-Semitism: 'La faute de Céline, qu'il a vainement tenté de racheter en s'identifiant de plus en plus à l'objet qu'il condamnait et en s'enfonçant de plus en plus dans l'infâme, est de n'avoir eu aucun sens de la responsabilité de l'écrivain' (André, *L'Imposture perverse*, p.353).

43 Kristeva, *Pouvoirs de l'horreur*, p.10.

44 *Ibid.*

45 Robert Llambias adds a valuable dimension to this analysis when he writes,

> Céline se rend [...] parfaitement compte de la précarité de sa situation, que les succès de *Voyage* et de *Mort à crédit* appartiennent à une époque révolue, et qu'il n'est plus qu'un spectateur impuissant de sa propre dérive. Il est remarquable qu'alors Céline, en authentique écrivain, ait immédiatement perçu que sa réinsertion possible dans l'Histoire ne pouvait s'accomplir que par l'écriture. Il va alors faire entrer l'histoire en force dans ses romans, mais cette entrée ne se fait que par une théâtralisation et un refus du réalisme historique: pour rejoindre l'histoire, il lui faut désormais l'inventer. (Llambias, 'Guerre, histoire et langage dans le récit célinien', p.96)

46 Factually, of course, Céline had had his royalties converted into gold and buried in Denmark, but this is not the version given in the fictional text:

> le plus grave maintenant, dans un sens, la frontière danoise... j'en avais parlé à personne mais j'y pensais je peux dire depuis Paris... même mon idée depuis toujours, preuve que tous les droits de mes belles œuvres, à peu près six millions de francs, étaient là-haut... pas

> au petit bonheur: en coffre et en banque... je peux le dire à présent *Landsman Bank... Peter Bang Wej*... ça risque plus rien... (*R*, p.886)

47 Deleuze and Guattari, *Kafka: pour une littérature mineure*, p.49.
48 See, for instance, *CA*, pp.45–46, quoted *infra*. p.137. Colin Nettelbeck points out that such a reading can even be extended to the apparently unambiguous motives behind the narrator's longing to reach Denmark:

> l'explication ouvertement donnée par le texte de l'attirance vers le Danemark—le fait que le narrateur avait mis tout son argent dans une banque danoise pour assurer sa sécurité—doit aussi se comprendre à un niveau symbolique, ce 'trésor' apparaissant comme le complément de celui que le narrateur et Lili ont porté avec eux, caché dans le double de la musette de Bébert [...] Les passeports, preuve d'identité; le livret de mariage, signe de l'intégration de l'expérience et de l'esprit de la danse; le pistolet et le poison, pouvoir sur la mort et, donc, relative indépendance vis-à-vis d'elle: autant d'éléments d'une disposition intérieure qui fait pendant au 'trésor' extérieur pour créer un moment de parfait équilibre entre la Matière et l'Esprit. (Nettelbeck, 'Un Art conscient', p.116)

49 Knapp, *Céline: Man of Hate*, p.200.
50 This same process can be seen in more condensed form earlier in the text: 'Hilda petite garce, surprise de Nature, était pas elle tarée du tout!... réussite coquine, diable au corps!... réussie?... enfin, 16 sur 20!... je parle de tout en vétérinaire, en sorte de raciste...' (*CA*, p.160); and later, 'mais le certain charme Aïcha!... moi qui suis extrêmement raciste je me méfie, et l'avenir me donnera raison, des extravagances des croisements... mais là l'Hilda, je dois admettre, c'était réussi!...' (*CA*, p.161), as well as in the narrator's evaluation of Laval:

> il était très brave... il haïssait les violences, pas pour lui, comme moi, que c'est décourageant, ignoble... moi qui l'ai traité de tout, et de juif, et qu'il le savait, et qu'il m'en tenait vachement rigueur que je l'avais traité de youpin, proclamé partout, je peux parler de lui objectivement... Laval était le conciliant-né... le Conciliateur!... et patriote! et pacifiste!... moi qui vois que des bouchers partout... lui pas! pas!... pas!... (*CA*, p.169)

51 The present discussion is not intended in the slightest to condone the text's methods, nor to deny that those methods may have unforgivable Political ramifications, but merely to suggest that, in the explicitly metafictional context in which they are placed, such techniques are employed not in order that the text be used for a Political end, but a political end (*polos* as opposed to *polis*), contributing, as they do, to the direct transmission of the aesthetic to the reader.

52 Debrie, *Il était une fois... Céline*, p.56. Denise Aebersold also suggests that, 'On voit Céline reprendre dans les dernières décennies de sa vie le thème de l'œuvre sacrificielle. Pour lui, la création, la seule digne d'un écrivain et dont il s'approprie la gloire exclusive, se paye par le don de soi-même. Elle signifie le martyre, le calvaire' (Aebersold, *Céline: un démystificateur mythomane*, p.103). Vincent Mahé, meanwhile, writes,

> Il y a un prix pour vivre: c'est de ne vivre qu'un jour et d'accepter l'oblitération totale de sa personne. C'est en se pliant à la loi de cette immédiate péremption que Céline touche l'éternité, ou du moins l'infini de beauté qui se refuse aux autres écrivains. Vivant d'un seul coup, il prend la vie toute entière, dans son intensité et dans son extension. (Mahé, 'Les deux temps du rigodon', p.161)

53

> Ce 'moi océanique', cette nostalgie d'une fusion avec les étoiles, cette souffrance d'avoir des contours, ce besoin de s'échapper du 'sac de peau pâle que le Bon Dieu nous a donné' trouve une espèce de résonance avec l'ascèse thibétaine qui parle de la peau comme du "résidu de l'égoïsme".
>
> > Si les choses nous emportaient en même temps qu'elles, si mal foutues qu'on les trouve, on mourrait de poésie.
>
> Mourir de poésie? Les textes céliniens laissent souvent apparaître cette tentation fusionnelle, se dissoudre—un terme familier à Céline—s'alléger, se désagréger, disparaître... [...] 'Mourir de poésie', restera un fantasme latent dans l'œuvre de Céline, exprimé le plus souvent comme une métamorphose rendant l'être humain assimilable à un souffle. L'eau, le ciel, les brumes, le vent, tout un univers fluide de formes transparentes qui se font et se défont, se conjuguent dans une cantate de dentelle pour enchanter ce grand départ vers une Cythère inconnue (Debrie, *Il était une fois... Céline*, p.107)

54 Nettelbeck, 'Journey to the End of Art', p.88.
55 It might be argued that Poulet's assertion that the narrator's discourse makes him laugh is proof of Nettelbeck's assessment of the comic nature of passages such as this; his laughter, however, would seem to be more of a nervous reaction, since the narrator tells us that Poulet was actually vexed by this conversation, an assertion which is supported by Robert Poulet's book, *Mon ami Bardamu* (Paris: Plon, 1971). This analysis is reinforced by one of the later diatribes (quoted below) in which Marcel laughs at the narrator's words in spite of his obvious anger (*R*, p.729).
56 Following the typographic conventions of the Pléiade edition, the stars here indicate a section break.
57 Nettelbeck, 'Journey to the End of Art', p.88.

58 In *Nord*, the narrator has already described History as the past devoid of desire: 'l'agréable du IVe Reich, si vous le jugez, *l'Histoire déjà, les vociférations éteintes*, c'est qu'ils pensaient aux moindres détails...' (*N*, p.489; my italics). Annie Gillain talks of this new desire-infused Historic temporality in terms of a Bakhtinian time of carnival. See Annie Gillain, 'Le grotesque du carnaval chez Céline', *Actes du colloque international de Paris, juillet 1976, Bulletin de la Société des Études céliniennes*, 1 (1978), 319–334.
59 De la Quérière, 'L'Écriture et le contre-courant', p.35.
60 The intention of this reinvestment of desire into the strata of History is, therefore, the opposite to that proposed by Albert Chesneau when he suggests that, in keeping open a line of communication—which, according to Chesneau, should never have even existed—between the worlds of personal myth and History, Céline perpetuates a non-sense (Albert Chesneau, 'Esquisse d'une conception de l'Histoire chez Céline', *Actes du Colloque international d'Oxford, septembre 1975, Australian Journal of French Studies*, 13.1–2 (1976), 126–133 (p.131)) in order to, 'nous égarer avec lui dans les dédales d'une reconstruction phantasmatique de l'histoire' (*ibid.*, p.129).
61 This notion of death as anti-production feeding into the process of production, as a pre-requisite for the attainment of a properly emotive style which disregards the logical constructs of the intellect, can also be found outside of the fictional corpus. Take, for instance, Céline's following comments, in which the abandonment of content and form in favour of style are said to be facilitated by his unfortunate status:

> Si vous vous mettez dans un cas tout à fait singulier comme le mien d'être traqué, et pas à la rigolade, pas traqué par les "passions", mais traqué à vous faire empaler et déchiqueter ou condamner en tant que repris de justice par vos frères, évidemment vous avez une histoire toute faite, vous n'avez plus d'efforts à fournir! Il n'y a plus qu'une question de style qui se présente. (*Cahiers Céline* 2, p.26)

62 The relationship between the narrator/protagonist Céline/Destouches is, therefore, even more complex than is suggested by Colin Nettelbeck who sees the separation of Céline in the narrative present and Docteur Destouches in the past as, 'un *procédé* qui sert à éclairer et à agrandir la distance entre les deux niveaux temporels du récit' (Nettelbeck, 'Un Art conscient', p.117).
63 See chapter two of the present study.
64 Day, *Le Miroir allégorique de Louis-Ferdinand Céline*, p.238.
65 'L'interrogation sur le titre [...] confirme cette impression de mise entre parenthèse du déplacement, juxtaposition de deux lieux sans liaison transitionnelle, affirmant finalement la différence du déplacement et du mouvement qui met l'accent sur ce qui se passe à l'intérieur d'un espace' (Cresciucci, *Les Territoires céliniens*, p.266).
66 Alain Cresciucci suggests something similar when he writes:

> Dans *Rigodon*, le train a d'abord pour fonction structurelle de définir le roman comme itinéraire. Avant d'être l'instrument capital du déplacement il réalise la métaphore du 'métro-tout-nerfs-rails-

> magiques-à-traverses-trois-points'. En ce sens la discordance expérience/roman se voit déconsidéré, car l'écriture ne relève que de son rapport à la chose ferroviaire. (Cresciucci, *Les Territoires céliniens*, p.274)

67 Luc Rasson, '"Le petit mot de trop": *D'un château l'autre*', in *Actes du colloque international de Toulouse, juillet 1990* (Tusson & Paris: Du Lérot/Société des Études céliniennes, 1991), pp.215–225 (pp.216–217). In these same pages, Rasson provides an excellent analysis of the castle.

68 On this subject, Philip Stephen Day has written that Céline,

> le naturaliste respecte l'être proche de l'harmonie universelle, plus apte que l'homme à en saisir les mystères; l'esthète ne se lasse pas d'admirer chez eux l'absence des défauts physiques qui nous diminuent. Dans le règne animal, c'est le chat qui réunit la perfection physiologique et formelle. Tous ceux-là sont des êtres privilégiés parce que, protégés du monde dur et hostile par leur harmonie interne, ils ont la possibilité de résonner avec elle, puis de s'évanouir dans le cosmos comme une onde musicale. (Day, *Le Miroir allégorique*, p.192)

69 Deleuze and Guattari, *Kafka: pour une littérature mineure*, pp.40–41. As will be seen from this quotation, a becoming-woman or a becoming-animal is, in essence, but a different intensity of a becoming-imperceptible. Indeed, as Deleuze and Guattari state elsewhere, 'Si le devenir-femme est le premier quantum, ou segment moléculaire, et puis les devenirs-animaux qui s'enchaînent avec lui, vers quoi se précipitent-ils tous? Sans aucun doute, vers un devenir-imperceptible. L'imperceptible est la fin immanente du devenir, sa formule cosmique' (Deleuze and Guattari, *Mille plateaux*, p.342).

70 It should be noted that Aïcha's complete mastery over her dogs merely reinforces her already obvious Fascist tendencies, for to train an animal in human ways, to Œdipalise it, is the very opposite of a becoming-animal. See Deleuze and Guattari, *Mille plateaux*, pp.292–295.

71 Colin Nettelbeck implies that the birth actually takes place (see Nettelbeck, 'Un Art conscient', p.111). This might explain the discrepancy between his interpretation of the novels' disrupted chronology and that of the present study. For further discussion of this subject, see note 74 below.

72 See also Bonnefis, 'Passage Céline', p.157:

> *Presque*. Il s'en faut de ce petit mot qu'au terminus tout enfin ne se termine, le voyage, et le livre, et l'œuvre peut-être... Comme si, à la toute dernière extrémité, *quelque chose* se refusait à la fin ou débordait de la fin. Un petit *quelque chose* qui fait que le roman va se clore avant terme. Car c'est ainsi que toujours il se clôt. Cette structure de l'avant terme est celle qui imprime à toutes les fins de

> Céline, fin de ceci ou de cela, fin de chapitre et fin d'ouvrage, fin de phrase, leur dimension si éminemment suspensive.

Seen in this way, the conclusions of *D'un château l'autre* and *Féerie pour une autre fois* would be in complete concordance, a view not shared by Colin Nettelbeck who suggests that, in spite of the parallel circularity of these two works, 'dans *Féerie*, il s'agissait de *restituer*, par les moyens de l'art, une réalité détruite, tandis que dans *D'un château l'autre*, il est question d'ouvrir la voie à quelque chose *qui n'a pas encore existé*, quelque chose de neuf' (Nettelbeck, 'Un Art conscient', pp.110–111). This point of contention rests more on Nettelbeck's analysis of *Féerie pour une autre fois* than that of *D'un château l'autre*, however.

73 Nettelbeck, 'Un Art conscient', p.107. To this list should be added the fact that, although not ready to die, having undergone a mastectomy, Mme Armandine's life is invested with death.

74 Colin Nettelbeck has also suggested that this disruption of the trilogy's chronology is performed with an aesthetic end in mind. He says,

> Céline disloque le temps parce que la vérité de son art l'exige. Or, sur le plan de l'art, le renvoi au passé ne concerne pas la vie de l'auteur mais son œuvre. En nous rejetant en arrière au-delà de *D'un château l'autre*, Céline nous ramène forcément à la fin de *Féerie*, comme le point de départ *commun* de *D'un château l'autre* d'une part, et de *Nord-Rigodon* d'autre part. [...] Il s'agirait ainsi de deux entreprises *parallèles*, *D'un château l'autre* ayant comme une valeur initiatrice pour la lecture des deux derniers. (Nettelbeck, 'Un Art conscient', p.112)

The present analysis will be in agreement with Nettelbeck in all respects, here, except with regard to his suggestion that *Nord* and *Rigodon* must be read as having the same purpose, for if the chronology of the trilogy is deliberately disrupted so as to send the reader back to the end of *Féerie* and to create a link between *D'un château l'autre* and *Nord*, then the first two volumes of the trilogy will reiterate the promise of the title of their predecessor, whilst *Rigodon*, chronologically posterior, will, eventually, fulfill that promise.

75 Day, *Le Miroir allégorique de Louis-Ferdinand Céline*, p.238. This idea of a movement without progress must not be confused with a nomadic trajectory governed not by movement but by speed. On this subject, Deleuze and Guattari write,

> Le nomade se distribue dans un espace lisse, il occupe, il habite, il tient cet espace, et c'est là son principe territorial. Aussi est-il faux de définir le nomade par le mouvement. Toynbee a profondément raison de suggérer que le nomade est plutôt *celui qui ne bouge pas*. Alors que le migrant quitte un milieu devenu amorphe ou ingrat, le nomade est celui qui ne part pas, ne veut pas partir, s'accroche à cet espace

> lisse où la forêt recule, où la steppe ou le désert croissent, et invente le nomadisme comme réponse à ce défi. Bien sûr le nomade bouge, mais il est assis, il n'est jamais assis que quand il bouge [...]. Le nomade sait attendre, et a une patience infinie. Immobilité et vitesse, catatonie et précipitation, "processus stationnaire", la station comme processus, ces traits de Kleist sont éminemment ceux du nomade. Aussi faut-il distinguer la *vitesse* et le *mouvement*: le mouvement peut être très rapide, il n'est pas pour cela vitesse; la vitesse peut être très lente, ou même immobile, elle est pourtant vitesse. Le mouvement est extensif, et la vitesse intensive. Le mouvement désigne le caractère relatif d'un corps considéré comme "un", et qui va d'un point à un autre; *la vitesse au contraire constitue le caractère absolu d'un corps dont les parties irréductibles (atomes) occupent ou remplissent un espace lisse à la façon d'un tourbillon*, avec possibilité de surgir en un point quelconque. (Deleuze and Guattari, *Mille plateaux*, pp.472–473)

76 These comments are applicable only to the narrator Céline, for the critical reception of *D'un château l'autre* had already changed the opinions of many with regards to the author himself, a shift which moved further still in Céline's favour with the publication of *Nord*. See note 77 below.

77 That this is the case is attested to by the work's critical reception. As Henri Godard remarks, '*Nord* fut d'autre part jugé supérieur à *D'un château l'autre* par la plupart des critiques, favorables ou défavorables, qui furent amenés à comparer les deux romans' (Godard, in *Romans* II, coll. La Pléiade (Paris: Gallimard, 1974), pp.1156–1157; for specific examples of such criticism, see Godard, 'La Réception critique', in *Romans* II, pp.1156–1159; see especially Maurice Nadeau and Robert Poulet, quoted in *ibid.*, p.1157).

78 See also *N*, pp.318–319, quoted *infra* p.167.

79 Deleuze and Guattari, *Mille plateaux*, pp.438–439.

80 *Ibid.*, p.519.

81 '[La pensée nomade] ne se fonde pas sur une totalité englobante, mais au contraire se déploie dans un milieu sans horizon comme espace lisse, steppe, désert ou mer' (Deleuze and Guattari, *Mille plateaux*, p.469).

82 It is interesting to note that in the Zenith Hotel, Lili and Bébert are able to move about freely, whereas the protagonist Céline/Destouches and La Vigue are only able to traverse this smooth space by a "becoming-Bébert": 'Bon!... je fais l'effort... à quatre pattes... je démolis un peu le bas du mur... La Vigue vient aussi, à quatre pattes...' (*N*, p.344).

83 After the passport photograph incident La Vigue dons the false identity of Norvins Étienne as though it were a role (*N*, p.364); upon discovering that his trousers have been ripped apart by rats in his room he states that he cannot believe that this is happening to him who once played the Misanthrope (*N*, p.575); when showing Célinc/Destouches a mark on his head that he insists is the result of an attack by a group of people, he is said to 'louche[r] comme dans son dernier film… même plus' (*N*, p.632); and, at the height of

his madness, he is described as being 'somnambule... [comme à] rue Lepic quand il se battait avec un rôle, qu'il le possédait pas... pas encore... absent... entre le réel et scène...' (*N*, p.648).

84 It should be remembered that there is an almost unequivocal equivalence between a schizophrenic mode and a nomadic mode for Deleuze and Guattari, the latter term replacing the former, in *Mille plateaux*, so as to avoid the misinterpretation to which their ideas on the schizophrenic (in the earlier *L'Anti-Œdipe*) were all too often subjected.

85 It is for this reason that the novel ends with a heated debate between Harras and Göring regarding the route taken by the German army's retreat from Russia (*N*, pp.706–707). For Deleuze and Guattari's discussion of this aspect of the nomadic trajectory, see *Mille plateaux*, p.471:

> Le nomade a un territoire, il suit des trajets coutumiers, il va d'un point à un autre, il n'ignore pas les points (point d'eau, d'habitation, d'assemblée, etc.). Mais la question, c'est ce qui est principe ou seulement conséquence dans la vie nomade. En premier lieu, même si les points déterminent les trajets, ils sont strictement subordonnés aux trajets qu'ils déterminent, à l'inverse de ce qui se passe chez le sédentaire. Le point d'eau n'est que pour être quitté, et tout point est un relais et n'existe que comme relais. Un trajet est toujours entre deux points, mais l'entre-deux a pris toute la consistance, et jouit d'une autonomie comme d'une direction propre.

As an aside, it might be suggested that the term 'philosophique accélérée' provides a perfect description of Deleuze and Guattari's nomadic thought system.

86 Day, *Le Miroir allégorique de Louis-Ferdinand Céline*, p.238.

87 One should, at this point, remember Colin Nettelbeck's assertion that, 'le Nord qu'il ne faut pas perdre est la direction qui rapproche de la Vie: c'est encore une métaphore de l'idéal artistique'. Quoted *infra.*, p.136.

88 The protagonist Céline/Destouches and Lili have already found themselves alone at certain points in the trilogy—although not quite as often as might be expected for a married couple—, but at such times, if any action or thought process takes place at all, then the emphasis is always on Céline/Destouches. The difference with this case, then, is that they *act* together as one, as is indicated by the first person plural.

89 Deleuze and Guattari, *Mille plateaux*, p.209, also quoted *infra.*, p.132. In the light of this quotation, it should be remembered that La Vigue has been said to indulge in faciality. It is thus by getting rid of him that the protagonist Céline/Destouches will 'échapper au visage, défaire le visage et les visagéifications'.

90 On this subject, Henri Godard writes in a letter to the author of this study: 'La page du manuscrit correspondant au passage à la page Pléiade 747 se trouve à la page 138. Ce n'est pas exclu que dans une version antérieure le passage ait figuré à une page 149 et que Céline se soit amusé à reprendre le numéro pour celui du bateau'.

91 All of these examples recall, of course, Céline's famous declaration that in writing, 'Il faut noircir, et se noircir' (quoted in J.C., 'Le Docteur écrit un roman', in *L'Herne*, pp.209–212 (p.211)).
92 Christ, it will be remembered, is the very epitome of the process of faciality. See *infra*, p.135 and note 24 to Chapter Three above.
93 Deleuze and Guattari, *Mille plateaux*, p.367.
94 *Ibid.*, p.390. Also quoted *infra.*, p.124.
95 *Ibid.*, p.361.
96 Deleuze and Guattari, *Mille plateaux*, p.365.
97 In the context of the present study, the underlined passage can be seen to refer not only to the two groups of protagonists in the *récit*, but also to the narrator and the reader, as a becoming-reader/text is entered into, and also to the protagonist Céline/Destouches and the narrator Céline as their respective temporal and topographical strata blend into eachother. To use Krance's terminology, it might also be said that at this point, 'the *je*, or the effective, existential self', fuses with, 'the *moi*, or what we might call the *ecstatic* self' (Charles Krance, 'Céline and the Literature of Extasis', p.180).
98 Nettelbeck, 'Journey to the End of Art', p.89.
99 Colin Nettelbeck also talks of a kind of becoming-music of the text through transposition into an alternative temporality when he writes,

> Mais qu'est-ce, au juste, que cette perception musicale de la réalité? En termes abstraits, on peut dire qu'elle est la synchronisation du temps affectif de l'individu avec le passage d'un autre temps qu'on peut caractériser d'extérieur à l'individu, de façon à produire dans l'individu une sensation d'harmonie et de continuité rythmique qui est musique. (Colin W. Nettelbeck, 'Notion et fonction de la "transposition" chez Céline et Proust', p.17)

100 Deleuze and Guattari, *Mille plateaux*, pp.367–368.
101 'Ce n'est pas l'enfant qui devient adulte, c'est le devenir-enfant qui fait une jeunesse universelle' (Deleuze and Guattari, *Mille plateaux*, p.339).
102 Nettelbeck, 'Journey to the End of Art', p.89. Although Nettelbeck also considers the children's role to be 'clearly positive', he seems to suggest that this is *in spite of* their cretinous characteristics rather than *because of* those very traits as the present study would suggest. See also Nettelbeck, 'Un Art conscient', pp.116–117.
103 Talking of this physical degradation, Serge André writes, 'plus Céline progresse dans ce travail de fétichisation de la langue, plus il se décompose lui-même corporellement' (André, *L'Imposture perverse*, p.416).
104 Cresciucci, *Les Territoires céliniens*, p.323.
105 *Ibid.*; my emphasis in bold typeface.
106 *Ibid.*; my italics. See also *ibid.*, p.338 where Cresciucci talks of death being the driving force of Céline's entire *œuvre* in similarly negative terms.
107 In the light of these comments, it may be no coincidence that Céline's completed prose works number twelve: *Voyage au bout de la nuit*, *Mort à crédit*, *Guignol's band* I,

Guignol's band II, *Bagatelles pour un massacre*, *L'École des cadavres*, *Les Beaux draps*, *Féerie pour une autre fois* I, *Féerie pour une autre fois* II, *D'un Château l'autre*, *Nord* and *Rigodon*.

108 The present analysis is not dissimilar to that of Colin Nettelbeck who writes,

> The passport, as proof of identity, signifies that Céline has arrived at the end of his life-journey intact. The marriage certificate symbolizes the total merging of the narrator with Lili, the marriage of experience with the spirit of the dance: hence the title of the work. Beyond history, beyond art, apotheosis has been reached. But total liberation is only possible in death, which explains the presence of the cyanide. Death, here, is no longer the negation of Life, but the peaceful end for one whose work has been completed. That Céline put the final touches on this novel the day he died is poignantly significant: there could be no reason for writing anything more. *Rigodon* is his *Nunc dimittis*, and, as such, is a fitting epilogue for the whole opus. (Nettelbeck, 'Journey to the End of Art', p.89)

Although it is doubtless tempting to speculate as to the deeper significance of Céline's timely death, however, to do so somewhat conflates fiction and biography. This is unfortunate, for by privileging the author's actual death as opposed to his acceptance of it, it is almost possible to infer from Nettelbeck's statements that *Rigodon* is some kind of suicide note.

109 Lucette Destouches quoted in *Romans* II, p.1183.

110 Many critics have commented on the double meaning of the word 'rigodon'. See especially Mahé, 'Les deux temps du rigodon'.

111 Bonnefis, 'Passage Céline', p.163.

112 Aebersold, *Céline: un démystificateur mythomane*, pp.119–120.

113 Deleuze and Guattari, *L'Anti-Œdipe*, pp.14–15.

114 Deleuze and Guattari, *Mille plateaux*, pp.189–190.

115 Massumi, *A User's Guide to 'Capitalism and Schizophrenia'*, p.150, footnote 29.

116 Ian Noble has talked of the points of suspension as a, 'degree zero of punctuation open to a variety of connections and subordinations which the reader is to supply', and which have the effect that, 'words appear to burst into existence out of a void, without an immediate context within which their meaning is fixed *a priori*' (Noble, *Language and Narration in Céline's Writings*, p.99). Something similar is suggested by Julia Kristeva, but in the context of a strangely structuralist reading that depends on precisely the kind of formalism that she argues is absent in the Célinian novel. See Julia Kristeva, 'D'une identité l'autre', *Tel Quel*, 62 (1975), 10–27, (p.23).

117 This primordiality of style, and especially of the three points, is also reiterated in interviews. To take but one example: 'Je n'ai pas la prétention d'apporter un message. [...] Je suis un technicien, un styliste, un point c'est tout...' (*Cahiers Céline* 1, p.157).

118 Deleuze and Guattari, *Mille plateaux*, p.397.

119 *Ibid.*, p.391.

120 On the lace-like structure of the Célinian text, Philip Stephen Day has written the following:

> Céline estime que le romancier contemporain n'a rien à apprendre à son lecteur au sujet de la vie. Il la trouve autour de lui; les journaux et la télévision le mettent en rapport avec pratiquement toute la réalité courante. Dès lors, il ne reste au romancier qu'à supprimer dans ce qu'il écrit, et même dans ce qu'il imagine, ce qu'un lecteur sait avant de lire: 'De là tous les trous qu'on voit dans mon style (...) Ce qui reste c'est la dentelle: la ligne essentielle, les points caractéristiques; et autour: des trous... La dentelle, ça me connaît: ma mère était dentellière [...] On fabrique maintenant de la dentelle à la machine. De la littérature aussi'. C'est la ponctuation de Céline qui évoque assez bien sa manière de concevoir un livre comme de la dentelle. Les signes qui séparent les mots sont commes les intervalles dans le feston, sans lesquelles la dentellière ne pourrait tracer son dessin. Ces poches de vide s'organisent à mesure que le tissu prend forme: elles 'aèrent' le récit, lui confèrent une apparence légère et délicate. Le rôle essentiellement logique de la ponctuation conventionnelle ne permet guère d'introduire des liens entre les images et les impressions qui se succèdent suivant le rythme d'un spectacle ininterrompu. Les points d'exclamation et les aposiopèses de Céline prolongent les mots verticalement et étendent leur sens horizontalement. Les pauses successives les font rebondir, comme autant de petites pierres plates lancées sur la surface lisse d'un lac. Les images se créent au fil de ce mouvement; la ponctuation les accélère, les ralentit, marque leur point de chute (!) et les ondes qu'elles dessinent [...]. Ces signes jouent donc un rôle pictural à mesure que l'aspect logique des phrases s'estompe et que les contours d'un mirage émotif remplacent le sens littéral des mots. (Day, *Le Miroir allégorique*, p.127)

121 Llambias, 'Guerre, histoire et langage dans le récit célinien', p.103.
122 *Ibid.*, p.104.
123 *Ibid.* Llambias goes on to suggest that,

> Céline se débarrasse à la fois du récit et d'un quelconque sens dont celui-ci pouvait être porteur. Par cet allègement, l'écrivain esquive une nouvelle fois l'Histoire, en la niant. Cette stratégie de l'écriture n'est-elle pas née (mais il est évident qu'il ne s'agit que de l'une de ses sources...) de cette culpabilité fondamentale à tout écrivain, dès lors que celui-ci a pensé, un seul instant, que son acte d'écrire retentirait sur l'Histoire, voire en infléchirait peut-être le cours? (*ibid.*)

This attribution of meaning to the act of writing a non-representational, emotive aesthetic, however, relies on the belief—already seen in Montaut's 'Médecine, théorie du "style" et antisémitisme chez Céline' (see note 9 to Chapter Three above), Murphy's 'Louis-Ferdinand Céline: Between Presence and Polyphony' (see *infra*, p.133), Yves de la Quérière's 'L'Écriture et le contre-courant' (see *infra*, p.152), Chesneau's 'Esquisse d'une conception de l'Histoire chez Céline' (see note 60 to Chapter Three above), and Kristeva's various essays—that there exists, in Céline's universe, a divorce between the ideological (real) and stylistic (fictional) aspects of the text which, in effect, renders irreconcilable the thematic and stylistic levels of the text (which have been seen, in the present study, consistently to complement each other), since, in a schizophrenic conception of style, the boundary between style and life no longer exists: 'Le style, chez un grand écrivain, c'est toujours aussi un style de vie, non pas du tout quelque chose de personnel, mais l'invention d'une possibilité de vie, d'un mode d'existence' (Gilles Deleuze, *Pourparlers* (Paris: Les Éditions de Minuit, 1990), p.138; previously quoted as an epigraph in the introduction to the present study). When Llambias restricts his comments purely to the transpositional space of the text, the present study can only be in agreement with him. He writes,

> Comme pour accélérer l'élimination d'une certaine Histoire, le texte se creuse de plus en plus, devient tissu de plus de vide que de plein, rejoignant alors la fascination de la femme-danseuse et de la mère-dentellière. Tout est danse car tout doit être léger, aérien, afin que le regard puisse à la fois surmonter la répugnance que lui inspire son époque, et se détacher de tout ce qui entrave. L'écriture peut alors vaincre la 'pesanteur spécifique' dont parle Nietzche, et devenir, quel que soit son objet, clarté [...]. Ce jeu du plein et du vide, dans lequel le plein ne se réalise que par le vide qui le crée, et vice-versa, l'écrivain n'en fait pas seulement la métaphore de toute écriture; sa broderie, qui rend compte de la lourdeur de notre monde, de sa complexité infinie, témoigne également de l'extrême sensibilité qu'il faut posséder pour ramener vers soi les fils emmêlés. Cet effleurement de fantômes si ténus que la moindre lourdeur les efface, comme ces corps miraculeusement conservés et qui tombent en poussière à l'ouverture de la tombe, cette recherche à fuir le sens engendre aussi du sens à l'infini. La guerre peut alourdir un monde déjà pesant, l'écriture en fait l'absent de toute fiction par un mouvement qui, pareil à celui de la danseuse, la libère pour toujours. (Llambias, 'Guerre, histoire et langage dans le récit célinien', pp.104–105)

Notes to the Conclusion

1 See Michel Foucault, *Les Mots et les choses: une archéologie des sciences humaines* (Paris: Gallimard, 1966), especially pp.366–398.

2 Sass, *Madness and Modernism*, p.338.

3 Donley, 'Céline musicien', p.76.

4

> Bacon n'a pas cessé de vouloir éliminer le "sensationnel", c'est-à-dire la figuration primaire de ce qui provoque une sensation violente. Tel est le sens de la formule: 'j'ai voulu peindre le cri plutôt que l'horreur'. Quand il peint le pape qui crie, il n'y a rien qui fasse horreur, et le rideau devant le pape n'est pas seulement une manière de l'isoler, de le soustraire aux regards, c'est beaucoup plus la manière dont il ne voit rien lui-même, et crie *devant l'invisible*: neutralisée, l'horreur est multipliée parce qu'elle est conclue du cri, et non l'inverse (Deleuze, *Francis Bacon: logique de la sensation*, p.29)

5 Louis-Ferdinand Céline, in *Cahiers Céline* 2, p.171.
6 Brian Massumi, Translator's Foreword, in Gilles Deleuze and Félix Guattari, *A Thousand Plateaus: Capitalism and Schizophrenia*, trans. by Brian Massumi (Minneapolis and London: University of Minnesota Press, 1987), p.xv.
7 *Ibid.*, p.xiv.
8 *Ibid.*
9 Yves Pagès, for instance, considers 'la distinction éculée de la forme et du fond' to be, 'un démenti aussi formel que paradoxal [...] une ultime pirouette' (Pagès, *Les Fictions du politique chez L.-F. Céline*, p.12), effectuated by Céline in order to maintain the racism of the pamphlets throughout the latter half of his career, whilst absolving himself of that very racism through the perpetuation of his own legend as a misunderstood stylist.
10

> Et s'il est vrai que le délire est coextensif au champ social, on voit dans tout délire les deux pôles coexister, et des fragments d'investissement schizoïde révolutionnaire coïncider avec des blocs d'investissement paranoïaque réactionnaire. L'oscillation entre les deux pôles est même constitutive du délire. Toutefois, il apparaît que l'oscillation n'est pas égale, et que le pôle schizoïde est plutôt potentiel par rapport au pôle paranoïaque actuel. (Deleuze and Guattari, *L'Anti-Œdipe*, p.451)

11 It should be remembered that the 'vision féerique' in the metafictional prefacing sections of *Guignol's band* has been seen to allude to the preface of *Voyage au bout de la nuit* in which is found the line, 'tout le monde peut en faire autant. Il suffit de fermer les yeux' (*V*, p.5). See *infra* p.40.

Bibliography

Works by Louis-Ferdinand Céline

Principle Editions Cited

Romans I (*Voyage au bout de la nuit*, *Mort à crédit*), ed. by Henri Godard, coll. La Pléiade (Paris: Gallimard, 1981)

Romans II (*D'un château l'autre*, *Nord*, *Rigodon*), ed. by Henri Godard, coll. La Pléiade (Paris: Gallimard, 1974)

Romans III (*Casse-Pipe*, *Guignol's band* I, *Guignol's band* II [*Le Pont de Londres*]), ed. by Henri Godard, coll. La Pléiade (Paris: Gallimard, 1988)

Romans IV (*Féerie pour une autre fois* I, *Féerie pour une autre fois* II [*Normance*], *Entretiens avec le professeur Y*), ed. by Henri Godard, coll. La Pléiade (Paris: Gallimard, 1993)

Books

L'Église (Paris: Denoël et Steele, 1933)

Mea Culpa, suivi de Semmelweis (Paris: Denoël & Steele, 1936)

Bagatelles pour un massacre (Paris: Denoël, 1937)

L'École des cadavres (Paris: Denoël, 1938)

Les Beaux draps (Paris: Nouvelles Éditions Françaises, 1941)

Ballets sans musique, sans personne, sans rien (Paris: Gallimard, 1959)

Chansons, ed. by Frédéric Monnier (Paris: La Flûte de Pan, 1981)

Arletty, jeune fille dauphinoise: scénario, ed. by Frédéric Monnier (Paris: La Flûte de Pan, 1983)

Lettres à son avocat: 118 lettres inédites à Maître Albert Naud, ed. by Frédéric Monnier (Paris: La Flûte de Pan, 1984)

Lettres à Tixier: 44 lettres inédites à Maître Tixier-Vignancour, ed. Frédéric Monnier (Paris: La Flûte de Pan, 1985)

Lettres à Joseph Garcin: 1929–1938, ed. by Pierre Lainé (Paris: Librairie Monnier/La Flûte de Pan, 1987)

Préfaces et dédicaces, ed. by Henri Godard (Tusson: Du Lérot, 1987)

Lettres à la NRF, 1931–1961, ed. by Pascal Fouché (Paris: Gallimard, 1991)

Lettres des années noires, ed. by Philippe Alméras (Paris: Berg International, 1994)

Lettres à Marie Canavaggia, ed. by Jean-Paul Louis, 3 vols (Tusson: Du Lérot, 1995)

Douze lettres à Eugène Dabit, ed. by Jean-Paul Louis (Tusson: Du Lérot, 1996)

Histoire du petit Mouck (Paris: Éditions du Rocher, 1997)

Lettres de prison à Lucette Destouches et à Maître Mikkelsen, 1945–1947, ed. by François Gibault (Paris: Gallimard, 1998)

Six lettres, Février 1947 (Paris: Gallimard, 1998)

Collected Volumes containing articles, correspondence and unpublished fragments

L.-F. Céline, ed. by Dominique de Roux, Michel Beaujour and Michel Thélia, *Les Cahiers de l'Herne*, 3 & 5 ([n.p.]: l'Herne, 1972) [a revised and composite edition of *Louis-Ferdinand Céline* I, *Le Cahier de l'Herne*, 3 (1963), and *Louis-Ferdinand Céline* II, *Le Cahier de l'Herne*, 5 (1965)]

Cahiers Céline 1, *Céline et l'actualité littéraire, 1932–1957*, ed. by Jean-Pierre Dauphin and Henri Godard (Paris: Gallimard, 1976)

Cahiers Céline 2, *Céline et l'actualité littéraire, 1957–1961*, ed. by Jean-Pierre Dauphin and Henri Godard (Paris: Gallimard, 1976)

Cahiers Céline 3, *Semmelweiss et autres écrits médicaux*, ed. by Jean-Pierre Dauphin and Henri Godard (Paris: Gallimard, 1977)

Cahiers Céline 4, *Lettres et premiers écrits d'Afrique, 1916–1917*, ed. by Jean-Pierre Dauphin (Paris: Gallimard, 1978)

Cahiers Céline 5, *Lettres à des amies*, ed. by Colin W. Nettelbeck (Paris: Gallimard, 1979)

Cahiers Céline 6, *Lettres à Albert Paraz, 1947–1957*, ed. by Jean-Paul Louis (Paris: Gallimard, 1980)

Cahiers Céline 7, *Céline et l'actualité, 1933–1961*, ed. by Jean-Pierre Dauphin and Pascal Fouché (Paris: Gallimard, 1986)

Cahiers Céline 8, *'Progrès' suivi de Œuvres pour la scène et l'écran*, ed. by Pascal Fouché (Paris: Gallimard, 1988)

Céline. Textes et documents 1 (Paris: Bibliothèque L.-F. Céline de l'université de Paris VII, 1979)

Céline. Textes et documents 2, Bibliothèque L.-F. Céline (Paris: Bibliothèque de littérature française contemporaine de l'université de Paris VII, 1982)

Céline. Textes et documents 3, Bibliothèque L.-F. Céline (Paris: Bibliothèque de littérature française contemporaine de l'université de Paris VII, 1985)

L'Année Céline 1990 (Tusson & Paris: Du Lérot / IMEC, 1991)

L'Année Céline 1991 (Tusson & Paris: Du Lérot / IMEC, 1992)

L'Année Céline 1992 (Tusson & Paris: Du Lérot / IMEC, 1993)

L'Année Céline 1993 (Tusson & Paris: Du Lérot / IMEC, 1994)

L'Année Céline 1994 (Tusson & Paris: Du Lérot / IMEC, 1995)

L'Année Céline 1995 (Tusson & Paris: Du Lérot / IMEC, 1997)

L'Année Céline 1996 (Tusson & Paris: Du Lérot / IMEC, 1998)

Secondary Works on Céline

Albums

Catalogue de l'Exposition Céline, Musée de l'Ancien Evêché de Lausanne (Lausanne: Edita, 1977)

Album Céline, ed. by Jean-Pierre Dauphin and Jacques Boudillet, coll. La Pléiade (Paris: Gallimard, 1977)

Collections of Articles

Louis-Ferdinand Céline: Voyage au bout de la nuit, special edition of *Roman 20–50: Revue d'étude du roman du xxe siècle*, 17 (1994)

Céline USA, ed. by Alice Kaplan and Philippe Roussin, special edition of *South Atlantic Quarterly*, 93.2 (1994)

Actes du Colloque international d'Oxford, septembre 1975, *Australian Journal of French Studies*, 13.1–2 (1976)

Actes du colloque international de Paris, juillet 1976, *Bulletin de la Société des Études céliniennes*, 1 (1978)

Actes du colloque international de Paris, juillet 1979, *Bulletin de la Société des Études céliniennes*, 3 (1980)

Actes du colloque international d'Oxford, juillet 1981, *Bulletin de la Bibliothèque L.-F. Céline de l'Université de Paris VII et de la Société des Études céliniennes*, 5 (1981)

Actes du colloque international de La Haye, juillet 1983, *Bulletin de la Bibliothèque L.-F. Céline de l'Université de Paris VII et de la Société des Études céliniennes*, 8 (1984)

Actes du colloque international de Paris, juin 1986 (Tusson & Paris: Du Lérot / Société des Études céliniennes, 1987)

Actes du colloque international de Londres, juillet 1988 (Tusson & Paris: Du Lérot / Société des Études céliniennes, 1989)

Actes du colloque international de Toulouse, juillet 1990 (Tusson & Paris: Du Lérot / Société des Études céliniennes, 1991)

Actes du colloque international de Paris, juillet 1992 (Tusson & Paris: Du Lérot / Société des Études céliniennes, 1993)

Actes du colloque international de Paris, juillet 1994 (Tusson & Paris: Du Lérot / Société d'Études céliniennes, 1996)

Actes du colloque international d'Amsterdam, juillet 1996 (Paris: Société d'Études céliniennes, 1998)

Louis-Ferdinand Céline 1: pour une poétique célinienne, ed. by Jean-Pierre Dauphin, La Revue des Lettres Modernes, 398–402 (Paris: Minard, 1974)

Louis-Ferdinand Céline 2: écriture et esthétique, ed. by Jean-Pierre Dauphin, La Revue des Lettres Modernes, 462–467 (Paris: Minard, 1976)

Louis-Ferdinand Céline 3: lectures de 'Féerie pour une autre fois', ed. by Jean-Pierre Dauphin, La Revue des lettres modernes, 462–467 (Paris: Minard, 1978)

Louis-Ferdinand Céline 4: lectures (2) de 'Féerie pour une autre fois', ed. by Jean-Pierre Dauphin, La Revue des Lettres Modernes, 560–564 (Paris: Minard, 1979)

Louis-Ferdinand Céline 5: vingt-cinq ans d'études céliniennes, ed. by Pascal Fouché, La Revue des Lettres Modernes, 849–856 (Paris: Minard, 1988)

Books and Articles (includes articles from collected volumes cited in the text)

AEBERSOLD, Denise, 'Céline et les intellectuels', *Actes du colloque international de Paris, juillet 1976, Bulletin de la Société des Études céliniennes*, 1 (1978), 185–196.

———, *Céline: un démystificateur mythomane*, Archives des Lettres Modernes, 185: Archives L.-F. Céline, 3 (Paris: Lettres Modernes, Minard, 1979)

ALMÉRAS, Philippe, 'Et la chair se fait verbe: coup d'œil sur la bibliothèque de Céline', in *Louis-Ferdinand Céline 2: écriture et esthétique*, ed. by Jean-Pierre Dauphin, La Revue des Lettres Modernes, 462–467 (Paris: Minard, 1976), pp.123–140

———, *Céline: entre haines et passion*, coll. Biographies sans masque (Paris: Robert Lafont, 1994)

ANDRÉ, Serge, *L'Imposture perverse*, coll. Champ Freudien (Paris: Éditions du Seuil, 1993)

BACH, Raymond, 'Céline, Anti-Semitism and the Limits of Textual Subversion', *Romance Notes*, 32.2 (1991), 119–126

BACHAU, B., 'Louis-Ferdinand Céline, écrivain de l'Apocalypse', *Les Lettres Romanes*, 36.3 (1982), 251–260

BEAUJOUR, Michel, 'Céline, artiste du laid', *The French Review*, 38 (1964), 180–190

———, 'La Quête du délire', in *L.-F. Céline*, ed. by Dominique de Roux, Michel Beaujour and Michel Thélia, *Les Cahiers de l'Herne*, 3 & 5 ([n.p.]: l'Herne, 1972), pp.285–302

BELLOSTA, Marie-Christine, *Le Capharnaüm célinien ou la place des objets dans 'Mort à crédit'*, Archives des Lettres Modernes, 164: Archives L.-F. Céline, 2 (Paris: Lettres Modernes, Minard, 1976)

———, '*Féerie pour une autre fois* I et II: un spectacle et son prologue', in *Louis-Ferdinand Céline 3: lectures de 'Féerie pour une autre fois'*, ed. by Jean-Pierre Dauphin, Revue des lettres modernes, 462–467 (Paris: Minard, 1978), pp.31–62

———, *Céline ou l'art de la contradiction: lecture de 'Voyage au bout de la nuit'* (Paris: Presses Universitaires de France, 1990)

BIAISIN, Gian-Paolo, 'Disease as Language: The Case of the Writer and the Madman', in *Medicine and Literature*, ed. by Enid Rhodes Peschel (New York: Neale Watson Academic Publications, 1980), pp.171–177

BLANK, Andreas, 'Un Voyage au bout du discours: Céline et l'acte parole', *Les Lettres Romanes*, 47.4 (1993), 265–277

BLONDIAUX, Isabelle, *Une Écriture psychotique: Louis-Ferdinand Céline* (Paris: A.G. Nizet, 1985)

BOISSIEU, Jean-Louis, 'Quelques effets "littéraires" ou archaïsants dans *Voyage au bout de la nuit*', in *Louis-Ferdinand Céline 2: écriture et esthétique*, ed. by Jean-Pierre Dauphin, La Revue des Lettres Modernes, 462–467 (Paris: Minard, 1976), pp.33–51

BONNEFIS, Philippe, 'De l'âme. L'hypothèse du ballon dans l'œuvre de Céline', *Revue des Sciences Humaines*, 71.200 (1985), 93–155

———, 'Passage Céline', *Revue des Sciences Humaines*, 69.198 (1985), 141–167

———, *Céline: le rappel des oiseaux* (Paris: Galilée, 1997)

BRÉE, Germaine, 'The Persona of the Doctor in Céline's *Journey to the End of the Night* and Camus' *The Plague*', in *Medicine and Literature*, ed. by Enid Rhodes Peschel (New York: Neale Watson Academic Publications, 1980), pp.88–97

BOUNAN, Michel, *L'Art de Céline et son temps* (Paris: Éditions Allia, 1997)

BUCKLEY, William K. (ed.), *Critical Essays on Louis-Ferdinand Céline* (Boston: G.K. Hall, 1989)

C———, J., 'Le Docteur écrit un roman', in *L.-F. Céline*, ed. by Dominique de Roux, Michel Beaujour and Michel Thélia, *Les Cahiers de l'Herne*, 3 & 5 ([n.p.]: l'Herne, 1972), pp.209–212

CARILE, Paolo, 'Notes pour une approche du comique célinien', in *Louis-Ferdinand Céline 2: écriture et esthétique*, ed. by Jean-Pierre Dauphin, La Revue des Lettres Modernes, 462–467 (Paris: Minard, 1976), pp.79–98

CARSON, Jane, 'The Biomorphic Structure of Céline's Imaginative Space', *Degré Second*, 8 (1984), 13–17

———, *Céline's Imaginative Space*, American University Studies: Series II, Romance Languages and Literature, 42 (New York: Peter Lang, 1987)

CHAPSAL, Madeleine, *Les Écrivains en personne* (Paris: Julliard, 1960)

CHESNEAU, Albert, *Essai de psychocritique de Louis-Ferdinand Céline*, Archives des Lettres Modernes, 129 (Paris: Minard, 1971)

———, 'Esquisse d'une conception de l'Histoire chez Céline', *Actes du Colloque international d'Oxford, septembre 1975*, *Australian Journal of French Studies*, 13.1–2 (1976), 126–133

COEN, Stanley J., *Between Author and Reader: A Psychoanalytic Approach to Writing and Reading* (New York: Columbia University Press, 1994)

CORNILLE, Jean-Louis, 'Céline, Elstir et le Christ', *Littérature*, 107 (Oct. 1997), 64–74

CRESCIUCCI, Alain, *Les Territoires céliniens: Expression dans l'espace et expérience du monde dans les romans de L.-F. Céline* (Paris: Éditions aux Amateurs de Livres, 1990)

———, 'Le Sens de la formule', *op. cit: Revue de littératures française et comparée*, 2 (1993), 121–125

DAMOUR, A.-C and J.-P, *L.-F. Céline: 'Voyage au bout de la nuit'* (Paris: Presses Universitaires de France, 1985)

DAUPHIN, Jean-Pierre (ed.), *Les Critiques de notre temps et Céline* (Paris: Garnier, 1976)

DAY, Philip Stephen, *Le Miroir allégorique de Louis-Ferdinand Céline* (Paris: Klincksieck, 1974)

———, 'Ponts et creux dans les premiers chapitres de *Guignol's band*: passages, plongées, émergences, inversions, réversibilités', *Actes du colloque international d'Oxford, juillet 1981*, *Bulletin de la Bibliothèque L.-F. Céline de l'Université de Paris VII et de la Société des Études céliniennes*, 5 (1981), 243–251

DEBRIE, Nicole, *Il était une fois... Céline: Les intuitions psychanalytiques dans l'œuvre célinienne* (Paris: Aubier, 1990)

DEBRIE-PANEL, Nicole, *Louis-Ferdinand Céline* (Lyon: Bitte, 1961)

DERVAL, André, 'Le Récit fantastique dans l'œuvre de L.-F. Céline', in *L'Année Céline 1990*, ed. by André Derval, Henri Godard, Jean-Paul Louis, Eric Mazet (Tusson & Paris: Du Lérot / IMEC, 1991), pp.195–223

———, 'D'un Voyage imaginaire', *op. cit: Revue de littératures française et comparée*, 2 (1993), 127–130

DONLEY, Michael, 'L'Identification cosmique', in *L.-F. Céline*, ed. by Dominique de Roux, Michel Beaujour and Michel Thélia, *Les Cahiers de l'Herne*, 3 & 5 ([n.p.]: l'Herne, 1972), pp.327–334

———, 'Céline musicien', in *Actes du colloque international de Paris, juillet 1994* (Tusson & Paris: Du Lérot / Société d'Études céliniennes, 1996), pp.71–79

DUNWOODIE, Peter, 'L'Espace Londonien: *Guignol's band* I et II, *Australian Journal of French Studies*, 19.2 (1982), 158–184

———, 'Merveilleux, étrange et fantastique dans les romans de Louis-Ferdinand Céline', *Les Lettres Romanes*, 37.1–2 (1983), 82–111

ENGLISH, Cheryl, 'La Description dans le roman célinien: étude de *Guignol's band*', in *L'Année Céline 1995* (Tusson & Paris: Du Lérot / IMEC, 1996), pp.233–235

ERLICH, Bruce, 'Céline's Last Voyage: Self and Mask in the Bourgeois Apocalypse', in *Travel, Quest and Pilgrimage as a Literary Theme*, Studies in Honor of Reino Virtanen, ed. by Frans C. Amelinckx, Joyce N. Megay (Ann Arbor, MI: Society of Spanish and Spanish-American Studies, 1978), pp.231–242

FERRANT, Alain, 'D'une compulsion l'autre: écriture et rhétorique de la confusion chez L.-F. Céline', *Revue Française de Psychanalyse*, 58 (1994), 483–492

FORBES, Jill, 'Symbolique de l'espace: le "Londres" célinien', *Actes du colloque international de Paris, juillet 1976*, *Bulletin de la Société des Études céliniennes*, 1 (1978), 27–40

FORTIER, Paul A., *'Voyage au bout de la nuit': étude du fonctionnement des structures thématiques: le "métro émotif" de L.-F. Céline*, Bibliothèque des Lettres Modernes, 33 (Paris: Minard, 1981)

FRIZOT, Daniel, 'The Clown Figure in Louis-Ferdinand Céline and Nathanael West or the Tragi-Comic in Modern Fiction' (unpublished doctoral dissertation, Purdue University, 1973)

———, 'Céline's *Guignol's band* I and II, Puppet Show and Grotesque', *Synthesis: Bulletin du Comité National de Littérature Comparée de la République Socialiste de Roumanie*, 6 (1979), 263–268

GIBAULT, François, *Céline 1: 1894–1932 le temps des espérances* (Paris: Mercure de France, 1985)

———, *Céline 2: 1932–1944 délires et persécutions* (Paris: Mercure de France, 1985)

———, *Céline 3: 1944–1961 cavalier de l'Apocalypse* (Paris: Mercure de France, 1985)

GILLAIN, Annie, 'Le grotesque du carnaval chez Céline', *Actes du colloque international de Paris, juillet 1976*, *Bulletin de la Société des Études céliniennes*, 1 (1978), 319–334

GIUSTO, Jean-Pierre, *Le Champ clos de l'écriture: Laforgue / Saint-John Perse / Céline* (Valenciennes: Presses Universitaires de Valenciennes, 1985)

GODARD, Henri, 'Un Art poétique', in *Louis-Ferdinand Céline 1: pour une poétique célinienne*, ed. by Jean-Pierre Dauphin, La Revue des Lettres Modernes, 398–402 (Paris: Minard, 1974), pp.7–40

———, 'Les Références au travail narratif dans le roman célinien', *Actes du Colloque international d'Oxford, septembre 1975*, *Australian Journal of French Studies*, 13.1–2 (1976), 7–17

———, *Poétique de Céline*, coll. Idées (Paris: Gallimard, 1985)

GREENBERG, Alvin David, 'The Novel of Disintegration: Paradoxical Impossibility in Contemporary Fiction', *Wisconsin Studies in Contemporary Literature*, 7 (1966), 103–108

GROVER, Frédéric, 'Le Romancier et l'histoire: le cas Céline', *L'Esprit-Créateur*, 15 (1975), 332–344

GUÉNOT, Jean, *Louis-Ferdinand Céline damné par l'écriture*, 2nd rev edn (Saint-Cloud: the author, 1984)

GUINEBERT, Jean-Marie, 'Présences de la danse dans *Guignol's band* et *Féerie pour une autre fois*', in *L'Année Céline 1991* (Tusson & Paris: Du Lérot / IMEC, 1992), pp.181–198

HANREZ, Marc, *Céline*, coll. Pour une Bibliothèque Idéale, 6 (Paris: Gallimard, 1961)

HARRIS, Frederick B., 'Linguistic Reality - Historical Reality: Genet, Céline, Grass', *Neohelicon: Acta Comparationis Litterarum Universarum*, 14.2 (1987), 257–273

HAUPTMAN, Robert, *The Pathological Vision: Jean Genet, Louis-Ferdinand Céline, and Tennessee Williams*, American University Studies, Series 3, vol. 5 (New York: Peter Lang, 1984)

HENRIC, Jacques, *Louis-Ferdinand Céline*, coll. Lieux de l'Écrit (Paris: Marval, 1991)

HEWITT, Nicholas, 'Narration and Desolidarisation in Céline's *Mort à crédit*', *Essays in French Literature*, 12 (1975), 59–69

———, 'Londres, la Capitale du vingtième siècle: esquisse d'une topographie de *Guignol's band*', *Actes du colloque international de Paris, juillet 1979*, *Bulletin de la Société des Études céliniennes*, 3 (1980), 31–44

———, *The Golden Age of Louis-Ferdinand Céline* (Leamington Spa: Berg Publishers 1987)

———, *The Life of Céline* (Oxford: Blackwell, 1999)

HINDUS, Milton, *The Crippled Giant: A Literary Relationship with Louis-Ferdinand Céline*, rev edn (Hanover: University Press of New England, 1986) [translated as, *Louis-Ferdinand Céline tel que je l'ai vu* (Paris: L'Herne, 1969)]

HOUDEBINE, Jean-Louis, 'Céline l'ancien', in *L'Année Céline 1993* (Tusson & Paris: Du Lerot / IMEC, 1994), pp.195–200

HUCHET, Jean-Charles, 'Le Voyage au bout de Noirceur-sur-la-Lys', *Littérature*, 37 (1980), 37–52

KAMINSKI, H.-E., *Céline en chemise brune* (Paris: Excelsior, 1938)

KNAPP, Bettina L., *Céline: Man of Hate* (Alabama: The University of Alabama Press, 1974)

———, 'From Hero to Horror: Louis-Ferdinand Céline, M.D.', in *Medicine and Literature*, ed. by Enid Rhodes Peschel (New York: Neale Watson Academic Publications, 1980), pp.18–27

KOLE, Ellen, 'Louis-Ferdinand Céline: Perspectives in Black Humor' (unpublished doctoral dissertation, New York University, 1978)

KRANCE, Charles, 'Céline and the Literature of Extasis: The Virtuosity of "Non-Genre"', *Language and Style*, 6 (1973), 176–184

———, '*Semmelweis*, ou l'accouchement de la biographie célinienne', in *Louis-Ferdinand Céline 2: écriture et esthétique*, ed. by Jean-Pierre Dauphin, La Revue des Lettres Modernes, 462–467 (Paris: Minard, 1976), pp.7–32

———, '*Guignol's band* et la rhétorique du geste célinien', *Actes du colloque international de Paris, juillet 1976*, *Bulletin de la Société des Études céliniennes*, 1 (1978), 123–140

———, *L.-F. Céline: The I of the Storm*, French Forum Monographs, 75 (Lexington: French Forum Publishers, 1992)

KRISTEVA, Julia, 'D'une identité l'autre', *Tel Quel*, 62 (1975), 10–27

———, 'Actualité de Céline', *Tel Quel*, 71–73 (1977), 45–52

———, *Pouvours de l'horreur: essai sur l'abjection*, coll. Points Essais (Paris: Éditions du Seuil, 1980)

LATIN, Danièle, 'Louis-Ferdinand ou le malentendu idéologique', *Les Lettres Romanes*, 28 ([n.d.]), 49–63

———, *Le 'Voyage au bout de la nuit' de Céline: roman de la subversion et subversion du roman: langue, fiction, écriture* (Bruxelles: Académie Royale de Langue et Littérature Françaises, 1988)

LeBLANC, James D., 'On Excrement, Time and Style in Céline's *Mort à crédit*', *Degré Second*, 12 (1989), 77–86

LINDBLAD, Diane Margaret, 'Louis-Ferdinand Céline: An Aesthetics of Anti-Semitism' (unpublished doctoral dissertation, University of Washington, 1989)

LLAMBIAS, Robert, 'Guerre histoire et langage dans le récit célinien', *Revue des Sciences Humaines*, 75.204 (1986), 89–105

LOSELLE, Andrea, 'Fading Images: The Touristic Itinerary and Spatial Representation in Céline's German Trilogy', *Symposium: A Quarterly Journal in Modern Foreign Languages*, 47.1 (1993), 16–35

LUCE, Stanford, 'Increment and Excrement: Céline and the Language of Hate', *Maledicta: The International Journal of Verbal Aggression*, 1.1 (1977), 43–48

——— (ed.), *Céline and his Critics: Scandals and Paradox*, Stanford French and Italian Studies (Saratoga, CA: Anma Libri, 1986)

MAHÉ, Henri, *La Brinquebale avec Céline* (Paris: La Table Ronde, 1969)

MAHÉ, Vincent, 'Les deux temps du rigodon: répétition et destruction dans l'œuvre de Louis-Ferdinand Céline', in *L'Année Céline 1990* (Tusson & Paris: Du Lérot / IMEC, 1991), pp.157–172

MANCEL, Yannic, 'De la sémiologie textuelle à la théorie du roman: Céline', *Dialectiques*, 8 (1975), 45–68

———, 'Sémiotiques de la folie et de l'écriture dans *Féerie pour une autre fois*', in *Louis-Ferdinand Céline 4: lectures (2) de 'Féerie pour une autre fois'*, ed. by Jean-Pierre Dauphin, La Revue des Lettres Modernes, 560–564 (Paris: Minard, 1979), pp.123–147

MATTHEWS, J.H., *The Inner Dream: Céline as Novelist* (Syracuse, NY: Syracuse University Press, 1978)

MAZET, Éric, 'D'un masque l'autre', in *L'Année Céline 1993* (Tusson & Paris: Du Lérot / IMEC, 1994), pp.211–222

McCARTHY, Patrick, *Céline* (Harmondsworth: Allen Lane, 1975)

———, 'La Multiplicité des narrateurs dans *Féerie pour une autre fois*', *Actes du colloque international de Paris, juillet 1976*, *Bulletin de la Société des Études céliniennes*, 1 (1978), 231–246

———, '*Féerie pour une autre fois*, le roman de la jalousie', in *Louis-Ferdinand Céline 4: lectures (2) de 'Féerie pour une autre fois'*, ed. by Jean-Pierre Dauphin, La Revue des Lettres Modernes, 560–564 (Paris: Minard, 1979), pp.75–91

MIROUX, Pierre-Marie, 'Féerie de la mort', in *Actes du colloque international de Toulouse, juillet 1990* (Tusson & Paris: Du Lérot/Société des Études céliniennes, 1991), pp.183–193

———, 'Esquisse du visage de la mort', *op. cit: Revue de littératures française et comparée*, 2 (1993), 137–143

———, 'S'éclater la tête', in *Actes du colloque international de Paris, juillet 1994* (Tusson & Paris: Du Lérot/Société d'Études céliniennes, 1996), pp.183–188

MONTANDON, Alain, 'Le Statut du lecteur dans *Voyage au bout de la nuit*', *op. cit: Revue de littératures française et comparée*, 2 (1993), 145–152

MONTAUT, Annie, 'Médicine, théorie du "style" et antisémitisme chez Céline', *Littérature*, 58 (1985), 42–59

MURPHY, Ann L., 'Louis-Ferdinand Céline: Between Presence and Polyphony' (unpublished doctoral dissertation, Brown University, 1988)

———, 'Célinian Esthetics and Narrative Polyphony', *French Forum*, 16.1 (1991), 67–79

MURAY, Philippe, *Céline*, coll. Tel Quel (Paris: Éditions du Seuil, 1981

———, 'D'un échec de Freud devant Céline', in *Alphonse Juilland: D'une passion l'autre*, Stanford French and Italian Studies, ed. by Brigitte Cazelles (Saratoga, CA: Anma Libri, 1987), pp.197–204

MURRAY, Jack, *The Landscapes of Alienation: Ideological Subversion in Kafka, Céline and Onetti* (Stanford, CA: Stanford University Press, 1991)

NETTELBECK, Colin W., 'Journey to the End of Art: The Evolution of the Novels of Louis-Ferdinand Céline', *PMLA*, 87.1 (1972), 80–89

———, 'The Antisemite and the Artist: Céline's Pamphlets and *Guignol's band*', *Australian Journal of French Studies*, 9 (1974), 180–189

———, 'Un Art conscient: structures, symboles et significations dans les derniers romans', in *Louis-Ferdinand Céline 2: écriture et esthétique*, ed. by Jean-Pierre Dauphin, La Revue des Lettres Modernes, 462–467 (Paris: Minard, 1976), pp.99–119

———, 'Coordonnées musicales de l'esthétique romanesque de Céline', *Actes du Colloque international d'Oxford, septembre 1975*, *Australian Journal of French Studies*, 13.1–2 (1976), 80–87

———, 'Notion et fonction de la "transposition" chez Céline et Proust', *Actes du colloque international de Paris, juillet 1976*, *Bulletin de la Société des Études céliniennes*, 1 (1978), 7–26

———, 'Céline devant l'an 40: *Les Beaux draps* et le début de *Guignol's band*', *Actes du colloque international d'Oxford, juillet 1981*, *Bulletin de la Bibliothèque L.-F. Céline de l'Université de Paris VII et de la Société des Études céliniennes*, 5 (1981), 67–80

———, 'Historical Vision in Céline's Last Novels', in *Critical Essays on Louis-Ferdinand Céline*, ed. by William K. Buckley (Boston: G.K. Hall, 1989), pp.268–278

NOBLE, Ian, *Language and Narration in Céline's Writings: The Challenge of Disorder* (Atlantic Highlands, NJ: Humanities Press International, 1987)

O'CONNELL, David, 'Jules, l'*alter ego* de Céline dans *Féerie* I', *Actes du colloque international de Paris, juillet 1976*, *Bulletin de la Société des Études céliniennes*, 1 (1978), 157–165

OSTROVSKY, Erika, *Céline and his Vision* (London: University of London Press, 1967: New York: New York University Press, 1967)

———, 'Louis-Ferdinand Céline: Creator and Destroyer of Myths', in *Critical Essays on Louis-Ferdinand Céline*, ed. by William K. Buckley (Boston: G.K. Hall, 1989), pp.92–100

PAGÈS, Yves, *Les Fictions du politique chez L.-F. Céline* (Paris: Éditions du Seuil, 1994)

POULET, Robert, *Mon ami Bardamu* (Paris: Plon, 1971)

QUÉRIÈRE, Yves de la, 'l'Écriture et le contre-courant: *Rigodon* de Céline', *Australian Journal of French Studies*, 19.2, (1982), 25–35

RACELLE-LATIN, Danièle, 'Louis-Ferdinand Céline et la psychocritique', *Revue des Langues Vivantes*, 40.2 (1974), 150–158

———, '*Voyage au bout de la nuit* ou l'inauguration d'une poétique "argotique"', in *Louis-Ferdinand Céline 2: écriture et esthétique*, ed. by Jean-Pierre Dauphin, La Revue des Lettres Modernes, 462–467 (Paris: Minard, 1976), pp.53–77

———, 'Création littéraire et économie de la libido dans *Voyage au bout de la nuit* de L.-F. Céline', *Actes du colloque international de Paris, juillet 1976, Bulletin de la Société des Études céliniennes*, 1 (1978) 259–280

RASSON, Luc, '"Le petit mot de trop": *D'un château l'autre*', in *Actes du colloque international de Toulouse, juillet 1990* (Tusson & Paris: Du Lérot/Société des Études céliniennes, 1991), pp.215–225

REMINGTON, Ann M., 'The Patterns of Guilt in Céline's *Mort à crédit*: A Psychoanalytic Study (unpublished doctoral dissertation, University of Wisconsin, 1974)

RICHARD, Jean-Pierre, 'Prendre le métro', in Jean-Pierre Richard, *Microlectures*, coll. Poétique (Paris: Éditions du Seuil, 1979)

———, *Nausée de Céline* ([n.p.]: Fata Morgana, 1980)

ROBERTSON, Alton Kim, 'The Grotesque Interface' (unpublished doctoral dissertation, University of Texas at Austin, 1991)

ROUX, Dominique de, *La Mort de Louis-Ferdinand Céline* (Paris: Christian Bourgeois, 1966)

SAUTERMEISTER, Christine, 'Pitreries et dérobades dans *Féerie pour une autre fois*', in *Louis-Ferdinand Céline 4: lectures (2) de 'Féerie pour une autre fois'*, ed. by Jean-Pierre Dauphin, La Revue des Lettres Modernes, 560–564 (1979), 93–105

SCHILLING, Gilbert, 'Images et imagination de la mort dans *Voyage au bout de la nuit*', *L'Information littéraire*, 2 (1971), 68–75

SCHOOLCRAFT III, Ralph, '*Honi soit qui mal y danse*: Circulation and Transport in Céline's Early Novels', *MLN*, 105.4 (1990), 833–856

SCULLION, Rosemarie, 'Social Spaces of Excluded Madness in the Writings of Louis-Ferdinand Céline' (unpublished doctoral dissertation, University of Wisconsin-Madison, 1987)

———, 'Madness and Fascist Discourse in Céline's *Voyage au bout de la nuit*', *The French Review*, 61.5 (1988), 715–723

SILK, Sally M., 'Caught in the Dialogic: The Célinian Narrator Silenced', *MLN*, 107.4 (1992), 795–805

SMITH, André, *La Nuit de Louis-Ferdinand Céline* (Paris: Bernard Grasset, 1973)

SOLOMON, Philip H., 'Céline's *Death on the Installment Plan*: The Intoxications of Delirium', *Yale French Studies*, 50 (1974), 191–203

———, 'The View from a Rump: America as Journey and Landscape of Desire in Céline's *Voyage au bout de la nuit*', *Yale French Studies*, 57 (1979), 5–22

STEINER, George, 'Cry Havoc', in *Critical Essays on Louis-Ferdinand Céline*, ed. by William K. Buckley (Boston: G.K. Hall, 1989), pp.198–204 [first publ. in *Extraterritorial* ([n.p.]: Atheneum Publishers & Faber and Faber, 1971)]

SZAFRAN, Willy, *Louis-Ferdinand Céline: essai psychanalytique* (Bruxelles: Éditions de l'Université de Bruxelles, [n.d.])

TALLON, Xavier, 'Thames and time: temps et narration dans *Guignol's band*', in *L'Année Céline 1990* (Tusson & Paris: Du Lérot / IMEC, 1991), pp.173–194

THIHER, Allen, *Céline: The Novel as Delirium* (New Brunswick, NJ: Rutgers University Press, 1972)

———, 'Le "je" célinien: ouverture, extase et clôture', *Australian Journal of French Studies*, 13.1–2 (1976), 47–54

———, '*Féerie pour une autre fois*: mythe et modernisme', in *Louis-Ferdinand Céline 4: lectures (2) de 'Féerie pour une autre fois'*, ed. by Jean-Pierre Dauphin, La Revue des Lettres Modernes, 560–564 (Paris: Minard, 1979), pp.107–121

THOMAS, Merlin, *Louis-Ferdinand Céline* (New York: New Directions, 1979)

UPDIKE, John, 'The Strange Case of Dr. Destouches and M. Céline', in *Critical Essays on Louis-Ferdinand Céline*, ed. by Willliam K. Buckley (Boston: G.K. Hall, 1989), pp.334–339

VANDROMME, Pol, *Louis-Ferdinand Céline*, coll. Classiques du XXe siècle (Paris: Editions Universitaires, 1963)

VERDAGUER, Pierre, 'Louis-Ferdinand Céline et l'obsession de la chair', *Stanford French Review*, 9.2 (1985), 201–221

———, 'Tendances fantastiques et merveilleux raciste chez Louis-Ferdinand Céline', *Symposium*, 39.4 (1985–6), 284–300

———, *L'Univers de la cruauté: Une lecture de Céline* (Geneva: Librairie Droz, 1988)

VITOUX, Frédéric, *Louis-Ferdinand Céline: misère et parole* (Paris: Gallimard, 1973)

ZAGDANSKI, Stéphane, 'Dieu, Proust et Céline: le roman comme machine de guerre', *L'Autre Journal*, 4 (1993), 51–53

Works by Deleuze and Guattari

Joint Works by Gilles Deleuze and Félix Guattari

L'Anti-Œdipe: capitalisme et schizophrénie, 2nd aug edn (Paris: Éditions de Minuit, 1973)

Kafka: pour une littérature mineure (Paris: Éditions de Minuit, 1975)

Mille plateaux: capitalisme et schizophrénie 2 (Paris: Éditions de Minuit, 1980); English edition (includes translator's foreword): *A Thousand Plateaus: Capitalism and Schizophrenia*, trans. by Brian Massumi (Minneapolis: University of Minnesota Press, 1987)

Qu'est-ce que la philosophie? (Paris: Éditions de Minuit, 1991)

Works by Gilles Deleuze

La Philosophie critique de Kant (Paris: PUF, 1963)

Proust et les signes, (Paris: PUF, 1964; 2nd rev edn, 1970; Quadridge / PUF, 1996)

Le Bergsonisme (Paris: PUF, 1966)

'Le Schizophrène et le mot', *Critique*, vol.24, 255–256 (1968), 731–746

Spinoza et le problème de l'expression (Paris: Éditions de Minuit, 1968)

Différence et répétition (Paris: PUF, 1969)

Logique du sens (Paris: Éditions de Minuit, 1969)

'Schizologie', preface to Louis Wolfson, *Le Schizo et les langues* (Paris: Gallimard, 1970), pp.5–23

Présentation de Sacher-Masoch (Paris: 10/18, 1971)

Nietzsche et la philosophie, 4th ed (Paris: PUF, 1973)

Empirisme et subjectivité, 3rd ed (Paris: PUF, 1980)

Francis Bacon: logique de la sensation, 2 vols (Paris: Éditions de la Différence, 1981)

Spinoza: philosophie pratique, 2nd aug edn (Paris: Éditions de Minuit, 1981)

Cinéma 1: l'image-mouvement (Paris: Éditions de Minuit, 1983)

Cinéma 2: l'image-temps (Paris: Éditions de Minuit, 1985)

Foucault (Paris: Éditions de Minuit, 1986)

Le Pli: Leibniz et le baroque (Paris: Éditions de Minuit, 1988)

Pourparlers: 1972–1990 (Paris: Éditions de Minuit, 1990)

Dialogues, with Claire Parnet, coll. Champs (Paris: Flammarion, 1996)

Works by Félix Guattari

L'Inconscient machinique (Paris: Éditions Recherches, 1979)

La Révolution moléculaire (Paris: 10/18, 1980)

Cartographies schizoanalytiques (Paris: Éditions Galilée, 1989)

Chaosmose (Paris: Éditions Galilée, 1992)

Chaosophy, ed. by Sylvère Lotringer (New York: Semiotext(e), 1995)

Secondary Works on Deleuze and Guattari

Collections of Articles

La Quinzaine Littéraire, 686 (1–15 fév., 1996), special edition on Deleuze.

A Deleuzian Century?, ed. and with an introduction by Ian Buchanan, special edition of *South Atlantic Quarterly*, 96.3 (1997)

Nomadic Trajectories, ed. by John Sellars, special edition of *PLI: Warwick Journal of Philosophy*, 7 (1998)

Books and articles

ALLIEZ, Éric, *Deleuze philosophie virtuelle*, coll. les Empêcheurs de penser en rond (Le Plessis-Robinson: Synthélabo, 1996)

———, *Gilles Deleuze: une vie philosophique*, coll. les Empêcheurs de penser en rond (Le Plessis-Robinson: Synthélabo, 1998)

BOGUE, Ronald, *Deleuze and Guattari* (London and New York: Routledge, 1989)

BUYDENS, Mireille, *Sahara: l'esthétique de Gilles Deleuze*, coll. Pour Demain (Paris: J. Vrin, 1990)

COLOMBAT, André, *Deleuze et la littérature*, American University Studies: Series II, Romance Languages and Literature, 132 (New York: Peter Lang, 1990)

GOODCHILD, Philip, *Deleuze and Guattari: An Introduction to the Politics of Desire* (London: Sage Publications, 1996)

GUILMETTE, Armand, *Gilles Deleuze et la modernité* (Québec: Éditions du Zéphyr, 1984)

HALLWARD, Peter, 'Gilles Deleuze and the Redemption from Interest', *Radical Philosophy*, 81 (1997), 6–21

HARDT, Michael, *Gilles Deleuze: An Apprenticeship in Philosophy* (London: UCL Press, 1993)

HEFFERNAN, Nick, 'Œdipus Wrecks? Or, Whatever Happened to Deleuze and Guattari: Rereading *Capitalism and Schizophrenia*', in *Redirections in Critical Theory: Truth, Self, Action, History*, ed. by Bernard McGuirk (London & New York: Routledge, 1994), pp.110–165

MacKENZIE, Iain, 'Creativity as Criticism: The Philosophical Constructivism of Deleuze and Guattari', *Radical Philosophy*, 86 (1997), 7–18

MASSUMI, Brian, *A User's Guide to 'Capitalism and Schizophrenia': Deviations from Deleuze and Guattari* (Cambridge, MA: MIT Press, 1992).

PATTON, Paul (ed.), *Deleuze: A Critical Reader* (Oxford: Blackwell, 1996)

PEARSON, Keith Ansell (ed.), *Deleuze and Philosophy: The Difference Engineer*, Warwick Studies in European Philosophy (London: Routledge, 1997)

ZOURABICHVILI, François, *Deleuze: une philosophie de l'événement*, coll. Philosophies (Paris: PUF, 1996)

Other Works Consulted

BARTHES, Roland, *Mythologies* (Paris: Éditions du Seuil, 1957), p.187.

BATAILLE, Georges, *L'Expérience intérieure*, coll. Tel, rev edn (Paris: Gallimard, 1954)

BENJAMIN, Andrew, *Present Hope: Philosophy, Architecture, Judaism* (London: Routledge, 1997)

BOYERS, Robert, ORRILL, Robert (eds.), *Laing and Anti-Psychiatry* (London: Penguin, 1972)

CARROLL, David, *French Literary Fascism: Nationalism, Anti-Semitism, and the Ideology of Culture* (Princeton, NJ: Princeton University Press, 1995)

CRITCHLEY, Simon, *Very Little... Almost Nothing: Death, Philosophy, Literature* (London: Routledge, 1997)

CULLER, Jonathan, *Structuralist Poetics: Structuralism, Linguistics and the Study of Literature* (London: Routledge, 1989)

DERRIDA, Jacques, *Memoires for Paul de Man*, trans. by Cecile Lindsay, Jonathan Culler, Eduardo Cadava and Peggy Kamuf, rev edn (New York: Columbia University Press, 1989)

DURAND, Gilbert, *L'Imagination symbolique*, 3rd edn (Paris: PUF, 1976)

EAGLETON, Terry, *Criticism and Ideology: A Study in Marxist Literary Theory* (London: Verso, 1978)

———, *Literary Theory: An Introduction* (Oxford: Blackwells, 1983)

FOUCAULT, Michel, *Histoire de la folie à l'âge classique: suivi de 'Mon corps, ce papier ce feu' et 'La Folie, l'absence d'œuvre'* (Paris: Gallimard, 1972)

———, *Les Mots et les choses: une archéologie des sciences humaines* (Paris: Gallimard, 1966)

———, *Language, Counter-Memory, Practice: Selected Essays and Interviews*, ed. by Donald F. Bouchard, trans. by Donald F. Bouchard and Sherry Simon (Ithaca, NY: Cornell University Press, 1996)

FREUD, Sigmund, *Jokes and their Relation to the Unconscious*, ed. by Angela Richards, trans. by James Strachey, The Penguin Freud Library, 6 (London: Penguin, 1991)

———, *Two Short Accounts of Psycho-Analysis: Five Lectures on Psycho-Analysis and the Question of Lay Analysis*, ed. and trans. by James Strachey (London: Penguin , 1991)

———, *On Metapsychology: The Theory of Psychoanalysis*, ed. by Angela Richards, trans. by James Strachey, The Penguin Freud Library, 11 (London: Penguin, 1991)

———, *On Psychopathology: Inhibitions, Symptoms and Anxiety and Other Works*, ed. by Angela Richards, trans. by James Strachey, The Penguin Freud Library, 10 (London: Penguin, 1993)

FRYE, Northrop, *Myth and Metaphor: Selected Essays 1974–1988*, ed. by Robert D. Denham (Charlotsville: University Press of Virginia, 1990)

GENETTE, Gérard, and TODOROV, Tzvetan (eds.), *Littérature et réalité*, coll. Points Essais (Paris: Éditions du Seuil, 1982)

HAYLES, Katherine (ed.), *Chaos and Order: Complex Dynamics in Literature and Science* (Chicago: The University of Chicago Press, 1991)

HEWITT, Andrew, *Fascist Modernism: Aesthetics, Politics and the Avant-Garde* (Stanford, California: Stanford University Press, 1993)

HOBSBAWM, Eric, *Age of Extremes: The Short Twentieth Century, 1914–1991* (London: Michael Joseph, 1994)

JAMESON, Fredric, *Marxism and Form: Twentieth Century Dialectical Theories of Literature* (Princeton, NJ: Princeton University Press, 1971)

———, *Fables of Aggression: Wyndham Lewis, the Modernist as Fascist* (Berkeley, Los Angeles: University of California Press, 1979)

———, *The Political Unconscious: Narrative as a Socially Symbolic Act* (Ithaca, NY: Cornell University Press, 1981)

———, *Postmodernism, or, the Cultural Logic of Late Capitalism* (London: Verso, 1991)

KAPLAN, Alice Yaeger, *Reproductions of Banality: Fascism, Literature, and French Intellectual Life*, Theory and History of Literature, 36 (Minneapolis: University of Minnesota Press, 1986)

LAING, R.D., *The Divided Self: An Existential Study in Sanity and Madness* (London: Penguin, 1990)

MACHEREY, Pierre, *A Theory of Literary Production*, trans. by Geoffrey Wall (London: Routledge, 1989)

MacLENNAN, George, *Lucid Intervals: Subjective Writing and Madness in History* (Leicester: Leicester University Press, 1992)

MOORE, F.C.T., *Bergson: Thinking Backwards*, Modern European Philosophy (Cambridge: Cambridge University Press, 1996)

RAY, William, *Literary Meaning: From Phenomenology to Deconstruction* (Oxford: Blackwell, 1984)

REICH, Wilhelm, *The Mass Psychology of Fascism*, ed. by Mary Higgins and Chester M. Raphael, trans. by Vincent R. Carfagno (London: Souvenir Press, 1972)

RIMMON-KENAN, Shlomith, *Narrative Fiction: Contemporary Poetics* (London: Routledge, 1983)

SAID, Edward W., *Representations of the Intellectual: The 1993 Reith Lectures* (London: Vintage, 1994)

———, *Culture and Imperialism* (London: Chatto and Windus, 1993)

SARTRE, Jean-Paul, *Réflexions sur la question juive*, coll. Idées (Paris: Gallimard, 1976

SASS, Louis A., *Madness and Modernism: Insanity in the Light of Modern Art, Literature, and Thought* (Cambridge, MA: Harvard University Press, 1992)

SCHALK, David L., *The Spectrum of Political Engagement: Mounier, Benda, Nizan, Brasillach, Sartre* (Princeton, NJ: Princeton University Press, 1979)

SERRES, Michel, *Le Parasite* (Paris: Bernard Grasset, 1980)

STOICHEFF, Peter, 'The Chaos of Metafiction', in *Chaos and Order: Complex Dynamics in Literature and Science*, ed. by Katherine N. Hayles (Chicago and London: The University of Chicago Press, 1991), pp.85–99

STORR, Anthony, *Human Destructiveness: The Roots of Genocide and Human Cruelty*, 2nd rev edn (London: Routledge, 1991)

TAYLOR, Ronald (ed.), *Aesthetics and Politics: The Key Texts of the Classic Debate Within German Marxism* (London: Verso, 1980)

THEWELEIT, Klaus, *Male Fantasies*, trans. by Stephen Conway, 2 vols: vol 1: *Women, Floods, Bodies, History*; vol 2: *Male Bodies: Psychoanalyzing the White Terror* (Cambridge: Polity Press, 1987)

TODOROV, Tzvetan, *Introduction à la littérature fantastique*, coll. Points Essais (Paris: Éditions du Seuil, 1970)

WRIGHT, Elizabeth, *Psychoanalytic Criticism: Theory in Practice*, aug edn (London: Routledge, 1987)

Currents in Comparative Romance Languages and Literatures

This series was founded in 1987, and actively solicits book-length manuscripts (approximately 200–400 pages) that treat aspects of Romance languages and literatures. Originally established for works dealing with two or more Romance literatures, the series has broadened its horizons and now includes studies on themes within a single literature or between different literatures, civilizations, art, music, film and social movements, as well as comparative linguistics. Studies on individual writers with an influence on other literatures/civilizations are also welcome. We entertain a variety of approaches and formats, provided the scholarship and methodology are appropriate.

For additional information about the series or for the submission of manuscripts, please contact:

Tamara Alvarez-Detrell and Michael G. Paulson
c/o Dr. Heidi Burns
Peter Lang Publishing, Inc.
516 N. Charles St., 2nd Floor
Baltimore, MD 21201

To order other books in this series, please contact our Customer Service Department:

800-770-LANG (within the U.S.)
212-647-7706 (outside the U.S.)
212-647-7707 FAX

or browse online by series at:

www.peterlang.com